PCs
6-in-1

by Lisa Bucki

A Division of Macmillan Computer Publishing
201 West 103rd Street, Indianapolis, Indiana 46290 USA

President
Roland Elgey

Senior Vice President/Publishing
Don Fowley

Publisher
Joseph B. Wikert

Publishing Manager
Brad Koch

General Manager
Joe Muldoon

Editorial Services Director
Carla Hall

Managing Editor
Thomas F. Hayes

Director of Acquisitions
Cheryl D. Willoughby

Acquisitions Editors
Nancy Maragioglio
Angie Wethington
Stephanie McComb

Product Development Specialist
Steve Schaefer

Production Editor
Julie A. McNamee

Editor
Elizabeth Barrett

Web Master
Thomas H. Bennett

Product Marketing Manager
Kourtnaye Sturgeon

Assistant Product Marketing Manager/Design
Gretchen Schlesinger

Assistant Product Marketing Manager/Sales
Karen Hagen

Technical Editors
John Purdum
Coletta Witherspoon

Media Development Specialist
David Garratt

Acquisitions Coordinator
Michelle R. Newcomb

Software Relations Coordinator
Susan D. Gallagher

Editorial Assistant
Virginia Stoller

Book Designer
Glenn Larsen

Cover Designer
Jay Corpus

Production Team
Marcia Deboy
Jenny Earhart
Tim Neville
Angela Perry
Julie Searls
Sossity Smith

Indexer
Tim Taylor

To Steve, for his boundless patience, wisdom, and love

Acknowledgments

This project provided unique challenges and rewards for me and my colleagues at Que. Our talents blended to ensure this book would suit the needs of many readers, and be a reliable resource for months and years. I hope the following folks will accept my sincere thanks.

Angie Wethington and Nancy Maragioglio provided the opportunity for me to write this book and a number of resources to keep the book moving forward despite an ambitious publishing schedule and summertime temptations.

Steve Schaefer and Julie McNamee, the development and production editors, improved the book's structure and grammar at every turn, and helped me manage to keep the many lessons in this book in order and in perspective.

Technical editors Coletta Witherspoon and John Purdum scrutinized the information you'll find here to ensure its accuracy, completeness, and ease of use.

The production department, as always, saved the day in the end, providing an attractive interior and beautiful illustrations, so you can enjoy the book's look as well as its contents.

Trademark Acknowledgments

All terms mentioned in this book that are known to be or are suspected of being trademarks or service marks have been appropriately capitalized. Que Corporation cannot attest to the accuracy of this information. Use of a term in this book should not be regarded as affecting the validity of any trademark or service mark.

We'd Like to Hear from You!

QUE Corporation has a long-standing reputation for high-quality books and products. To ensure your continued satisfaction, we also understand the importance of customer service and support.

Tech Support

If you need assistance with the information in this book or with a CD/disk accompanying the book, please access Macmillan Computer Publishing's online Knowledge Base at **http://www.superlibrary.com/general/support**. If you do not find the answer to your questions on our Web site, you may contact Macmillan Technical Support by phone at **317/581-3833** or via e-mail at **support@mcp.com**.

Also be sure to visit QUE's Web resource center for all the latest information, enhancements, errata, downloads, and more. It's located at **http:// www.quecorp.com**.

Orders, Catalogs, and Customer Service

To order other QUE or Macmillan Computer Publishing books, catalogs, or products, please contact our Customer Service Department at **800/858-7674** or fax us at **800/882-8583** (International Fax: 317/228-4400). Or visit our online bookstore at **http://www.mcp.com/**.

Comments and Suggestions

We want you to let us know what you like or dislike most about this book or other QUE products. Your comments will help us to continue publishing the best books available on computer topics in today's market.

Lisa D. Wagner
Senior Product Director
QUE Corporation
201 West 103rd Street, 4B
Indianapolis, Indiana 46290 USA
Fax: 317/581-4663 E-mail: *lwagner@que.mcp.com*

Please be sure to include the book's title and author as well as your name and phone or fax number. We will carefully review your comments and share them with the author. Please note that due to the high volume of mail we receive, we may not be able to reply to every message.

Thank you for choosing QUE!

Contents

Part V: Choosing and Installing Peripherals   399

Part VI: Troubleshooting   473

Part VII: Appendixes 579

Introduction

"It's a big decision."

"I'm not sure if it's worth the cost."

"I don't know where to start."

Starting to work with computers, deciding to purchase your first personal system, or working with your system hardware can all be intimidating steps. Even if you consult magazines, talk to colleagues and friends, or visit a number of computer stores, you still may not find the answers you want to make decisions and proceed with confidence.

Working effectively with a computer on your own may seem like it requires you to be part mechanic and part mystic. You not only have to know how to put the parts together or break them down when something goes wrong, you have to understand the software that makes the thing run. With all the different components and options available in today's computer systems, it can be tough to get started and keep up.

That's where *PCs 6-in-1* can help.

Using This Book

PCs 6-in-1 is designed to help you learn about six different aspects of choosing, using, and maintaining a computer quickly and easily. You don't have to spend time figuring out what to learn. All the most important tasks are covered in this book. Learn the skills you need in short, easy-to-follow lessons, each of which takes about 10 minutes to complete.

This book is organized in six parts, so that you can jump right to the part you need:

> Part I, "PC Hardware Overview," introduces you to the components of a personal computer (PC) system, and gives you hints for choosing and buying a new system. Lessons here also explain how to set up and clean up your system.

Part II "Operating Systems—How Windows 95 Fits In" explains how to get around in Windows 95 (OEM Service Release 2, or OSR 2), and jump to the DOS prompt if you need to.

Part III "Maximizing Your Applications" gives you a crash course in using key features of the Windows 95 applications you use to get your work done. The steps you learn in these lessons apply in almost every Windows 95 application, making the time you spend with this part a worthwhile investment.

Part IV "Using the Internet" explains how to set up your system to dial into an Internet account, and how to use the software that comes with Windows 95 OSR 2 to work with e-mail, read news, and browse for information.

Part V "Choosing and Installing Peripherals" shows you how to enhance your system by adding new or better components, like a fax/modem or Zip drive.

Part VI, "Troubleshooting" lends a helping hand when your computer goes on the fritz. Lessons here address problems at startup or with components such as the monitor, as well as techniques for making a disk more efficient or dealing with viruses.

The book concludes with reference appendixes listing buyers' resources and troubleshooting resources.

This book covers a lot of ground. Beginners can tackle all the lessons—even those that cover operations normally only attempted by more experienced users. The lessons also provide the latest technical information and tips to benefit computer users of all experience levels.

Conventions Used in This Book

Each of the short lessons in this book includes step-by-step instructions for performing specific tasks. The following icons (small graphic symbols) are included to help you quickly identify particular types of information:

 TIP   These icons indicate ways you can save time.

These icons point out definitions of words you'll need to know in order to understand how to work with hardware or a software feature.

CAUTION

Caution icons help you avoid making mistakes.

In addition to the icons, **on-screen text**, **entries you type**, and **items you select** are all formatted with bold type to make them easier to identify.

PC Hardware Overview

Pinning Down Your Computer Needs

This lesson covers the tasks you can handle with a computer, and helps you begin identifying what type of computer system you need.

What Do You Need a Computer for, Anyway?

Before you buy a personal computer (which in this book means an IBM-compatible computer), you need to ask yourself the same kinds of basic questions you'd ask before buying a tool or household appliance. Consider this question first: "What am I going to use it to accomplish?"

You can use a personal computer for entertainment, education, keeping track of personal finances, and more. You can also use your computer to work at home, write letters, do your taxes, run a small business, or handle the demands of your job.

When you're thinking about what you want to do with the computer you're about to buy, take a look at different *software programs*. You'll find programs you want to start using right away and others you may want to experiment with in a few months or when the need arises. Either way, knowing what types of programs you want to use will help you decide what kind of computer to buy. Each piece of software requires particular pieces of computer hardware (*components*), or hardware with particular capabilities. Deciding which software you want to use first can help you make a shopping list of the system components you'll need and how powerful they need to be. The rest of this lesson helps you choose software and discover how it may affect the system you decide to buy. Lesson 10 of this part, "Making the Big Purchase," will share more about making your actual software and hardware purchases.

 Software programs Sometimes called simply *software* or *programs*, each program gives your computer the instructions to get a particular job done.

 Hardware The equipment components that make up your computer system. For example, the keyboard is a piece of hardware.

Choosing Different Types of Programs

Personal computers are very capable, but they're not very smart. A computer needs programs—including basic software that lets the computer start up—to tell it what to do. Literally thousands of programs exist for you to choose and install on your computer. Some programs only perform one, limited activity, such as letting you calculate numbers. Other programs offer a range of sophisticated capabilities, letting you create and format complicated documents or organize and reorganize information.

Most software programs can be grouped into familiar types or categories that describe the tasks each program in the category handles:

- **Run the computer.** The operating system software tells your computer how to start up, communicate with all its devices, and work with other software. Every personal computer comes with the operating system software. Microsoft Windows 95 ships on most new personal computers today, and is the primary operating system I'll cover in this book.

 TIP This book covers a specific version of Windows 95 known as OEM Service Release 2 (OSR 2). If you aren't using OSR 2 you can still use this book but some of the features and functions will be different than those described here.

- **Process words.** Use a *word processing* program to type, edit, and apply attractive formatting to text, and even add graphical pictures to documents, as shown in Figure 1.1. The leading word processing programs include Microsoft Word for Windows, Lotus WordPro, and Corel WordPerfect.

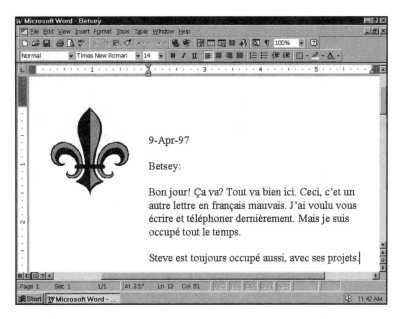

Figure 1.1 Get your words on paper and spruce them up with a word processing program.

- **Crunch numbers.** Use a *spreadsheet* program to organize numbers in a grid and add formulas to perform calculations. You may hear the Microsoft Excel, Lotus 1-2-3 for Windows, and Corel Quattro Pro programs mentioned in this category.

- **Manage data.** Use a *database* to store and sort lists of information, such as phone lists and home inventories. Database programs are used more often for business than pleasure, so you may need the Microsoft Access and Lotus Approach programs only at the office.

- **Communicate.** Use a piece of hardware called a *modem* with your special programs to transmit data over phone lines. You can send and receive faxes and electronic mail (*e-mail*), chat with other users, or access a wealth of data available through online services and the Internet, shown in Figure 1.2. Part 4 of this book covers how to use your computer and easily available software to access the Internet.

- **Educate and entertain.** Have fun (mindless or otherwise) searching for treasure, learning from an illustrated online encyclopedia, and more. Today's more powerful computers have led to elaborate computer games, educational programs, and entertainment resources that use pictures, animation, and sound. There are hundreds (or maybe even thousands) of programs for education and entertainment.

Figure 1.2 Use your modem and special communications software to find information online.

 TERM **Multimedia Programs** Programs that combine text, pictures, sound, full-motion video, and animation, to lend excitement and realism to the user's experience.

- **Manage time, money, and more.** Use computer programs to organize your time, manage your contacts with others, or even write checks and budget your money. Specialized programs can help you track your diet or fitness level and even plan landscaping and home renovation projects. The Microsoft Outlook and Lotus Organizer programs enable you to create to-do lists, and more. Intuit's Quicken and Microsoft Money provide money-management and check writing features.

- **Present and publish information.** Use a *presentation graphics* program to create presentations and pages that convey a message with style. Figure 1.3 shows an example from Microsoft PowerPoint, which leads the market along with Lotus Freelance and Corel Presentations. Use a *desktop* *publishing* program like Microsoft Publisher or Adobe PageMaker to create newsletters, flyers, and publications. Other programs let you create and work with drawings and *fonts* (fancy lettering). You can even capture, edit, and print digital photos and video.

Figure 1.3 Any number of graphics, presentation graphics (PowerPoint is shown here), and publishing programs enable you to create flyers and other documents with punch.

- **Maintain your computer and its files.** Use utility programs to back up files, check for *viruses* (data-destroying programs that can infect your computer), compress or zip files so they take up less disk space, and perform more disk-management activities to keep your computer healthy.

TIP **Programs At Work and At Home** If you use a particular program at work, like Microsoft Word for word processing, it's probably best to buy the same program for your home system so you can seamlessly work on files in both places.

TIP **Program Sneak Preview** Most computer stores have various software installed on demo systems, so you can try before you buy. Some software publishers let you download trial or demo versions of software.

Looking at Software Requirements

After you've chosen the software programs you want to use, you'll need to figure out how powerful your computer has to be to run them. The programs you want to run may also require you to have certain other kinds of software on your computer. Fortunately, software publishers give you a hand with figuring out what your program needs by providing you with a list.

Check the software product box for a section labeled something like "Recommended Hardware and Software Requirements" or "To use this program, you need…" This section usually appears on the side or back of the box, and it tells you several important things (such as whether the program requires Microsoft Windows 95). Don't worry if you don't understand some of the techie terms you find on the box. You'll learn more about Windows 95 in Part 2 of the book, and you'll learn more about selecting hardware in the rest of this part.

CAUTION **Meet the Minimum!** The system you buy should meet the most demanding minimum hardware and other requirements for any software you want to use. You can't take the requirements for all the programs and somehow "average" them. If your computer doesn't meet the minimum requirements, the software may run unreliably or may not run at all. Even if your computer meets the minimum, the program may not run to your satisfaction. Often the system that runs the program best exceeds the guidelines on the software box.

Here are the requirements you need to consider; they're outlined on the package for each software program you purchase.

What Type of Computer Do You Need?

To run software created for a Macintosh computer, you must have a Macintosh, commonly called a "Mac." To run software created for an IBM-compatible (Windows-compatible) computer, you need that kind of computer. IBM- or Windows-compatible computers are generally called PCs. This book focuses on PCs only, not Mac systems.

How Powerful Must the Computer Be?

Usually the box will tell you what kind of *central processing unit* (the *CPU* or "brain") your computer needs to have. This is designated by a number for the CPU such as "386" or "486". In general, a higher number indicates a more powerful processor. The leading CPU manufacturer, Intel, calls its most common desktop processor the *Pentium,* although you'll sometimes see the Pentium called a "586". Intel also offers two even more powerful CPUs, the Pentium Pro and Pentium II.

A number such as "133MHz" or "160MHz" indicates how fast the processor is. In general, higher numbers designate faster processors. (Although a more powerful processor makes a difference; for example, a 90MHz Pentium might perform a bit better than a 486-based machine rated at 100MHz.) Many PCs have the processor type and speed stamped on the front.

Your computer's CPU must be *at least* as powerful and as fast as the one required. If you have any doubts about how the processor will work, ask the retailer to demo the software you want. Many reputable dealers will show you how the software runs on a system with a processor like the one you're considering buying.

Do You Need a Multimedia or Business System?

Most PC manufacturers give you the choice between a few broad categories of IBM-compatible systems. The first category, *business* or *workstation* systems, includes systems that are very powerful and may be set up to connect to a network of other computers. The other, *multimedia* or *home* systems, include special components for handling sound and more intensive video (features of many home-oriented programs such as games or educational software). For the best of both worlds, you may need a *professional* system. Such systems include the power and networking capabilities of a business system, while adding multimedia.

Generally, businesses seek more cost-effective, straightforward systems because business users don't necessarily need to run multimedia components included in business software. So some business systems may come without certain multimedia components or may have less powerful multimedia components. In contrast, home consumers seek a system that can handle a wide range of software and serve family educational and entertainment needs for several years.

So, most home-oriented systems do include multimedia and communications capabilities. Special business challenges require a professional system. For example, a sales person may need a system that can both deliver multimedia presentations for clients and connect to a network. Professional systems are more expensive, but they offer the greatest degree of flexibility.

Which Operating System Does It Use?

Most of you will be buying computers that run under the operating system called *Windows 95*. Windows 95 includes an underlying version of MS-DOS, the *Disk Operating System* from Microsoft that provides basic control of your computer. If your computer uses Windows 95, don't buy programs made for the OS/2, UNIX, or System 7.6 (Macintosh) operating systems. If you have a computer that's running an older version of DOS and Windows 3.11, make sure you have the right version of DOS to run the program. For example, if a program requires MS-DOS 5.0 to run, you must have MS-DOS with version number 5.0 *or higher*. Many newer programs need to be run under Microsoft Windows 95.

CAUTION

Get Windows 95 OSR 2 New computer systems have a more recent version of Windows 95 called OEM Service Release 2 (OSR 2), or Windows 95 B. This update of Windows 95 better manages large hard disk drives (where files are stored), has improved power management features, and more. If you buy a new system, make sure it has OSR 2 installed. If the system you're considering has an older version of Windows and DOS installed along with Windows 95, the Windows 95 version may not be OSR 2, so you might want to consider buying another system that does have OSR 2.

How Much Memory and Storage Should the Computer Have?

Random-Access Memory, or *RAM*, holds the instructions and data you're working with while your computer is turned on. When you install a program and save your work, both are stored on the computer's *hard drive*, a semi-permanent storage area that lets you access the program or data later. Programs require a minimum amount of RAM to run correctly. They also take up a certain amount of storage space on the hard drive; make sure you have enough hard drive space available to install the program. (See Lesson 2 in this part for recommendations about how much RAM and storage to look for in a new system.)

What Kind of Input Device and Monitor Are Needed?

Some programs require a mouse for selecting commands; you can better work with many game programs using an alternative device called a joystick. The software box will say which is best. Monitors (and the internal *video cards* they connect to) come in several flavors, depending on the *resolution* each provides. The two types of monitors sold with most new systems today, from lowest to highest resolution, are VGA (Video Graphics Array) and SVGA (Super VGA). Programs with generous graphics generally require better-resolution monitors such as Super VGA.

Are There Optional Programs or Equipment That Can or Should Be Used?

Some programs may require a sound card and speakers to take full advantage of the program's features. Most communications programs require a modem or fax/modem; if any special equipment is required or recommended, the software box will usually say so. Some programs also require that you have a particular Windows 95 component (such as Windows networking capabilities) or some other type of software like a page layout program installed.

In this lesson, you learned that you should choose what kind of software you want to run before you buy a computer, because all programs require a minimum amount of computing power to run. The next lesson takes you inside the system box, to teach you vital information about the CPU, RAM, and System Unit.

Powering Up: The CPU, RAM, and System Unit

This lesson teaches you what the three most important parts of a computer system do and gives you hints for choosing these items when you buy a new system.

Giving the Computer a Brain: the CPU

A PC's *central processing unit (CPU)* executes all commands and controls the flow of data, providing the "brain" that enables the PC to calculate and perform operations like sorting information more quickly than a human could. The CPU makes perhaps the greatest contribution to a PC's speed and power. The CPU chip plugs into a socket on the motherboard, a circuit board that holds the key electronic components of the computer. The CPU is generally the largest chip on the motherboard, making it easy to identify. Figure 2.1 shows an example CPU chip.

A two-part name like "486DX4 100 MHz" or "Pentium 133MHz" identifies most CPUs. The first part ("486DX4," "Pentium") indicates the type of CPU the system has. As you learned in the last lesson, the most powerful processors offered by market leader Intel are the Pentium (a.k.a. the "586"), Pentium Pro, and Pentium II. (So far, Pentium Pro and Pentium II CPUs are sold mostly in high-end business systems, but they could become the most common CPUs offered at your local computer store.) To make it even more confusing, other CPU manufacturers use slightly different numbering systems, such as the Cyrix 5x86—roughly comparable to an Intel 486, Cyrix 6x86—meant to compete with the Pentium, and AMD K5 and K6 CPUs—which take on the Pentium and Pentium Pro.

Figure 2.1   A CPU like this one serves as a PC's brain, performing all calculations and commands.

CAUTION

CPU Promises   AMD, Cyrix, or IBM/Cyrix usually claim their CPUs actually run faster than Pentium chips with a comparable speed rating. (Several computer magazines use special testing software to compare CPU speeds.) Even so, don't base your purchase decision on CPU speed and power alone. Consider the full system package and the reputation of the manufacturer. The AMD and Cyrix chips are often found in systems offered by less-established, smaller manufacturers.

The second number in the processor's name (such as "100 MHz" or "133 MHz") indicates the CPU's speed in megahertz. You don't need to know many technical details about CPU speed; just keep in mind that higher is better when comparing two processors of the same type. Each type of CPU is usually released in several different speeds. Table 2.1 lists several CPU types and the speeds you'll find for them.

Table 2.1   CPU Speeds

Processor type	Speed ratings (MHz)
486DX2	66, 80
486DX4	75, 100, 120
Pentium	90, 100, 120, 133, 166, 200
Pentium Pro	166, 180, 200
Pentium II	233, 266, 300

Some CPUs now offer *MMX technology*. CPUs with MMX are optimized to run multimedia applications and, therefore, offer faster multimedia playback than standard CPUs. However, when manufacturers introduce any new hardware technology, the software makers need to catch up. At the time of this writing, most applications can't yet take advantage of MMX capabilities. So before you pay the extra $200 or so for an MMX system, make sure the software you want to run requires it or that there's a good chance you'll need the MMX capabilities later.

TIP **A Pro Plus** A Pentium II CPU is essentially a faster Pentium Pro, with MMX technology.

TIP **Pick a Processor** If you're shopping for a new system, it should at the very least have a Pentium 166MHz, and if you plan to run a lot of games or multimedia CD-ROMs it should have MMX.

Counting Up the RAM You Need

A computer's *random access memory (RAM)* consists of a bank of chips (see Figure 2.2) that act as "working memory," holding program instructions and data only while your computer's on. Unless the instructions and data are saved to a disk, RAM forgets them when you turn your computer off. RAM is measured in *megabytes (M)*. Each megabyte is equivalent to over one million characters of data. Most computers today come with 32M of RAM, though some sell with only 16M installed. There are a few different flavors and speeds of RAM, as well. One of the most prominent today is Extended Data Output (EDO) RAM, but an even faster type of RAM that has just hit the market is called SyncDRAM.

RAM Enough A system with at least 32M of RAM will seamlessly run the newest programs and serve your needs for the near future. Most software programs list a lower RAM requirement today, but if you buy less than 32M, CAUTION your system could become outdated quickly.

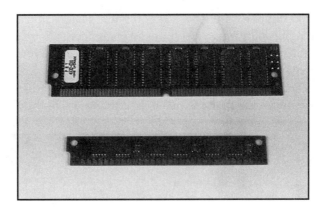

Figure 2.2 A "bank" or module of RAM (memory) is called a SIMM, short for Single Inline Memory Module.

You also will hear about what's called a *cache* when you hear about RAM and the CPU. A cache is an extra holding area for program instructions that need to be frequently used by the CPU or swapped in and out of RAM. Your CPU can usually access those instructions from the cache more quickly than it could from a hard disk or even RAM, so a cache helps the system work more effectively. Most systems sold today offer either a 256K or 512K cache. When deciding between two systems or configurations, pick the system with the most cache.

Sizing Up the System Unit

All instructions flow through the components stored in the *system unit*—the box or case that holds the CPU, motherboard, and other internal components. The system unit of a traditional desktop PC has a fairly large *footprint*, which means it takes up a lot of desk space. *Tower* units stand vertically and can be tucked away under a desk. Many manufacturers are moving toward selling tower units or slightly shorter *minitower* units only. Figure 2.3 shows a minitower system unit.

The system unit houses the computer's main circuit board—the *motherboard*. Data travels in a computer along circuits called *buses* on the motherboard. Although three main buses (data bus, address bus, and control bus) manage the computer's operation, often these are collectively called *the bus*. The bus carries instructions back and forth between the CPU and other devices in the system. The now-standard *PCI Local Bus* carries data along at least 32 lines, that is, at

19

least 32 bits at a time. *Local bus* computer designs add special buses so the CPU can communicate directly with key components like the monitor, resulting in much better performance. You should look for PCI local bus capabilities in any system you buy, especially PCI local bus video (which helps the monitor display more quickly). You'll also want the system to be able to handle fast hard disk drives, so look for what's called an Enhanced IDE (EIDE) hard drive controller.

Figure 2.3 Space-saving tower or minitower system units are becoming more prevalent today.

Expansion slots on the motherboard within the system unit enable you to plug in additional adapters for new devices, such as a scanner, that you add to your computer. You'll need these to add components to or upgrade your computer, especially if you don't buy a computer that's multimedia-equipped. Most new systems offer at least five expansion slots (two ISA slots for older expansion boards and three PCI slots for current and future technology).

New systems also should support Universal Serial Bus (USB), a new method for connecting peripheral devices to the system. With USB technology, you don't have to install a new adapter for each device you want to connect to your computer. You would simply plug the first device into the USB port (a receptacle on the back of the system unit where you plug in the cable for a USB device), then plug the next device into the first one, and so on to form a chain of up to 127 devices. For example, you could plug a keyboard into the USB connection, plug a mouse into the USB receptacle on the keyboard, and so on. There aren't many USB add-on devices available, but you'll want your system to be able to deal with them in the future. Make sure any new system you buy supports USB; many new systems come with one or two USB connections (ports) available on the back of the system unit.

Adapter   An *adapter*—also called an expansion board, expansion card, or adapter card—is a small circuit board that installs in expansion slots on the motherboard. Once you've installed a particular adapter, you connect a new device such as a scanner to it. Some adapter's cards are themselves the new device—for example, internal modems and sound cards.

Ports are simply receptacles (on the back of your system unit) to plug in equipment such as printers. Most computers now come with separate mouse, keyboard, and monitor ports. *Parallel* ports (labeled LPT1, LPT2, and so on) are usually for plugging in printers; *serial* ports connect a mouse (if a dedicated mouse port doesn't exist), an external modem, or a printer. Serial ports are also sometimes called COM (short for COMmunications) ports, and are labeled COM1, COM2, and so on. Some computers also provide special game ports for joysticks.

One last key feature found "in the box" is the *BIOS*. This specialized program (stored on a chip) is designed to work with your system's particular motherboard and it can be an issue if you ever want to upgrade your system. So, ask the computer seller how recent the BIOS version is; and make sure a reputable company—AMI and Phoenix are the leaders—made the BIOS.

BIOS   This is the Basic Input/Output System. This is a chip on the motherboard that contains the instructions for starting up, or booting, the computer, and more.

You've just learned about the key components—CPU, RAM, and system unit—that make a PC tick. The next lesson covers storage devices that keep your programs and other information on file for you.

Storing Your Work: Hard and Removable Disks

3

In this lesson, you learn how a PC saves information for later use on a hard or floppy disk, and why disks are vital PC components.

Understanding Disk Basics

When you're using your computer, your data exists only in the computer's *Random Access Memory* (RAM). RAM holds the data and program instructions your computer is working with while the computer is turned on. Turn the computer off, and RAM's contents are lost.

To work with that data again, you need to save the data in a more permanent way; you put it in *storage*. Disks are your computer's storage area. They hold your data for you until you delete it or move it. When you save information, your computer takes what's in RAM and writes it to a disk. When you want to use stored data again, your computer looks at that data on the hard disk drive and reads a copy of it back into RAM. If you change your data, you'll need to save it to the hard disk drive again to preserve your changes, and so on.

New users frequently use the terms "floppy disk" and "hard drive" to refer to the two main storage tools of the computer. A "disk" and a "drive," however, are not the same things.

The *disk* is the spinning platter of magnetic material that holds the stored data. The hard "drive" within your computer actually holds a stack of these magnetic disk platters—that's how it holds so much data. In contrast, the spinning "platter" that you can see within a floppy disk is actually a tough film coated with magnetic material.

The actual collection of mechanisms that spins the disk, writes information on the disk, and reads information from the disk is the *disk drive*. The hard disk drive in your computer has a sealed case that holds both the drive and the stack of disks. You can insert and remove disks from floppy disk drives and other removable drives through a slot on the front of the drive (and the front of the system unit).

How Disks Store Information

At its most basic level, your computer can only understand two digits: 0 and 1. The computer combines 0s and 1s to create unique characters, and then those characters are combined to form words, values, commands, and so on.

Whether hard or floppy, your disks are coated with tiny magnetic particles, each of which can be magnetized by an electrical charge. Each of these particles is known as a *bit*—short for *BInary digiT*. When a bit has a high charge or is magnetized (the "on" state), the computer reads it as a 1. When a bit has a low charge or is not magnetized (the "off" state), the computer reads it as a 0. A combination of eight bits forms a *byte*, which is one character of data. There is a unique set of bits for each letter of the alphabet, for every single-digit number, and for many special characters (like $).

The capacity of every disk and memory chip can be measured in bytes. A *kilobyte* is just over 1,000 bytes. A *megabyte* is just over 1,000,000 bytes, and a *gigabyte* is over a billion bytes (or a thousand megabytes).

These magnetic bits aren't just floating around on the disk's surface. They're actually formatted or arranged in a very specific pattern to make it easy for the disk drive to store and find data. Each disk has concentric rings called *tracks* dividing it. To further organize the data, the disk has *sectors*, pie-shaped wedges separated by imaginary lines radiating from the center of the disk, as shown in Figure 3.1.

Formatting a Disk   You format a disk—arrange the magnetic bits into tracks and sectors—so your computer can write information to the disk. A PC usually comes with the hard disk already formatted. But, you may need to format a floppy disk before using it. To learn how to do this, see Lesson 14, "Formatting a Disk," in Part 2.

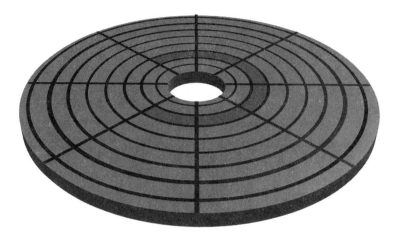

Figure 3.1   Magnetic information is arranged into concentric rings called tracks, which are divided into wedges called sectors.

Tiny magnetic codes on the disk identify the tracks and sectors that store every group of bits. Your system manages data in units called *clusters* or *allocation units*. Each cluster might hold one or more sectors. Under older versions of DOS (operating system software) and Windows, the smallest cluster size possible for hard disks over 256M is 8k (8,000 bytes or characters). Because all your files won't necessarily contain even multiples of 8,000 characters, some space is wasted. For example, a file with 8,001 bytes would occupy two full clusters, even though most of the second cluster is wasted. Windows 95 OEM Service Release 2 (OSR 2), which has shipped on new computers since the fall of 1996, uses the more efficient FAT32 system with smaller 4K clusters. With 4K clusters, you can pack 10 – 15 percent more information on the same drive. This is yet another reason to ensure any new computer you buy uses OSR 2, not the original release of Windows 95. As a bonus, the new FAT32 system supports much larger hard disks than earlier file systems. You'll learn more about what the FAT does in later lessons.

File   This is a named collection of information, stored on a disk. You can think of a file as a single document, such as a letter from a word processor, a budget worksheet from a spreadsheet program, or a picture file created in a graphics program.

How a Drive Reads and Writes Information

When a drive *writes to* a disk, it's actually magnetizing selected bits to create bytes, or characters. When the drive *reads from* a disk, it reads the bits comprising each byte and places a copy of that information in RAM. A mechanical part called the *read/write head* is connected to an arm that floats over the disk surface (much like the tone arm on old record turntable), magnetizing bits or reading their magnetic charges, as shown in Figure 3.2.

Figure 3.2 The read/write head magnetizes bits on a disk and reads magnetic charges.

The drive's read head is smart and fast. It knows exactly where the different parts of a file are stored and finds them all to load them into RAM. (Lesson 8 of Part 6 explains why a file might become divided into pieces on a drive.) Similarly, it's adept at finding available space on a disk to copy a file to. A disk drive's speed is called its *access time*. Smaller access times indicate faster drives. For example, you should look for a hard drive with an access time of 12 ms (milliseconds) or less. Otherwise, you'll find yourself tapping your toe while you're waiting for your drive to perform various operations.

Selecting a Hard Disk Drive

Your computer stores information semipermanently on the *hard disk* (also called the *hard disk drive* or *hard drive*), which consists of several metal disks in an airtight case. When you install a program, it's placed on the hard disk so it can be retrieved into RAM for use over and over. Hard disks can store more information than floppy disks and tend to be more reliable (because they take less abuse), so you should also store important data files on the hard disk instead of a floppy. You can later delete programs and data to reuse the space they occupied.

Hard disk capacities are measured in megabytes (1,000M equals a *gigabyte*, or *1G*). A too-small hard drive limits the number of programs you can install; these days the minimum is usually 1.2G. You also want to consider a hard drive's *access time*. A slow hard drive can slow down your whole system, no matter how fast the processor is. A lower access time indicates a faster drive (10ms is faster than 12ms). Most drives available today are Enhanced IDE (which are faster than the older IDE drives), but some systems come with faster SCSI hard drives.

Install   To make a program available on your computer, you must install it to the hard disk. Each program offers a setup or install file that automates the installation process, copying the program's files to your disk and altering key files on your system to make sure the program will run correctly. Lesson 1 in Part 3 explains how to install and remove programs under Windows 95.

TIP   **Bigger Is Better**   Don't underestimate how rapidly you'll fill your hard drive. To have enough space for your current needs and the long term, buy at least a 2.5G drive, with 12ms access time or better.

Working with Floppy Disks

Like a hard drive, a floppy disk lets you store data and program instructions semipermanently. The difference: *floppy disks* store data on portable disks you can slide in and out of a slot in the system unit. Floppies enable you to move files from one computer to another, such as when you want to take a memo home from work to edit it on your home system. Older floppy disk drives used flexible 5.25-inch disks, which are now almost obsolete. Recent floppy drives use 3.5-inch HD (high-density) disks that hold 1.44M of data; these have hard plastic shells that better protect your data.

Floppy Capacity

You may have noticed that your floppy disks or disk labels have "HD" or something similar on them. These hieroglyphics refer to the disk's *density* or *capacity*, which is as important as the floppy's size. Both affect how much data a floppy disk can hold.

Manufacturers indicate this amount in *kilobytes* (each K is just over 1,000 characters) and *megabytes* (each M is more than one million characters). All floppy disks sold today are *double-sided* (DS); they store data on both sides (many early floppies were single-sided) and hence store more information.

The disk's capacity depends on how efficient its magnetic storage material is. The newer *high-density* (HD) disks hold more data than *double-density* (DD) disks of the same size. For a comparison of various disk capacities, see Table 3.1.

Table 3.1   Floppy Disk Capacities

Size	Type	Capacity
3.5-inch	DSDD, double-sided double-density	720K
3.5-inch	DSHD, double-sided high-density	1.44M
3.5-inch	ED, extra-high-density	2.88M
5.25-inch	DSDD, double-sided double-density	360K
5.25-inch	DSHD, double-sided high-density	1.2M

To translate the capacity of any disk into real-world terms, think of each byte as a character. A 3.5-inch HD (high-density) floppy disk holds 1.44 megabytes, which is roughly 1.4 million characters. So if the average page of data has 35 lines of 65 characters each (2,275 characters), a single 1.44-megabyte disk can hold more than 600 pages of data (2,275 characters times 600 pages equals 1,365,000 characters), which is about as many pages as there are in this book—if the data doesn't have a lot of fancy formatting.

Inserting and Removing a Floppy Disk

Floppy disks give you almost unlimited (if not completely convenient) capacity for storing files. When you want to use the files on a floppy, you need to insert it into the floppy disk drive on the system unit. When you're finished working with the floppy, you then remove it from the disk drive. Follow these steps to insert and remove a floppy disk:

1. Turn your 3.5-inch disk so the label side is up. Grip the edge opposite the edge covered by the sliding door. (If you were inserting a 5.25-inch disk, you would need to hold it label up, with the square notch to the right and the side with two smaller notches facing the drive slot.)

2. Insert the leading edge of the disk (it's covered by the metal sliding door on a 3.5-inch floppy) into the drive slot (Figure 3.3). Push it (gently) all the way into the drive. When the disk seats, the drive's eject button pops out. (For a 5.25-inch disk, you may have to press the drive lever down until it clicks in place in front of the slot.)

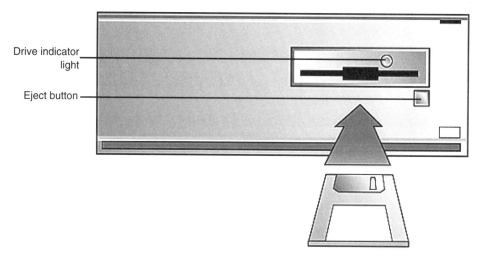

Figure 3.3   Insert the leading edge of the floppy disk into the floppy drive slot on the system unit.

3. To finish using the disk, save your work on it. After the drive's indicator light goes out, you can remove the disk (which you should do before you use another one or shut down your computer).

4. Press the drive's eject button (or lift the lever if your 5.25-inch drive has one); the disk pops part of the way out.

5. Pull the disk the rest of the way out and store it in a safe place.

Drive Light Never remove a floppy disk from the drive when the drive indicator light is still on. Doing so usually damages your files, and you could lose data permanently.

CAUTION

Adding Removable Disks to the Mix

Some applications today create huge files. A single graphic image file, for example, can be a few megabytes in size. In fact, even a word processing document with fancy formatting can greatly exceed 1M. This created a problem in transferring files between computers. These large files don't fit on the typical 1.44M floppy disk.

In the last few years, hardware manufacturers have come to the rescue, offering floppy-like drives that use larger disks or cartridges. The most common removable disk drives include the 100M Zip drive and 1G Jaz drive created by Iomega), 230M EZFlyer and SyJet 1.5G from SyQuest, and 90M and 150M drives from Bernoulli. The drives themselves range in price from $149 for the ZIP to $400 or more for a larger, faster removable drive. The disks or cartridges themselves start at about $15 for the 100M ZIP disk to more than $90 for a 1G Jaz cartridge.

Figure 3.4 This compact Jaz drive (external model shown) uses 1G cartridges that store more than the typical hard drive available a few years ago.

At this point, you have to add most of these removable disk alternatives after you purchase a system, but some systems now include a Zip drive for extra removable storage. Some models connect to a parallel (printer) port. You plug the drive in, plug your printer into the back of the drive, and install the software that runs the drive. Other models must be used with a SCSI (Small Computer Systems Interface) adapter, a faster type of disk and device connection that isn't standard on most PCs. If you don't have a SCSI adapter, you'll need to install one to use a SCSI removable drive (see Lesson 4 in Part 5). If you don't have a SCSI adapter and don't want to buy and install one, make sure you buy a parallel port model.

SCSI An acronym for Small Computer Systems Interface, SCSI is a type of disk and device connection. SCSI usually offers the fastest method for devices like disk drives to communicate with the system, so it's a faster type of connection. In addition, one you've installed a SCSI adapter, you can create a "daisy chain" of devices; plug the first device into the adapter, then plug the next device into the first one, and so on. Lesson 4 in Part 5 covers SCSI in more detail.

Note that the parallel models are external—you don't have to install them inside the system unit, so you can use them with more than one computer as long as you've installed the software for the drive on each. SCSI models are usually internal, or installed in the system unit.

Safe Ejection Inserting a removable disk resembles the process for inserting a floppy. Generally, you just gently push the disk in until it clicks into place. You may also need to close a lever, as for some SyQuest drives. While you simply reverse the process to eject the removable disk, be aware that some removables require you to use software to unlock or unmount the drive before you remove it. Failing to unlock the drive could result in lost files.

Referring to Disk Drives: By the Letter

As you've already noticed, your computer probably has at least two drives. Your computer uses a simple system to tell them apart: the ABCs. You'll need to know your computer's naming system when you want to save, retrieve, or otherwise work with data files. Here's how to identify your system's drives:

- If your computer has only one floppy disk drive, it's drive *A*. If your system has two floppy disk drives, the one that's to the left or on top is usually drive *A* (although this may not be true if the leftmost floppy drive is oriented vertically).

- On a system with two floppy disk drives, the bottom or right one is usually drive *B*.

- Generally, the hard disk drive inside your computer is drive *C*. If you have multiple hard disk drives, the first will be *C*, the second will be *D*, and so on. Hard disks are assigned drive letters before CD-ROM drives, removable disk drives, and any network drives your system can access.

- Your CD-ROM drive, if you have one, is usually drive *D*. However, if you have multiple hard disks or removable drives attached to your system, the CD-ROM drive will usually be bumped to a later letter. For example, one of my systems has three hard disks, a Syquest removable disk drive, and a CD-ROM drive. The three hard disk drives are *C*, *D*, and *E*; the Syquest is *F*, and the CD-ROM is *G*. If your system is attached to a network, the drives on the network normally are assigned a much higher letter, such as *I* or *H*.

This lesson introduced you to hard, floppy, and other removable disks, that enable PCs to store information. The next lesson covers devices you use to give the computer information, or input.

Putting Information In: Keyboards, Pointers, and Scanners

This lesson gives you information to help you choose and use the devices that let you control the computer by giving your input: a keyboard, a mouse or other pointing device, and a scanner.

Giving Input with the Keyboard

If you've ever seen a typewriter, then you know what a keyboard looks like: a device with a bunch of keys, each of which corresponds to a particular letter, number, character, or special function like backing up and erasing a character. The keyboard plugs into the system unit via a flexible cord. You use the keyboard to enter characters that appear on-screen in the program (and file) you're presently working with. Other keys enable you to edit information, or perform commands. Keyboards offer several different types of keys:

- **Alphanumeric keys.** These keys include our basic letters and numbers and the Shift key for creating upper-case letters and special characters, arranged in the traditional QWERTY layout used for typewriters.

- **Arrow keys.** These keys move the insertion point (a blinking line that tells you where characters you type will appear) or highlight around on-screen. Some keyboards only offer arrows for moving up, down, left, and right. Other keyboards including diagonal arrow keys. The arrow keys appear to the right of the alphanumeric keys.

- **Numeric keypad.** This keypad offers numbers arranged like a 10-key calculator. It appears at the far-right end of the keyboard, and is particularly handy for entering numeric data.

- **Esc (Escape) key.** Usually located at the upper-left corner of the keyboard, this key cancels whatever you're currently doing.

- **Ctrl (Control) and Alt (Alternate) keys.** You press one of these keys and hold it down, then press another key, usually to execute some type of special command. For example, pressing Alt+F4 closes the current program window in Windows 95. You also often press the Shift key in conjunction with these keys. Look for these keys both at the lower-left and lower-right corners of the keyboard on each side of the space bar.

- **F (Function) keys.** Pressing one of these keys, either alone or with Ctrl or Alt, executes a command. These keys appear in a row along the top of most keyboards. Some keyboards offer a second set of function keys along the left side. I find the keys at the left easier to use than those along the top row.

TIP **Keyboard Tryout** The numerous keyboards on the market all offer the same basic keys, but they can differ greatly in terms of the size and responsiveness of the keys. If your computer use will involve a lot of typing, make sure you tryout the keyboard before making a purchase. If a system meets your needs but you don't like the keyboard, you can purchase another keyboard for generally less than $100.

TIP **Make the Connection** Lesson 12 of this part explains how to connect a keyboard, mouse, or other pointing device to your system. In addition, Lesson 2 of Part 5 explains how to install a new keyboard or mouse on your system, including how to set up the mouse or keyboard under Windows 95.

In the last few years, keyboard comfort has garnered much attention due to carpal tunnel syndrome—a strain injury caused by typing and other repetitive action. So, manufacturers have designed keyboards and other computing devices that are more ergonomically correct (that is, designed for more healthy and safe use). Figure 4.1 shows an ergonomic keyboard that's widely available.

Figure 4.1 The split design of this ergonomic keyboard helps you keep your wrists straight, relieving wrist strain while you type.

Choosing Your Pointer: Mouse or Trackball

Computers do so much these days—in terms of graphics, games, music, and so on—that the keyboard alone doesn't cut it as the only input device. A *mouse* or *trackball* makes it easier to work in most programs, saving you the trouble of remembering arcane commands or keystroke combinations.

As you move the mouse around on your desk, a smooth ball within the mouse rolls and transmits your movements to a pointer on-screen, as shown in Figure 4.2. The pointer mirrors the way you move the mouse. An upside-down version of a mouse called a *trackball* lets you roll a ball to move the pointer. Using either device you can move the pointer smoothly from one edge of the screen to the other instead of wearing out your finger pressing the arrow keys. Depending on the program you're using, the pointer can take various shapes, including an arrow, a box, a vertical hash mark, an hourglass, and a *crosshair* (crossed lines resembling a plus sign).

Use the mouse or trackball to point to things on-screen, click to make selections, and drag items from place to place; use a joystick to control computer games. You'll learn more about specific pointer techniques in Part 2, Lesson 1 of this book.

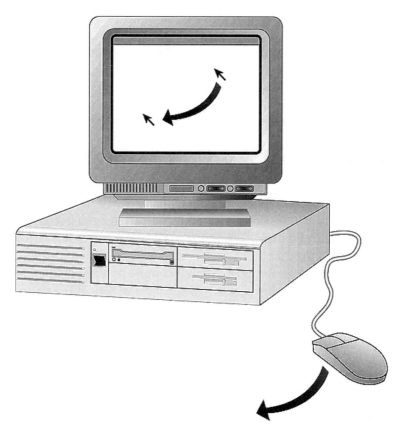

Figure 4.2 Moving the mouse on your desk (or rolling the ball on a trackball) moves the pointer on-screen.

Choose a device that operates smoothly and feels comfortable. If you have wrist and hand problems, consider a choosing a trackball, which can be less fatiguing because you don't have to push it around on the desk.

TIP   **Mouse Comfort**   In the future, you'll be seeing more alternate mouse and pointer devices to reduce hand and wrist injuries. Microsoft's new Intellimouse now offers Glidepoint technology to make the mouse work with less effort. And, some laptops offer touchpad or similar devices so you can move the pointer with a single finger.

TIP **Digitizing Tablets** Graphic artists sometimes use another type of input device called a *digitizing tablet.* Tablets include a pencil-like stylus. When you draw on the tablet with the stylus, your work appears on-screen. Digitizing tablets make generating electronic drawings and paintings much easier and more natural; using a mouse or trackball can be awkward and yield much less attractive results.

Choosing and Adding a Joystick

If you or anyone else using your computer will be playing a lot of games, then you may want to consider adding a joystick. A *joystick* is a small desktop device with a handle-like stick. To control the on-screen character, plane, or gun in your game, you move the stick around. Pressing the stick forward and slightly to the left sends the character up and to the left on-screen for example. While joysticks don't provide smooth control like a mouse or trackball, they're preferred by gamers because they let you change the direction of the on-screen object you're controlling much more quickly. And, it's not practical to use a joystick to move a mouse in regular applications like a word processor. For that kind of work, use your mouse or trackball, instead.

Figure 4.3 A joystick lets you move characters and objects in game programs.

Adding a joystick to your system is usually as simple as plugging it in to the back of your computer. Your system will have either a dedicated game port for the joystick, or there will be a receptacle for it on your sound card. Follow these steps to connect a joystick:

1. Turn off your computer.

2. Look for the joystick port (receptacle), which might be labeled as the game port on your system, which will be slightly D-shaped and have 15 holes. It will match the size and shape of the plug at the end of the joystick cable, which will have 15 pins.

3. Plug the joystick in and restart your system. Then you can start your game software and use the joystick.

4. If the software asks you to calibrate the joystick, you'll simply have to move the stick to the upper-left and lower-right as directed by the program.

Using a Scanner to Capture Images

Scanners use light to convert an optical image to a digital image that you can view or save using your computer. You can choose either a *hand-held* scanner (which you drag over the image much like a mouse) or a *flatbed* model that looks and works much like a photocopier. Color and *grayscale* (black-and-white) models are available; higher resolutions (more dots per inch—higher dpi) produce crisper images.

Special scanner models are designed specifically for scanning color photos or slides into your system; some of these are installed right in the system unit or on the system monitor.

Hand-held scanners only let you scan an image that's about 4 inches in width at a time. Photo scanners likewise handle small images. Desktop scanners let you scan a full 8.5-inch×11-inch (or larger) page in a single pass, and often provide better quality because the original image remains perfectly still. A hand-held scanner requires steady, slow dragging and takes practice; in some photo scanners, the image moves and can shift around as it's scanned.

Scanners are definitely optional equipment. Home computer users can get away with a hand-held 400-dpi color scanner or photo scanner; professional publishers should choose color flatbed units with 1000-dpi or better resolution.

Some manufacturers have released devices that combine scanning with other functions such as faxing, copying, and printing (see Figure 4.4). In other cases, a scanner might be integrated into a monitor or keyboard. If you're considering buying a "combination" device, keep a couple of caveats in mind. First, these combination devices often are much slower or offer lower quality than their standalone counterparts, which you trade off for the convenience and cost-efficiency of the combination device. If your combination device goes on the fritz, you can be left without all its functions until you repair or replace it. Finally, you may spend more money overall in the long run as you replace the various functions of the combination device with a better printer, then scanner, and so on.

Figure 4.4 Combination devices that scan, fax, copy, and print provide convenience, but often sacrifice quality or speed.

This lesson covered devices you use to give your computer input (information and commands): keyboard, mouse, trackball, joystick, and scanner. The next lesson shows you how your computer provides information to you in the form of output from video displays and printers.

Getting Information Out: Video and Printers

In this lesson, you learn how a PC's video display and printer provide you information on-screen and on paper. The lesson also provides guidance for selecting a display and printer to suit your needs.

Viewing Information with a Monitor

The monitor displays your program and data visually (like a TV screen) and connects to a graphics or video card inside your computer. The monitor's *resolution* and other capabilities must match those of the video card. When you're buying a standard office or home system, this isn't usually much of an issue because both components come with the system. However, if you ever consider upgrading your monitor or video card, compatibility does require some investigation. The rest of this section covers some monitor and display features that you should be familiar with before buying any new system or monitor or display upgrade.

 Video or Display When you see a computer ad listing the system's *video* or *display* specifications, the ad is referring to the capabilities of the graphics (or video display adapter) card, which has more to do with the display speed and consistency than the monitor itself.

TIP   **Monitor Sold Separately?**   Many computer stores—especially larger retailers—don't include a monitor with some systems. If a monitor isn't included with the system you buy, make sure the monitor that you do buy is compatible with the graphics card in the system. You'll learn more about this in the rest of this section and in Lesson 9 of Part 5.

Sizing Up a Monitor

Today's monitor manufacturers realize how fatiguing it can be to work with a bad monitor. In fact, eyestrain and neck strain still bother most computer users at one time or another. And because people are spending more and more time with computers every day, comfort is becoming an important issue.

Monitors come in several different sizes (see Figure 5.1). The most common sizes today are 14 inch, 15 inch, 17 inch, 20 inch, and 21 inch; monitors up to 42 inch are available. Like TVs, a monitor's size is measured diagonally, from corner to corner of the case. The actual viewing area of the screen, then, is smaller than the monitor's overall size. A 14-inch monitor has up to a 13.1-inch viewing area, a 15-inch monitor has up to a 13.7-inch viewing area, a 17-inch monitor has up to a 15.8-inch viewing area, and so on. So, when you're shopping for a monitor, make sure to verify its actual viewing area. It may be smaller than you think on some models! Most users will find a 15-inch monitor the best bargain, but anyone performing a lot of graphics work should choose at least a 20-inch monitor and be prepared to pay premium prices. Monitors over 17-inch jump rapidly in price for successively larger sizes.

Figure 5.1   Larger monitors let you view full pages on-screen and are becoming increasingly affordable, but keep in mind that they require more desktop and vertical space.

The next important monitor measurement is *resolution*, or how detailed the picture on a monitor is. Most monitors can display in several *pixels-per-inch* (*ppi*) modes: 640×480, 800×600, 1024×768, 1280×1024, or more.

Pixel Shorthand for "picture elements," pixels are the small dots of colored light that a monitor uses to compose an image. Each pixel actually is a group of three illuminated phosphors: red, green, and blue. For the most part, your eye interprets each pixel as a bright dot.

Dot Pitch The gray space between the phosphor pixels that create a monitor's image is called the dot pitch. A higher dot pitch means there's more gray space between dots, yielding a fuzzier image that's harder on the eyes.

Your monitor's controls can help you use your monitor more safely and comfortably; see Lesson 12, "Setting Up Your System," later in this part to learn more about monitor adjustments.

Gauging a Graphics Card

A few important measurements apply to graphics or video cards. First up is resolution; the card and monitor both must be capable of the same resolution. The next important card measure, *color depth* or *bit depth*, simply means the number of colors that the video card can generate and display on-screen (most can display at more than one bit depth):

- **4-bit (16 colors).** Most video can handle more than 16 colors today, and in fact, Windows 95 doesn't look too great with only 16 colors. Only a couple of years ago, most laptop systems only offered a 16-color display.

- **8-bit (256 colors).** Even though most systems are capable of displaying more colors now, 256 is enough for most computing tasks.

- **16-bit (65,536 or 64K colors).** If you're planning to use newer edutainment CD-ROMs or dabble in graphics, 16-bit color looks great. 16-bit color is also called *high color*. (Some adapters also offer 15-bit depth—32,768 or 32K colors.)

- **24-bit (16,777,216 or 16.8M colors).** For professionals and other color connoisseurs, this is the best display possible. It's so good, it's also referred to as *true color*.

VGA and SVGA   Video cards some times are labeled according to industry standard names. *VGA (Video Graphics Array)* cards handle up to 640×480 resolution and 256 colors. SVGA (Super VGA) displays handle resolutions of at least 800×600 and up to 256 colors.

Each video card contains its own RAM (which may be described as VRAM, DRAM, or EDO RAM). Graphics cards in new systems should offer at least 2M of RAM; otherwise, graphics-intensive applications like multimedia programs will run very slowly, as the card will have trouble drawing images quickly enough on the monitor.

Newer video cards also are accelerated, meaning the video card has a special coprocessor chip that handles the video data rather than letting the CPU handle it. Offloading this task to the video card makes the system perform better. On most new systems, graphics are accelerated to 64-bit speeds, although 128-bit video cards are on the market.

Bigger Bit Depths?   If you see a card that's labeled "64-bit," that measurement is referring to the card's data (coprocessor) speed, not it's color depth. Remember from Lesson 2 of this part that the system's bus speed is also measured in bits. So, a "PCI 64-bit" card is faster, but doesn't offer more than 16.8 million colors.

CAUTION

One last video feature that's becoming more standard is 3D enhancement. Basically, 3D video cards make on-screen textures and objects seem more realistic while being drawn on-screen much more quickly. This feature makes display on newer systems greatly superior, enhancing the viewing experience for (you guessed it) multimedia programs and games.

To learn more about changing the color and resolution settings for your display, see Lesson 15, "Controlling the Desktop Appearance," in Part 2.

Printing

Printers make *hard copies* (printouts) of your work in black and white or color. *Inkjet* or *bubblejet* printers blow liquid ink at the page in precise patterns, creating characters on single sheets of paper. *Laser* printers (Figure 5.2), generally more expensive, use an electrically charged drum to transfer *toner* (dry ink) onto paper, much like a photocopier. Both inkjet and later printers can print in black and white. Some inkjet models come capable of both color and black and white printing; other models enable you to add on color printing capability. Laser printers, generally, are either black and white or color, with color models being substantially more expensive.

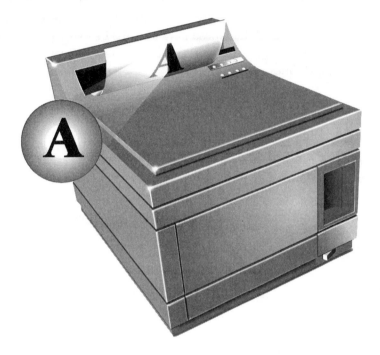

Figure 5.2   Laser printers are more expensive but offer greater resolution and speeds.

Like display resolution, printer output quality is measured by the dots you see, or dots-per-inch (dpi). Inkjet printers offer lower resolution (starting at about 300 dpi), and laser printers offer the best (up to 1200 dpi). Generally, higher dpi capabilities mean a printer will cost more than a similar laser or inkjet model.

Also consider a printer's speed, measured in *pages per minute (ppm)*. Inkjet printers have different speeds depending on whether you're printing in black and white or color; the low end I've seen is 1.7 ppm in color and 3 ppm in black. Laser printers can print at 8 ppm or more, in contrast.

A few of things affect a laser printer's speed: it's internal processor, memory, fonts, and connection. You can usually upgrade the memory or add more fonts (or PostScript capabilities for graphics) to improve performance and reduce printer errors. Look for a minimum of 1M of memory in a laser printer.

All printers connect via a parallel (LPT) or serial (COM) port. (Make sure your system has the right type of port available so you can connect the printer you'd like to buy.) Serial printers have traditionally been faster than parallel printers. However, the EPP (Enhanced Parallel Port) LPT connections found on newer systems perform much faster, if you buy a printer that also takes advantage of EPP capabilities.

TIP **Hook It Up** Lesson 12 of this part, "Setting Up Your System," explains how to connect a printer to your system. In addition, Lesson 1 of Part 5 explains how to install a new printer for your system, including how to set up the mouse or keyboard under Windows 95.

Entry-level prices for inkjet printers are attractive, at around $200 for black and white and $300 for color, which makes them economical and versatile printers. But laser printer prices have fallen, too, to around $400 for a basic model; however, in this category, you can easily spend over $1,000.

There are just a couple more printing capabilities worth mentioning. A *dot-matrix printer* creates letters by pressing patterns of pins against a printer ribbon; they offer either 9 or 25 pins, with 25-pin models offering higher quality. These printers use continuous-feed paper, which is more expensive and prone to paper jams. They also tend to be noisier and slower than other types of printers. On the up side, they are inexpensive to buy (some new models are still around for less than $100), and their ribbons are cheap.

Many inkjet printers claim photo-quality, or offer add-on packages for printing photos. Technology is improving in this area, and you should make sure you see samples from one of these printers before purchasing it. Always ask to see an actual print sample—don't rely upon samples in the product's marketing brochure!

TIP **Even Better Printing** Other printers are even more high-end than laser printers or very specialized. These include dye sublimation and thermal transfer printers, and plotters. While most users don't need to purchase such a printer, if you ever need a specialized print job, check the phone directory for a print shop or engineering shop that has one of these printers and can print your document for a fee. They'll tell you how to prepare and transfer the file to them for printing.

This lesson explained the equipment your computer uses to display and print images, documents, and multimedia animation. Continue to the next lesson to explore how computers can communicate via modems.

Communicating with a Modem

In this lesson, you learn how a modem enables a PC to communicate with other computers.

Understanding Modem Basics

Modems let computers communicate and transfer data over telephone lines. A modem converts a computer's digital data to analog (wave-based) information that can be sent and received on phone lines. When a modem receives information, it converts it back from the wave format to the digital format your computer understands. With a modem, you can:

- Exchange electronic mail and files with other computer users.
- Send and receive faxes (if you have a fax/modem) or files.
- Talk with others over the phone (for voice-capable modems).
- Use a (voice-capable) modem as a phone messaging system.
- Connect to online services such as America Online, CompuServe, or the Internet to gather information.

Modems can be *internal* (on an adapter card inside the system unit) or *external* (a box connecting to a COM or communications port). Notebook computers can have either an internal modem, an external modem, or what's called a PC card modem; you'll learn about PC cards in Lesson 9 of this part. External modems can be easier to install and can be used with more than one computer, and also have indicator lights to cue you as to the modem's operating state. Internal modems, on the other hand, cost less and don't require a separate cable or free COM port; the Windows 95 software can display a limited modem indicator on-screen for you.

Modems require special software to work. Basic software called a driver file works with Windows 95 to handle basic modem operations. From there, you need special software to handle particular modem jobs: sending and receiving files, connecting to the Internet or an online service, handling special Internet functions, faxing, and so on. Usually, the modem or system will come with all the software you need to take advantage of the modem's full range of capabilities.

Most new computers—even notebook or laptop models—include modems, because almost all computer users now want to connect to the Internet or an online service to share e-mail and retrieve information. It's quite a phenomenon, with millions of new users going online each year.

If your computer doesn't have a modem, see Lesson 5 in Part 6 to learn how to add one. Whether you're adding a modem to an existing system or want to choose the best modem for a new system, the rest of this lesson will teach you what you need to know about modems.

TIP **What about Hayes?** A company called Hayes Technologies made some of the most widely-used early modems and therefore became the industry standard. Most modems sold today are Hayes-compatible and use the *Hayes command set*, alphanumeric command strings used behind the software scenes to control the modem's operation.

Modem Speeds

Modems transfer data at a rate measured in *bits per second* (*bps*); higher numbers mean a faster modem. Modem speeds have been increasing rapidly as folks crowd onto the Internet. A faster modem means on-screen graphics transmit faster to the computer, and hastens e-mail exchange.

Earlier modems operated at 2,400bps and 9,600bps. Today's slowest modems operate at 14,400bps, with other available modems working at 28,800, or 33,600. (You'll sometimes see modem speeds abbreviated in ads. For example, a 33,600bps modem might be called a *33.6, 33.6K,* or *33.6kbps* modem.)

A new technology called "x2" makes modems capable of *downloading* (receiving information only) at about 56,000 bps. This technology was developed by U.S. Robotics, a leading modem manufacturer. A couple of cautions are in order about x2. First, not all online services and Internet connections let you take advantage of 56K speeds. And, remember that you can only download (receive) data at 56K; you can only send data at a slower speed, usually 33.6K. So, make sure you need the faster download speed before you pay for it. Second, some modems actually need to be upgraded to the x2 standard, which right now costs about $60. Finally, modems connect only as fast as the local phone lines, phone traffic, and other conditions allow, so even if you pay for this speediest modem, it won't necessarily be able to connect at top speed in your area.

 TIP **A Small Price to Pay...** Prices for top-speed modems usually hover around the $200 mark. So, if you're spending a lot of time online and your modem isn't keeping up, a modem upgrade generally is worthwhile.

 TIP **Better in a Flash** If a modem offers "Flash ROM Upgradability," that means you'll be able to improve its speed later by installing upgrade software from the modem manufacturer. You can either download such an upgrade or request it on disk.

Other Modem Standards

Features that describe how and how quickly a modem works include modulation, data compression and error correction. Modulation describes exactly how a modem sends signals over the phone line, (indicated with "V." plus a number and perhaps "*bis*"). Plain V.32 modems work at around 9600 bps. V.32bis modems transfer at speeds up to 14.4K, while V.34 or V.Fast modems operate at 28.8K or above.

Modems that have *data compression* make the data more compact before sending it (so they can send more of it), and they *decompress* data when they receive it. The top standard in data compression today is V.42bis, and any modem you choose should support that standard. A modem's throughput describes how much data it can transfer when it's operating at its top speed, with compression working. For faster modems, throughput can be 115,200 or 230,400 bps!

Error correction means your modem automatically senses mistakes in data and retransmits it as needed; the standard to meet here is V.42.

A last buzzword you may hear or see is 16550 UART. For a modem to work effectively while Windows is running, the PC's COM port (or the internal modem) needs to support 16550 UART. Most do, but if you're considering connecting an external modem to a COM port on an older system, check the system documentation or check with the manufacturer to make sure your system can handle 16550 UART.

 TIP **Got It?** To summarize, you should look for a modem with V.34, V.Fast, or better modulation for the fastest transfer speeds; V.42bis data compression; and V.42 error correction.

Faxing with a Modem

A fax/modem or data/fax modem can send and receive faxes using special software. Windows 95 comes with faxing software called Microsoft Fax (Figure 6.1), but most fax/modems also come with different types of faxing software that may offer more features than Microsoft Fax. (See Windows 95 online help, described in Lesson 6 of Part 2, to learn to use Microsoft Fax.) You also can purchase faxing software like WinFax Pro from other software publishers.

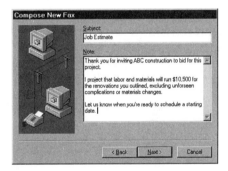

Figure 6.1 The Windows 95 Microsoft Fax application walks you through the process of addressing and composing a fax.

There are certain advantages and disadvantages to using a fax modem, and these can affect whether you rely on a fax/modem alone or use it as a supplement to a dedicated fax machine. Fax/modems aren't great for receiving, because faxes that you receive are often saved in special graphical formats. To be able to use a received fax for practical purposes, you then have to print it out, which can be time-consuming. Also, if you want to use your fax/modem as your only fax, you'll have to leave your computer on around the clock, which may consume more power than the few faxes you receive are worth. Lastly, receiving faxes can be distracting if you're performing other computer work.

On the other hand, fax/modems are a cost- and space-saving alternative for small or home offices, and a must for professionals on the road. They also save paper, because you fax without printing. If you fax infrequently, a fax/modem can be a good alternative.

Fast Faxing? A fax/modem's top speed varies depending on what it's doing. Even though fax/modems may be able to transmit online data at 33.6Kbps or 56Kbps, the top fax speed for most fax/modems is 14.4Kbps, just as most older fax machines only can send at about 9.6Kbps.

CAUTION

Using a Modem Like a Phone

Another new modem technology is *DSVD* (*Digital Simultaneous Voice and Data*), also called *VoiceView*. Modems that support this technology are often called voice-capable, voice-enabled, or voice/data/fax modems. This technology lets a modem handle regular voice calls, for hands-free phone conversations (see Figure 6.2), as on a regular office speakerphone. (*Full-duplex* modems let both parties talk simultaneously— a feature you should look for.) Of course, you'll also need a microphone to be able to talk through the modem, if one isn't integrated with your system.

Figure 6.2 My Compaq Presario came with a DSVD modem. Here, I'm using it and its accompanying software to dial the phone and place a hands-free call.

DSVD also enables the modem to do two things at once, like show video while you talk, so you can video conference (in which case the modem or system will come with a small video camera for that purpose). With the right software, some voice-capable modems can even serve as answering machines/voice mail systems, as long as you're willing to leave the PC on 24 hours a day. DSVD or

VoiceView is a nice feature for home office systems, and is now included in many system packages without a significant price difference when compared to other systems without a voice-capable modem.

CAUTION

I Can't See You   To video conference with someone else via computer, the person you're calling must have a voice-capable modem and video camera that's compatible with the one installed in your system.

Adding an Extra Phone Line

A modem must be connected to a phone line jack, which is a problem if you're using the computer at home and only have one phone line. You only have three alternatives to deal with this situation:

- **Plug the phone into the modem.** Most modems have an extra jack or receptacle so you can plug one line into the phone line and one line into your phone, so that both the phone and modem work. The problem with this is that when you're online, incoming calls get a busy signal or no answer, or can even disrupt your connection. Also, you (and your housemates) can't use the phone and be online simultaneously.

- **Install an additional phone line in your house or office.** Make sure to place the new jack or receptacle in a location that's convenient for your computer. The obvious drawback is the extra expense of the new phone line.

- **Buy a switching device.** See Lesson 11 in this part to learn how a phone line switch can let you conveniently use a phone, modem, and even fax machine on a single phone line.

Looking at High-End Modems

A few other options exist for making modem or "modem-like" connections to exchange data at high speed. The first is *ISDN (Integrated Services Digital Network)* modems. ISDN modems transfer data at up to 128Kbps, roughly twice the speed of an analog 56K modem. But ISDN also requires that a special ISDN phone line be run to your house. An ISDN line actually operates like two phone lines, so you can transfer data and talk at the same time, but these lines can be expensive and aren't available in all areas of the country. Call your local phone company to see if you can get ISDN. ISDN modems are also more costly and require a faster connection to the computer; finally, only a limited number of Internet Service Providers (companies that let you connect to the Internet) allow more-expensive ISDN connections. So, there are numerous issues to consider before you buy into this technology.

Some "modems" actually connect to the cable television company's coaxial cable that's wired to your house or apartment if you receive cable service. Some of these connections only display information on your TV (not your computer); you use a special keyboard or remote to operate the cable receiving box that connects to the TV. Cable companies are increasingly offering Internet access via this type of modem because it can receive information rapidly (up to 30M per second), but the jury is still out as to whether this communications method will take hold.

The last type of modem, still in its infancy, lets you download information rapidly via a small satellite dish. Speeds are amazing here, but the communication is strictly one way and the dish is expensive. I'd wait before buying this technology, unless you plan to spend several hours a day downloading information or browsing the Internet.

You've just learned how modems communicate via phone lines to enable you to gather and share electronic information. The next lesson covers CD-ROM drives, sound cards, and other features that qualify a computer as a multimedia machine.

CD-ROM Drives and Multimedia

This lesson explains what multimedia is and how it enhances your computing experiences, as well as the components that give a computer multimedia capabilities, such as a CD-ROM drive.

What Makes a Multimedia System?

Multimedia programs combine text, pictures, sound, full-motion video, and animation. Hundreds of multimedia games, educational products, and reference products are now offered to teach and entertain you. Examples include Microsoft's Encarta 96 Encyclopedia and World Atlas. More companies are using sales kiosks that sell via multimedia presentations. Many companies, such as car companies, will mail you promotional animations showing you how their latest products work and sound. Salespeople even now carry laptop computers that let them use interactive on-screen presentations to close a deal. World Wide Web sites on the Internet increasingly include sound and animation to hold your attention.

To take advantage of the power of multimedia programs, your computer must have certain extras (such as a sound card), and be fairly powerful in order to handle the demands of multimedia. The standards for multimedia compliance aren't as hard and fast as they used to be, so you should always check the system requirements for the software you'd like to run. In general, you'll want a fast CPU like a Pentium and an ample 32M of RAM (see Lesson 2); a video card with at least 2M of memory, acceleration, and 3-D capabilities; and a fast CD-ROM drive and fully-featured sound card, which you'll learn more about in the rest of this lesson.

TIP **What about Clips?** As you use your computer more and more, you'll increasingly encounter sound and video clips online or from other sources. For the most part, under the older Windows 3.11, you had to obtain special software to play back clips. Windows 95 does a much better job of supporting multimedia, enabling you to play audio CDs as well as sound and video files—each in a couple of different file formats.

MPEG MPEG refers to a standard for compressing and decompressing digital video and audio. Multimedia systems need to support MPEG. MPEG-2 is fast becoming the most common "flavor" of MPEG, although an emerging MPEG (MPEG3) is being used for compressed sound files placed on the Internet.

Spinning Sound and Data from a CD-ROM Drive

Many computer users experience a thrill the first time they play an audio CD—or a multimedia CD-ROM computer program—from their PC's CD-ROM drive. The CD-ROM drive revolutionized personal computers, giving them the capability of handling text, graphics, video, animation, and sound—making the PC a true multimedia machine. The CD-ROM drive reads the data on the disc by quickly spinning it and bouncing a laser off the surface.

CD-ROM A CD-ROM drive uses lasers to read a *CD-ROM* (*Compact Disc Read-Only Memory*). Most CD-ROM drives hold one CD at a time, but some multi-disk changer units are on the market.

Until just a few years ago, multimedia escaped the reach of most computers because video, animation, and sound take huge amounts of storage space. Each reflective CD-ROM holds over 650M, room for quite a bit of sound and video. CD-ROM drives that can write as well as read data have become widely available (as an add-on for your system) and relatively affordable, although not as affordable as a drive that reads or plays only.

Like the audio CDs you use with a home stereo or boom box, computer CD-ROMs are 4.5-inches in diameter, plastic but metallic-looking platters. Each disc can hold more than 650M of data. Most new systems come with an internal

CD-ROM drive, and they are also optional on most laptop models. The performance of a CD-ROM drive depends on its *access time* and *transfer rate*—how fast it can get and deliver information. Look for a high transfer rate (in kilobytes per second) and a small access time (in milliseconds). Relative drive speed is generally referred to in shorthand, with "Single-speed" or "1X" representing the speed of the original drives on the market. *Six-speed* (6X) CD-ROM drives (which are about six times as fast as 1X drives) are common now, and the fastest drives are 16X or more. Whether you're buying a new system or replacing your older CD-ROM drive, you should look for a drive that's at least 8X, like the one shown in Figure 7.1.

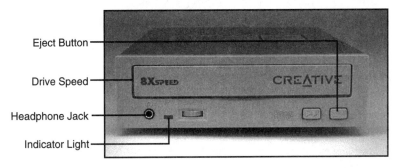

Figure 7.1 Most CD-ROM drives have an eject button, and some even feature a plug so you can plug in headphones for private listening.

 TIP **Fast Filing** CD-ROM drives spin the disc so fast that your computer can grab data from any spot on the disc almost immediately. Data (program) CDs organize information in folders and files, just like hard and floppy disks. You'll learn more about files and folders in a later lesson.

Doing DVD

The next generation of CD media will be the *DVD (digital versatile disc or digital video disc)*. This format will have four or more times the density of today's CD-ROMs (up to about 17 gigabytes)—enough to hold a full motion picture, with the soundtrack in four different languages. DVD players that attach to televisions are now available; as the format gains acceptance, look for DVD players to begin appearing in PCs. DVD players can play conventional CD-ROMs in addition to the DVD.

Inserting and Removing a CD

Some CD-ROM drives use a *disk caddy*; you have to put the disc in a caddy before you put it in the drive. Drives without a caddy have a drawer for the disk that slides in and out, much like the CD player attached to your stereo. A brand new type of CD-ROM drive on the market doesn't have such a drawer; you simply insert the disc directly into a slot in the drive, much like a floppy disk drive. Use these steps to insert and remove a CD-ROM disk:

1. Check the shiny side of the CD for fingerprints, clinging hairs, or other debris. If you find any, wipe the CD gently with a soft cloth. Wipe from the center hole to the outside edges; do *not* wipe in a circular motion.

2. Open the CD-ROM drive by pressing its eject button; if your drive uses a caddy, flip open the CD-ROM caddy.

3. Grip the CD lightly (with your fingertips around its edge) and pick it up; the printed side should face your palm.

4. With your palm (and therefore the shiny side of the CD) pointing down, carefully center the CD and place it in the drive drawer or the CD caddy. You should be able to see the printed side of the CD, facing up. If you're using a caddy, close its lid and insert it into the slot in the drive.

CAUTION

Upside Down   Some CD-ROM drives require the CD-ROM to be loaded in with the label facing down. These drives are a vast minority, but be sure to check your drive's documentation if you have problems reading a CD-ROM.

5. Gently push the drive drawer closed as shown in Figure 7.2, or push the caddy into the drive slot until it locks in place. (Alternatively, you can press the eject button again.) The drive will close and the disc will be ready to use.

6. When you're finished using the CD-ROM, make sure you close any files from it that are open on-screen, or stop the disc if an audio CD is playing. Wait for the drive indicator light to go out; that means the CD has stopped spinning.

7. Press the CD-ROM drive's eject button. The drawer or caddy will slide out. Remove the CD or caddy from the drive. If the CD has a drawer, press it gently so it retracts into the drive, or press the eject button again to close it.

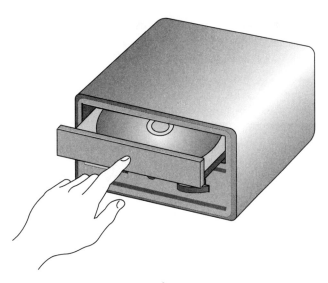

Figure 7.2 Give the CD-ROM drawer a gentle push to finish inserting it.

Reducing Wear and Tear with Program Controls

In life, you can count on the fact that mechanical parts wear out and break. Your CD-ROM drive has several mechanical parts, especially if it uses a drawer rather than a caddy. For example, buttons like the eject button on audio equipment and computers are notorious for wearing out. Similarly, too much downward pressure on a drive drawer can move it out of alignment or break it.

To prevent such disasters, some publishers of software for use with CDs provide ways to use the software to open and close the drive door. Here's how the basic process works:

1. If the program requires it, insert the CD manually into the drive. If you try to run the program and there's no disc in the drive, you'll see an error message. Use the CD as needed, such as copying files from it, or playing it if it's an audio CD.

2. Before you try to eject the CD, make sure you're finished using it. (You don't want to try to eject the CD while it's spinning.) If it's an audio CD, stop playing it. If you're running a program from the CD, use the **File**, **Exit** command to close the program.

3. Open the drive or eject the caddy by clicking in the appropriate place or by choosing the appropriate menu command. For example, you may have to click an eject icon (a symbol or picture), as shown in Figure 7.3. (You can click the eject icon again to close the drawer in such a case.) To eject a program CD-ROM, double-click the **My Computer** icon on the desktop. In the My Computer window that opens, right-click the CD-ROM drive icon with the mouse (see Lesson 2 in Part 2 to learn more about using the mouse), and then choose **Eject** from the menu that appears.

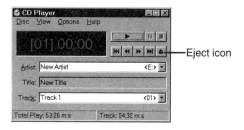

Figure 7.3   Click an eject icon like this one to have the software eject the CD.

Handling Sound with Hardware

A sound card, speakers, and microphone enable your computer to play and record sound. The *sound card* is an adapter card that plugs into a slot in the system unit; it runs speakers, a microphone, and even specialized music equipment that uses MIDI (Musical Instrument Digital Interface). Sound cards also may include a game port for plugging in a joystick, as shown in Figure 7.4.

Most sound cards offer 16-bit sound quality and provide a kind of output called *wavetable*. The more wavetable "voices" the card offers, the higher its quality. Cards with 32 and 64 voices are now on the market. In addition to a MIDI/game port, the card should offer 3-D Surround Sound. For smooth operation, a sound card also should offer its own RAM module. Whatever the card's specifics, it should be compatible with the popular Sound Blaster card (meaning that it supports the same capabilities as the Sound Blaster, not that you have to have two sound cards).

Other Sound Card Components

The speakers also affect sound quality. Get at least 10-watt speakers, and upgrade to better ones with extra features like subwoofers if you're a connoisseur. Better quality speakers even feature separate bass and treble volume controls. Also check to see whether the speakers you're buying require separate batteries; some do. Some audio equipment manufactures are also introducing mini speakers that can connect to a stereo system or a sound card. No matter what, make sure the speakers you use are appropriate for use with a computer. Without the proper magnetic shielding, the magnets in some power-ful speakers could actually damage information on your hard and removable disks. Finally, if you can't find a plug for your headphones on the system unit or near the CD-ROM drive, look for it on the back of a speaker.

Figure 7.4 Speakers, a microphone, and even a MIDI device or joystick plug into the sound card installed in a PC.

See Me, Hear Me Some newer systems have speakers integrated into the monitor. As I noted in an earlier lesson, you do make some trade-offs (like lower speaker power) in buying such a combination device, and one of its compo-nents could break. But the pro of an integrated speaker/monitor setup is free desk space.

CAUTION

In terms of inputting sound so the sound card can capture and record it, a huge variety of microphones are on the market. Microphones range from the more basic stand-alone mics like the one in Figure 7.4 to headset models that keep the microphone a consistent distance from your mouth. For recording short sounds or voice messages in business, an inexpensive model will usually do. If you intend to create production-quality sounds, invest in a headset or amplified microphone.

Sound Software

As noted earlier, Windows 95 does offer some basic applets for playing standalone multimedia files. It even lets you record basic sound files in the common .WAV file format. Most sound cards also come with additional software with more sophisticated sound capture and editing features. For example, a recording/editing program might let you add echo or convert a sound file to different formats. All sound cards offer a program for adjusting the sound levels ("mixing the sounds") from the various input and playback sources; better mixers also enable you to adjust the bass and treble mix. Still other sound cards will create software for creating MIDI files or creating playback lists for audio CDs. If your sound card doesn't offer the software you need, various types of sound software is widely available.

CAUTION

Can I Capture Video? Not usually. While multimedia systems let you capture and play back sound and play back animation and video, it's not standard to equip a PC to capture video. That capability requires a video-capture card and other TV equipment.

This lesson helped you understand how CD-ROM drives, sound cards, and speakers transform your glorified calculator (PC) into an entertaining, interactive machine. You also learned about the features to look for in multimedia hardware. The next lesson covers a grab bag of other peripheral devices.

Other Devices You Might See

This lesson covers common add-ons or extra devices that you might see on new computer systems. You'll learn about their features to help you decide whether you need a particular type of device.

Tape Backup Drives

Backing up your computer's hard disk means copying all of its files and folders to another disk or storage medium. Usually, backup software uses a special format for the backup file(s), so you have to use the backup software to *restore* the backed-up information when it's needed. Backing up provides safety for a couple of reasons: you can store the back up media in a location away from your computer and it's not likely that you'd accidentally delete backup information. Some new systems include a tape backup drive, to provide greater safety and save you the trouble of adding a tape backup drive later. Prices for add-on tape drives range from about $130 to $400 or more.

These drives use tape cartridge to hold the backup, recording the data on magnetic tape within the cartridge in a linear fashion, just as songs are recorded on an audio tape one after another. This enables the tape backup drives to transfer data relatively quickly (up to 19M per minute, depending on the model), but makes retrieval slower than other media, because the drive has to run sequentially through the tape to find the file(s) you want to restore.

Tapes hold anywhere from 125M to several gigabytes of information. First called QIC (quarter-inch cartridges) tapes, tape cartridges come in a variety of widths and formats today. Most are still QIC-compliant and so are called names like QIC-3010 and QIC-3020 and QIC-Wide. Other types of cartridges can include Travan and 4mm DAT. There are so many flavors that they can't all be covered here. Just be sure to get a drive that's large enough to accommodate the size of your hard disk and that you get the correct tapes for it.

External tape backups usually attach to the parallel (printer) port on your system. Internal tape backups attach to either a SCSI or IDE or Enhanced IDE (ATAPI) controller within your system. Figure 8.1 shows an example of an internal tape backup drive. Tape backup drives come with backup software (Windows 95 also offers Microsoft Backup), that lets you backup and restore files, or schedule a backup operation for a time when you won't be working with your system, such as overnight.

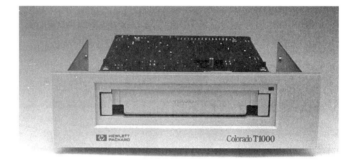

Figure 8.1   Internal tape backup drives like this one attach to an adapter card inside the computer.

Digital Cameras and Video Cameras

The next part of our computing lives that's "going digital" is photography and video recording. If you are planning to use your computer to play with images, want to e-mail family photos to a relative across the country or world, want to include personal images in letters to relatives, or are simply interested in digital photography and its capabilities, consider a digital camera. At about $400 for a decent entry-level model, you can add a digital camera to your system. These cameras look and snap photos much like familiar 35mm cameras; instead of storing the images on film, however, they store the digital images in memory cards in the camera until you download them to your computer via a connection to a special card you install or another port on your system. Once you copy a digital photo to your system, you can edit and print it just as you would any graphic image. Most even come with image editing software.

These cameras capture in varying resolutions and color depths, and they can hold varying numbers of images—all depending on how much memory the camera has. Look for a camera that uses 640×480 resolution or better, 24-bit color (16.7 million colors), stores 60 images at standard resolution, and has expandable storage (via what are called Flash Memory Cards). Better models offer video preview, autofocus lenses, and even voice annotation so you can record your thoughts about your shots as you take them.

Digital video cameras are still a bit primitive. While these aren't yet suited for capturing home movies, you can use them to make video conference calls or to grab still images. Many newer systems with voice-capable (also called DSVD or VoiceView) modems include a video camera for video conferencing. These small cameras cost a few hundred dollars and connect to a video capture card installed in your system; they can be mounted on top of the monitor. Some newer models plug right into a USB (Universal Serial Bus) port. For video conferencing, other users must have a camera and software that's compatible with yours. However, there's not much variation between models at this point, and the video shots aren't necessarily that smooth, detailed, or flattering.

Figure 8.2 shows an example of a digital camera and digital video camera.

Figure 8.2 Digital cameras (left) and video cameras help you digitally trap and store still shots and moving shots.

TIP **Photo Prints** While digital images are fun to display on-screen or e-mail to friends, you'll also want hard copies of your prized shots. Several specialized photo or photo-realistic printers have hit the market. For example, the Sony Color Photo Printer (about $500) uses dye sublimation and prints in 16.7 million colors. You send images directly to this printer via a wireless connection from Sony's DSC-F1 Digital Still Camera.

Infrared (Wireless) Ports

In the past, users have been lucky to have a single desktop computer with a mouse, printer, and maybe another device or two added to it. Now, we're all hardware hogs, with decked-out desktop units, notebook (and smaller) computers, digital cameras, and more. So, transferring information between devices is becoming more of an issue. It's cumbersome to have to connect a digital camera or laptop to download images or files to a desktop system. Plus, you always have to have the right cable on hand, or an easy way to access the ports on the back of your desktop system.

Wireless technology may slowly replace the wired-up world. Basically, wireless uses infrared waves to transmit data. Major manufacturers like IBM are offering wireless data transfer on both desktop and notebook units. You may see a wireless mouse on the market, or add-ons for wireless printing. Just keep in mind that both devices you want to transfer information between have to be equipped for wireless use.

TERM **Infrared...** *Infrared ports* or *infrared transceivers* handle the data transfers, so look for these buzzwords if you're shopping for this feature. *IrDA* stands for *Infrared Data Access*, so that acronym can clue you in, as well as *infrared-ready.*

Touch Controls

Compaq, Sony, and some other PC manufacturers are offering more buttons—either on the monitor or on the system unit—to control features like sound card volume, CD-ROM playback, and more. These buttons work in conjunction with software on your system. These buttons offer fast control, because you don't have to hunt around to find a software volume control, for example. Such touch controls may be a good choice for beginning or intimidated users, who aren't yet comfortable with the mouse or using software features.

If these buttons are on the monitor, they're almost always at hand. However, if your system uses a tower case and the buttons are on the case, the case (and thus the buttons) may be out of reach.

I don't use the touch controls on my Compaq Presario often. As I've noted in other instances, buttons are mechanical, and therefore they can break. I don't want to wear them out more quickly than they would normally. My system even lets me turn the button controls off, which I typically do.

Television Connections

A rare but potentially interesting option is a connection that lets you hook your TV to your system unit, so you can display your computer information on the television. Other computers may come equipped to simply display a TV picture in a small window on-screen, or with a large screen that can function both as a TV and monitor, as on a system recently offered by Gateway2000. Some of these setups even let you record information from your computer to VCR tape. Such an add-on may be right for you if:

- Your computer is in a central location in your house, and you want to see information on a larger screen when browsing on the Internet, for example.
- For professional reasons, you need to watch television as you work.
- You use your computer for gaming and want to see the action on a larger screen.
- You'll be using your computer both for regular computing and pure entertainment, you might want TV capability.

As cable TV companies and companies putting content on the Internet try to get more home users to surf the Web, you may see even more opportunities for choosing and using computer/TV setups. One example is WebTV, which wraps up television, Internet browsing, and some computing capabilities in one.

This lesson covered several newer and more interesting devices that you may find in newer computer systems. The next lesson covers one last issue to consider before making your computer purchase—whether to buy a desktop or notebook system.

Choosing Between a Desktop and Notebook

In this lesson, you take a closer look a notebook computers, what they offer, and whether or not you may want to buy one. You'll learn about a notebook's unique features, as well as laptop-specific components.

Learning about Unique Notebook Features

If you need to use your computer while traveling or have a profession that requires you to perform computer tasks in the car or in airports, consider a notebook (sometimes called *laptop*)—a computer that's compact, opens like a paper notebook, and folds back down to a compact rectangle for travel. Figure 9.1 shows an example notebook computer.

Notebook or Laptop Computer   A notebook or laptop computer is compact and designed to be portable and easy to use when desk space is limited. To use a notebook, you open it or flip up its monitor. When you need to carry it to a new location, you fold it closed. Notebooks also can run for a few hours on battery power, making them ideal for use in remote locations (like construction worksites) or on planes.

Figure 9.1 A notebook computer opens for use and folds to a more compact size for travel.

Once a novelty item, notebook computers are moving more into the mainstream as prices come down and features improve. While many notebook models could cost $10,000 when then were introduced, notebooks now cost about $1,000 more than comparably-equipped desktop systems. Laptops offer the display and keyboard, some type of mouse or pointing device, parallel and serial ports (for printers and other devices), as well as other ports for adding an external monitor, mouse, or more. Most notebooks also offer additional hardware, covered next.

On the technology side of the equation, one of the worst parts of early laptops was the display. Because it's difficult to create a readable, response screen in a flat panel format, early notebook displays were slow and muddy, even though they were only monochrome. Today's *dual scan* or *active matrix* color displays keep up with the system's speed and offer as many colors as full-blown monitors. Still, you should be sure to carefully compare the displays on various notebook models before settling on your purchase.

Another issue that's been overcome in notebook technology is multimedia. First-generation notebooks had small hard disks, a floppy drive, the display and keyboard, and not much more, even though they were larger in size and much heavier. Now, sound card, microphone, and CD-ROM hardware is small enough to be included in notebook systems. Most notebooks now provide full-blown multimedia, which makes them ideal for sales people who travel and need to give multimedia presentations and demonstrations.

CAUTION

Removable Drives   On many notebooks, the floppy drive is removable, meaning you can take the drive out and slide in another removable device, such as a hard disk, CD-ROM drive, or extra battery. You have to be careful, because some systems offer one slot for removable devices, and both the floppy drive and CD-ROM have to use it; on such systems, you can use either the floppy disk drive or the CD-ROM drive, but not both simultaneously.

Manufacturers have made great strides in powering notebook systems. All of them come with an AC adapter, so you can power the system by plugging it into a regular wall socket. For true portability, laptops also can be powered via battery. Systems typically offer either a NiMH (Nickel Metal Hydride) or an even better Lithium Ion battery. Even if a system uses a different type of battery, systems typically let you recharge a battery by plugging it in via AC adapter while the system is turned off.

You also can buy separate battery charger units and extra batteries. Some batteries will slide into the same slot used by other removable devices, so that you can have two batteries available to power the system for a longer time period. When charged, a typical battery lasts up to four hours, assuming you're using power management features to conserve power by putting the system in "sleep" mode when it's been idle for a few minutes.

Although notebooks offer some ports for connecting devices, they have traditionally been more difficult to upgrade because you can't crack open the case and insert an adapter card. To work around this problem, notebook manufacturers developed bus slots for PC Cards (formerly called PCMCIA cards). PC Cards are adapters that are about the size of a credit card. You slide the PC Card into a slot (and perhaps install software, if needed) to install a PC Card device such as a modem, more RAM or storage space, network adapter, or hard disk.

You'll encounter three types of PC Cards today: Type I, Type II, and Type III, with each higher number designating a newer standard that accommodates a thicker card. Most systems today offer a slot that will accommodate either one Type III or two Type II cards. So, before you buy any device that uses a PC Card, make sure you have an available slot. To learn more about working with a PC Card device, consult the documentation that comes with the notebook computer and the device.

 TIP **The Modem's In There**... Internal modems are finally becoming available on notebooks, which is about time because many travelers need to be in touch with others. When a notebook has an internal modem, you don't have to fill a PC slot with a modem, and can use it for other devices. The down side is that it'll be tough or perhaps even impossible to upgrade an internal modem.

You can even use some notebooks as a desktop or a portable system. If this is a capability you may need, consider a notebook model for which you can purchase a *docking station*. To use the notebook with the docking station, you fold the notebook closed and slide it into the big slot on the docking station. The most important advantage to this approach is that you can use a larger monitor and keyboard, for greater working comfort. And, you don't have to repeatedly transfer your data between computers—whether you're using the system as a laptop or a (docked) desktop, you're accessing the same hard disk.

Considering a Computer on the Go

If you're thinking about a notebook purchase, it's usually because you already think you have enough need for its convenience to justify the extra cost. In case your own reasons don't convince you, here are several reasons why a notebook might be preferable to a desktop system:

- You can use a notebook almost anywhere, weather permitting.
- If both your computing needs and workspace are limited (such as if you live in a small apartment) but your budget is flexible, a notebook will serve you well without filling up every available inch.
- With a notebook, a computing desk at home becomes optional.
- Because of the PC Card slots, some upgrades are easier on a notebook, such as adding a network adapter.

- If you already have a relatively powerful desktop system, a notebook makes a good second system, giving you travel flexibility and saving you the trouble of finding more space for a second desktop.

CAUTION

Get a Carrying Case You might be tempted to transport your laptop using an old, large briefcase or book bag to save the $100 or so a laptop case will cost. This isn't a great idea. Laptop cases not only provide special padding and insulation to protect your machine, but also offer numerous nooks and crannies for laptop cables and accessories. You don't want to *forget* a key item (like a spare battery) when you take that important business trip.

Reconsidering a Computer on the Go

While you might yearn for the cachet of a notebook, your more conservative side may prevail when you consider these potential drawbacks:

- If price is really an issue for you, then you should definitely opt for the desktop system.
- Though they're made to be beat up to some degree, all computers and notebooks have fragile aspects and require care. For example, if you bounce a notebook around too much while you use it, you can cause the hard disk read/write head to crash into the disk, possibly causing permanent damage. Notebooks also are sensitive to extremes of heat, cold, and wetness, and can be damaged if left too long in a car that's hot, cold, or wet. Lastly, you don't want to expose any computer or its drives to too much dirt and debris; because you lug a laptop around, it, by definition, can come into greater contact with potentially damaging substances.
- Notebooks have typically been more difficult—or impossible—to upgrade. Opening the unit to upgrade it would void the warranty. You were stuck with the RAM, CPU, hard disk and other elements you bought, unless you're using a PC Card, which of course can be swapped. This limitation is changing. Some manufacturers now offer systems that use the same RAM as desktop units, upgradeable CPUs, and more. Definitely look for upgradeable features if you'll be buying a notebook.
- Notebooks are more easily stolen; in fact, this is quite a problem at airports.
- Most notebook models no longer use a mouse or trackball-like device. In fact, most use a "trackpoint" type pointing device, which resembles a stubby joystick amidst the keys. Still others use a touchpad type device,

where you drag your finger over a rectangular membrane to move the mouse pointer. These devices can be difficult to get used to, and aren't appropriate for some types of uses, like intensive graphical design.

- A notebook might not be ideal for your favorite computer game, because most notebooks don't offer you a port to plug in a joystick.

- While it's a definite plus that most notebooks offer sound, keep in mind that the sound quality on some models may not be up to snuff. If you'll be using your laptop to give multimedia customer presentations, make sure you're satisfied with its sound capabilities.

- You make some compromises when it comes to the keyboard. Notebook keys are often smaller and closer together. They may also have a lower profile and a less snappy rebound, so they can cause you to make typos or type more slowly. Also, notebook keyboards usually don't have all the keys that are available on a full-sized system, such as the numeric keypad to the right of the alphanumeric keys.

- While displays are better, notebook display size and quality is still an issue. Make sure you find a display you're comfortable with. The two most common display standards are *dual scan* and *active matrix*. Dual scan displays are less expensive and generally consume less power, but they're also less bright and a bit slower. Active matrix displays offer the highest quality on a laptop, but you pay more for them, and some of them draw a lot of power—a minus if you'll be running from the battery a majority of the time.

This lesson covered notebook (laptop) computers, and why one may or may not be a sound alternative to a desktop system. The next lesson helps you put the knowledge you've accumulated so far into play—by making a computer purchase.

Making the Big Purchase

In this lesson, you learn more about computer purchase considerations and get pointers that will help you select a vendor.

Making a Final Decision About Your Needs

Once you've chosen the software you want to use (and know its hardware and additional software requirements), you should have a good starting point for choosing a computer. Lessons 2 through 9 should've helped you determine which components you may want step up a notch or two in either power or capacity, so you'll have a system that suits your needs now but also will accommodate you for the next few years. Before you go shopping, make a list of all the requirements you want your computer system to have.

Today, most manufacturers offer fully equipped home multimedia systems. These packages are very comparable in price and performance, so your decision may come down to being based on one or two minimum requirements from your list.

Your budget also has an impact on your computer purchase decisions. Obviously, there's no need to mortgage your house to buy a top-of-the-line setup, but you also don't want to buy a system that'll be obsolete as soon as you bring it home. Allow yourself room to grow with your computer. As a rule of thumb, decide what system you need now, add $500 to your budget, and then buy a system that's faster than the one you need now and has more memory and storage space.

Zeroing in on Your Purchase

When you choose where to buy your computer, compare factors like the type of seller you'll be dealing with, manufacturer, price, service, and warranty. Be sure you're comparing apples to apples where possible—compare prices on systems from the same manufacturer with the same features, or on comparable services. The rest of this section covers the primary factors to consider.

Deciding Where to Buy It

You have to choose where to buy your new computer, and this decision isn't as straightforward as it may seem. In the last few years, dozens of manufacturers and sellers have jumped into the fray, offering a variety of computer components through retail and mail order outlets.

Where you decide to buy your computer depends not only on the kind of computer you want to buy, but also on your computing confidence and what you expect to happen after the sale, as outlined in Table 10.1. Computer magazines and your local newspaper offer advertisements for a variety of computer sellers. While the ads may look the same, there are great differences in what you get from various computer sellers.

Table 10.1 Where You Can Buy Your Computer

Seller	Description
Catalog companies	Sell equipment and software from a variety of manufacturers. Offer convenience but minimum of service or technical support (for the catalog brands). For more experienced users. Purchase with credit card.
Manufacturer direct	Manufacturers sell their own equipment by phone, mail, or the World Wide Web. Convenient, with competitive pricing and warranty. Knowledgeable sales staff. For experienced users or those who want to purchase a particular brand. Purchase with credit card.
Appliance/department store	Offer computers alongside other electronic equipment. Typically, selection, service, and the salesperson's knowledge are limited, although financing may be offered. For moderately experienced users.

Seller	Description
Computer discount stores	These computer superstores offer the broadest selection and best pricing available from retailers. Knowledgeable sales force and financing help smooth the sale. Most offer carry-in repair and upgrade service. Inexperienced users can comfortably buy a computer here.
Value-added resellers (VARs)	These sellers include small retail computer stores and companies that sell computers direct to businesses. Typically, their salespeople are most knowledgeable, and they offer the highest level of after-sale service. Many perform warranty work for computer manufacturers. All this service costs more, though. For very inexperienced users, businesses, or those who want to purchase a high level of after-sale support.

Choosing the Manufacturer (Brand)

Make sure you're buying a computer from a reputable manufacturer. Go to the library and check computer magazines such as *PC World* to find the top brands that offer the most reliable products. Reliability ratings may vary depending on whether you're buying a desktop or laptop system. Also, check with friends, relatives, and business associates who own personal computers. They may have horror stories to help you steer clear of a bad brand, or have stories of great experiences with a particular manufacturer. Remember, all manufacturers make systems sound great in advertisements; you have to do your own leg work to learn which systems last.

Getting a Sweet Deal with Suites

Most sellers offer *preconfigured* systems with everything you need, including the operating system (Windows 95 OSR 2 for most new PCs) and multimedia software for the sound card. Also compare the free software offered with a system.

Many manufacturers and dealers include several pieces of software with every new system. This software can save you hundreds of dollars (because you won't have to purchase it yourself), so shop around for a package that offers the applications you want and need. Most packages also include a starter membership with one or more online services or *Internet Service Providers* (ISPs), companies that provide access to the Internet. However, you can usually get free membership startup deals directly from online service or ISPs, even if they don't come with your computer. You also may get games and reference programs. If the software program you want to use comes with the computer, rest assured that the computer can run it.

Some major manufacturers offer suites of software, where the applications in the suite are designed to work smoothly together and provide a broad range of capabilities. Microsoft Office, Lotus SmartSuite, and Corel's WordPerfect Suite are included with new computer systems from selected manufacturers. If your company uses applications from one of the three leading publishers, it's smart to have the same ones on your personal system. However, if the computer you want doesn't come with the software you prefer, don't write the system off. All the big three suites let you "upgrade" from a competitor's suite at a reduced price. Also, each suite may have different versions. For example, Microsoft Office 97 comes in Standard, Professional, and Small Business versions. If the system you want doesn't come with the right version of the suite that you want, try negotiating to get the suite you need or get a better price. (Yes, some manufacturers will subsitute one suite for another.)

Suite   A software suite is a group of programs bundled by a software publisher and sold for a competitive price. Basic suites usually offer a word processor, spreadsheet, and presentation graphics program, perhaps along with some unique tools from the publisher. "Professional"-level suites also include a database.

Integrated Software   If your new computer doesn't offer all the software you want and you have a broad range of needs, consider an *integrated package*. The leading integrated package, Microsoft Works for Windows, offers word processing, spreadsheet, database, and communications capabilities. It gives the help you need at an entry-level price, and you can upgrade later to a full suite if needed.

Pricing Comparable Systems

In the last two years, computer pricing has become much more comparable between the various computer sellers; catalogs and manufacturers don't necessarily offer the best prices. Sometimes, you can get the best deal when an appliance store puts a model on sale or offers a rebate. Compare prices from a few sources and make sure you're getting the best deal.

If one system lacks a particular feature or capacity that you really want, make sure you find out how much it would cost to upgrade the system; most sellers will upgrade the RAM or hard disk on a new system for a nominal fee (or free, as you're shelling out more money for a component), saving you the trouble of doing so later.

For each system, verify whether certain extras and necessities are included in the price; sometimes shipping, printer cables, or even the monitor will cost extra.

Finally, don't be afraid to ask for a better deal. Some major appliance and computer discount stores will meet or beat competing prices, or give you a rebate if you find your system advertised for less within a certain period after your purchase. If you can't negotiate on the purchase price, see if you can get the retailer to discount any added purchases, such as a printer or accessories.

Financing Your Find

Department stores, appliance stores, and computer discount stores frequently offer financing or special deals like "six months same as cash" (in addition to credit card purchasing). Be careful with store financing: interest rates can be as high as credit card rates—or higher. Mail-order catalog companies, manufacturers, and VARs typically let you use a credit card to purchase your computer.

Looking at the Warranty and Return Policy

Most manufacturers offer a warranty (one year minimum) on parts and labor. Generally, the warranty covers *on-site* repairs—a repair representative will come to you to fix your system. However, in some cases, you'll need to transport the system to the store where you purchased it (or to an authorized dealer), or you might have to ship it (or a component) back to the manufacturer for repair. Most warranties require that repairs or upgrades be performed by an authorized dealer; using any other repair service (or doing it yourself) voids the warranty.

CAUTION

Warranty for Sale   Many dealers offer an extended warranty that covers the system up to three years, starting when the manufacturer's warranty expires. These warranties generally cost a few hundred dollars, so they can

continues

continued

> actually be pricier than simply paying for repairs that are later needed. You do not have to buy an extended warranty immediately; you usually can buy it any time before the manufacturer's warranty expires. If you really want an extended warranty, don't finance it; the finance charges you'll pay would definitely make the warranty a bad deal.

If you decide that a computer doesn't meet all your needs or that you don't need the system for some reason, most sellers offer some type of return policy. Usually, you can return the entire system within 30 days of purchasing it. You'll be required to return the system in its original packaging in most instances. If you purchased the system from a manufacturer or mail order catalog, you may need to pay to return the system. Be sure you understand the seller's return policy.

Don't buy a system unless it includes at least a one-year on-site warranty from the manufacturer and a 30-day unconditional return policy from the seller. Otherwise, if some catastrophic problem strikes the system, you could be stuck with a $2,000 junk pile.

After Sale Service

You can purchase additional computer services (for example, upgrading your system) from computer superstores, VARs, and computer repair companies. In general, a computer superstore's fees will be much lower than a VAR's or repair company's.

The superstore requires you to carry your system in, while a VAR or repair company will come to you (for a fee, of course). Superstores offer some services (such as adding a modem to your system) at a flat rate rather than an hourly fee. And if the technician encounters a problem while performing the service, you don't have to pay for extra time used to fix the problem. Be sure to have an authorized dealer perform repairs and upgrades to your system if it's still under warranty.

Considering Computer Resellers

Secondhand stores of all types have always been around, but only recently have stores that sell used and refurbished computers and peripherals begun to boom. In most cases, I wouldn't recommend that a beginner buy a used system; for novices, the warranty, service, and online documentation provided with newer computer systems is invaluable.

However, you might want to consider a used computer if:

- You have a friend who can help you work with or upgrade a slightly older system, or you're not worried about a warranty.
- You want to get your feet wet with basic word processing or spreadsheet use, so you don't want to spend much.
- You're buying a starter system for your kids to beat up.

It also can be a good compromise to buy a used printer or other component, to allow you to spend more on the system itself. For example, I picked up a used dot matrix printer a few years ago, and it still works like clockwork.

Check the phone book for a store in your area that sells used computers. Before you buy a used system, make sure you research the cost of a somewhat comparable new system and check the classifieds for other used systems that are for sale, so you have an idea of what you should be paying for the used system.

Leasing Your System

Some computer sellers—particularly computer discount stores and VARs—will lease you a system that fits your needs. Some companies will even let you rent a system for a week or so in an emergency.

Leasing a system is usually not a good idea for a home user, because a lease is much more expensive in the long run. However, businesses often choose to lease systems, because computing technology changes so rapidly and leasing tends to make it more convenient to upgrade to a newer system. Leasing can also be an option if you're just starting a small business and don't have the capital to buy your system(s) right off the bat, or if you're bringing in a temporary worker for an undetermined time frame. If you're considering leasing a computer for business, consult your accountant about the tax and other implications before setting on leasing (versus purchasing).

This lesson offered facts to help you select a system to purchase based on the manufacturer and package, and provided guidance concerning where to buy it. The next lesson reviews a few accessories for use with your system that you might want to pick up.

Accessorizing for Maximum Efficiency

In this lesson, you learn about necessary and optional accessories for use with a computer.

Providing a Sturdy Base

Even if you purchase a notebook computer, you'll need a clean, level work area for using the system and keeping your floppy disks in order. For a desktop system, you need to provide a more permanent work center, as it's simply to cumbersome to repeatedly take apart and reassemble a heavy desktop system. The next few sections cover the items to consider buying to support a desktop system.

Computer Workstation

You need a wide, stable surface for your system unit, monitor, and printer. While you can place a computer on a traditional table or desk, specialized workstations (see Figure 11.1) offer monitor shelves, slide-out keyboard shelves, system unit holders, cable openings, and more special features to accommodate a computer's parts. Some workstations are mounted on casters to make them mobile. You can spend as little as $150 or up to a couple thousand for decorator-style units. And make sure you have a comfortable chair with good support and adjustable height. Your best bet is to visit an office, computer, or furniture store (rather than shopping from a catalog) and try out several computer desk and chair models before you buy yours; the extra comfort will be well worth the extra shopping time. Also, measure to make sure the hutch or shelving on the workstation allows enough space for the monitor (this can be an issue for 17-inch and larger monitors), and ample room for the system unit (again, measure to confirm).

Figure 11.1   A computer workstation helps you better arrange a computer's components.

CPU stand

If you're buying a desktop unit that has the older, horizontal-style case, and you don't want to use the system unit to support your monitor, you can buy a CPU stand to hold the system unit in a vertical orientation. This enables you to tuck it under the workstation and save space; doing so without such a stand can leave your system unit unstable or place it in contact with static electricity from the floor.

Vertical or Not   Once you've chosen how to orient a horizontal system unit, you should stick with that orientation. Changing repeatedly between laying it on the desktop or standing it on end can cause the hard disk to get out of

CAUTION

alignment and crash. However, CD-ROM drives are intended for use only in a horizontal orientation. So, when a horizontal desktop unit has a CD-ROM drive, you generally can't stand the system unit on its end, because doing so would also stand the CD-ROM drive on end and likely damage the drive.

Printer Cart or Stand

If you purchase a smaller workstation with little surface area, it'll be essential to add some kind of cart or stand to hold the printer and a supply of paper. You often can find models to match your workstation, or models that hold two printers. Some roll so you can use them in multiple rooms or with different printers, or have a drawer for storage. Printer stands start at around $100.

Power Protection and Other Connections

You'll have a lot of connections to make when you set up your PC (see the next lesson to learn more). There are a few accessories that provide greater power safety or connection options:

- **Surge suppresser.** Surge suppressers (see Figure 11.2) protect against sudden spikes in power that can zap your computer and data. This is one accessory that's *not optional*. Surge suppressers also give you additional plugs for your computer's components and even your modem's phone line. Basic models start at about $8.

CAUTION

Strip Sense Be careful: Not *all* plug-in strips are surge suppressers. The ones sold in general merchandise discount stores may simply be multi-receptacle plugs. Also, *never* plug suppressers into one another; doing so defeats the surge suppresser circuitry.

- **UPS (uninterruptible power supply).** A UPS feeds electrical current to your computer in the event of a power loss (commonly called a *brownout*) that could cause data in RAM to be lost. Figure 11.2 also shows a UPS. These start at about $125, but are a good investment if there are frequent power losses in your area.
- **Switch boxes.** If you want to use two computers with a single printer, or vice versa, you could spend a lot of time plugging in and unplugging cables. Instead, invest about $25 in an idiot-proof switcher. Once you've plugged in all the cables, you simply turn or flip a switch to route information to the right device.

Figure 11.2 A surge suppresser (top) protects your computer against power zaps, while an uninterruptable power supply provides power during a brownout.

- **Phone line switches.** If you want to plug your phone and computer modem or phone, modem, and fax machine into a single phone line, you can buy a switching unit to enable all your devices to share the line. Features vary by model, but some models will automatically evaluate incoming calls and send them to the right device, phone or fax in particular. Entry level models start at about $50, and one with automated features will set you back $120 or so.

Enhancing Your Environment

Some last accessories help you work more smoothly and with greater comfort. You may not need all of these immediately, but you should be aware of these helpful accessories:

- **Mouse pad.** For best results, you should have a mouse pad (purchased separately, if one doesn't come with your system) under your mouse. The mouse's roller ball easily grips the pad's rubberized surface, which helps keep mouse movement smooth and even.

- **Keyboard drawer.** If your workstation doesn't provide a movable shelf for your keyboard, you can buy one that adds on. These either mount under the workstation surface or are contained within a case that you can place under your system unit or monitor. Keyboards free up additional workspace and enable you to stow your keyboard away when it's not needed. These cost from $50 to $100.

- **Anti-glare screens.** If you find yourself suffering from eyestrain when you use your computer, you may want to add an anti-glare screen. These reduce glare and improve screen contrast. Although these are less necessary with today's high-quality monitors, the lighting in your workspace may warrant one. Starting at about $25, these can make your life more pleasant.

TIP **Another Glaring Solution** You can use an ordinary manila file folder to cut glare. Simply put it on top of the monitor, fold it down both sides, and then tape it in place so it protrudes a few inches past the front of the monitor, shading the monitor to prevent any glare.

- **Copy holders.** If you retype documents a lot or have little desk space to hold materials you need to review while working, you can buy a copy holder for about $50. This device mounts to the side of your monitor and has a clip for holding relevant papers.

- **Comfort (ergonomic) devices.** Manufacturers have been improving keyboard designs, but some users still experience lower arm fatigue and pain when using the computer for an extended time. You can buy devices like wrist rests to alleviate such strain. If you're having any type of comfort problem, check with your local computer store for advice and a solution.

- **Disk storage.** Floppy disks can be damaged, so it's best to store them in a safe location. You can buy numerous types of boxes and holders to store and catalog your floppies and other removable disk cartridges.

You've just learned about a number of accessories that enable you to keep your PC safe and yourself comfortable. Lesson 12 in this part guides you in setting up a system.

Figure 11.3   This keyboard drawer includes wrist pads for comfort and support while using the mouse and keyboard.

Setting Up Your System

12

This lesson leads you through all the steps involved in connecting the parts for your computer system.

Deciding Where to Put a New Computer

Like any tool, your computer requires that you observe a few guidelines to use it comfortably and safely. Following these rules will prolong the life of your computer by protecting it from damage.

You should be particularly careful about where you place a computer within your home. Let common sense guide you. If the computer is for your whole family, put it in a room where you can easily supervise the kids while they use it. Make sure the kids can seat themselves at it comfortably without grabbing or leaning on any of the components. If you'll be using your home computer for business, put it in a more secluded spot (such as a den or home office) where you can have solitude while you work.

Likewise, you should use common sense with regard to what you place on and around your computer. Avoid bringing beverages around your computer; a spilled drink can fry a keyboard or burn up a CPU. You don't want to pile a ton of books on your system unit or get crumbs in a disk drive. You should also avoid smoking around your computer; smoke residue can clog and gunk up your disk drives. Following are the common-sense guidelines you need to follow in deciding where to put your computer:

- **Make sure there's room for your computer workstation, chair, and accessories.** Computer workstations are designed to use space economically, but keep in mind how much equipment and extras you have. You don't want to be continuously bumping into things or running over cables with your chair.

- **Keep it cool and dry.** Excessive heat can damage your computer, particularly the hard drive. Likewise, humidity (or worse, dripping water) can zap your computer or make it behave erratically. Avoid placing your computer in damp areas like basements, hot rooms like attics, or other areas that aren't air-conditioned. Don't place the computer in front of a window that receives heavy, direct sunlight, which can overheat the system and cause uncomfortable glare. Also, make sure there are several inches of clearance behind the system unit so its exhaust fan can draw in fresh air to cool the computer when it runs.

- **Avoid dust and pet hair.** The system unit's fan tends to suck in dust along with fresh air; sliding a disk into a drive can push in dirt and hair as well. Keep the area around your computer free from dust, hair, or equipment that attracts either of these (like a clothes dryer). If you can't avoid dust, consider buying plastic dust covers for your system components.

- **Provide proper lighting.** Place your computer so the room's light source is above and slightly behind the monitor. Improper lighting that falls on the monitor from the front or sides causes glare and reflections on the monitor, which can strain your eyes and make the screen hard to read.

- **Use a stable electrical outlet.** Never plug your computer into an outlet that's on a household circuit used by other appliances—even small ones like a toaster or blow-dryer. These can suck current away from the computer, causing power drops that will make the system lose data.

- **Put a modem-equipped computer near a phone line.** If your computer system has a modem, be sure to put the system near a phone jack or a location where one can be installed. If you'll be a heavy modem user, you may want to have a second phone line installed, with a jack (plug) for it near your computer. See Lesson 6 in this part for more about modems.

- **Keep it away from family traffic.** Use common sense. Don't place the computer where anyone can trip over the power or mouse cords, put the groceries down on the keyboard accidentally, throw things at the monitor, or the like.

Unpacking a New Computer

Use a reasonable amount of care when unpacking your system to avoid damaging any of the components. Also, take the time to do things that will ensure you can take advantage of your computer's warranty—register the system and (horrors) keep a few things you would normally throw out.

TIP **Parts, Too** The advice in this task also applies when you purchase up-grades or replacements for individual pieces of hardware. Take the steps recommended here before installing the device.

Follow these steps to unpack a new system:

1. Carefully open the boxes containing the computer components by pulling off the outside tape. Avoid slitting the box with scissors or a knife, which can scratch the components.

2. Remove each component from its box, placing it carefully on a computer desk or other flat, secure surface. Place any paperwork from the boxes in a handy location nearby. Also remove any cardboard protectors from the floppy disk drives. Check the box carefully for all cables, manuals, screws, and other vital items from the manufacturer. You don't want to pack away or accidentally discard anything you might need to properly set up and run your computer.

TIP **It's Stuck!** If a heavy component is surrounded by Stryrofoam and you're having trouble getting the component out of the box, carefully turn the compo-nent and box over, while firmly pressing the top of the component so it doesn't unexpectedly slide out of the box, and set it on a sturdy surface. With the weight of the component holding down the Styrofoam, you should be able to slide the box up and off.

3. Return all cardboard, Styrofoam, and plastic packing materials to the boxes, including the floppy disk protectors. Store the boxes in a safe, dry place. You'll use these if you ever need to transport the computer. (Also, some companies will not allow returns unless the computer is packed in its original boxes.)

4. Take the packing slip or receipt from the pile of papers you put aside and check it to make sure you received all the pieces you paid for. Review the setup instructions quickly. Have you received all the connectors you need? If something's missing, contact the seller immediately.

5. Inspect all components for damage. If you find problems, call the seller immediately.

6. Fill out and mail your Registration Card. Alternatively, some manufactur-ers provide an online registration process that begins automatically when you start the computer the first time. If you want to get technical support from the manufacturer or seller, you must follow its registration process.

7. Take all the paperwork that came with your computer—packing slip, invoices, receipts, and warranty information—and file it with your other important personal papers.

Connecting the Components

Connecting a computer system's components is a matter of plugging the right connector into the right socket. The sockets and connectors have similar shapes (and corresponding numbers of holes and pins), so matching them up is easy. Some computer manufacturers even label the various sockets on the back of the system unit for you.

You may need a few tools to assemble your computer. These are primarily used to tighten connectors into place. So before you start, gather up a medium-sized Phillips-head screwdriver, a medium-sized flat-head screwdriver, and a small flat-head screwdriver. Also grab a small envelope or plastic baggie for leftover screws and the like; file these away with the paperwork that came with your computer.

 TIP **Lay It All Out** Take the time to lay out all the parts where you want them so that you won't have to untangle cables after you've connected components. For example, if you want to place the mouse to the right of the keyboard and the printer somewhere to the left (or the reverse if you're left handed and want your mouse on your left), arrange them that way before making the connections.

Just remember, if you feel you're having to force a connector into position, back off. You may be trying to plug it into the wrong socket, and you may risk breaking pins off the connector if you force it. One more tip: Avoid getting magnetic or electrical fields too close to the computer (don't even use magnetic-head screwdrivers), and *don't turn on any component until you have the whole system assembled and you have plugged the system into a surge protector.*

CAUTION **The Plug Doesn't Fit!** Most computer manufacturers provide documentation identifying the various sockets and connectors on the back of the system unit. If you have any doubts about where things go for your computer specifically, check the documentation.

Here are the basic assembly instructions:

1. **Connect the keyboard.** Find a round socket (port) on the back of the computer that accommodates a connector with five or six pins and a square in the center of the connector (see Figure 12.1). Make sure that you find the socket that's labeled for the keyboard, as the mouse may use the same type of connector. The socket also will have a slot at the top or bottom. Align the keyboard plug's pins with the holes in the socket; this should also line up the ridge on the keyboard plug with the slot in the socket. Press the plug gently into place.

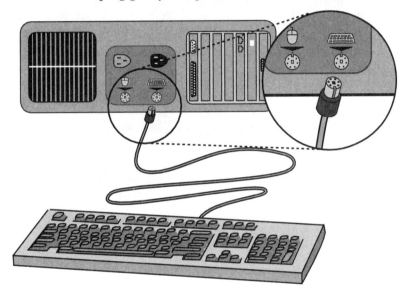

Figure 12.1 The keyboard and mouse usually plug into round receptacles.

2. **Connect the mouse.** The connector will look like the round keyboard plug or will be an oblong shape (with 15 or fewer pins). Align the mouse plug's pins with the holes in the socket; press the plug gently into place. If you have an oblong connector with screws, gently tighten the screws.

3. **Connect the monitor.** It has two cords: One has an oblong plug with 15 or fewer pins, and the other plugs into a source of power (on the back of the system unit or on a surge suppresser). Plug in the oblong connector and the power cord as shown in Figure 12.2; *do not* turn on the monitor yet.

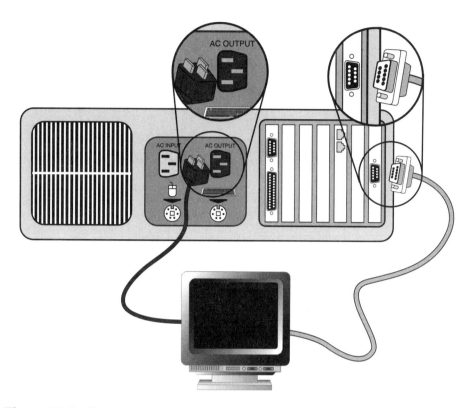

Figure 12.2 The monitor may plug into two places on the system; one plug powers the monitor. Otherwise, the monitor will have one plug that plugs into the back of the system, and another that plugs into the surge suppresser.

4. **Connect the printer.** Most likely, its cord will have a *parallel* connector with 25 pins that plugs into a socket with 25 holes on the system unit. Printers using serial ports have 9- or 25-pin connections; in this case, the system unit has the pins and the connecting end of the cable has the holes. Check your printer's cable: Which connection do you have? Ease the plug into place, tightening the screws or clicking the metal clips. Plug your printer's power cord into a surge suppresser, but *do not* turn on the printer yet. (It's preferable to use a separate surge suppresser plugged into a wall outlet other than the one you're using for the surge suppresser handling the rest of the system. That's because both the system itself and the printer draw a lot of power, and you don't want to overtax the wall outlet.)

5. **Set up your modem.** You may need to make several connections if the modem is external. Using a cord that ends in plastic clips like those on a

phone cord (*RJ-11 connections*), plug one end into the jack labeled Line on the back of the modem; plug the other end into your home's phone-line jack. Take the serial cable that comes with the modem and plug one end into the serial port on the back of the modem. Plug the other into the corresponding 25-pin socket on the back of your computer. Finally, plug the modem power cord (if any) into the surge suppresser. For internal modems, use an RJ-11 cord to connect the Line jack on the back of the system unit to the wall phone jack. If your modem has an extra jack labeled "Phone," you can plug your phone into it.

6. **Plug in the speakers and microphone.** Connect them to the sound card at the back of the system unit. Plug the microphone into the "Mic In" jack, and plug the speakers into the "Spk Out" jack. (Refer to Figure 7.4 in Lesson 7 of this part to see how these items connect.) If you're not using batteries for the speakers, you may need a power adapter unit; plug one end into the power jack on the back of one of the speakers and the other end into the surge suppresser (*don't* turn on the speakers yet!).

 TIP **Boxy Plugs** The plug for some power adapters is a large, square box. When you plug it into a surge suppresser, it can cover other receptacles on the adapter. To avoid this, try plugging the big adapter plug into one end of the suppresser strip or the other.

7. **Finally, plug the system unit itself into your surge-suppresser power source.** The cable for the system unit has one end with prongs and one with slots. Plug the end with slots into the receptacle with prongs (sometimes labeled "AC Input"). Plug the normal end of the cable into the surge suppresser.

At this point, you should be ready to turn on the juice to your computer. Lesson 1 in Part 2 describes in detail how to properly start up or boot your system.

Adjusting Your Monitor

Even though you can adjust your monitor, you may still encounter screen glare once you start up your computer, as described later in this book. Changing daylight coming through a window can cause glare at particular times or during certain outdoor conditions. Of course, you can do the obvious: Close the curtains or blinds to adjust the daylight coming in. Most people, however, find natural daylight restful—especially if the interior is lighted by fluorescent fixtures. Don't worry. You can try a couple of tricks to get the best of both worlds.

TIP   **A Better Resolution**   Most monitors can display in several resolutions, depending on which display driver file you install and use. To learn how to change your monitor's resolution in Windows 95, see Lesson 14 "Controlling the Desktop Appearance" in Part 2.

Use these steps to adjust your monitor:

1. Place the monitor at the appropriate height and distance in relation to where you sit. The monitor should be about two feet from your eyes, at eye level or slightly below. If necessary, use a monitor stand or a few books to raise the monitor to eye level.

2. Most monitors have a tilt-and-swivel base. If necessary, use it to adjust the screen even if you can't place it exactly at eye level.

3. To adjust the brightness, look for the knob labeled **Bright** or indicated with a "sun" icon.

4. To adjust the contrast (the difference between light and dark), look for the knob labeled **Contrast** or indicated with a half-dark and half-light icon.

5. If the screen image is cut off or fuzzy on one side, you need to adjust the H-phase (horizontal control). Look for a knob and turn it to center the image on-screen. Some systems have two knobs: one that controls the horizontal width of the image and one that controls the horizontal position of the image.

6. If the screen image appears smashed or stretched vertically, you need to adjust the V-size (vertical control). Look for a knob and turn it to adjust the height of the image on-screen; you may need to turn a second knob to adjust the vertical position of the image.

Reducing Your Stress While Using Your PC

No matter how expensive your system was, or how you adjust your monitor, or what type of accessories you've added for comfort and safety, you should still pay attention to your physical comfort when you use your computer. Before you realize it's happening, you can develop a headache, burning eyes, or a stiff neck.

The best defense is to take a break after every half-hour to hour of work (or play). Get up from the computer and walk around the office a bit. Take that coffee or restroom break. In addition, you can do some simple exercises to release stress and rest your muscles—even your eye muscles. Push yourself away from the computer for a moment to take a break and try these exercises:

- Release the tension in your neck by moving your head gently. In a seated position, place your hands in your lap and relax your shoulders. Slowly drop your chin to your chest, and then raise it back up until you're looking to the joint where the wall meets the ceiling. Drop your head back down, and then look slowly to the left and right, past each of your shoulders. Repeat as needed.

- Squint your eyes hard and hold for a few seconds. Release and repeat as needed.

- To prevent dry eyes, force yourself to blink often.

- Make a fist and point your index finger toward the ceiling. Hold the finger about four inches from your eyes; focus on the finger until you can see it clearly. Slowly move your hand away from your face, keeping your eyes focused on your finger, until you've fully extended your arm. Then slowly bring your hand back to its original position, keeping your eyes focused on your finger. Repeat as needed.

You learned the steps for setting up and adjusting a PC in this lesson. The final lesson in this part shows you how to maintain your PC.

Maintaining Your System

This lesson explains how to protect the investment you've made in your system. You learn basic routines for cleaning the system unit, monitor, keyboard, mouse, and more.

Cleaning the System Unit

The system unit is one of the most important components to clean regularly. That's because its internal fan tends to suck dust toward and into the system unit. Dust particles inside the system unit and its air ventilation slots blocks the flow of air, causing internal parts to overheat and wear out prematurely. You should keep the area around your system as dust free as possible, and clean the system unit about once a month. If you notice heavy enough dust buildup or if you have pets, you might want to clean the system unit twice a month or more.

Turn It Off!   Turn the computer off before you clean any of its parts. You don't want to get a shock or cause potential damage.

CAUTION

Follow these general steps to clean the system unit:

1. Using the soft-brush attachment of your vacuum, clean around the system unit. Vacuum the ventilation slots on the front of the computer, as shown in Figure 13.1.

2. Also with the vacuum soft-brush attachment, clean the ventilation slots for the fan. If needed, detach all cable connections and vacuum the connectors, too. Never use a wet cleaner on cable connectors.

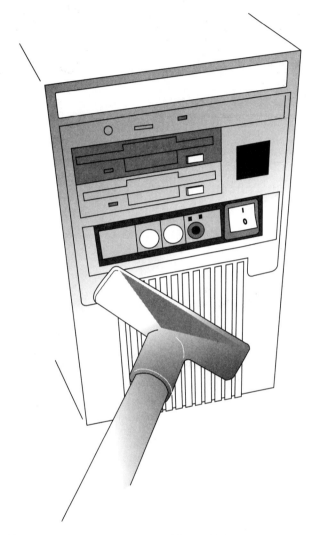

Figure 13.1 You can vacuum the system unit's ventilation slots with a vacuum's soft brush attachment.

3. Spray a household cleaner like Fantastik or Formula 409 onto a clean, soft cloth. (Do not spray the cleaner directly on the system unit, because you don't want liquid to drip inside.) Wipe the case thoroughly, and use another dry cloth to soak up any excess cleaner.

Cleaning the Monitor

A monitor attracts dust more than any other component because it creates and electrostatic field that acts like a magnet for dust and small particles. Like the system unit, your monitor has ventilation slots that you need to keep free from dirt. Use this routine to clean your monitor:

1. With the vacuum soft-brush attachment, clean the ventilation slots for the monitor.

2. Spray a household cleaner like Fantastik or Formula 409 onto a clean, soft cloth. Wipe the monitor case thoroughly, and use another dry cloth to soak up any excess cleaner. *Do not* wipe the screen with the cleaner, because you could damage it.

CAUTION   **No Cleaner on the Screen**   Never use any type of household cleaner (especially glass cleaner) on the monitor's screen, unless your monitor's manufacturer says it's OK to do so. Such cleaners are designed for glass, and can damage the plastic anti-glare coatings on many monitors.

3. If you see any grime still caught in nooks or crannies like the ventilation slots, lightly moisten a cotton swab and wipe it away.

4. To clean the screen itself, moisten a fresh cloth with plain distilled water or a screen cleaning solution, available at computer stores. You may also find pre-moistened towelettes for cleaning the screen. Wipe the screen thoroughly, and let it dry on its own.

TIP   **Static Buster**   Computer stores sell anti-static cloths that are ideal for wiping off your screen between cleanings.

Cleaning the Keyboard

Although it's not obvious, keyboards collect a lot of dirt and crumbs. You'd be surprised how much pet hair can find its way into a keyboard, too. If you start to notice keys sticking or see an obvious buildup of gunk around the keys, it's time to clean the keyboard. Follow these steps to do so:

1. Lay out some newspaper or paper toweling, then turn the keyboard over and shake out the particles trapped in it. You also can lightly tap on the keyboard to dislodge any stuck particles.

2. Use a soft, 1/4 inch-wide artist's brush to sweep out any remaining hair or dirt particles (see Figure 13.2).

Figure 13.2 Sweep the keyboard with a soft brush.

3. Spray a clean cloth with household cleaner, or wet it lightly with distilled water. Wipe the tops and sides of the keys, and the keyboard case. You can moisten a cotton swab to clean up tight spots between keys.

4. Use a dry cloth to wipe away any excess cleaner.

Cleaning the Mouse or Trackball

As you glide the mouse over its mousepad, the mouse's rubber ball tends to catch small pieces of dirt and hair. Once these particles are trapped inside the mouse, then can make the mouse skip as it rolls or cause the on-screen pointer to move in a jerky fashion. If you're seeing such symptoms or the mouse feels a bit sticky, you can use the following steps to clean the mouse or trackball:

1. Turn the mouse over and carefully remove the rubber mouse ball. To do so, twist the plastic ring around the mouse ball a quarter to a half turn in the direction of the arrow labeled "Open" on the ring. You can then lift the

ring out of its slot and remove the mouse ball. Trackballs generally lift straight out of their chassis. You may have to rotate a retaining collar to release the ball, much like a mouse.

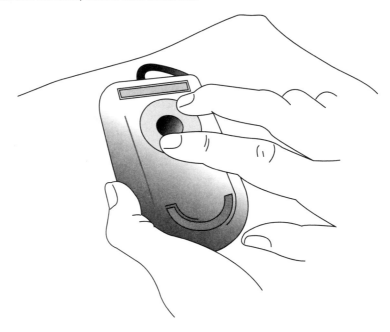

Figure 13.3 Turn the plastic ring around the mouse ball to remove both it and the mouse ball.

2. Turn the mouse right-side-up and tap it to help out any dust and debris. Then turn the mouse back over and use a soft brush to sweep out remaining dirt, lint, or hair. Follow the same procedure for a trackball.

3. Inspect the rollers within the mouse or trackball. These make contact with the rubber ball and transmit its actions to your computer. If you see any dirt on these, remove it with a pencil eraser or a toothpick. Turn the mouse back over to tap out any remaining bits of eraser or crud.

4. Use a facial tissue or lint-free cloth to wipe off the rubber mouse ball. If the rubber ball is very dirty, use a small amount of distilled water to wipe it off. If you're cleaning a hard plastic trackball, you can wipe it off with some household cleaner.

CAUTION

Mouse Ball Care Even though the mouse ball is rubber, it's fairly delicate. Dropping it can deform it. Also, do not use regular household cleaner, glass cleaner, or any detergent- or alcohol-based cleaner on it. You should only clean the mouse ball with distilled water or a special cleaning solution especially made for mouse balls.

5. Place the roller ball back into the mouse or trackball. Replace the plastic• ring and twist it back into place.

Cleaning the Printer

To clean a printer's exterior, you use the same basic process as for cleaning other components. Remove the paper or paper tray, then vacuum the printer with the soft brush attachment. Spray some household cleaner on a clean cloth, and wipe off the exterior.

Use the release button to open a laser or inkjet printer, and remove the toner or ink cartridge. For a dot matrix printer, open the top if needed and remove the ribbon. Use a soft brush or vacuum with the soft brush attachment to sweep out dirt, toner, and paper dust that has accumulated inside the printer. Put the toner or ink cartridge or ribbon back into the printer, and close it up.

To clean the critical parts of the printer, buy printer cleaner paper from your computer store. Load the paper into the printer, turn it back on, and use the Print command on the File menu of any word processor (such as Windows Notepad) to print a blank page. For best results, send the cleaner paper through a few times to thoroughly clean the parts.

Cleaning the Drives

You've got to keep dust out of a disk drive or CD-ROM drive to keep it in good working order. Dust not only can damage the drive's parts but also any floppy disks or CDs you insert into the drive. In addition to vacuuming the slot or drawer of any drive to keep it free from dust, you can buy a cleaning kit for your drive from your local computer store and use it every couple of months or so. Make sure you get the right kit—either for the floppy drive or CD-ROM drive that you want to clean.

To use the drive cleaning kit, turn the computer on and remove any disk or CD from the drive. Take the cleaning disk that comes in the kit and lightly coat it with the kit's cleaning spray; for a floppy drive, coat both sides of the cleaning disk, and insert the disk into its carrier, if needed. Insert the cleaning disk in the drive. Double-click the **My Computer icon** on the Windows 95 desktop (you'll learn more about Windows 95 in the next part). In the window that opens, **double-click the icon for the drive** you're cleaning. Windows displays a message that there's no disk in the drive. That's OK. Click **Retry** a few times, then click **Cancel**. Remove the cleaning disk from the drive.

Taking Care of Your Floppy Disks

While floppy disks aren't as fragile as they used to be, they aren't indestructible, either. Use a reasonable amount of care and caution when handling floppy disks. Here are some guidelines:

- Avoid touching the magnetic disk surface when it's exposed. Skin oil and other substances can damage the disk's magnetic properties.

- Avoid placing the disk anywhere near dust, dirt, or liquid; these can damage magnetic material. If you insert a dirty disk into a disk drive, the gunk on the disk can damage the drive.

- Keep the disk well away from magnets, electrical wires, electronic appliances, computer components, or anything that might be magnetized—like paper clips. That's right—never clip a disk to your paperwork. Electric power generates a magnetic field that can affect the disk's magnetic material. It also is a safe practice to keep your telephone away from your disks and the computer, as telephones also have magnets.

- Keep disks away from heat sources (like photocopiers) that can warp them.

- For 5.25-inch disks, make sure you write on the label with a felt-tip pen before sticking it on the disk. A sharp pencil or ballpoint could dent a disk's magnetic surface.

- *Write-protect* your disks to preserve data. This procedure lets the disk drive read what's on a disk, but prevents the drive from altering the data in any way. You write-protect a 3.5-inch disk by sliding a small tab (you'll see this if you look at the back of the disk) to open the little tab window. To write-protect a 5.25-inch disk, bend a piece of tape (or a write-protect tab) over the rectangular notch near one corner of the disk.

This lesson showed you the basic cleaning steps that will keep your computer in good working order. The next lesson, which launches Part 2, explains how to start, restart, and shut down your system.

Operating Systems—How Windows 95 Fits In

Starting Up, Restarting, and Shutting Down Your System

This lesson provides the proper steps for starting up, restarting, and shutting down your computer and Windows 95.

Starting Your Computer and Windows 95

As with any electronic device, you have to turn on your computer to get it to work. This simple process involves several steps you should practice religiously. Although you might not damage your computer if you do it differently, turning on the system components in the right order can help prolong the life of your system.

Starting your computer is also called *booting up* (because your system "pulls itself up by its bootstraps"). The computer reads built-in startup instructions from the operating system and some special chips, and then it performs a Power-On Self-Test (POST) to check its ability to "talk" to the system components.

Many users and experts debate when you should turn your computer on and off. Some insist that we all should conserve energy, turning a computer off every time we've finished using it. At the other extreme, some people think computers should never be shut down; they think all this powering up and down wears out the computer's components faster. You should follow the recommendation of your system's manufacturer. For example, some systems with voice messaging capabilities are meant to be left on all the time, and go into a "sleep" mode when not in use to conserve energy.

When you start a newer system, the Windows 95 operating system loads, and you'll see the Windows desktop on-screen. Other systems may display a special menu or screen installed by the manufacturer. In still other instances, the manufacturer may have installed a multimedia presentation that runs the first time you start the computer. After you view this information the first time, the computer will start normally, skipping the presentation.

Windows 95 In addition to being the *Disk Operating System* that manages your computer's basic functions, Windows 95 is a *graphical user interface* (*GUI*). It's called a GUI because you use a mouse and on-screen *graphics* (pictures) known as *icons* to control your computer, as opposed to a simple blank screen where you type arcane commands.

For best results, use the following steps to start off your computing day:

1. Make sure the floppy disk drive is empty. Otherwise, the computer will try to start itself from the floppy disk it finds in drive A (most of which will not have any system-startup instructions).

2. Make sure the surge-suppresser strips for the system and printer are plugged into wall socket and that all system components are plugged into the main system surge suppresser. Turn on the surge suppressers.

3. Turn on the monitor's power. If the power switch is on the back of the monitor, it will probably have a I (vertical hash mark) on the top half and an **O** (circle) on the bottom half. To turn the monitor on, press down the half with the I mark. Other monitors have a knob or button on the front that you can simply press.

No Startup Shortcuts Some users like to plug all their computer components into the surge suppressor and leave all the power switches on so they can turn on the whole system just by flipping the surge suppresser switch. This is a *bad* idea because it sends a power surge into the individual components, zapping them slightly and causing excess wear.

4. If you have a printer that you need to turn on manually (these days, some power up on their own when you print a document), turn it on next; the power switch is usually on the back or right side. After a brief power up test, the **Online** indicator for the printer should light up, indicating that it's ready to go. Also turn on other devices attached to your system, such as scanners and Zip drives, before continuing.

5. Time to turn on the system unit. Find the On/Off switch on the back, right, or front side of the system unit; turn it to **On** or press it to the "on" position.

6. Watch the monitor; you may see several self-test messages flash on the screen. When the computer finishes its self-test, you'll see the Welcome to Windows 95 screen with the Windows 95 desktop beneath it. Simply click the **Close** button to display the desktop by itself (see Figure 1.1).

Figure 1.1 When you start your system, the Windows 95 desktop appears.

Resetting (Warm-Booting) a Computer

You can be working happily along on your computer system, and it can suddenly stop working or start behaving erratically. Your computer can have such symptoms for a variety of reasons, although it usually happens because software instructions conflict, and your computer can't decide what to do—or because too many instructions come flying at your computer at once, and it just gets paralyzed.

When your computer begins behaving erratically or you need to restart it for another reason, your only option is to *reset* or *reboot* it. Rebooting the system clears out whatever was jamming the computer and takes the computer back through the operating system startup instructions. Unfortunately, if you restart your system and you haven't saved what you're working on, that work is lost. Therefore, save your work often—every 10 minutes or after making any major changes to an important piece of work.

Most often, you will reboot by *warm-booting* your system. It's called a warm-boot because the computer's already warmed up; you just use some commands to reset the system without cutting the power flow to the computer, as described in the following steps:

1. Remove any disks that are in floppy disk drives. If you don't, your computer will try to read from the floppy disk instead of your hard drive when it restarts.

2. Click the **Start** button in the lower-left corner of the screen, and click **Shut Down**, as shown in Figure 1.2. If you don't know how to click, refer to the next lesson, where you'll learn more about using the mouse.

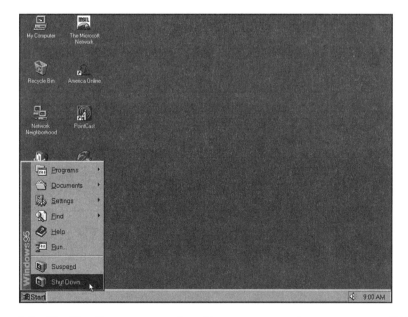

Figure 1.2   The Shut Down command enables you to warm-boot your system if it's having problems.

3. In the Shut Down Windows dialog box that appears (Figure 1.3), click **Restart the Computer?**, and then click **Yes**. Whatever was on-screen will be wiped off. The computer will go through its startup process all over.

Figure 1.3   Use the Restart the Computer command to warm-boot the system.

TIP   Other Rebooting   You should warm-boot to restart your system whenever possible. However, if the steps here don't work (because the mouse isn't responding or some other problem), you can cold-boot or try another restarting method (a special keystroke combination called Ctrl+Alt+Delete). You also can restart an application rather than the whole system. See Lessons 3 and 4 in Part 6 to learn about these other methods for restarting the system.

Shutting Down Windows 95 and Your System

When you shut down your computer, resist the temptation to just turn off the components' power switches because you could lose work if you haven't saved properly. For the greatest safety, make sure you save all your work first—and then exit all programs—before shutting down your computer.

To make sure you don't lose any work you're creating with a particular software application, save it to a file on the hard disk so you can work with it later. (Copy it to a removable disk, if needed, too.) Otherwise, when you shut down the system, your work will be cleared out of Random Access Memory (RAM) and lost forever.

Also, it's important to shut down your applications before quitting. Quitting with an application running can leave temporary (.tmp) files on your hard disk. These files can be large and your system can accumulate a number of them; these files needlessly decrease available hard disk space and could even cause the Windows 95 operating system to have performance problems. Use the following steps for the cleanest and safest way to shut down Windows 95 and your system:

1. Save your files by opening the application's **File** menu and choosing **Save**. The program will ask you to specify a name and location for the file holding your work. (For more information, see Lesson 4, "Creating, Naming, and Saving Documents" in Part 3.)

2. Quit (exit) any programs you're using by opening the **File** menu and choosing **Exit** or **Quit**. Your computer closes the program and removes it from your screen. (See Lesson 2, "Starting, Exiting, and Switching Between Applications," in Part 3.)

3. To exit Windows 95, click the Start button in the lower-left corner of the screen to open the Start menu, and then choose Shut Down (refer to Figure 1.2).

4. The Shut Down Windows dialog box appears, asking you to confirm that you really want to shut down. Make sure **Shut down the computer?** is selected (Figure 1.3), and then click the **Yes** button.

5. After a few seconds, an on-screen message tells you it's safe to turn off your computer. Turn off the power switch on the system unit first. Then turn off the power switches on the monitor, printer, and other devices.

6. Turn off the surge suppresser's power switch.

You can use the steps you learned in this lesson to start up and shut down your system in the safest way possible. The next lesson introduces you to the Windows 95 desktop and using the mouse.

Understanding Windows 95

In this lesson, you'll learn about the parts of the Windows 95 desktop and how to use a mouse to manipulate items on the desktop.

Understanding the Windows 95 Desktop

As you learned in the last lesson, Windows 95 starts and displays the Windows 95 desktop each time you start your computer. New systems shipping from manufacturers today have the most recent version of Windows 95 called OEM Service Release 2 (OSR 2), or Windows 95 B. This update of Windows 95 better manages large hard disk drives (where files are stored), power management features, and more. If you buy a new system, make sure it has OSR 2 installed. The lessons in this book cover the features of OSR 2.

As you can see in Figure 2.1, the Windows 95 desktop is made up of several components. These components are used throughout Windows 95 and Windows applications to make it easy for you to get your work done. You can customize the desktop by adding more components so that Windows 95 works the way that you do (see Lesson15, "Controlling the Desktop Appearance).

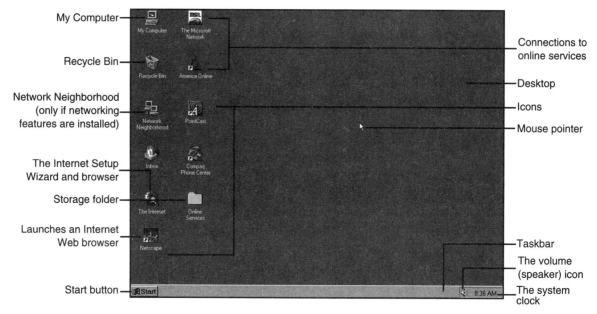

My Computer
Recycle Bin
Network Neighborhood
(only if networking
features are installed)
The Internet Setup
Wizard and browser
Storage folder
Launches an Internet
Web browser
Start button

Connections to
online services
Desktop
Icons
Mouse pointer
Taskbar
The volume
(speaker) icon
The system
clock

Figure 2.1   The Windows 95 Desktop serves as your launch pad for starting programs and accessing Windows 95 features.

The components of the desktop include:

Icons and Shortcuts   Icons are pictures that represent programs (Microsoft Excel, WordPerfect, and so on), files (documents, spreadsheets, graphics), printer information (setup options, installed fonts), and computer information (hard and floppy disk drives). Shortcuts, which have a small arrow in the lower-left corner work like icons, and enable you to create many ways to start a program or open a document. Icons and shortcuts are used throughout Windows 95 and Windows applications. Icons come in two sizes, large and small, and Windows 95 uses four types of icons: program, file, printer, and computer. Each type of icon will be pointed out as it is introduced in the book.

Desktop   This is the area that takes up the entire background of the screen. Items sit on the Windows desktop, much as the desk in your office serves as a holding place for useful tools and files.

Mouse pointer   The on-screen pointer (usually an arrow) that you use to select items and choose commands. You move the pointer by moving the mouse across your desk or mouse pad. You'll learn how to use the mouse later in this lesson.

110

My Computer   The My Computer icon gives you access to a window in which you can browse the contents of your computer or find information about the disk drives, control panel, and printers that you have on your computer.

Recycle Bin   The Recycle Bin serves as your electronic trash can. You drag unwanted files, folders, or other icons to the Recycle Bin, and the Recycle Bin appears to have papers spilling over the top of it. To permanently delete the items, first double-click the **Recycle Bin** icon to open its window. Select the items you want to delete, open the **File** menu and choose **Empty Recycle Bin**. Windows asks you for your confirmation. (As a shortcut, you can click with the right mouse button on the Recycle Bin icon, then click **Empty Recycle Bin** in the menu that appears.)

Start button   Click the **Start** button to display the Start menu, which contains a list of commands that enable you to get to work quickly and easily. The Start menu contains commands for launching programs, opening the most recently used files, changing settings, finding files or folders, accessing Help topics, running a program by entering a specific command line, and shutting down Windows 95.

Taskbar   Click a button on the taskbar to either launch a program (use the Start button) or switch to a different task. For each application that you open, a button appears on the taskbar. When you use more than one application at a time, you can see the names of all the open applications on the taskbar. At any time, you can click the appropriate button on the taskbar to work with the open application.

Initially, the taskbar appears at the bottom of the screen. However, you can move it to the top, left, or right side of the screen to suit your needs. For example, if you were using the Microsoft Word for Windows program and the taskbar appeared below the status bar, you might want to drag the taskbar to the top of the screen and position it above the toolbars, where it is more convenient.

A system clock in the tray at the right end of the taskbar displays the current time. This tray also may display icons for certain pieces of hardware (like your system speakers or the printer) when they're active, or icons for some programs (like the Lotus 97 SmartSuite) to give you easy access to program features. For example, the Volume Control feature enables you to control the volume for sounds played through your computer speaker and multimedia devices.

111

Network Neighborhood   If Windows 95 networking features are installed on your system (some of which are required for connecting to the Internet whether or not your system is connected to a network), you'll have a Network Neighborhood icon, as shown in the picture. If your computer is on a network, you can double-click the **Network Neighborhood** icon to browse through your network and see what it contains. This icon also provides information on mapped drives and interfaces.

In Box   The In Box starts the Windows Messaging application, which functions as a traffic cop for getting and storing information from various information services (such as CompuServe), electronic mail systems, and the Microsoft Fax software. Double-click the **In Box** icon to use Windows Messaging to send and receive mail on your network or send faxes with your modem.

Internet   The Windows 95 OSR 2 desktop offers you the Internet Setup Wizard, which you start by double-clicking the icon labeled **The Internet**. The first time you use this icon, it sets up your system to connect to the Internet. Thereafter, the icon starts the Internet Explorer 3.0 Web browser program that's also included in OSR 2. You may also see an icon for another Web browser, like the Netscape icon. Your desktop may include other icons (like The Microsoft Network or America Online*)* for connecting to online services.

On your system, you may see icons or shortcuts (like PointCast or Compaq Phone Center) that launch other programs. You may also see icons for folders (like Online Services in Figure 2.1) or specific files on the desktop. In Windows 95, you can store folders and files (and parts of files called *scraps*) directly on the desktop.

TIP   **Extra Stuff**   Keep in mind that PCs typically come with a wealth of software packages pre-installed by the manufacturer. So your desktop may include different, more, or fewer icons than the desktop pictured throughout this book. And you may see different selections on the Start menu's submenu, Programs.

Using the Mouse

You can use the mouse to quickly select an icon or window, among other things. The process involves two steps: pointing and clicking.

To *point* to an object (icon, window title bar, and so on), move the mouse across your desk or mouse pad until the on-screen mouse pointer is on top of (or touches) the object. You may have to pick up the mouse and reposition it if you run out of room on your desk.

To *click*, point the mouse pointer at the object you want to select, and then quickly press and release the left mouse button, as shown in Figure 2.2. If the object is an icon or window, it becomes highlighted.

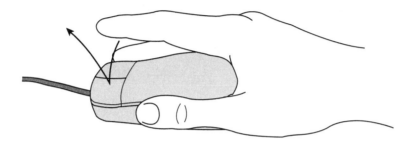

Figure 2.2   Press the left mouse button once to "click."

When you're pointing at an object, you can also click the right mouse button (*right-click*) to select it. Simply press and release the right mouse button once. If the object is an icon, it becomes highlighted. If you right-click the desktop, the taskbar, or a taskbar button, a menu opens. You can perform many shortcuts in Windows 95 by right-clicking. These shortcuts are mentioned throughout the book.

When you *double-click* an item, you point to the item and press and release the left mouse button twice in rapid succession, as shown in Figure 2.3. Double-clicking is often the easiest way to perform a task; for example, you can open a window by double-clicking its icon.

You can also use the mouse to move an object (usually a window, dialog box, or icon) to a new position on-screen. You do this by dragging the object. To *drag* an object to a new location on-screen, point to the object, press and hold the left mouse button, move the mouse to a new location, and release the mouse button. The object moves with the mouse pointer while you hold the button down.

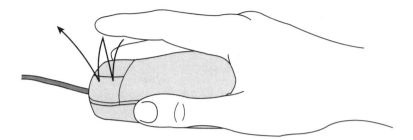

Figure 2.3   Press the left mouse button twice to "double-click."

In this lesson, you learned about the parts of the Windows 95 desktop and how to use the mouse to manipulate items on the desktop. In the next lesson, you'll learn how to work with windows.

Working with Windows

In this lesson, you will learn how to open a window, use scroll bars, resize a window, move a window, tile and cascade windows, and close a window.

What Is a Window?

Windows 95 uses *windows* on-screen to organize information and commands, as described here:

- Program icons and choices on the Start menu open windows that hold programs and documents.
- Dialog boxes are windows; you can move them around on-screen.
- A window opens when you start My Computer or Windows Explorer to manage files and disks or when you start any other application from Windows. You'll learn more about managing files with My Computer and Explorer in the next section of this book.
- Each file you open within an application opens in its own document window.

A *window* is a rectangular area of the screen in which you view program folders, files, or icons. The window is made up of several components (see Figure 3.1) that are the same for all windows in Windows 95 and Windows applications and make it easy for you to manage your work.

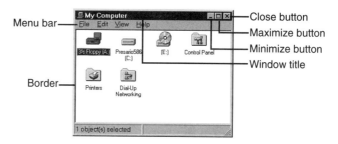

Figure 2.1   The My Computer window shows you the elements of a typical window.

Opening Windows

To open a window from an icon, double-click the icon. For example, point at the **My Computer** icon on the desktop and double-click. If you do it correctly, the My Computer icon opens up to the My Computer window.

You can also use a shortcut menu to open a window. Just point to the icon for the window and click the right mouse button; a shortcut menu appears. Select **Open** on the shortcut menu, and the icon opens into a window.

Using Scroll Bars

Scroll bars appear along the bottom and right edges of a window when text, graphics, or icons in a window take up more space than the area shown allows. Using scroll bars, you can move up, down, left, or right in a window.

Figure 3.2 shows an example. Because the Control Panel's contents are not fully visible in the window, scroll bars are present on the bottom and right sides of the window. The following steps show you one way to use the scroll bars to view items outside the window:

1. To see an object that is down and to the right of the viewable area of the window, point at the **down arrow** located on the bottom of the vertical scroll bar.

2. Click the **down arrow** and the window's contents scroll up.

3. Click the **scroll arrow** on the right end of the horizontal scroll bar, and the window's contents move left.

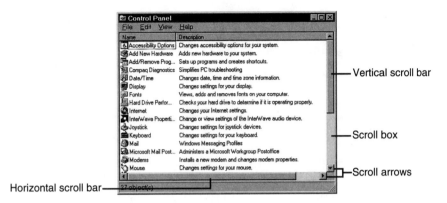

Figure 3.2 Scroll bars enable you to view other window contents, if all the contents won't fit in the window simultaneously.

Through its location within the scroll bar, the scroll box depicts how much of a window is not visible. If you know approximately where something is in a window (maybe two-thirds of the way down, for example), you might want to drag the scroll box. To drag a scroll box and move quickly to a distant area of the window (top or bottom, left or right), use this technique:

1. Point to the scroll box in the scroll bar and hold down the left mouse button.

2. Drag the scroll box to the new location.

3. Release the mouse button.

Sometimes you might need to move slowly through a window. You can move the contents of a window one window-full at a time by clicking in the scroll bar on either side of the scroll box.

 TIP   **Empty Window?**   Don't worry if text, graphics, or icons don't appear in a window. Use the scroll bar to bring the text, graphics, or icons into view.

Sizing a Window with Maximize, Minimize, and Restore

You may want to increase the size of a window to see its full contents, or you may want to decrease a window's size (even down to button form on the taskbar) to make room for other windows. One way to resize a window is to use Maximize, Minimize, and Restore. If you use the mouse, you will use the Maximize, Minimize, and Restore buttons located on the right side of the window's title bar. If you use the keyboard, you can use the Maximize, Minimize, and Restore menu commands on the Control menu. The following list defines the purpose of each of these buttons and commands:

- Select the **Maximize button** or command to enlarge the window to its maximum size.

- Select the **Minimize button** or command to reduce the window to a button on the taskbar.

- Select the **Restore button** or command to return a window to the size it was before it was maximized. (The Restore button and command are available only after a window has been maximized.)

Figure 3.3 shows the My Computer window maximized to full-screen size. At full size, the Minimize and Restore buttons are available. At any other size, you see the Maximize button instead of the Restore button.

To maximize, minimize, or restore a window with the mouse, click the appropriate button. To maximize, minimize, or restore a window with the keyboard, follow these steps:

1. Press **Alt+Spacebar** (for an application window) or **Alt+–** (for a document window) to open the window's Control menu.

2. Select the **Restore**, **Minimize**, or **Maximize** command from the menu. To select a menu command, press the down arrow key to highlight the command you want, then press Enter. Or, press the underlined letter in the command name.

 TIP **Document Windows Are Different** In the next part, you'll learn to open documents within applications. To access the Control menu for a document window, press **Ctrl+–** (minus sign).

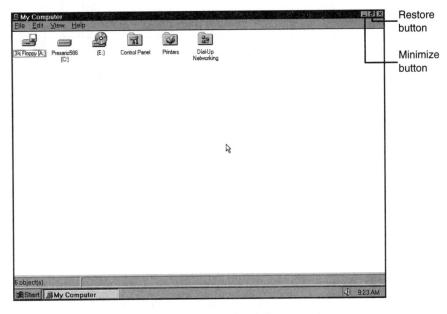

Restore
button

Minimize
button

Figure 3.3 The My Computer window maximized to full-screen size.

Sizing a Window's Borders

At some point, you may need a window to be a particular size to suit your needs. If so, simply drag the window border to change the size of the window.

To use the mouse, follow these steps:

1. Place the mouse pointer on the portion of the border (vertical, horizontal, or corner) that you want to resize. When the mouse pointer is positioned correctly, it changes into one of the shapes described here:

The vertical double-headed arrow appears when you position the mouse pointer over the top or bottom window border. It enables you to resize the window's height by dragging the border up or down.

The horizontal double-headed arrow appears when you position the mouse pointer over either side of the window border. It enables you to resize the window's width by dragging the border left or right.

The diagonal double-headed arrow appears when you position the mouse pointer over any of the four corners of the window border. It enables you to resize the window's height and width proportionally by dragging the corner diagonally.

119

2. Press the mouse button and drag the border. If you drag slowly enough, a faint line appears, indicating where the border will be when you release the mouse button.

3. Once the border is in the desired location, release the mouse button. The window is resized.

To resize a window using the keyboard, follow these steps:

1. Press **Alt+Spacebar** (for an application window) or **Alt+–** (for a document window) to open the window's Control menu.

2. Press **S** to choose the Size command. The pointer becomes a four-headed arrow.

3. Use the arrow keys to move the pointer to the border or corner you want to resize. The mouse pointer turns into a different shape.

4. With the pointer on the border or corner, press the arrow keys to resize the window. A gray shaded outline appears showing the new border location.

5. When the shaded outline appears to be the size you want, press **Enter**. To cancel the operation, press **Esc**.

Moving a Window

When you start working with multiple windows, moving a window becomes as important as sizing one. For example, you may need to move one or more windows to make room for other work on your desktop.

You can move a window with the mouse or keyboard. To move a window using the mouse, point at the window's title bar, press and hold the left mouse button, and drag it to a new location. To use the keyboard, follow these steps:

1. Press **Alt+Spacebar** (for an application window) or **Alt+–** (for a document window) to open the window's Control menu.

2. Press **M** to choose the Move command. The pointer changes to a four-headed arrow.

3. Use the arrow keys to move the window to a new location.

4. When the window is located where you want it, press **Enter**. To cancel the operation and return the window to its original location, press **Esc**.

Arranging Windows

In Windows 95, you can use more than one application at a time, and in each Windows application, you can work with multiple document windows. As you can imagine, opening multiple applications with multiple windows can make your desktop pretty cluttered. That's why it's important that you know how to manipulate and switch between windows. The following sections explain how to do just that.

When you have multiple windows open, some windows are inevitably hidden by others, which makes the screen confusing. You can use the commands on the taskbar's shortcut menu (which you access by right-clicking the taskbar) to arrange windows from the desktop:

- **Cascade.** When you choose this command, Windows lays all the open windows on top of each other so that the title bar of each is visible. Figure 8.1 shows the resulting cascaded window arrangement. To access any window that's not on the top, simply click its title bar.

Each title bar is arranged in a cascading group

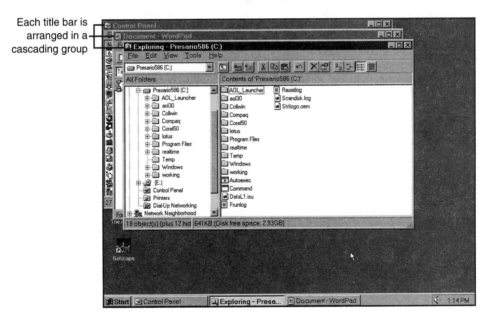

Figure 3.4 Cascaded windows overlap in a stack, but you can see the title bar of each window.

- **Tile.** If you need to see all of your open windows at the same time, use one of the Tile commands on the shortcut menu. When you choose one of these commands, Windows resizes and moves each open window so that they appear side by side horizontally or vertically. Right-click a blank area on the taskbar and choose the **Tile Horizontally** command from the shortcut menu to create an arrangement similar to that shown in Figure 3.5. To arrange the windows in a vertically tiled arrangement, right-click a blank area on the taskbar and choose the **Tile Vertically** command.

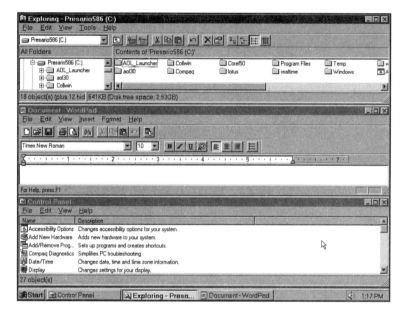

Figure 3.5 Horizontally tiled windows like these enable you to view at least some of the contents of each open window.

- **Minimize All Windows.** If you want to minimize all the windows at once, right-click a blank area on the taskbar and choose **Minimize All Windows**. The opened windows disappear from the desktop, but the application buttons remain visible on the taskbar.

TIP   **Quick Minimize**   The keyboards for many newer desktop systems offer a special new key called the Windows key. The Windows key is usually near the Spacebar, and has a Windows 95 logo on it (the logo looks like a wavy window). To quickly minimize all open program windows to buttons on the taskbar, press **Windows key+M**.

To arrange windows within an application, open the Window menu and choose **Tile** or **Arrange All**.

Closing a Window

When you're finished working with a window, you should close it. This can help speed up Windows, conserve memory, and keep your desktop from becoming cluttered. In particular, if your computer has 16M of RAM or less, you should close programs when you've finished working with them, because too many running programs could substantially slow down your system.

To close a window with the mouse:

1. Click the **Control menu** icon to display the Control menu.

2. Choose (click) the **Close** command to close the window.

 TIP **Quickie Close** To quickly close a window with the mouse, click the **Close** button. If you have multiple My Computer windows on-screen (see Lesson 9 in this part, "A Brief Look at My Computer," for more about opening My Computer Windows), press and hold the Shift key, and click the Close button for the topmost window.

If you'd rather use the keyboard, select the window you want to close (by pressing Alt+Tab repeatedly, until you see the window you want) and press **Alt+F4**.

In this lesson, you learned how to use windows. In the next lesson, you'll learn how to choose commands from a menu.

Entering
Commands

4

In this lesson, you learn how to select and open menus, choose menu commands, and read a menu.

What Is a Menu?

A *menu* is a group of related commands that tell Windows 95 what you want to do. Menu commands in Windows 95 and Windows 95 applications are organized in logical groups. For example, all the commands related to starting your work in Windows 95 are on the Start menu. The names of the available menus appear in the Start menu or on the menu bar in an application window or other window (like a My Computer window).

Most software publishing companies have agreed to use *common user access* standards, which means they design their Windows 95 applications to be easy to use and to work like other Windows 95 applications. All Windows 95 applications offer a *graphical user interface* (GUI) just like Windows 95. Familiar visual cues help you get around in the program.

Whenever possible, Windows 95 applications put their menus in much the same place on-screen and offer similar commands. The File menu tends to be first on the menu bar, for example, and it usually offers New, Open, Save, and Exit commands—no matter which Windows 95 application you're using. Normally you'll also find a Window menu that lists the names of open documents; to switch to the document you want to work on, choose it. Most applications also provide a Help menu at the far right end of the menu bar. Once you're familiar with where commands are in one program, it'll be fairly easy to find them in another program.

In telling you to choose commands from a pull-down menu, this book uses the format *menu title, menu command*. For example, the statement "choose **File, Open**" means to "open the **File** menu and select the **Open** command."

> **Pull-Down Menu**   A menu that appears to "pull-down" from the menu bar. You access the menu by clicking its name in the menu bar.

Choosing Menu Commands with the Mouse

To choose a menu command with the mouse, click the menu title in the menu bar. The menu opens to display the available commands. To choose a particular command, simply click it. For example, to see the Help options available for My Computer, click the **Help** menu title in the My Computer menu bar. The Help menu appears (see Figure 4.1). You can close a menu by clicking anywhere outside of it.

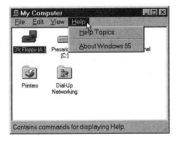

Figure 4.1   Click a menu name to open the menu.

To select a command on a menu that you've displayed, click the command. For example, to see the available topics from the Help facility, you click the **Help Topics** command, and a Help window appears. (Remember, to close this or any window, click the **Close** button.) For more information on using Help, refer to Lesson 6 in this part.

Choosing Menu Commands Using the Keyboard

You also can open menus and select menu commands with the keyboard. To open a pull-down menu, press **Alt** to activate the menu bar of the active window. The first menu title becomes highlighted, indicating that the menu bar is active. With the menu bar active, you can open a menu using either of two methods:

- Use the arrow keys to highlight the menu title you want, and then press **Enter**.
- Press the key that corresponds to the underlined letter in the menu name. For example, to open the Help menu, press **H**.)

Once the menu is open, you select a command from the menu using the same techniques you used to open the menu. Highlight the command you want with the arrow keys and press **Enter**, or press the key that corresponds to the underlined letter to select the command you want.

To open the Control menu with the keyboard, press **Alt+Spacebar** in an application window (such as Microsoft Word or My Computer), or press **Alt+–** (hyphen) in a document. Then highlight your selection using the arrow keys and press **Enter**, or press the key that corresponds to the underlined letter of the command. To close the Control menu (or any menu for that matter), press **Esc** twice.

Commands, Options, or Selections?   Commands, menu options, and menu selections all refer to the same thing: items you choose from a menu. Further, commands may be "performed," "executed," or "selected." This simply means that the computer carries out the instructions associated with the command (whether it is to display another menu or perform an operation).

Understanding Menu Symbols

Windows 95's menus (and those of most other Windows applications) contain a number of common elements. For example, *selection letters* (letters that you press to choose a command) appear underlined. Figure 4.2 shows a number of these common menu elements.

When a command doesn't have any symbol beside it, it simply runs when you choose it. For example, choosing the Exit command on a File menu would prompt you to save any unsaved work, then exit (close) the program.

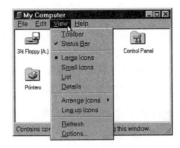

Figure 4.2 This menu shows a number of common menu elements.

Some commands *toggle* on and off (turn on or off) when selected, like the Status Bar command in Figure 4.2. When a command like this is toggled on, a check mark appears to the left of it. Choosing the command again toggles it off and removes the check mark.

Sometimes horizontal divider lines separate commands into groups. If you see a round dot to the left of a command in a group, that means only one command in the group can be selected (toggled on). The Large Icons command shown in Figure 4.2 is the command that's currently selected in the second group. If you choose a different command, the dot appears next to that command and not the Large Icons command.

Some commands have a right-pointing triangle to the right, like the Arrange Icons command. Choosing such a command by pointing to it with the mouse or pressing its selection letter displays a *submenu* (sometimes called a *cascading* menu) that offers more options, like the one shown in Figure 4.3. In that submenu, click the option you want.

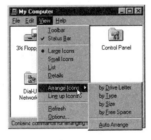

Figure 4.3 Pointing to a command with a triangle beside it displays a submenu.

Some menu commands may appear grayed-out or dimmed, which means that you cannot currently use them. These commands are only available for use under certain circumstances; usually, you need to perform some other action to activate the command. For example, you cannot select the Copy command if you have not first selected an object to copy.

Another menu element you will see often to the right of a command is the *ellipsis* (…). An ellipsis appears after a command to indicate that Windows 95 needs more information in order to complete the command. To get that information, Windows 95 displays a *dialog box*. For more on dialog boxes, see Lesson 5 "Using Dialog Boxes."

Using Shortcut Keys Instead of Menus

Some menu commands list *shortcut keys* that you can use to bypass the menus; shortcut keys are displayed to the right of their associated commands. (Shortcut keys aren't available for every menu option; generally, they are available for such common commands as Open, Save, and Print.) When you first get started, you'll need to use the menus to view and select commands. However, once you become familiar with Windows 95, you'll probably want to use shortcut keys for commands you use often. Shortcut keys enable you to select a command without using the menus. Shortcut keys generally combine the Alt, Ctrl, or Shift key with a letter key (such as W). If a shortcut key is available, it is listed on the pull-down menu to the right of the command.

For example, Figure 4.4 shows the Edit menu from the My Computer window. Notice that you can choose Edit, Select All to select everything in the window, or you can press the shortcut key Ctrl+A to bypass the menu.

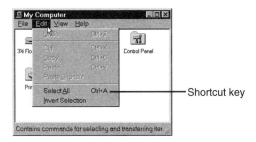

Figure 4.4 Use shortcut keys to bypass menus.

Using Toolbar Buttons Instead of Menus

Consistent with the promise that Windows 95 programs are easy to use, many programs offer *buttons* (icons) you can click instead of choosing a command from a menu. Often, you'll find these in a row called a *toolbar*. Each button performs exactly the same action as a particular typed command or a menu selection; it's just simpler and faster to use. Some toolbar buttons even let you skip a few steps (dialog boxes, for example). Each button has a picture that suggests what its command does. For example, the button for printing shows (surprise!) a printer. The following table shows some common buttons you might see in Microsoft applications; toolbar buttons from other software publishers will look and function much like these.

Starts a new document or opens an existing document.

Saves the current document to disk.

Prints the current document.

Lets you preview what the current document will look like when you print it.

Cuts out the text or data you've selected and puts it in the Windows Clipboard (a temporary storage location).

Copies the selected text or data you've selected and puts the copy in the Windows Clipboard.

Pastes what's in the Clipboard onto the screen at the location of the insertion point.

Undoes the previous command or action.

Applies bold, italic, or underline formatting to the text you've selected.

Changes the alignment of the paragraph you've selected to left-, center-, or right-alignment.

Skipping the Menu Bar with a Shortcut Menu

Windows 95 offers an even more accessible command feature: shortcut menus. If you right-click any icon, object, or selection in any window (or even a blank space on the Windows desktop), a menu pops up displaying the options available for the item you selected. You can then click the desired command to execute it or to see a dialog box that asks for additional input. So if you ever have a question as to what you can do with a particular object, simply right-click it; you don't have to scan all the menus to find out what's available.

In this lesson, you learned how to use menus and other methods to choose commands. In the next lesson, you'll learn how to use dialog boxes.

Using Dialog Boxes

In this lesson, you learn how to use the various dialog box components, including lists for selecting and working with files.

What Is a Dialog Box?

Windows 95 uses *dialog boxes* to exchange information with you. As you learned in Lesson 4 of this part, a menu command followed by an ellipsis (…) indicates that when you select the command, a dialog box will appear asking you for the information the program needs to complete the operation.

Windows 95 also displays dialog boxes to give you information. For example, Windows 95 might display a dialog box to warn you about a problem (for example, to say **File already exists, Overwrite?**) or to confirm that an operation should take place (for example, to confirm that you're ready to shut down).

Using the Components of a Dialog Box

Dialog boxes vary in complexity. Some simply ask you to confirm an operation before it is executed (in which case you select **OK** to confirm the operation or **Cancel** to abort it). On the other hand, some dialog boxes are quite complex, asking you to specify several options.

The following list briefly explains the components of a dialog box, and the rest of the lesson describes the components and how to use them in greater detail.

> **Text box**   A text box provides you with a place to type an entry, such as a name for a file you want to save or a value such as the number of copies of a document to print.

List box   A list box presents a list of possible choices from which you can choose. Scroll bars often accompany a list box so you can scroll through the list. In addition, a text box is sometimes associated with a list box: the list item that you select appears in the text box associated with the list.

Drop-down list box   This box is a single-line list box with a down-arrow button to the right of it. When you click the arrow, the drop-down list box opens to display a list of choices.

Option buttons   Option buttons (sometimes called radio buttons because of their resemblance to the radio buttons in old cars) present a group of related choices from which you can choose only one. Simply click the option button you want to select, and all others become deselected.

Check boxes   Check boxes present a single option or group of related options. Check boxes toggle an option on and off (a check mark or an **X** appears in the box when the option is turned on). To select or deselect a check box, click it. Even though check boxes may be grouped, you can select all the options in the group, none of them, or any combination of them.

Command buttons   When selected, command buttons carry out the command displayed on the button (Open, Help, Cancel, OK, and so on). If there is an ellipsis on the button (such as Options…), choosing it will open another dialog box. The most common command buttons are OK, Cancel, and Apply. Choosing OK accepts the options you selected and closes the dialog box. Choosing Cancel closes the dialog box without running a command. Choosing Apply accepts your dialog box options without closing the dialog box, so you can view on-screen changes and make additional selections if necessary.

Tabs   Tabs represent multiple sections of a dialog box. Only one tab is displayed at a time, and each tab contains related options. Choosing a tab changes the options that appear in the dialog box.

Icons   For some dialog box options, the dialog box displays an *icon* for each choice or a graphic or palette showing a variety of choices. Simply click the choice you want.

 TIP   **Keyboard Moves**   To move between dialog box controls with the keyboard, you can press the **Tab** key repeatedly until a dotted-line highlight surrounds the option you want to work with. If the option has a *selection letter* (underlined letter), you can move to it by pressing and holding the **Alt** key and pressing the selection letter. Just be careful—sometimes Alt+selection letter just moves to the control, and in other cases it executes the control.

Using Text Boxes

You use a text box to enter the information that Windows 95 needs to complete a command. This information is usually a file name or some type of formatting choice. Figure 5.1 shows a text box and list boxes in the Font dialog box (accessed from the Windows 95 WordPad Format menu).

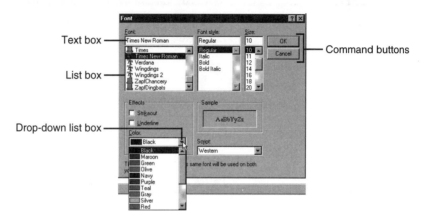

Figure 5.1 A text box and list boxes in the Font dialog box.

To activate a text box using the mouse, simply click in the text box. Notice that the insertion point (the flashing vertical line that indicates where the text you type will appear) appears in the active text box. Some text boxes include *increment or spinner buttons* that let you increase or decrease a value instead of having to type it in. Click the **up arrow** to increase the value. Click the **down arrow** to decrease the value. (Click and hold a spinner button to change the value more quickly.) You also may see a *slider*, on which you drag a bar to increase or decrease a value.

To activate a text box using the keyboard, press **Alt+*selection letter***. For example, to activate the File Name text box shown in Figure 5.1, press Alt+N.

Once you have activated a text box and typed text into it, you can use several keys to edit the text. Table 5.1 outlines these keys.

Table 5.1 Editing Keys for Text Boxes.

Key	Description
Delete	Erases the character to the right of the insertion point.

continues

Table 5.1 Continued

Key	Description
Backspace	Erases the character to the left of the insertion point.
End	Moves the insertion point to the end of the line.
Home	Moves the insertion point to the beginning of the line.
Arrow keys	Moves the insertion point one character in the direction of the arrow.
Shift+End	Selects the text from the insertion point to the end of the line.
Shift+Home	Selects the text from the insertion point to the beginning of the line.
Shift+Arrow key	Selects the next character in the direction of the arrow.
Ctrl+C	Copies selected text to the Clipboard.
Ctrl+V	Pastes selected text from the Clipboard.

Using List Boxes and Drop-Down Lists

You use a list box to make a selection from a list of available options. For example, you use the Font list box in the Font dialog box (see Figure 5.1) to choose a font to apply to the text that's selected in your document.

To select an item from a list box using the mouse, click the appropriate list item. For a drop-down list, click the drop-down list arrow to open the list, then click the choice you want. In the Font list box, notice that the item you select is automatically displayed in the linked text box above the list box. Click **OK** or press **Enter** to accept the selection; click **Cancel** or press **Esc** to close the dialog box without making the selection.

 TIP **Scroll It** Whenever a dialog box can't display all the available choices in a list, it displays one or more *scroll bars*. Use the scroll bars to move through the list to see the rest of the choices.

To select an item from a list box using the keyboard:

    1. Press **Alt+selection letter** to activate the list box. For example, to activate the Font list box displayed in Figure 5.1, press **Alt+F**. Or, press the Tab key to move to the list.

2. Press the **up** and **down arrow keys** or **PageUp** and **PageDown** to move through the list. Each list item appears highlighted as you come to it.

3. When the item you want is highlighted, press **Enter** to accept the selection and close the dialog box. (Or click the **Apply** button if the dialog box offers one to accept the choice and leave the dialog box open.)

To select an item from a drop-down list box using the mouse, open the list box by clicking the down-arrow, and then click the appropriate list item.

To select a drop-down list box item using the keyboard:

1. Press **Alt+selection letter** to activate the list box.

2. Press the **down arrow** key to open the drop-down list box.

3. Press the **up** and **down arrow keys** or **PageUp** and **PageDown** to scroll through the list.

4. Press **Enter** to make your selection and close the dialog box. (Or click the **Apply** button if the dialog box offers one to accept the choice and leave the dialog box open.)

Using Option Buttons

Option buttons enable you to make a single choice from a list of possible command options. For example, the Word Wrap options displayed in Figure 5.2 enable you to choose how text is wrapped in the WordPad window. The active option (the Wrap to Ruler option in Figure 5.2) is indicated by the small filled-in circle.

To select an option button with the mouse, click the circle for the option you want. To use the keyboard, press **Alt+selection letter** for the option you want. For example, you could press Alt+N to activate the No Wrap option shown in Figure 5.2.

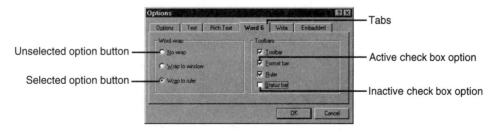

Figure 5.2 Option buttons and check boxes in WordPad's Options dialog box.

Using Check Boxes

Command options that you can select (activate) or deselect (deactivate) are usually presented as check boxes. When a check box is selected, a check mark appears in the box, indicating the associated command option is active (see Figure 5.2).

To select or deselect a check box with the mouse, click its box. Using the keyboard, press **Alt+selection letter** to select or deselect a check box. For example, press Alt+s to activate the Status Bar option shown in Figure 5.2. You also could press **Tab** to move to the check box, then press **Spacebar** to toggle the check box on and off.

Using Command Buttons

You use command buttons to perform operations like closing the dialog box to accept its settings, canceling the dialog box, or even opening another dialog box. To select command buttons with the mouse, simply click the appropriate command button. Figure 5.2 shows two common command buttons: OK and Cancel. Select the **OK** command button to accept the information you have entered or to verify an action and close the dialog box. (Pressing Enter is equivalent to selecting the OK button.) Select the **Cancel** command button to leave the dialog box without executing the information you provided in the dialog box. (Pressing Esc is the keyboard equivalent to selecting the Cancel button.)

Accidents Happen   If you accidentally select the Cancel command button, don't worry. You can always reenter the dialog box and continue. Be careful when you select OK, however: The instructions you have entered in the dialog box will be executed.

CAUTION

Using Tabs

Windows 95 uses tabs to organize the options in a dialog box into categories (like a set of index dividers in a notebook). Tabs appear across the top of some dialog boxes, and each tabbed section contains a different set of options. Click a tab to go to that area of the dialog box and access that tab's set of options. Figure 5.2 shows six tabs.

Using Dialog Box Icons

Some dialog boxes make selecting an option even more obvious. Some dialog boxes, like the one shown in Figure 5.3, present a palette of choices or icons. Simply click the choice you want, then click **OK** to accept it and close the dialog box. Using the keyboard, press **Alt+selection letter** or press the **Tab** key to select the group of choices. Use the arrow keys to highlight the choice you want, then press **Spacebar** to select it. To accept your choice and close the dialog box, press **Enter**.

Figure 5.3 When a dialog box like this one from Windows Paint shows a number of small choices, click the one you want.

Working with Folder and File Lists in Dialog Boxes

Whenever you issue a command to perform a *file operation* (such as the Open or Save command on the File menu), the dialog box that appears usually includes a Look In drop-down list box, with another list box below it.

The Look In list enables you to navigate a folder tree for all the disk drives attached to your system, with the Desktop being the topmost level (because you can store files and folders on the Windows 95 desktop). A small icon identifies each disk drive, folder, and subfolder. An open-file icon indicates which folder you're currently viewing. Closed-file icons identify other folders. The files and subfolders in the currently selected folder generally appear in the list below the Look In list. Use the following steps to navigate through the levels of a Look In drop-down list box when you encounter one in a file-handling dialog box:

1. Click the **drop-down arrow** to open the Look In list.

2. To go to the main folder (root directory) of a drive, click its drive icon in the tree, as shown in Figure 5.4. The Look In list closes, and the first-level folders and files in the selected folder appear in the list below.

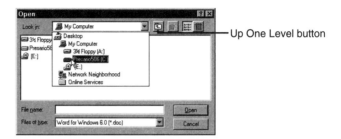

Figure 5.4 Use the Look In drop-down list to select the disk drive that holds the file you want to work with.

3. To move "down" one level in the tree (display the files in a subfolder of the current folder), double-click the folder or subfolder in the Look In list of files and folders that appears in the dialog box.

4. To move "up" one level in the tree, click the **Up One Level** button at the top of the dialog box. To jump up by more than one level, open the **Look In** drop-down list and click any higher-level folder on the same disk (which would have an open-file icon beside it) or another disk drive icon.

5. When the file you want appears in the list below the Look In list, double-click the file to open it.

 TIP **Filing Shortcuts** Within a file handling dialog box, you can right-click any file or folder icon in the list below the Look In list for a shortcut menu. The shortcut menu lets you work with the folder or file—deleting it, renaming it, and more.

In this lesson, you learned how to use the different components of dialog boxes. In the next lesson, you'll learn how to use Windows 95's Help system.

Using Windows 95 Help

In this lesson, you learn how to get help, use Help's shortcut buttons, and use the What's This? help feature.

Getting Help in Windows 95

Windows 95 offers several ways to get *online help*, instant on-screen help for menu commands or other tools. Online help is Help information that appears in its own window whenever you request it. The Help feature is organized like a reference book with three tabs: Contents, Index, and Find. The Contents and Index features show you, step by step, how to use commands and functions and how to perform operations in Windows 95's applications and accessories. The Find feature enables you to search for specific words and phrases in a Help topic.

Whether you use the keyboard or the mouse to access Help, help information is always available at your fingertips. If you do not know or cannot remember how to perform some task, you can use Windows 95's Help system to find out.

To get help on common tasks, follow these steps:

1. Click the **Start** button on the taskbar. The Start menu appears.

2. Click **Help** in the Start menu. The Help Topics: Windows Help window appears, showing a list of Windows Help topics.

3. Click the **Contents tab** to browse through the Help topics listed in the Help window, or click the **Index tab** to search for a specific Help topic. You can click the **Find tab** to search for specific words or phrases in a Help topic.

TIP   **Fast Help**   You can press **F1** at any time to access a program's help file from within the program.

Using the Contents Feature

You can get help with common tasks using Help's Contents feature. The Contents feature displays the top level groups of information covered in Help, such as How To and Tips and Tricks. When you open a major group, a list of main topics appears. As you can see in Figure 6.1, both the major groups and the main topics in each group are represented by book icons, and subtopics are represented by page icons (with a question mark). You can simply select a book to see a list of the subtopics.

Follow these steps to use Help's Contents feature:

1. Click book icon for the main group that contains the Help topic you want to open. The group's name becomes highlighted.

2. Click the **Open** button to open the group. A list of chapters in that group appears. (In place of steps 1 and 2, you can simply double-click a book icon to open it.)

Double-click a page icon to display a Help window.

Double-click a book icon to display a list of topics.

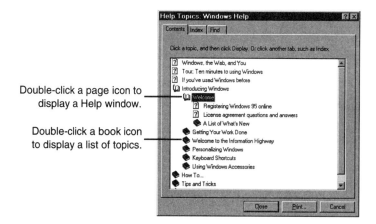

Figure 6.1   The Help Topics: Windows Help window.

3. Click book icon for the chapter that contains the Help topic you want to open. The chapter name becomes highlighted.

4. Click the **Open** button to open the chapter. A list of subtopics appears below the open chapter. (In place of steps 3 and 4, you can simply double-click a chapter book icon to open it.)

5. Click the subtopic you want to display and click the **Display** button that appears. (Or, double-click the subtopic icon.) A window appears, displaying the Help information.

6. After you read the explanation, click the **Close** button in the Windows Help window's title bar to close the Windows Help window.

If you want to print the list of Help topics in the Help Topics: Windows Help window, click the **Print** button at the bottom of the window. The Print dialog box appears. Click the **OK** button to print the list of help topics and subtopics.

Using the Index Feature

Help's Index feature provides a list of Help topics arranged alphabetically in the Index list box. In Figure 6.2, for example, the "copying" topic appears in the topic text box and is highlighted in the topic list. In some cases, Windows 95 displays more than one related topic in the topic list, and you can select which topic you need more information on. The Index is especially useful when you cannot find a particular Help topic in Help Contents' list of topics.

To use the Help Index, follow these steps:

1. Click the **Index** tab in the Windows Help window. The Index options are displayed.

2. Type a topic in the topic text box at the top of the dialog box. This enters the topic for which you want to search and scrolls to the first entry that matches the word you typed. That topic appears highlighted in the topic list.

3. Click on a subtopic, if necessary. Then click the **Display** button. (Or, double-click the subtopic.) Windows 95 displays the selected Help topic information in a Windows Help window.

4. When you are finished reading the Help information, click the **Close** button to close the Windows Help window.

 TIP   Topic List   Instead of typing something in the text box, you can scroll through the topic list and select the topic you want from the list.

Figure 6.2 The Index tab in the Windows Help window.

Using the Find Feature

You can search for specific words and phrases in a Help topic instead of searching for a Help topic by category.

The first time you use the Find tab, you have to help Windows create a list that contains every word from your Help files. A special dialog box will guide you. Then you can search for words and phrases similar to existing words and phrases in a Help topic. The Find feature is especially useful when you cannot find a particular help topic in Help Contents' or Index's list of topics.

To build a word list (the first time only), follow these steps:

1. Click the **Find** tab in the Windows Help dialog box. The dialog box that appears gives an explanation of the Find feature and gives you these options: Minimize database size, Maximize search capabilities, and Customize search capabilities.

2. Click **Minimize Database Size** to create a short word list, choose the **Maximize Search Capabilities** option to create a long word list, or choose **Customize Search Capabilities** to create a shorter word list if you have limited disk space.

CAUTION

Accidents Happen   If you don't want to use the first list that Windows created, don't worry. You can rebuild that list to include more words or exclude words. Simply click the **Rebuild** button and choose a word list option to recreate the word list.

3. Click the **Next** button to continue.

4. Click the **Finish** button to create the word list.

After Windows creates the word list, the Find tab contains a text box, a word list, and a topic list.

To search for words or a phrase in a Help topic:

1. Type the word you want to find in the first text box at the top of the Find tab. This enters the word for which you want to search and scrolls to the first entry that matches the word you typed. The word appears highlighted in the word list.

2. (Optional) Click another word in the word list to narrow the search if necessary.

3. Click a topic in the topic list, and then click the **Display button**. Windows 95 displays the selected Help topic information in a Windows Help window.

4. When you are finished reading the Help information, click the **Close (X)** button to close the Windows Help window.

TIP   **Topic List**   Instead of typing something in the top text box, you can scroll through the word list and select the word you want from the list. If you want to find words similar to the words in a Help topic, click the **Find Similar** button.

Using Help Windows

When you display any Windows Help option, a button bar appears at the top of the Help window, and it always remains visible. This button bar includes three buttons: Help Topics, Back, and Options. Click the **Help Topics** button to return to Help's table of contents. Click the **Back** button to close the current Windows Help window and return to the preceding one. Click the **Options** button to display a menu with the following commands:

Annotate   Select this command if you want to add notes to the text in the Windows Help window. A dialog box appears, in which you can type and save your text. When you save the annotation, a green paper clip appears to the right of the Help topic to indicate that it has an annotation. Click the paper clip to view the annotation.

Copy   Select this command if you want to copy Help text to the Clipboard.

Print Topic   Select this command to display the Print dialog box. Then click the **OK** button to print the topic using the current printer settings, or click the **Properties** button to change printer settings.

Font   Select this command to change the size of the font displayed in the Windows Help window. When you select this command, another menu appears from which you can select Small, Normal, or Large. A check mark indicates the current size.

Keep Help on Top   Select this command if you want the Windows Help window to always be in the foreground of your screen. When you select this command, another menu appears from which you can select Default, On Top, or Not On Top. A check mark indicates the current selection.

Use System Colors   Select this command if you want Windows to use the current system colors for Help windows. Otherwise, Help uses the colors from the default Windows color scheme, which has a yellow background and may be less readable for you. (Lesson 15 in this part explains how to change system colors.) When you select this command, a dialog box appears, informing you that you must restart Help for the color change to take effect. Choose **Yes** to close Help or choose **No** to return to the Windows Help window.

Help windows often display shortcut buttons as well. Using shortcut buttons, you can jump to the area of Windows 95 to which the Help information refers. For example, suppose you're reading a Help topic that contains information on how to change the wallpaper on the desktop (see Figure 6.3). You click the shortcut button (the button with an arrow that curves up and to the left) to jump to the Control Panel's Properties for Display dialog box from within Help. There you can make the necessary changes and get on with your work.

To use a shortcut button, simply click it. You're immediately taken to that area of Windows 95.

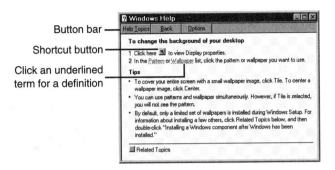

Button bar

Shortcut button

Click an underlined
term for a definition

Figure 6.3   The shortcut button in the Help window.

Getting Help in Dialog Boxes

The What's This? feature provides a handy way of getting more information about dialog box options. You activate this feature by clicking the ? icon, which appears on the right side of the title bar in all Windows 95 and many application dialog boxes.

The following steps tell you how to use the What's This? feature to display a description of any option in a Windows 95 or application dialog box.

1. Click the **?** icon in the upper-right corner of the Windows 95 dialog box. A large question mark appears next to the mouse pointer.
2. Click any option in the dialog box. Windows 95 displays a pop-up box containing a short description of the item you selected.
3. When you are finished reading the Help information, click anywhere on the screen to close the pop-up box.

 TIP   **Quick Description**   If you right-click an option in a dialog box, a shortcut menu appears displaying one menu command: What's This? Click **What's This?** to view a description of the option.

In this lesson, you learned how to access Windows 95's Help system. In the next lesson, you'll learn how to work with the accessories and programs that come with Windows 95.

Starting a Built-In Windows Application or Accessory

In this lesson, you learn about the accessory programs Windows offers and how to start them.

Looking at the Windows 95 Programs

Windows 95 comes with a host of free programs, commonly called *applets* (small application programs) or accessories used to do real work in Windows. Although some of these programs are not state-of-the-art and won't provide you with the advanced options you'll find in other commercial programs, they do give you the power to do basic jobs in Windows, such as writing letters, drawing pictures, and dialing your phone. The latest release of Windows that ships on new PCs, OEM Service Release 2 (OSR 2), offers a few new applets that didn't appear in the original Windows 95 release, helping you tackle more tasks than ever before.

 TIP   **Maintenance Programs**   Windows also includes a set of *utilities* to help you properly maintain your computer. For instance, ScanDisk can help repair damaged disks, and Disk Defragmenter can reduce file fragmentation and speed up your hard disk.

Detailed instructions on how to use all the Windows 95 applets could easily consume another 600-page book. So, instead of that, Table 7.1 lists the most commonly used applets and utilities and a brief description of each. As you run these applets, keep in mind that the Windows Help system is close at hand. For instructions on how to use any of these applets, simply open the **Help** menu and click a topic.

Table 7.1 Applets and utilities offered in Windows 95 OEM Service Release 2 (OSR 2)

Icon	Applet Name and Description
Calc	**Calculator** is just like a hand-held calculator.
Charmap	**Character Map** lets you copy and insert special characters that do not appear on your keyboard.
Clipbrd	**Clipboard Viewer** displays the contents of the data that you cut or copy from a document. (The Clipboard stores data temporarily so you can paste it into another location.)
Dial-Up Networking	**Dial-Up Networking** is a *remote-computing* program, which lets you connect two computers (for example, your home and office computers) over the phone line. Each computer must have a modem.
Filexfer	**File Transfer** enables you to send files while simultaneously talking to someone on the phone by using your voice-enabled modem. This applet is new to OSR 2.
Directcc	**Direct Cable Connection** lets you connect two computers with a cable and transfer files between the two computers. This is especially useful if you have to transfer files between a laptop and desktop computer.
Hyperttrm	**HyperTerminal** is a modem communications program that connects you to another computer or to online services.
Wangimg	**Wang Imaging** for Windows, new to OSR 2, enables you to view graphics files in a variety of formats such as JPG, XIF, TIFF, BMP, and FAX. You also can scan images directly into this applet.
Notepad	**Notepad** lets you create and edit plain text files, which can be opened in almost any program.
Mspaint	**Paint** offers a complete set of tools for drawing and painting pictures on your screen. You can also use Paint to create your own background designs for the Windows desktop.

Icon	Applet Name and Description
Dialer	**Phone Dialer** is a programmable phone keyboard. You can use it (along with a modem) to dial phone numbers for you. After Dialer places the call, you can pick up the receiver and start talking.
WordPad	**WordPad** is a more sophisticated word-processing program than Notepad. It allows you to style text to make your documents more attractive.
Awfxex32	**Fax** is a new program that can transform your computer (equipped with a fax modem) into a fax machine. You can then receive faxes and send the documents you type to other fax machines.
Freecell	**Games** is a group of computer games including FreeCell, Hearts, Minesweeper, and Solitaire. Most of these games are very addictive, but they do help hone your mouse skills.
Iowconn1	The **Get on the Internet** choice runs the Internet Connection Wizard, which helps you set up your computer to connect to an Internet service provider. These and the next three Internet features are only bundled in OSR 2.
The Internet	The desktop icon labeled **The Internet** launches the Internet Connection Wizard the first time you select it, and thereafter launches Internet Explorer, a Web browser program.
Internet Mail	**Internet Mail** is an easy e-mail program for use with an Internet e-mail account.
Internet News	**Internet News** enables you to browse Internet newsgroups, online "bulletin boards" where users can post and read messages.
Conf	**Microsoft NetMeeting,** new in OSR 2, enables multiple users to hold an online conference by typing using an on-screen Whiteboard where users can draw and type text. NetMeeting also enables a group of users to chat online, share applications on-screen, transfer files, and transmit audio and video.

continues

Table 7.1 Continued

Icon	Applet Name and Description
	Multimedia consists of several programs that control your sound card and CD-ROM drive. CD Player lets you play audio CDs. Media Player plays computerized movie clips and sound recordings. Sound Recorder lets you plug a microphone into your sound card and record voices and other sounds. Volume Control allows you to crank up the volume of your sound card or CD player.
	Backup is a utility that copies the files on your hard disk, compresses them (so they take up less space), and places the compressed files on a set of floppy disks or a backup tape. If anything happens to your files, you can use Backup to restore the backed up files to your hard disk.
	Disk Defragmenter rearranges the parts of each file on your hard disk so your disk drive doesn't have to hunt all over for them. This increases the speed of your drive and the overall speed of your computer. Run this monthly.
	DriveSpace compresses files on a disk, so they take up less space, and decompresses the files automatically when you need them. Note that you can't presently use DriveSpace on FAT32 hard drives under OSR 2, which means you'll only be able to compress floppy and removable disks, unless you have a second hard disk that's not using the FAT32 file management system.
	ScanDisk looks for lost pieces of files on a disk and for bad spots on the disk itself. It can help you recover lost data, repair floppy disks, and reduce future data loss by preventing Windows from storing data on any bad areas of the disk.
	Windows Messaging (formerly Microsoft Exchange) is a one-stop electronic mailbox for all your network e-mail and e-mail that you receive from online services.
	The Microsoft Network is an online service offered by Microsoft Corporation. If you have a modem, you can subscribe to the service and use it to connect to other computer users, do research, shop, send and receive mail, and much more.

149

TIP **Missing Applets** If you don't find some of the applets listed in Table 7.1 on your system, that means they haven't been installed. Use Windows Help system to learn more about installing other Windows components.

Starting Built-In Windows Programs

You start a Windows 95 applet much as you would start any other Windows 95 application. (You'll learn more about working with applications under Windows 95 in Lesson 2 of Part 3.) Follow these steps to find out where to look for and how to run Windows applets:

1. You can get to all Windows applets via the Start button. Click the **Start** button, point to **Programs**, and then point to **Accessories**.

2. At the bottom of the Programs menu are a couple of applets, but the Accessories menu is the place where most applets hang out, as shown in Figure 7.1. At the top of the Accessories menu are the names of additional submenus. If the applet you want is on a submenu, point to the submenu name to display its applets.

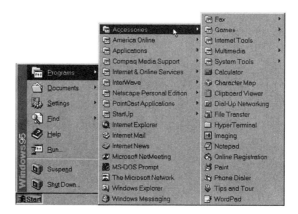

Figure 7.1 The Accessories submenu of the Programs menu holds most Windows 95 applets and utilities.

3. When you see the name of the applet you want to run (either in the Accessories menu or one of its submenus), click it.

4. Windows runs the applet and automatically closes the Start menu. The applet displays its own window, complete with title bar and menu bar, so you can start performing a task.

This lesson introduced you to the applets and utilities offered in Windows 95, and showed you how to find applets to start them. The next lesson shows you how to use Windows Explorer to work with files.

Viewing Drives, Folders, and Files with Windows Explorer

8

In this lesson, you will learn how to use Windows Explorer to view a disk's contents.

Understanding Drives, Folders, and Files

A *drive* is the hardware that seeks, reads, and writes information from and to a disk. A hard disk and its drive are considered one inseparable unit, while a floppy disk can easily be removed from its drive and replaced with a different disk.

Drives are given letter names. For most computers, drives A and B are floppy disk drives, used to store and retrieve data on floppy disks. Drive C generally designates the hard disk inside the computer. (Because hard disks and their drives are not easily separated, the terms *disk* and *drive* are often used interchangeably when referring to hard disks.) If the computer has more than one hard disk, or if the hard disk has been divided into multiple partitions (sections), the additional drives are usually labeled D, E, F, and so on. (See Lesson 3 in Part 1 for more about hard and removable disks.)

Because so much information can be stored on a hard disk, hard disks are usually divided into folders. For example, drive C probably has a separate folder for every program you have. Floppy disks can contain folders too, but they usually don't. (Because of their limited capacity, it is easy to keep track of files on a floppy disk without using folders.)

Disk space is not set aside for individual folders; in fact, folders take up hardly any disk space at all. If you think of a disk as a file drawer full of papers, folders are like tabbed file folders used to organize the papers into manageable groups.

Folders What Windows 95 refers to as *folders*, Windows 3.1 referred to as *directories*. You still may encounter the term "directories" from time to time.

Folders hold files, just as paper file folders hold pieces of paper. Files come in two varieties: *program* (or *executable*) *files* and *document files*. A program file contains the instructions the computer needs to perform. A document file contains a text document that you can read. Regardless of the type of files you're working with, you can use Windows Explorer (and My Computer, which you'll learn about in the next lesson) to view and control files and folders.

TIP **Long File Names** File names in Windows 95 can have up to 255 characters and do not require a file extension; file names in Windows 3.1 can only have up to eight characters and usually have a file extension with a maximum of three characters. To display the file extensions for file names, choose **View**, **Options** from Explorer, My Computer, or any open folder menu. In the Options dialog box, click the **View** tab, and click the **Hide MS-DOS file extensions for file types that are registered** check box. The check mark disappears from the check box. Choose **OK** to display the file extensions.

Starting Windows Explorer

To start Windows Explorer, follow these steps:

1. Open the **Start** menu and choose **Programs**.
2. From the Programs menu, choose **Windows Explorer**. (You'll usually find the Windows Explorer choice at the bottom of the Programs menu.) The Windows Explorer window appears (see Figure 8.1).

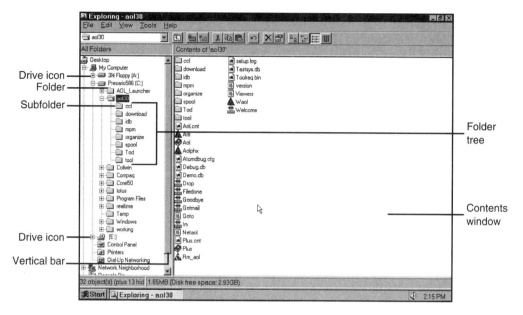

Figure 8.1 The Windows Explorer window, displaying the folder tree.

Using the Windows Explorer Window

Figure 8.1 shows the Windows Explorer window. The folder tree (the left side of the screen) shows all the folders on the selected drive (in this case, drive C).

The left pane of the Windows Explorer window contains the folder tree, a graphical representation of the folders and subfolders on your system. (The folder list on your screen will probably contain folders different from those shown in Figure 8.1.)

Folders and Subfolders The folder that leads to all other folders (much like the trunk of a tree leads to all branches and leaves) is the *main folder*. In Figure 8.1 the main folder is C:\. Any folder can have a subfolder. *Subfolders* are like file folders within file folders; they help you organize your files. In Figure 8.1, *download* is a subfolder of *aol30*.

The right side of the window contains a list of the files in the folder that's currently highlighted in the folder list. Notice that the folder icon next to the *aol30* folder (the highlighted folder) appears as an open folder. In Figure 8.1, the

154

files in the *aol30* folder are listed in the right half of the Windows Explorer window.

Selecting Folders

When you select a folder using the folders tree, its contents are displayed on the right side of the Explorer window. To select a folder with the mouse, simply click the folder you want. Table 8.1 lists the keys you can use to select a folder with the keyboard.

Table 8.1   Keys for Selecting a Folder in the Folder Tree.

Key	Function
↑	Selects the folder above the selected one.
↓	Selects the folder below the selected one.
←	Closes the selected folder.
→	Opens the selected folder.
Home	Selects the first folder in the folder list.
End	Selects the last folder in the folder list.
First letter of folder name	Selects the first folder that begins with that letter. Press the letter again if necessary, until you select the folder you want.

Opening and Closing Folders

In Figure 8.1, the folder tree shows the subfolders of the *aol30* folder. You can *collapse* (decrease the detail of) the folder tree so that subfolders do not appear, or you can *expand* (increase the detail of) the folders list so that folders many levels deep will show. A plus sign (+) next to a folder indicates that there are subfolders to display; a minus sign (–) next to a folder indicates that the folder has been opened and can be closed. Click the plus or minus sign beside any folder icon in the folder tree to expand or collapse its subfolders.

To open or close a folder with the mouse, just double-click the folder icon. To open or close a folder with the keyboard, select the folder using the arrow keys and press + (plus) to open it or – (minus) to close it.

CAUTION

It's Only for Show   Collapsing and expanding affects this display only; it doesn't alter your folders in any way.

Changing Drives

You can change drives to see the folders and files contained on a different disk. To change drives with the mouse, click on the drive icon in the folder tree. Using the keyboard, press the first number for the drive type (for example, press **3** for a 3.5-inch floppy drive). To change to drive C, use the arrow keys to highlight (C:).

Changing the Windows Explorer Display

The commands in Windows Explorer's View menu enable you to change how the folders window and the files list window display information. You can control the size of the windows, whether or not the toolbar and status bar are displayed, and how the files in the files list window are displayed.

When you change the Windows Explorer's display settings to suit your needs, Windows remembers those settings. They remain the same every time you start Windows (until you change them again).

Sizing the Windows

In the Windows Explorer screens you've seen so far, both the folder tree and the list of files were shown. You can change the way each is shown by changing the amount of window space allotted to each. For example, you may want to see more files and less white space around the folders list. Follow these steps to change the way the window space is divided between the panes:

1. A vertical gray bar is the divider between the two panes. Point to the gray bar, and the mouse pointer changes to a vertical bar with two arrows.

2. Drag the line to where you want it. The window display changes accordingly (see Figure 8.2).

Vertical bar has been moved to make Contents window larger

Windows Explorer toolbar

Mouse pointer

Status bar

Figure 8.2 You can drag the gray pane divider to resize the window panes, as shown here.

Changing the File List Display

By default, the Windows Explorer shows only the file names and icons for each folder. However, you can change the display to include more information about each file if you want. The View menu provides you with four options you can use to customize the file list display: Large Icons, Small Icons, List, and Details.

The View, List command tells Windows to display only the icons and file names for each folder (as shown in Figure 8.2). This is the default display.

Choose **View**, **Details** to have Windows display the following information about each file:

- Size in bytes
- File type (to describe the file—such as Folder, Application, Help, Settings, and so on)
- Last modification day and date

You can also change the size of the icons that Windows displays in the files list window. Choose **View**, **Large Icons** to display large icons with the file names

157

beneath the icons. Choose **View**, **Small Icons** to display small icons with the file names to the right of the icons.

 TIP **Sort by Column** When you display file details in the right pane of Windows Explorer, you can use the Name, Size, Type, and Modified column headings that appear to sort the list of files and folders. For example, click the Name column heading to re-sort the files and folders in descending alphabetical (z to a) order. Click the Name column heading again to redisplay the files and folders in ascending alphabetical order.

Controlling the Order of the Display

As you can see in Figure 8.2, the files in the folder are listed in alphabetical order by file name. If you prefer, you can have Windows arrange the icons by the following methods:

- Choose **View**, **Arrange Icons**, by **Type** to arrange files alphabetically by their file type.
- Choose **View**, **Arrange Icons**, by **Size** to arrange files by size from smallest to largest.
- Choose **View**, **Arrange Icons**, by **Date** to arrange files alphabetically by date from newest to oldest.

Using the Explorer Toolbar

Windows Explorer provides a toolbar at the top of the Windows Explorer window (as shown in Figure 8.2). You can toggle the display of the toolbar on and off by choosing **View**, **Toolbar**. Then you can click the buttons on the toolbar instead of choosing menu commands. Table 8.2 shows the buttons on the Windows Explorer toolbar.

Table 8.2 Windows Explorer's Toolbar Buttons

Button	Name	Description
🔼	Up One Level	Displays the folder one level above the folder currently displayed in the Folder text box.
✂	Cut	Cuts the selected file or folder and places it on the Clipboard.

Button	Name	Description
	Copy	Copies the selected file or folder to the Clipboard.
	Paste	Pastes the contents of the Clipboard to the location selected in the list.
	Undo	Undoes last file or folder operation.
	Delete	Deletes the selected file or folder.
	Properties	Displays the properties of the selected file or folder.
	Large Icons	Displays large icons in the contents window.
	Small Icons	Displays small icons in the contents window.
	List	Displays a list of files and folders with names and icons.
	Details	Displays a detailed list of files and folders.

Displaying the Status Bar

Initially, Windows displays the status bar at the bottom of the Windows Explorer window (as shown in Figure 8.2). If you want to hide the status bar, open the **View** menu and select **Status Bar** (to deactivate it). To redisplay it, choose **View**, **Status Bar** again.

Closing Windows Explorer

If you're not going to use Windows Explorer again right away, you should close it instead of minimizing it, to conserve system resources. To close Windows Explorer, click the **Close** button or double-click the **Control menu icon**. Or, choose **File, Exit**.

In this lesson, you learned how to use Windows Explorer to examine the contents of a disk. In the next lesson, you'll learn about another tool for working with files and folders: My Computer.

A Brief Look at My Computer

In this lesson, you will learn how to use the My Computer window to examine the contents of your hard, floppy, and CD-ROM drives.

Viewing a Disk's Contents with My Computer

My Computer enables you to view all files, folders, disk drives, and printers on your computer as icons. This feature is similar to Windows Explorer. Using My Computer, you can browse through your computer to find the files you want to open right from the desktop. Follow these steps:

1. Double-click the **My Computer** icon on the Windows 95 desktop to open the My Computer window. This window contains icons for all the disk drives on your computer as well as the Control Panel and Printers folder, and a Dial-Up Networking folder if Dial-Up Networking features are installed on your system.

2. Double-click the icon for the drive or folder you want to examine. A window opens that displays that drive's or folder's contents.

3. Select the folder you want to browse by highlighting its icon and choosing **File**, **Open** or by double-clicking its icon. You can select additional folders in the same way.

By default, each folder you select opens in its own window, as shown in Figure 9.1. To organize the screen and prevent one window from being hidden by the others, you can arrange the windows on the desktop any way you want. Simply drag each window by its title bar to a new location. For more on arranging multiple windows, refer to Lesson 3 "Working with Windows" in this part.

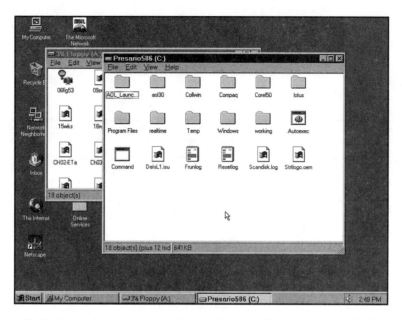

Figure 9.1   Browse the contents of the A drive and C drive from the My Computer window.

Changing the My Computer Display

By default, when you browse through folders in the My Computer window, Windows displays a separate window for each folder. However, you can control how Windows displays information in the My Computer window. For example, you can set up My Computer as a single window, and you can use the commands on My Computer's View menu to change the size of the icons and how they're displayed.

Setting Up a Single Window

If you don't like having all those windows on-screen while you're browsing through your files, you can set Windows 95 to display a single window that changes as you open each folder. Then, no matter how many disks or folders you select, you will only see one window on the desktop at a time.

To set Windows 95 so that you only see a single window as you browse using My Computer, follow these steps:

1. Open the current window's **View** menu and select **Options**. The Options dialog box opens.

2. Click the **Folder** tab if needed. The Folder options appear (see Figure 9.2).

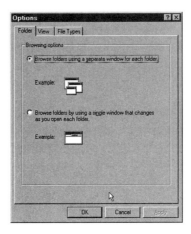

Figure 9.2 Browse options in the Options dialog box.

3. Select the second option (**Browse Folders By Using a Single Window that Changes as You Open Each Folder**).

4. Click the **OK** button. From now on, when you select a different folder from a window, Windows 95 displays its contents in the current window, rather than opening a new window.

If you want to change back to the default view in which Windows displays multiple browsing windows, repeat the preceding steps but choose the first option (**Browse Folders Using a Separate Window for Each Folder**) from the **Folder** tab.

Arranging Icons

By default, the items in the My Computer window (and any windows you open from this window) appear in Large Icon view. If you have a lot of icons in a window, you may want to open the **View** menu and choose **Small Icons** so you can view more icons at a glance. (You can always change back to the default view later by choosing **Large Icons** from the **View** menu.)

When arranging a window to suit your needs, you may need to move your icons out of the way by dragging them with the mouse. However, suppose that later you want to return your icons to their original positions. No problem! Choose **View**, **Arrange Icons**, **Auto Arrange** (a check mark appears next to the option when it's selected), and Windows 95 arranges the icons for you automatically. To turn off auto-arrange, select the same command sequence again; the option is deselected, and the check mark disappears.

You can use the other choices on the Arrange Icons submenu to sort the items in the window by Drive Letter, Type, Size, or Free Space, depending on the view you select.

To sort the icons in the current My Computer window, follow these steps:

1. Open My Computer's **View** menu.

2. Choose **Arrange Icons**, and a submenu appears.

3. Choose the sort type you want (**Drive Letter**, **Type**, **Size**, or **Free Space**). Windows rearranges the icons in the window accordingly.

Current Window Only   The file sorting and icon arrangements you choose apply to the current My Computer window only, not all open My Computer windows.

CAUTION

Another way to clean up the icons in the window is to arrange the icons so that they line up in rows. To do so, choose **View**, **Line up Icons**, and Windows 95 arranges the icons neatly in rows.

Closing My Computer

To close any open My computer window, click the **Close** button in the upper-right corner of the window. The window closes, or in the case of the initial My Computer window, shrinks to an icon on the desktop. If you have multiple My Computer windows and want to close them all, press and hold the Shift key, and click the title bar of the topmost window.

In this lesson, you learned how to view the contents of the drives on your computer by using the My Computer window. In the next lesson, you learn how to add and remove files and folders.

Creating and Deleting Files and Folders

In this lesson, you learn how to create, select, open, and delete files and folders.

Creating a File or Folder

Some files and folders are created automatically when you install a program. For example, when you install the Word 97 Windows program, the setup program creates a folder on your hard drive and places the Word 97 files in that folder. However, you can also create files and folders yourself.

There are several reasons you may want to create a folder. Many application installation programs create a folder when you install the application on your computer. If one of your application installation programs does not, you need to create a folder for that application.

A more common reason to create a folder is to store document files. For example, you may want to create a folder to store documents you create with WordPad so the document files won't be scattered among the more than one hundred Windows program files in the Windows folder. Having a separate folder for WordPad documents makes it much easier to find and manipulate the documents you create.

Creating a Folder with Windows Explorer

To create a folder using the Windows Explorer, follow these steps:

1. Open the **Start** menu and choose **Programs**.

2. From the Programs menu, choose **Windows Explorer**. The Windows Explorer window appears.

3. Click to select or highlight the folder in the folder tree under which you want to create the new folder. (The folder you create will be a subfolder of the folder you select.) If you don't want the new folder to be a subfolder of another folder, select the icon for the drive itself (such as C: or A:).

4. Open the **File** menu, and point to **New.** Then choose **Folder.** A folder icon named New Folder appears at the bottom of the contents list.

5. Type the new folder name using up to 255 characters (including spaces) in the text box that appears next to the new folder icon. (For more on file and folder naming, see Lesson 13 in this part.) The name you type replaces the words "New Folder" as you type, as shown in Figure 10.1.

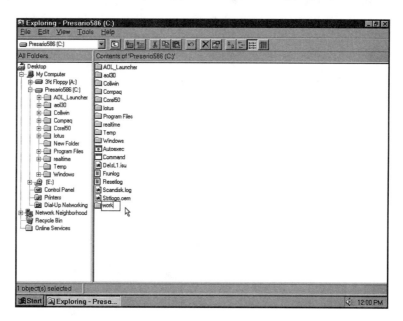

Figure 10.1 When you add a new folder, simply begin typing to name it.

6. Press **Enter**, and Windows renames the new folder.

Creating a Folder with My Computer

To create a folder with My Computer, follow these steps:

1. Double-click the **My Computer** icon on the desktop to open My Computer.

2. In My Computer, double-click the icon for the drive in which you want to create a folder. If needed, double-click the icon for the folder that you want to hold the new folder.

3. Open My Computer's **File** menu, and point to **New**. Then choose **Folder**. Windows creates a new folder icon.

4. Type a new name for the folder and press **Enter**. (For more on file and folder naming, see Lesson 13 in this part.)

Creating a File

Within either Windows Explorer or My Computer, you can create files as well as folders. The applications installed on your system determine what kinds of files you can create. Creating a new file from Explorer or My Computer lets you skip opening the program to create and name the new file. Of course, the file will be empty until you later open it in its application. Follow these steps to create a file in either Explorer or My Computer:

1. Launch Windows Explorer or open My Computer.

2. Select the drive in which you want to create a folder. If needed, open the folder that you want to hold the new file.

3. Open the **File** menu in either Explorer or My Computer, and point to **New**. In the New submenu, click the type of file you'd like to create, as shown in Figure 10.2.

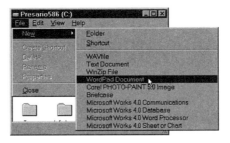

Figure 10.2   You can create a file for one of the applications installed on your system, such as WordPad.

4. The file's icon appears in the Explorer or My Computer window. Type a new name for the file and press **Enter**. (For more on file and folder naming, see Lesson 13 in this part.)

Selecting Files and Folders

The last two lessons showed you how to open (select) folders in the Explorer folder tree and in the My Computer window to see the contents of the folder. This section covers selecting again, but from a different perspective: Here, you learn how to select a folder or file to perform some type of operation with it, such as deleting it.

Selecting a single file or folder in Windows Explorer or My Computer is easy: Simply click its icon in the folder tree, contents list, or current window. You need to know additional techniques for selecting multiple files or folders (in any combination), described next.

To really speed up operations, you will want to select multiple files or folders and then execute commands that affect the entire group. For example, you may want to select several files to copy to a disk. Copying them all at once is much faster than copying each file individually. The following sections explain how you can select multiple files and folders.

Selecting Adjacent Files and Folders

Adjacent files or folders appear in sequence, or next to each other, in any Explorer or My Computer window. Whether you're working in the Explorer folder tree or contents list, or a My Computer window, the technique for selecting adjacent files and folders is the same. To do so, follow these steps:

1. In Explorer or My Computer, display (select) the folder holding the files and subfolders you want to select.

2. Click the icon for the first (top) file or subfolder in the group you want to select. In a My Computer window, you can think of this as the upper-left file or subfolder in the group that you want to select.

3. Press and hold **Shift**, and then click the icon for the last file or subfolder in the group you want to select. In a My Computer window, you can think of this as the lower-right file or subfolder in the group that you want to select. Windows selects (highlights) the adjacent files and folders.

TIP   **Box Them In**   To select adjacent files and folders in a My Computer window, you can drag to create a box around them. As you drag, all the files and folders are highlighted.

Selecting Nonadjacent Files and Folders

Although you can sort files and folders in a number of different orders, the files and folders you want to work with may not appear in a neat arrangement. Nonadjacent files and folders are those that don't appear within a contiguous list or block in Explorer or My Computer. You can select nonadjacent files and folders using the following steps:

1. In Explorer or My Computer, display (select) the folder holding the files and subfolders you want to select.
2. Click the icon for the first file or subfolder that you want to select. Note that this doesn't necessarily have to be the top file or folder in the list. It actually can be any file or folder in the collection that you'd like to select.
3. Press and hold **Ctrl**, and then click the icon for the next file or subfolder you want to select. Windows highlights it, as shown in Figure 10.3.

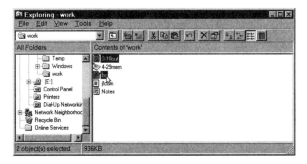

Figure 10.3   Press and hold the Ctrl key, then click to select nonadjacent files and folders.

4. Use **Ctrl+click** to select any additional files and subfolders.

Opening (Starting) a File

When you open (start) a file in Explorer or a My Computer window, Windows runs the file (if it's a program file), or opens it (in the application in which it was created) if it's a data file. The result of opening a file depends on the kind of file you open, as follows:

- Opening an executable file with an .EXE, .COM., .PIF, or .BAT extension runs the program that the file is supposed to start. If you opened a file called Msworks.exe, for example, Windows would run Microsoft Works for Windows.

- Opening a document file associated with an application starts the application on-screen and then loads the document file. For example, opening a file called Work.txt would launch Notepad and then open the Work.txt file in Notepad.

TIP   **File Types**   The icon for each file gives you a clue as to what kind of file it is. But if you want to see the file name extensions for your files in Explorer or My Computer, open the **View** menu and select **Options**. Click the **View** tab, and then click **Hide MS-DOS File Extensions for File Types That Are Registered**. This removes the check mark from the box. Click the **OK** button to put the change into effect.

Windows 95 offers a few different ways to open a file in the file list of Windows Explorer or in a My Computer window:

- Double-click the file.

- In Explorer, press **Tab** to move the highlight to the file list. Use the **arrow keys** to highlight the file you want to open, and then press **Enter**.

- When you see the file you want to open, click it to select (highlight) it. Then choose the **File, Open** command. Or, right-click the selected file to display its shortcut menu and click **Open**.

If you want to open an application and load a particular file in it, you can do it in Explorer or My Computer: Drag the document's file name and drop it on top of the executable file's name. If, for example, you dragged a file named Notes.txt until it was over the file Notepad.exe, Windows Notepad would start and load Notes.txt.

Deleting a File or Folder

There will come a time when you need to delete a file or folder. For example, you may have created a file or folder by mistake, you may want to remove the files or folder for an application you no longer use, or you may need to make more room on your hard drive.

CAUTION

Fatal Errors NEVER delete the following files from your hard disk: Command.com, Auto.exec.bat, Config.sys, User.dat, and System.dat. If you get rid of these files, you won't be able to boot your computer! Also, avoid deleting files with .BAT, .EXE, .COM, .PIF, .DLL, .DAT, and .INI file name extensions, unless you're sure of what you're doing. These files execute programs or give them more instructions to work properly; without one of these files, your application may not work.

CAUTION

Better Safe Than Sorry Before you delete anything, it's a good idea to make a backup copy of any files or folders you might need later. See Lesson 12 in this part for directions on how to copy files and folders. You should be especially careful when deleting any program folder; make sure the folder doesn't contain files the program needs to run.

To delete a file or folder, follow these steps:

1. In a My Computer window or the Windows Explorer folder tree or contents list, select the file or folder—or any combination of files and folders—to delete. Be aware that when you delete a folder, Windows 95 deletes all files in that folder.

2. Choose **File**, **Delete** or press the **Delete** key. The Confirm Folder Delete or Confirm File Delete dialog box appears as shown in Figure 10.4, indicating what will be deleted and asking you to confirm the deletion.

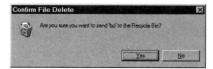

Figure 10.4 Confirm that you'd like to delete the file or folder.

3. Check the Confirm Folder (File) Delete dialog box carefully to make certain you are deleting what you intended to delete.

4. Click **Yes**.

CAUTION   **I Didn't Mean to Do That!**   If you delete a folder or file by mistake, immediately choose **Edit**, **Undo Delete** to restore the deleted folder(s) and file(s).

When Windows 95 deletes files and folders from Explorer or the My Computer window, it moves them to the Recycle Bin. Then, from the Recycle Bin you can restore any files you might need, as described in the next lesson.

In this lesson, you learned how to create, select, open, and delete files and folders. In the next lesson, you'll learn how to restore deleted files.

Using the Recycle Bin

In this lesson, you learn what the FAT is and what it has to do with deleted files, as well as how to use the Recycle Bin to delete and restore files.

What's the FAT, and What Does It Have to Do with Deleting?

FAT stands for *File Allocation Table*. Every formatted disk has specialized hidden files holding the FAT. So what does the FAT do, you ask? The FAT keeps track of where all the bytes for each file are physically stored on the disk. Let's look at this in more detail.

FAT A disk's *FAT (File Allocation Table)* is a special hidden file that tracks exactly where on a disk each piece or cluster of information is stored. The clusters may be adjoining, or they may be noncontiguous.

As you learned in Part 1, Lesson 3 "Storing Your Work: Hard and Removable Disks," the surface of a disk is divided into tracks (concentric circles) and sectors (each of these is shaped like a wedge of pie). Adjacent sectors on a track form a *cluster*. The smallest space that a file can occupy is a cluster. Depending on the size of the file, it can take up one cluster or many clusters. The FAT keeps track of the clusters that hold the contents of each file.

Deleting a file means you erase its contents so you can't use them anymore, which sounds like it wipes the data from the disk immediately. Well, that's not completely true. When you delete a file, its contents remain on the disk. In the FAT, the file's *location* is deleted, so that the FAT *thinks* there isn't anything in that spot on the disk. Later, when you save another file, the computer writes its contents on the clusters that are marked available, wiping out each cluster's previous contents (that is, the contents of the file you deleted).

With Windows 95, deleted files are tracked in the Recycle Bin. As long as a file appears in the Recycle Bin, you can restore it if you later decide you want to use it again. Basically, the Recycle Bin works with the FAT to ensure that the data you want remains somewhere on the disk. Under an older version of MS-DOS (version 5.0 or later) or Windows 3.11, you can restore a file only if you have a utility program for undeleting files. You have to use an undelete utility *immediately* after deleting a file; otherwise, the FAT will use the clusters the deleted file held if you save more files.

TIP   **Recycle It!**   To delete selected files and folders, you can drag them from any Explorer or My Computer window and drop them on the desktop Recycle Bin icon.

Working with the Recycle Bin

The files you delete in Windows are stored temporarily in the Recycle Bin. You can retrieve files from the Recycle Bin if you decide you need them again, or you can purge the deleted files when you're sure you no longer need them. By purging deleted files, you make more room on your disk.

TIP   **Paper Trail**   The Recycle Bin icon on the desktop changes to reflect whether or not you've deleted any files. When the Recycle Bin is completely empty, the icon is an empty wastebasket. When the Recycle Bin holds files you can retrieve, its wastebasket icon holds wadded-up paper.

Using the Recycle Bin to Restore a File

Retrieving (or *restoring*) a file or folder from the Recycle Bin places it back in its original location: on the same drive, and in the same folder. To retrieve files you've deleted from the Recycle Bin, follow these steps:

1. Double-click the **Recycle Bin** icon on the desktop. (If you see a Recycle Bin choice for the current disk in the Explorer or My Computer window, you can double-click it there, too.) The Recycle Bin window appears, as shown in Figure 11.1.

173

Name	Original Location	Date Deleted	Type	Size
106FIG01	C:\COLLWIN\shots	6/16/97 5:07 PM	Bitmap Image	54KB
106FIG02	C:\COLLWIN\shots	6/16/97 5:07 PM	Bitmap Image	81KB
201FIG01	C:\COLLWIN\shots	6/16/97 5:07 PM	Bitmap Image	31KB
201FIG02	C:\COLLWIN\shots	6/16/97 5:07 PM	Bitmap Image	35KB
201FIG03	C:\COLLWIN\shots	6/16/97 5:07 PM	Bitmap Image	408KB
202FIG01	C:\COLLWIN\shots	6/16/97 5:07 PM	Bitmap Image	31KB
203FIG01	C:\COLLWIN\shots	6/16/97 5:07 PM	Bitmap Image	47KB
203FIG02	C:\COLLWIN\shots	6/16/97 5:07 PM	Bitmap Image	73KB
203FIG03	C:\COLLWIN\shots	6/16/97 5:07 PM	Bitmap Image	32KB
203FIG04	C:\COLLWIN\shots	6/16/97 5:07 PM	Bitmap Image	76KB
203FIG05	C:\COLLWIN\shots	6/16/97 5:07 PM	Bitmap Image	78KB

42 object(s)   2.67MB

Figure 11.1   The Recycle Bin holds deleted files and folders.

2. The Recycle Bin works much like the file details view in any Explorer or My Computer window. Use the scroll bar at the right side of the Recycle Bin window to display the files and folders you'd like to restore.

3. Click the first file or folder you want to retrieve. To select multiple files or folders, hold down **Ctrl** and click each additional file or folder.

4. Open the **File** menu and choose **Restore**. Windows restores the files to their original locations.

5. Click the **Close** button or choose **File**, **Exit** to close the Recycle Bin window.

CAUTION

Files from Floppies?   When you delete files or folders from a floppy disk or some types of removable disks, Windows DOES NOT place the files in the Recycle Bin. In fact, unless you have a special utility to restore such deleted files, you will not be able to get them back. So, before you delete a crucial file or folder from a floppy or removable disk, make sure you have a current copy of the file on another floppy or your hard disk.

Note that you can change the way files are listed in the Recycle Bin by using the choices on the Recycle Bin's View menu. These choices work just as those discussed for Windows Explorer and My Computer in Lessons 8 and 9.

Emptying the Recycle Bin

If you're sure that you won't need to use certain deleted files ever again or you need to free up some disk space, you can remove deleted files from the Recycle Bin. Doing so removes the files from the drive permanently.

Follow these steps to purge deleted files in the Recycle Bin:

1. Double-click the **Recycle Bin** icon on the desktop. (If you see a Recycle Bin choice for the current disk in the Explorer or My Computer window, you can double-click it there, too.) The Recycle Bin window appears, as shown previously in Figure 11.1.

2. Open the **File** menu and select **Empty Recycle Bin**. A confirmation dialog box appears, as shown in Figure 11.2.

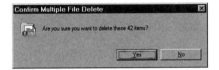

Figure 11.2 Windows asks you to verify that you want to delete files from the Recycle Bin, because removing them from the Recycle Bin permanently deletes them.

3. Choose **Yes** to delete all the files.

4. Click the **Close** button or choose **File**, **Exit** to close the Recycle Bin window.

To delete only one file from the Recycle Bin, select the file, open the **File** menu, choose **Delete**, and click **Yes**. Windows purges that file only. Or, to delete multiple files, you can press and hold **Ctrl**, then click multiple files to select them before choosing **File**, **Delete**.

As you learned in this lesson, the Recycle Bin works with your system's FAT; you learned to use the Recycle Bin to store and recover deleted files. The next lesson shows you how to move and copy files and folders.

Moving and Copying Files and Folders

In this lesson, you learn how to copy and move files and folders and how to use toolbar buttons and shortcut menus to work with files.

Understanding Drag and Drop

To move or copy files or folders through Windows Explorer or My Computer, the fastest method is to use *drag and drop*—that is, you select the items you want from your *source* folder, "drag" them to the *destination* folder, and "drop" them there. You'll learn the details of using this technique later in this lesson.

Before you move or copy, make sure the source file or folder is visible, so you can select the file(s) or folders you're going to drag. Also, make sure that the destination drive or folder is visible. In Figure 12.1, *work* (the source folder), the *Notes* file (the *source* file), and the empty *projects* folder (the *destination* folder) are all visible.

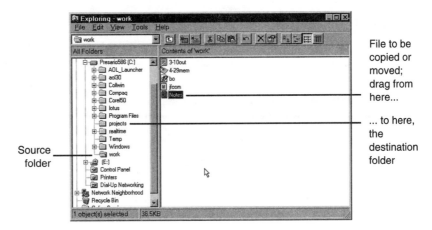

Figure 12.1 The selected file can be moved or copied.

Understand Dragging Within and Between Disks

The easiest technique for copying and moving files and folders is to drag the selection from one disk or folder icon to another. You need to know some simple rules when dragging your selections in Explorer or between My Computer windows:

- Whenever you drag between two folders on the *same* disk drive, Windows assumes you want to *move* the selection unless you tell it otherwise. Windows helps prevent you from cluttering up a disk with multiple copies of the same file(s) or folder(s).

- Whenever you drag between locations on *different* disk drives, Windows assumes you want to *copy* the selection unless you tell it otherwise. In this instance, Windows helps ensure the integrity of your files, as moving between drives can result in data loss; if you copy instead, your original file(s) and folder(s) will remain intact.

This lesson provides very specific steps for performing copy and move operations. You'll learn how to override Windows' natural tendencies—to copy a selection between folders on the same disk or move a selection from one disk to another.

Copying Files and Folders

Copying a file or folder creates an exact copy of the file's or folder's contents, and places it in the folder on the disk you specify, leaving the original intact. Copying is one of the computer's great convenience features. Not only does it save you work, but it enables you to move your work from one computer to another (or share it) when those computers aren't connected.

Copy versus Move   When you *copy* a file or folder, the original file or folder remains in its original location, and a copy of the file or folder is placed in a second location. When you *move* the file or folder, it no longer exists in its original location, but only in the new location.

Copying with the Mouse

With the mouse, use this procedure to copy:

1. Select the files or folders to copy.

2. To copy between disks, simply drag the selection to the destination folder on the destination disk. To copy between folders on the same disk, press the **Ctrl** key and drag the files or folders to the destination folder. When you're dragging to copy, Windows displays a plus with the mouse pointer, as shown in Figure 12.2.

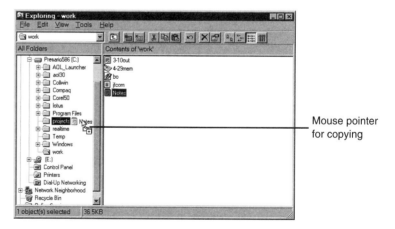

Mouse pointer
for copying

Figure 12.2   A plus sign by the mouse pointer indicates you're copying the selection that you're dragging.

3. Release the mouse button and the **Ctrl** key if you used it.

TIP   **Quick Copy**   If you need to copy to a floppy disk, right-click the selection, point to **Send To** in the shortcut menu, then click the floppy disk choice in the submenu.

Copying with the Commands

Instead of dragging with the mouse, use this procedure to copy:

1. Select the files or folders to copy.

2. Open the **Edit** menu and choose **Copy** (**Ctrl+C**).

3. Select the destination drive or folder.

4. Open the **Edit** menu and choose **Paste** (**Ctrl+V**). Windows pastes the copied files and folders in the destination folder.

CAUTION   **The File Is Already There**   If you attempt to copy a file or folder to a location in which a file or folder with the exact same name exists, Windows 95 lets you know with a message that says **This folder already contains a file called 'filename'. Would you like to replace the existing file with this one?** Choose **Yes** to replace the existing file or **No** to stop the copy operation.

Moving Files and Folders

Moving a file or folder removes it from the disk and folder where it's presently stored and places it on a new disk in the folder you specify. As with copying files, you can move most files by dragging them to different folder icons with the mouse.

Knowing how to move files gives you a lot of control over the contents of your hard disk. It's also a more efficient method of repositioning a file than copying and then deleting the original.

CAUTION   **Moving Caveat**   Be careful when moving certain files (or avoid moving them entirely). If you move a file that a program needs, such as a specialized data file, a template or style sheet file, or the startup file, you'll get error messages when the program tries to access the file and can't find it where it's supposed to be.

More About Moving Folders

Once you create a folder or subfolder, it's not set in stone on the folder tree. You can move it to a new location. You can even move a folder so it's contained within another folder, *demoting* the original folder to a subfolder. Or, you can move a folder to *promote* it, so it's no longer a subfolder of a particular folder.

When you move a folder, you move its total contents—not only its files, but its subfolder (along with any files and subfolders they contain). So, avoid moving program folders; doing so can cause the program not to run.

Moving with the Mouse

You use the same techniques whether you want to move folders or files: Drag the folder's icon to a new location on the Explorer folder tree or in a My Computer window.

With the mouse, follow these steps to complete a move:

1. Select the files or folders to move.
2. To move the selection between folders on the same disk, drag the files or folders to the destination folder in the folder tree or in a My Computer window. If you press **Shift** while dragging, you can move the selection to another disk. When you're dragging to move, Windows does not display a plus with the mouse pointer.
3. Release the mouse button.

Moving with Commands

Complete a move using these command steps:

1. Select the files or folders to move.
2. Open the **Edit** menu and choose **Cut (Ctrl+X)**.
3. Select the destination drive or folder.
4. Open the **Edit** menu and choose **Paste (Ctrl+V)**.

CAUTION

Wrong Move or Copy? If you move or copy the wrong files or folders, you can choose **Edit**, **Undo Copy** from the Explorer or My Computer menu bar, or click the **Undo** button on the Explorer or My Computer toolbar to undo the operation.

Using Toolbar Buttons and Shortcut Menus to Work with Files and Folders

The toolbar of the Explorer window or any My Computer window, when displayed, offers some key buttons that you can use to quickly work with selected files and folders. (Choose **View**, **Toolbar** to display the toolbar if it doesn't appear.) These buttons resemble similar ones you'll see in other Windows applications for copying and moving text and data:

Click the *Cut* button to remove the selected file(s) and folder(s) from their current location and place them on the Windows Clipboard, a temporary storage area. Then you can paste the selection to a new location.

Click the *Copy* button to place a copy of the selection on the Windows Clipboard, so you can paste a copy of the selection to a new location.

Use the *Paste* button after you cut or copy files and folders and select a new location for them. Pasting then places them in that new location. (The Paste button won't have any effect if you haven't previously cut or copied a selection.)

Click the *Undo* button when you realize your prior action was a mistake.

To move selected files and folders to the Recycle Bin, click the *Delete* button.

In addition to using toolbar buttons to work with selected files and folders, you can right-click any selected file or folder to display a shortcut menu of commands for working with that selection. The shortcut menu will typically offer Cut, Copy, and Delete commands that are the equivalent of the toolbar buttons with the same name. After you copy or cut a selection, if you right-click a disk or folder icon, you'll also see a Paste command on the shortcut menu that appears.

TIP **Still More Shortcuts** As you learned in "Using Dialog Boxes," Lesson 5 earlier in this part, many dialog boxes in Windows 95 applications list files and folders. You can right-click a file or folder icon *within* such a dialog box listing to display a shortcut menu with choices for copying and renaming files, and more. Also, many file dialog boxes include toolbar buttons you can use to change the file listing, such as seeing the details or list view.

In this lesson, you learned how to copy and move files and folders, using drag and drop, menu commands, toolbar buttons, or shortcut menus. In the next lesson, you'll learn how to rename and find files and folders.

181

Renaming and Finding Files and Folders

In this lesson, you learn how to rename and find files and folders.

Understanding File and Folder Names

File names must be unique in order for your computer to be able to tell them apart. With Windows 95, you can ignore most of the old file name rules, either when you're naming a file within an application or working in Windows Explorer or My Computer. Windows 95 and its applications let you use long file names (up to 255 characters). Folder names also can be long and can include special characters. In addition, you can use spaces, but you can't use any of the following characters: \ ? : * " < > |. Windows 95 (but not its DOS) recognizes upper- and lowercase letters in file names. So with Windows 95, you can use file names like "Letter to Mortgage Company 09/05/96" and "Phone List for Little League." Even though you don't usually see file name extensions (the three characters that follow the period in a file name) in Windows 95, it does use them behind the scenes to identify each file's type.

The file name extension can give you a clue about what a file is used for or what program it comes from. Table 13.1 lists a few of the common file extensions.

Table 13.1 File Name Extensions for Common File Types

Extension	File Type/Program It Comes From
.AVI	Video for Windows video file
.BAK	Backup file
.BAT	Batch file (a collection of commands)
.BMP	Windows bitmap graphic file
.COM	Program command file
.DAT	Data file
.DOC	Document file from Microsoft Word or another word processor
.DOT	Microsoft Word template file
.EXE	Executable program file
.GIF	Graphics Interchange Format graphics file
.HLP	Help file
.HTM	HyperText Markup Language (HTML) Web page file
.JPG	JPEG graphic file
.MDB	Database file from the Microsoft Access program
.MID	MIDI music file
.PPT	Microsoft PowerPoint presentation file
.PCX	PC Paintbrush or Windows Paint file
.TXT	Plain text (ASCII) file
.WAV	Sound file
.WKS, .WK1, .WK2, or .WK3	Lotus 1-2-3 file
.WP or .WPF	Document file from WordPerfect
.XLS	Spreadsheet file from Microsoft Excel
.ZIP	A file containing one or more files compressed with the PKZIP file-compression program

The file name may also include the *path* for the file. The path includes the letter for the drive where a file is stored, followed by a colon, followed by the folders and subfolders (called directories and subdirectories under Windows 3.11 and older versions of DOS) leading to the one holding the file. Folder and subfolder names are separated with backslashes (\). If, for example, a file were on drive C: in the \TEMP subfolder within the \WINDOWS folder, the full path would be C:\WINDOWS\TEMP.

Renaming Files or Folders

You may need to change the name of a file or folder to reflect changes in your work. For example, if you copy a file from one folder to another, you may want to rename the copy to make sure you can easily distinguish the files while working. To rename your files, follow these steps:

1. In the Explorer or My Computer window, select the file or folder you want to rename.

2. Choose **File**, **Rename**. Or, you can right-click the file or folder and choose **Rename** from the shortcut menu. A box appears around the file or folder name, and the name is highlighted.

3. Type the new name for the file or folder. As you type, the new name replaces the old name. Press **Enter** when you finish typing.

It Worked Yesterday   Never rename program files. Many applications will not work if their files have been renamed.

CAUTION

Searching for a File

As you create more files, the ability to find a specific file becomes more critical. You can search for either a single file or a group of files with similar names using the **Tools**, **Find, Files or Folders** command in Explorer. To search for a group of files, use the asterisk wild card (*) with a partial file name to narrow the search. You can also perform a partial name search without wild cards, search by last modification date, save complex searches, and do a full text search. Table 13.2 shows some search examples and their potential results.

Wild Cards   When you're not sure of the file name you want to find, you can use the asterisk wild card (*) to replace multiple characters in the file name or the question mark wild card (?) to replace one character in the file name.

Table 13.2 Search Examples and Their Results

Characters Entered for Search	Sample Search Results
mem?.doc	mem1.doc, mem2.doc, mem5.doc
mem1.doc	mem1.doc
mem*.doc	mem1.doc, mem2.doc, mem11.doc
c*.exe	calc.exe, calendar.exe
*.exe	calc.exe, calendar.exe, notepad.exe
c*.*	calc.exe, calendar.exe, class.doc

To search for a file, follow these steps:

1. From the Windows desktop, click the **Start** button, point to **Find**, and select **Files or Folders**. The Find dialog box appears (see Figure 13.1). (Alternatively, if you want to search from a particular folder, select the folder in the Explorer; choose **Tools**, point to **Find**, then click **Files or Folders**.)

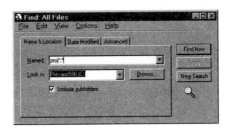

Figure 13.1 The completed Find dialog box.

2. In the **Named** text box, enter the characters you want to find, using wild cards to identify unknown characters.

3. If you want to search an entire disk drive, choose it from the **Look In** drop-down list (if it's not already there) and make sure the **Include Subfolders** check box is selected. Figure 13.1 shows my C: disk drive selected.

   If you want to search only the main folder, make sure the **Include Subfolders** check box is not selected.

4. If you want to search for a file according to its last modification date, select the **Date Modified** tab and select the date options you want.

5. If you want to search for a certain type of file, select the **Advanced** tab and choose a file type from the **Of Type** drop-down list.

6. Click the **Find Now** button to begin the search. The search results window appears under the Find dialog box, showing the files that were found (see Figure 13.2).

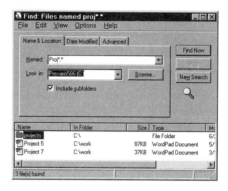

Figure 13.2 The search results.

Using Your Search Results

After you perform a search, Windows displays the search results, a list of the file(s) matching the criteria for your search. This list isn't just for show. You can perform certain file operations within it, which can save you from having to open a new window for a file that's been found. You can do any of these things with found file(s) in the list:

- Select one or more files (as you would in any other window) to perform file-related operations.
- Right-click the selected file(s) to display a shortcut menu of commands you can use to work with the file.
- Use the **Cut** command on the shortcut menu to move the file(s) elsewhere.
- Use the **Copy** command to copy the file(s) elsewhere.
- Use the **Delete** command to remove the file(s) from your disk.
- Rename the file(s) using **Rename**.
- View file details using the **Properties** command.

Saving and Rerunning a Search

Windows 95 enables you to save the criteria you create for a search so that you can later run the same search with only a couple of simple steps. When you save a search, Windows adds an icon for the search to the desktop. (Of course, you can move the icon to another location if you prefer.) To restart the search, all you have to do is double-click the icon. Use these steps to save a search:

1. Set up all your criteria and run the search.

2. You can save the search criteria only, or you can save the search criteria and the results. To include the results in the saved search, open the **Options** menu in the Find dialog box and click **Save Results** to toggle that command on.

3. To save only the search, open the **File** menu in the Find dialog box and click **Save Search**.

4. Click the **Close** button to close the Find dialog box. You'll see the icon for the saved search on the Windows desktop, as shown in Figure 13.3.

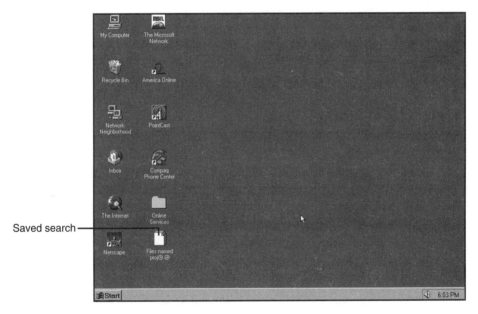

Saved search ─

Figure 13.3 Double-click the icon for a saved search to rerun the search.

5. Double-click the icon for the search, and the Find dialog box opens. If you saved the search criteria only, click the **Find Now** button to rerun the search. If you saved the search results, they automatically appear. Work with the listed files, and then close the Find dialog box when you finish.

In this lesson, you learned how to rename a file or folder and search for a file or folder. In the next lesson, you'll learn how to format a disk.

Formatting a Disk

In this lesson, you learn how to format a disk to prepare it to hold files.

Understanding Why You Format Disks

You'll recall from Lesson 3 "Storing Your Work: Hard and Removable Disks" (Part 1) that all disks are covered with a magnetic material. Your computer's disk drive gives an "on" or "off" state to tiny pieces of this material to create readable characters of information. To enable your drive to handle such a delicate operation, the magnetic material needs to be precisely arranged on the disk's surface. *Formatting a disk* is the process of arranging the magnetic material on the disk so it can store information.

 TERM **Format a Disk**   When you use Windows 95 to format a disk, it arranges the magnetic material on the disk so the drive can write files to the disk and read those files later.

Formatting not only organizes the magnetic storage information on a disk, it also sets up the *File Allocation Table* (FAT) that your computer uses to keep track of which parts of which files are stored on specific parts of the disk. (For more on the FAT, see Lesson 11 "Using the Recycle Bin" in this part.) Each disk has a specific capacity of storage space based on the density of the magnetic material. Different floppy drives are specifically geared to handle disks of a particular density. (More on this in a moment.) After you format a disk, you can save and copy files on it.

You can format disks that already have information on them to "freshen" them up and deal with minor errors on the disk's surface. Use caution when reformatting floppies and removable disks, however. *Formatting wipes out any information that exists on the disk and clears out the contents of the FAT.* You don't want to format a disk that holds data you need, which means you almost never want to format a hard disk, especially drive C.

CAUTION

Look Before You Format   If you accidentally format a disk that has data you need, that data is lost forever. There's no way to restore the data, and it's not put in the Recycle Bin so that you can retrieve it. Always double- or even triple-check to make sure that you're not formatting a floppy disk that you need or a hard drive that has important data and programs. (In general, Windows won't let you format your boot disk, usually drive C, so that you don't wipe out Windows and important files for booting your system.)

Explorer and My Computer let you format any floppy disk that matches the size and capacity of your floppy disk drive. You also can set a few other disk options. You can format many removable disks (like Zip and SyQuest cartridges), too, but sometimes the removable drive manufacturer provides a utility program that does the job better. When the manufacturer provides one, be sure to use that utility program.

TIP   **Forget Formatting**   Because formatting is a tedious operation, you can buy preformatted disks. However, if you don't want to spend a few extra cents for this convenience, you can format your own disks.

Choosing Format Options

The Format dialog box (shown in Figure 14.1) offers three choices in the Format Type area that enable you to control how the format operation is performed.

Let's look at those choices before you actually format a disk so you understand what each choice does to the disk:

> You can choose **Quick (Erase)** to reformat a disk that's been formatted before. Quick formatting is faster because it deletes files, cleans up the disk storage, and clears out the FAT, but it doesn't scan for bad sectors (information) on the disk. If you think a disk has bad sectors, perform a full format.

> Perform a **Full** format if a disk hasn't previously been formatted or has been formatted for a Macintosh. This is also the best option to choose if you suspect other problems with the disk, such as if the disk's files may be

infected with a virus. This formatting prepares the disk's surface for file storage and then scans the disk for bad sectors.

If you've already formatted a disk and just want to copy system files to it, choose **Copy System Files Only**. Windows copies the system files to the disk without deleting any existing files from the disk. This option makes the disk *bootable*; that is, if you insert the disk in drive A and start your computer, it reads the floppy disk for startup information.

Figure 14.1 The Format dialog box offers several choices you need to understand when you format a disk.

The Other Options area at the bottom of the dialog box offers choices that aren't crucial to the format operation. However, those options (described here) can help you catalog and work with formatted disks.

Label You can enter a label for the disk (which is also called a *volume label* in old DOS lingo). To add a label, first clear the check beside the **No Label** check box (if necessary), and then make your entry in the **Label** text box. Your label can have up to 11 characters including spaces, but it *cannot* include tabs or these characters:

  * / \ | . , ; : + = [ ] ( ) & ^ < > "

Display Summary When Finished Check this option if you want to see a report when the formatting is finished. The report tells you the disk's available space, the space occupied by the system files if you copied them to the disk, and space taken up by bad sectors. The latter tidbit is good to know; if a disk has a lot of bad sectors, its magnetic media may be going bad, so you should consider discarding it. For information about correcting errors on disks, see Lesson 6, "Using ScanDisk on a Damaged Disk" in Part 6.

Copy System Files   Select this to have Windows both format the disk and copy system startup files to the disk instead of simply copying the system files.

Choosing Disk Capacity

You may have noticed that your floppy disks or disk labels have "HD" or "DD" or something similar on them. These hieroglyphics refer to the disk's *density* (capacity), which is as important as the floppy's size. Disks of differing capacity and size combinations hold differing amounts of data. (Table 14.1 provides a review, but see Lesson 3 in Part 1 to learn more about different floppy disk capacities.)

Table 14.1   Floppy Disk Capacities

Disk Size	*Type*	*Capacity*
3.5-inch	DSHD, double-sided high-density	1.44M
3.5-inch	DSDD, double-sided double-density	720K
5.25-inch	DSHD, double-sided high-density	1.2M
5.25-inch	DSDD, double-sided double-density	360K

The disk's capacity depends on how efficient its magnetic storage material is. High-density (HD) disks hold more data than do double-density (DD) disks of the same size. Older disk drives can only work with DD disks. Computers built in the last few years, however, have high-density floppy disk drives that can work with both HD and DD disks of the right size (5.25-inch or 3.5-inch). One caution: Unless you tell Windows otherwise, it will try to format a DD disk as high-density. If you format a disk this way, it might work okay for a while, but eventually it'll cause you to lose data. Play it safe and format DD disks as DD disks and HD disks as HD disks.

CAUTION

Format Faux Pas   Formatting a DD disk as HD can slow down the format-ting process drastically toward the end, which may clue you in to the fact that you've specified the wrong disk capacity for formatting.

Performing a Disk Format

Now that you have a clear picture of what formatting does and how to use the formatting options that Windows 95 presents, you can follow these steps to format a disk:

1. If you're formatting a disk you've used before, double-check to make sure you've copied any files you might need from that disk. Insert the floppy or removable disk in the appropriate drive, if needed.

2. Click **Start**, point to **Programs**, and click **Windows Explorer** to start Explorer. Or, double-click the My Computer icon on the desktop to open the My Computer window.

3. In the Explorer folder tree or in the initial My Computer window, right-click the disk icon for the disk to format and click **Format**, as shown in Figure 14.2. (In My Computer only, you can alternatively click the disk icon once, open the **File** menu, and select **Format**.)

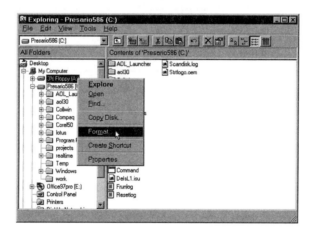

Figure 14.2 To start the format, right-click the drive in Explorer or My Computer and click **Format**.

4. In the Format dialog box that appears, use the **Capacity** drop-down list to specify the correct capacity of the floppy disk you're formatting.

5. Specify any formatting options you desire (they're described in detail earlier in this lesson), and then click **Start** to begin the format.

6. Windows shows you the formatting progress. If necessary, click **Cancel** to stop formatting.

7. When it's finished formatting the disk, Windows displays the Format
Results summary (if you specified that a summary should be displayed),
shown in Figure 14.3. Click **Close** to close the summary after reviewing it.

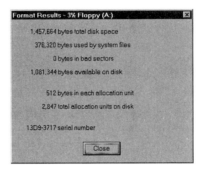

Format Results - 3½ Floppy (A:)

1,457,664 bytes total disk space

376,320 bytes used by system files

0 bytes in bad sectors

1,081,344 bytes available on disk

512 bytes in each allocation unit

2,847 total allocation units on disk

13D9-3717 serial number

Close

Figure 14.3   Windows informs you when the format is complete.

8. Click **Close** again to close the Format dialog box.

TIP   **A Gentle Reminder...**   If you try to select a disk that isn't formatted in either
Explorer or My Computer, Windows displays a message telling you that the disk
isn't formatted and asking whether you want to format it. Click **Yes** to display
the Format dialog box.

This lesson showed you the steps for formatting a disk, and explained the
available formatting options. The next lesson reveals how you can change the
look of your Windows desktop.

Controlling the Desktop Appearance

Work through this lesson to learn how to adjust the desktop's color and pattern, turn on a screen saver, adjust Windows' colors, choose various other settings, and change the display resolution.

Changing the Desktop's Background Color and Design

If you work in a large office, you probably walk past computers every day and see some sort of funky color scheme or design on the monitor. Maybe you've wondered how your colleague has managed to decorate his or her screen so expertly, and you have a secret desire to give your screen a custom look. Use these easy steps to add a background pattern or wallpaper:

1. To change any of the display properties, right-click a blank area of the Windows desktop and click **Properties**. (Another way to change display properties is to click the **Start** button, point to **Settings**, click **Control Panel**, and then double-click the **Display** icon.)

2. The Background tab appears up front. From the **Pattern** list, click the desired background pattern, as shown in Figure 15.1. A pattern gives some texture to the background, such as bricks or pillars. (Click (None) in the Pattern list to remove the current pattern from the desktop.)

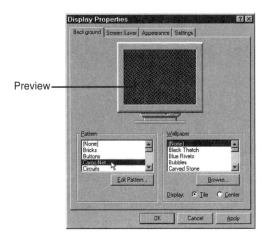

Figure 15.1   Choose a pattern for the desktop.

3. In the **Wallpaper** list, click the desired wallpaper design. Wallpaper is any graphic that lays on top of the desktop. Windows comes with several wallpaper designs from which you can select, or click (None) to remove the current wallpaper.

4. Select **Tile** to have the wallpaper design fill the screen, or select **Center** to have one section of the design placed in the middle of the screen.

5. The preview area shows how the screen will look with the new settings. Click **Apply** if you want to see how the desktop looks and think you might want to pick another design (repeat steps 2-4). To finish, click **OK** to save your changes.

CAUTION

Dueling Desktops   If you choose a wallpaper image for the desktop, the wallpaper will cover the pattern wherever it appears. When the wallpaper is tiled or full-screen size, it covers all the pattern. In such a case, you might as well remove the pattern; you can't see it, but it's taking up space in RAM.

TIP   **Wallpaper Wiz**   You can create your own wallpaper by using the Paint program that comes with Windows (**Start**, **Programs**, **Accessories**, **Paint**). After creating your picture, open the **File** menu and select one of the **Set As Wallpaper** options.

Turning on a Screen Saver

A screen saver displays moving pictures that can prevent a stagnant image from burning into your screen. Although with today's monitors this is less of a concern, you may want to display a screen saver for fun. Or, a screen saver offers a convenient way to hide your work from prying eyes; if you assign a password when you enable the screen saver, you have to type that password to stop the screen saver display so you can resume working.

To turn on a Windows screen saver, follow these steps:

1. Right-click a blank area of the Windows desktop and click **Properties**.
2. Click the **Screen Saver** tab to display its options.
3. Windows comes with several basic screen savers. Open the **Screen Saver** drop-down list and click the desired screen saver, as shown in Figure 15.2. Pick (None) if you don't want to use any screen saver.

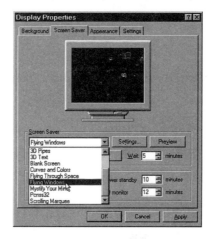

Figure 15.2 Select a screen saver to jazz up your desktop when you're not working.

4. To change the settings for the selected screen saver, click the **Settings** button, enter your preferences, and click **OK**. (Preferences vary depending on the screen saver; for example, if you turn on Flying Windows, you can specify the number of flying windows and the speed at which they fly.)
5. Click the arrows next to the **Wait ___ Minutes** spin box to specify how long your computer should be inactive before the screen saver kicks in.

6. To use the screen saver to protect your computer from unauthorized use, select the **Password Protected** check box. Then click the **Change** button, type your password in the **New Password** and **Confirm New Password** text boxes, and click **OK**. (Whatever you type appears as asterisks so nobody can read the password over your shoulder as you type it.)

7. If you have an energy smart monitor, you can pick one of the following options to have Windows power down the monitor during periods of inactivity: **Low-Power Standby** triggers the monitor's power saving feature. The monitor remains on. Use the **Minutes** spin box to specify how long the computer must remain inactive before the power saver kicks in. **Shut Off Monitor** turns the monitor off after the number of minutes you specify in the **Minutes** spin box.

8. Click **OK** to save your changes.

Changing the Appearance of Windows

Windows offers you a great deal of control over how its on-screen elements look. For example, you can change the color of title bars, the thickness of window borders, and the size of text for on-screen elements. Windows comes with several predesigned schemes that provide attractive settings for all the on-screen elements. You can choose an existing scheme to give the desktop a whole new look. Or, for more subtle changes, you can change the look of individual elements (objects).

 Scheme   A *scheme* is a collection of settings for the elements of the Windows screen, such as the color for title bars, the font used in menus, and the size of desktop icons.

Follow these steps to change the appearance of the Windows desktop:

1. Right-click a blank area of the Windows desktop and click **Properties**.

2. Click the **Appearance** tab to display its options.

3. To use one of these schemes, open the **Scheme** drop-down list and click the desired scheme, as shown in Figure 15.3.

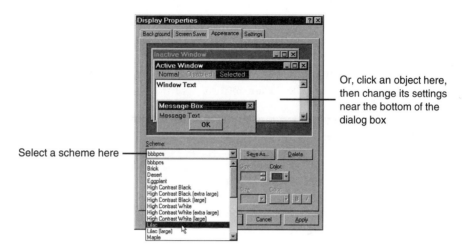

Select a scheme here

Or, click an object here, then change its settings near the bottom of the dialog box

Figure 15.3 Choose a new scheme to give Windows a more lively—or subdued—appearance.

4. Click an object to adjust in the preview area. The **Item** drop-down list shows the name of the selected item, enabling you to change its look.

5. To change the size of the selected item, click the arrows to the right of the **Size** spin box.

6. To change the color of the selected item, open the **Color** drop-down list and click the desired color.

7. If the selected item has text in it (as in a title bar or menu), you can use the **Font**, **Size**, and **Color** drop-down lists to control the appearance of the text.

8. To save your settings as a new color scheme, click the **Save As** button, type a name for the new color scheme, and click **OK**.

9. Click Apply if you want to see how Windows looks and think you might want to make more changes (repeat steps 3-8). To put your changes into effect, click **OK**.

Changing the Display Resolution

Display resolution and color settings control the quality of the display. As you learned in Lesson 5 of Part 1, most monitors can display in a few different resolutions and in a few different color settings (each of which controls how many colors the screen displays).

199

The settings you should pick depend on how you'll be using your computer. Higher resolutions (for example, 1024-by-768) display more information on the screen but display smaller objects than do lower resolutions (such as 640×480). So, while a higher resolution might be great for multimedia games, a lower resolution might be easier on the eyes for word processing.

For routine work in your applications, 256 colors will do. To play video clips and view pictures, pick High Color or True Color, if available. (When you pick more colors, more memory is required to display those colors.)

Use these steps to adjust the resolution and color settings in Windows:

1. Right-click a blank area of the Windows desktop and click **Properties**.

2. Click the **Settings** tab to view the current resolution and color settings.

3. Open the **Color Palette** drop-down list and select the number of colors you want your monitor to display.

4. Drag the slider under **Desktop Area** to the right to increase the screen resolution or drag it to the left to decrease resolution.

Choose the number of colors here ——— 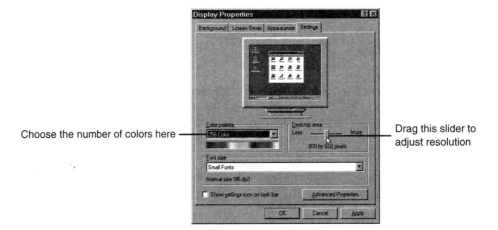 ——— Drag this slider to adjust resolution

Figure 15.4   Adjust the colors and resolution of the Windows display to make your screen more comfortable to view.

5. If you picked a higher resolution (Desktop area), you can use the **Font Size** drop-down list to select a large or small font for the display. (You might want to pick a larger font size so you can read the type.) Or, click the **Other** choice in the Font Size drop-down list, specify a **Scale** percentage for the fonts, and click **OK**.

6. Click **OK** to save your settings. Windows might tell you that you have to restart Windows to put your changes into effect. Click **Yes** to restart.

 TIP **Resolve Your Resolution** Just because you *can* choose a higher resolution for your monitor doesn't mean you *should*. Using the highest possible resolution (say 1280×1024) for a small monitor makes on-screen items appear tiny, straining your eyes. Stick with a comfortable resolution such as 800×600 on a 15-inch monitor or 1024×768 on a 17-inch monitor.

You now can select a desktop color and pattern, use a screen saver, change screen colors, and change the display resolution. The next lesson helps you make similar adjustments to the taskbar and Start menu.

Controlling the Taskbar

Here, you learn how to glean information from the taskbar, move and resize the taskbar, change taskbar options, and add and remove programs on the Start menu.

"Reading" the Taskbar

Notice that the right end of the taskbar displays the current time and a small icon of a speaker (if you have a sound card). When you see an icon or item in this area of the taskbar, take one of the following steps to control it:

- Point to the **time display** to view the current date, including the day of the week.

- Double-click the **time** to view a dialog box that lets you set the time and date on your computer.

- Click the **speaker** (**Volume**) icon for a simple volume slider (see Figure 16.1), or double-click the icon to change the volume and balance for individual items like your sound card, microphone, and CD-ROM drive.

- If you see a printer icon, you are currently printing one or more documents. To see which documents are printing, double-click the **printer** icon. For more details, see Lesson 12, "Printing and Controlling Print Jobs" in Part 3.

Figure 16.1   Click the speaker (Volume) taskbar icon to quickly adjust sound card volume.

Moving and Resizing the Taskbar

By default, the taskbar appears along the bottom of the Windows 95 desktop. This middle-of-the-road choice was intended to satisfy most users. Yet, right-handed users might find it awkward to point to the far left to start programs. Or, left-handed users might prefer to have the whole taskbar along the left edge of the screen. You can move the taskbar to the left or right edge of the screen, or even the top.

To move the taskbar to a different place on the desktop, point to a blank space on the taskbar (not to a program name or the time), hold down the left mouse button, and drag the taskbar to the left, top, right, or bottom of the desktop. When you release the mouse button, the taskbar snaps to the new location, as shown in Figure 16.2.

You'll also notice in Figure 16.2 that the taskbar buttons are too narrow to read. When you run more programs and the taskbar is along the bottom or top of the screen, it gets awfully crowded, making it difficult to see what each taskbar button says. You can change the size of the taskbar for easier reading.

To resize the taskbar, drag an edge of the taskbar up, down, right, or left to make it fatter or skinnier. Figure 16.3 illustrates how to resize the taskbar.

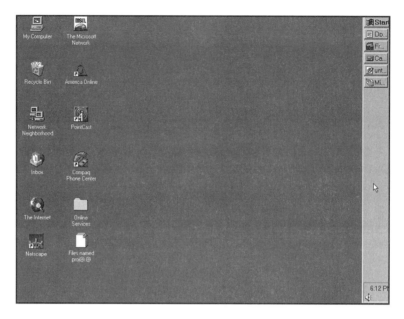

Figure 16.2 You can move the taskbar to a more convenient location on-screen.

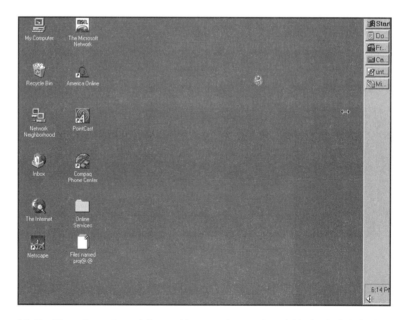

Figure 16.3 Drag the edge of the taskbar to change its width (or height), depending on its current location on-screen.

Changing Taskbar Options

Like other elements of the Windows screen, the taskbar has several options (properties) you can change to adjust how it looks and behaves. You can change other properties of the taskbar, to hide the time or keep the taskbar on top, for example. Follow these steps to change the taskbar properties:

1. Right-click a blank area of the taskbar and click **Properties**. (You also can click **Start**, point to **Settings**, and click **Taskbar**.) The Taskbar Options tab is selected by default (see Figure 16.4).

Figure 16.4 You can change options that control how the taskbar looks and acts.

2. Click to check or clear the options that you want. (A check mark indicates an option is turned on.) Here's what each check box does:

   Always on Top keeps the taskbar in the front of all windows.

   Auto Hide shrinks the taskbar so you have to move the mouse pointer to the edge of the screen where the taskbar is located (the bottom by default) to bring it into view.

   Show Small Icons in Start Menu controls the size of icons on the Start menu.

   Show Clock turns the time display on or off.

3. Click **OK** to close the dialog box and accept the new taskbar settings.

TIP   **Wide Load**   If you've sized the taskbar so that it's really wide or deep, it's a good idea to enable the Auto Hide property so that the Taskbar isn't constantly—and needlessly—hogging desktop space. Or, disable the Always on Top choice so that the taskbar doesn't cover vital parts of your program windows; keep in mind that when you do this, you'll have to minimize open programs to see the taskbar.

Adding and Removing Start Menu Programs

The Start menu that displays when you click the Start button at the left end of the taskbar is designed to be a convenience feature. In theory, the Start menu should enable you to start your programs with just a few mouse clicks, saving you the trouble of searching through Explorer or My Computer to find the program startup file. You'll really become speedy if you take the time to add and remove programs to the Start menu, so that it offers exactly the startup choices you need.

TERM   **Shortcuts**   Windows also calls the Start menu program startup commands shortcuts.

Adding a Program

As you'll learn in the first lesson in Part 3, when you install most programs with Windows 95, the install process automatically adds a startup command for the program to the start menu. In rare instances (such as when you install a game under DOS), you'll need to add a startup command manually. Follow these steps to do so:

1. Right-click a blank area of the taskbar and click **Properties**.

2. In the Taskbar Properties dialog box, click the **Start Menu Programs** tab.

3. Click **Add**. The Create Shortcut dialog box appears. You can type the full path and startup file name in the **Command line** text box. Or, click the Browse button and use the Browse dialog box to navigate to the startup file. (See Lesson 5 in this part to learn more about working with file lists in dialog boxes.) Click **Open** to select the file and close the dialog box.

4. Once the appropriate Command line is entered, click **Next**.

5. In the Select Program Folder dialog box that appears, a "tree" of the Start menu folders appears, as in Figure 16.5. You can simply click the folder where you want to place the program startup choice. Or, select the folder within which you want to add a new folder, click the **New Folder** button, and type a name for the folder.

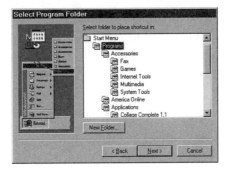

Figure 16.5 Click the desired folder on this "tree" to place the new program on the Start menu.

6. Click **Next** to display the Select a Title for the Program dialog box.

7. If needed, edit the name for the program startup command that appears in the text box at the top of the dialog box.

8. Click **Finish**. Windows adds the command to the Start menu.

9. Click **OK** to close the Taskbar Properties dialog box.

Removing a Program or Folder

If your Start menu seems too full and you have difficulty finding the commands to start your programs, you may want to remove some programs from the Start menu. Use these steps to do so:

1. Right-click a blank area of the taskbar and click **Properties**.

2. In the Taskbar Properties dialog box, click the **Start Menu Programs** tab.

3. Click **Remove**. The Remove Shortcuts/folders dialog box appears. This dialog box offers a tree that works just like the folder tree in Explorer. For example, you click the plus beside a folder to expand it and display its contents in the tree.

207

4. Use the tree to navigate to the folder or program you want to remove, then click it.

5. Click **Remove**. Windows removes the shortcut from the menu.

6. Repeat steps 4 and 5 to remove additional folders.

7. Click the **Close** button to close the Remove Shortcuts/Folders dialog box.

8. Click **OK** to close the Taskbar Properties dialog box.

Windows Applets I don't recommend removing any of the Windows applets or utilities from the Start menu. You never know when you might need them....

CAUTION

This lesson taught you how to work with, move, and resize the taskbar; set taskbar options; and add and remove Start menu programs. Turn the page to learn how to work at the DOS prompt should the need arise.

Working at the DOS Prompt If You Must

This lesson explains how to display the DOS prompt, enter DOS commands, change drives and directories, and start DOS programs.

Displaying the DOS Prompt (Window)

If you need to run DOS programs, you can visit the *DOS prompt*. DOS (which rhymes with "gloss" and stands for *Disk Operating System*) is a set of computer instructions that works in the background to help your computer do its job.

The DOS prompt is a symbol (or what techies call a command prompt) on the screen that tells you that you can type a command to run a program or do some work in DOS. In Windows 95, you should be able to avoid the DOS prompt altogether. If you need to run a DOS program, you can use Windows Explorer or My Computer to display the program's icon, and then double-click it.

DOS Prompt   A symbol (usually the current drive, a colon, and the \> symbols, as in C:\>) that tells you that you can enter commands.

A plain vanilla DOS prompt looks like **C:\>**. However, when you display the DOS prompt in a window from the Windows 95 desktop, the prompt includes the name of the Windows folder or directory (the *current* folder), as in **C:\WINDOWS>**. The following steps show you how to display and close the DOS prompt:

1. Click the **Start** button, point to **Programs** to display its submenu, and click **MS-DOS Prompt**.

2. The DOS prompt appears in a window, as in Figure 17.1. To make the window bigger, click the **Maximize** button. You can enter commands at the DOS prompt as described later in this lesson.

Full Screen button ——

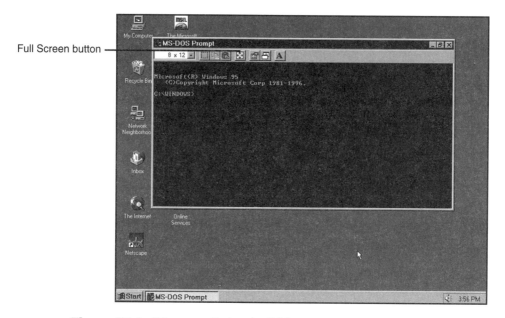

Figure 17.1   When you display the DOS prompt from Windows 95, the prompt appears in its own window.

3. To resize the DOS window, pick a size from the drop-down list at the left end of the toolbar, or click the **Full Screen** button, which is fourth from the left. (If the toolbar is not displayed, right-click inside the title bar and select **Toolbar**.) When the DOS prompt is in a window, switch between applications with the taskbar.

4. To exit the DOS window, click the **Close** button, or type **exit** at the DOS prompt and press **Enter**. Be sure to exit any DOS programs before you shut the DOS prompt window. If you don't, you may see a warning message telling you to exit the running DOS program.

TIP   **Full Screen Size**   You can quickly change the DOS display from full screen to a window by pressing **Alt+Enter**. DOS uses less memory in full screen view.

Using Commands in DOS

You type a command at the DOS prompt, and then press **Enter** to run the command. This sounds simple enough, but the commands you type have to be entered absolutely correctly, and when you use a file name in a command, you generally need to include the full *path* for the file. Otherwise, DOS will display the message **Bad command or file name**.

 TERM **Path or Path Name** The path or path name includes the disk drive letter plus a colon, a backslash for the main folder (root directory), any folder and subfolder names (separated by backslashes), the file name, a period, and the extension, as in C:\ALLWORK\MEMOS\4-14.DOC.

Decoding DOS Command Rules

DOS calls the rules for entering commands its command *syntax*. There are specific parts to a DOS command, and they must be entered in the right order and typed correctly. All the parts of a DOS command make up a *command line*. Here are the parts:

First type the **command** itself. It must be spelled correctly. For example, you use the COPY command to copy files. Some commands, like COPY, consist of an entire word. Other commands are abbreviations (*mem*) or acronyms (*md*).

Add **parameters**. *Parameters* tell DOS which file or other object to perform the command on (some commands require them, some don't). To delete a file, for example, you have to type the file name, including the path and three-letter file name extension.

Add **delimiters**, if they're needed. *Delimiters* include special characters you add, like the backslash (\), forward slash (/), and colon (:). These "punctu-ate" the command line for DOS. For example, you need to use the \ and : characters correctly in the path statement for a file, as in **c:\work\file1.txt**. Delimiters usually appear within parameters.

Add **switches** to the end of command lines. *Switches* fine-tune how the command works (some commands let you use switches, others don't). You can add a **/p** switch to a DOS **del** (delete) command, for example, so that DOS will prompt you to verify that you want to delete the file. Available switches vary, and you can use more than one switch at a time. Some switches even can be fine-tuned by adding a colon and a parameter.

For example, to display a list of files in a directory and sort the files by their three-letter extension, you would use the **dir** command and add the **:e** parameter to the **/o** switch. The full command with switch and parameter would be **dir /o:e**.

TIP   **On the Case**   You can type commands in uppercase or lowercase letters in DOS. The one thing DOS doesn't care about is which case you use.

TIP   **Need to Know More?**   To get help with a single DOS command, at the DOS prompt, type the name of the command, press the **Spacebar**, and then type either **/?** or **/help**. Press **Enter**, and DOS displays a description of the command and information about the parameters and switches you can or should use with the command.

Entering Commands at the DOS Prompt

The following steps demonstrate how to enter a command (in this case, the one that copies a file from the hard disk to a floppy disk):

1. At the DOS prompt, type **copy** (the command). Then press the **Spacebar**.

2. Type the name of the file you want to copy, including the drive, folder, and full file name with three-letter extension. This is a parameter required for the command, and it includes delimiters. In this case, you would type **c:\work\letter.doc**. Then press the **Spacebar**.

3. This particular command requires a second parameter: the drive letter of the disk you want to copy to, followed by the folder you want to copy to (if any). To copy to drive A, for example, type **a:** and press the **Spacebar**. (Make sure you have a formatted floppy disk in the drive you want to copy to.)

4. After you've entered the command and its parameters, enter any switches you want to use with the command. In this case, type **/v** so DOS will prompt you to verify the copy operation. Figure 17.2 shows the full command at the prompt.

Figure 17.2 Here, I've entered the copy command, along with a parameter (the full file name) and switch.

5. Press **Enter** to run the command.

6. If a prompt appears asking you for additional information before it can run a command (such as verifying the file copy in this case), respond to the prompt to finish the operation.

CAUTION

Cancel It! DOS doesn't offer an "undo" feature. To cancel a DOS command that's already running, press and hold the **Ctrl** key, press **C**, and then release both keys. Many DOS commands execute very quickly, though, so you may not have time to cancel them.

Understanding File Names at the DOS Prompt

Under Windows 3.11, an older version of DOS, or at the Windows 95 DOS prompt, certain *conventions* govern file naming. When you name a file in DOS, you give it a base name of up to eight characters and an optional three-character extension (which tells what kind of file it is), creating what's called an "8.3" file name. You can't use spaces or some characters in a file name's base name or extension. These forbidden characters are reserved for the system and commands:

" . / \ [ ] : * < > | + ; . ? space

If you go to the DOS prompt from Windows 95, you have to use 8.3 file names to refer to files. This becomes a problem when you want to refer to a file with a Windows 95 long file name. At the Windows 95 DOS prompt, a file name like "My Glossary.doc" is abbreviated to "myglos~1.doc." If you have multiple file names that are similar, you'll have trouble distinguishing them under DOS; DOS will abbreviate and sequentially number the files, as in "myglos~1.doc," "myglos~2.doc," and so on. There's really no easy way to work around this issue. If you'll need to work frequently at the Windows 95 DOS prompt, your best bet is to conform to the old 8.3 file name convention when working with Windows 95 programs so you'll be able to tell your files apart at the DOS prompt.

Changing Which Drive Is Active

To perform work with the files on the disk in a particular drive, you need to *change* to that drive or *log on* to it. If you don't log on to the appropriate disk drive before trying to perform a DOS command on a file on that disk, DOS displays a **File not found** error message after you press **Enter** to execute the command.

As you learned earlier in this book, most computers have two disk drives. The floppy drive is usually named *A*, and the hard disk drive is usually named *C*. If your computer has a CD-ROM drive or a second hard disk drive, it will be named *D* or *E*. You can log on to any drive that's connected to your system. Here are the steps:

1. If you want to log on to a floppy disk drive or CD-ROM drive, insert a floppy disk or CD-ROM in that drive with the files you want to work with.

2. At the DOS prompt, type the drive letter, followed by a colon. For example, to log on to floppy drive A:, type **a:**.

3. Press **Enter**. The computer logs on to that drive and redisplays the prompt, which now shows the new drive letter, indicating that it has logged on to the new drive.

Avoiding Error Messages

When you log on to a disk drive, it must contain a disk, and the disk must be formatted. You can encounter problems, however, when you try to log on to a floppy drive or CD-ROM drive. Let's say you try to log on to drive A, and you get an error message like this one:

```
Not ready reading drive A
Abort, Retry, Fail?
```

This message usually means that there is no disk in the drive. In this case, you can insert a disk in the drive and press **R** for Retry or **F** for Fail. To quit, you either press **F** for Fail twice, or you can press **A** for Abort, which gives you a message telling you the drive isn't active. Then type the name of another drive plus a colon, and press **Enter**.

Let's say you try to log on to drive A: and get an error message like this:

```
General failure error reading drive A
Abort, Retry, Fail?
```

This message means the disk in the drive you're trying to log on to isn't formatted or is in Macintosh format. In this case, you can insert a disk with the correct format in the drive and press **R** for Retry. To quit, you can press **A** for Abort, which gives you a message telling you that drive isn't active. Then type the name of another drive plus a colon, and press **Enter**.

Skipping the Log On

Suppose you want to work with a file on a disk in some drive other than the one DOS is currently logged on to. You would simply specify the full path name, including the drive letter. For example, let's say you have a floppy disk that you insert in drive A, and the disk holds a file called Memo.txt that you want to delete.

You can use a shortcut method to delete the file. At the DOS prompt, type **del a:\memo.txt** and press **Enter**. DOS removes the file from the disk in drive A. You don't need to log back on to drive C, though, because you never logged off it and onto drive A.

You can use this faster technique with other DOS commands like COPY and DIR. Don't worry if this confuses you. As you become comfortable working in DOS, it'll all become second nature. If not, you can work in the Windows 95 Explorer or Windows 3.11 File Manager if that's more comfortable.

Changing Which Folder (Directory) Is Active

The folder structure of your hard disk resembles a tree. The main folder or root directory (signified by a backslash, \) contains your system's startup files and other folders (directories).

All *folders* (*directories*) branch from the main folder (*root directory*) and hold files or other folders. You can create folders with the names you want, such as an **\ALLWORK** folder to hold work-related files you create. The Install or Setup programs for applications create folders to hold the files for the programs. For example, the directory that holds the Windows program files is called **\WINDOWS**.

Folders (directories) can hold *subfolders* (*subdirectories*), which are also called child folders. These help group specialized files. For example, within the **\ALLWORK** folder you create, you might want to add subfolders to organize various types of work, such as **\ALLWORK\MEMOS**, **\ALLWORK\ LETTERS**, and **\ALLWORK\BUDGETS**.

Just as you need to log on to the drive with the disk holding the files you want to work with, you also need to change to the folder where your files are located before you can work with them in DOS. The following steps explain how:

1. To move up to the main folder (root directory) from the C:\WINDOWS folder, which is the current folder when you display the DOS prompt, type **cd..**, and then press **Enter**. The prompt for the main folder (root directory), C:\>, appears. (CD.. always moves up one folder level.)

2. From the main folder, you usually need to move back down to a folder where your files are located. So, at the C:\> prompt, type **cd**. Then press the **Spacebar**.

3. Type the name of the folder to change to, such as **windows**. (If you pressed **Enter** now, you would change to the C:\WINDOWS folder.)

4. *(Optional)* If you're changing to a subfolder as well, type a backslash (\) followed by the name of the subfolder. For example, you could add **\system** to your command line.

5. Press **Enter**, and DOS displays a new prompt indicating the folder (and subfolder) you've changed to. In this case, it's C:\WINDOWS\SYSTEM>.

6. Use a similar process to move from a folder to one of its subfolders. Type **cd**, press the **Spacebar**, and type the name of the subfolder (for example **cd system**). Then press **Enter**.

There are some limitations if you're moving among folder (directory) levels. Let's say you've just jumped to the DOS prompt, and the current folder is C:\WINDOWS (the prompt being C:\WINDOWS>). If you want to change to a folder on your system called C:\ALLWORK, how do you get there?

The main folder (root directory) is the top level. The folders within the root directory are sometimes called *first-level* folders; they're one level "below" the main. (Subfolders are one level "below" the folders that contain them.)

You can move up and down through the folder tree, but you can't really move "sideways" from one branch to another. To get to another branch (directory), you'd have to tell DOS to go back up a level, move over, then go down a level.

If you type **cd..** and press **Enter**, DOS moves up one level in the folder tree. (CD was an acronym for Change Directory under older DOS versions.) If you type **cd ** and press **Enter**, DOS returns you all the way to the main folder (root), even if you're starting from a subfolder two or more levels down the tree.

So, there are two ways to move between folders in different branches of the folder tree, as in the example mentioned above:

- Starting from the C:\WINDOWS> prompt, you could type **cd..** and press **Enter** to move back to the main folder. Then you could type **cd allwork** and press **Enter**. You'd change to the \ALLWORK folder, and the prompt would look like this: C:\ALLWORK>.

- Starting from the C:\WINDOWS> prompt, you could type **cd \allwork** and press **Enter**. The \ preceding **allwork** tells DOS to move back to the main folder before trying to change to the ALLWORK folder. The prompt would look like this: C:\ALLWORK>.

Starting a DOS Program from the DOS Prompt

Instead of using icons to start DOS applications, you need to know the right startup command and enter it at the DOS prompt. To start a DOS application, you log on to the drive and folder that contains the program files. Then you type the startup command and press **Enter**. The startup command for most DOS programs really is the name of a program file called an *executable file*. Executable files contain program instructions and have the .EXE, .BAT, or .COM file name extensions. You generally don't have to type the file name extension when you type the program name to start the program.

 Executable Files   These are program files and contain program instructions. Executable files have the .EXE, .BAT, or .COM file name extensions. Most application programs you launch have the .EXE file name extension.

The name for the executable file usually resembles the program's name, and so does the name of the folder that holds the program's files. Sometimes these names are abbreviations of the program's name. Table 17.1 offers a list of some common startup commands for DOS applications (most of which are much older versions than their Windows-based counterparts), along with the folder where you might find those startup commands.

Table 17.1   DOS Startup Commands for Common Programs

Program Name	Directory Name	Startup Command
America Online	\aol	aol
Quicken	\quicken	quicken or q
Lotus 1-2-3	\123	123
The Norton Utilities	\nu	norton
QuickLink Fax	\ql	qlmain
Microsoft Word 5.0	\word5	word
Microsoft Works	\msworks	works
Doom	\doom	doom
WordPerfect	\wp50	wp

 TIP   **Find the Startup File**   When you have identified the folder holding your program files and have changed to that folder, use **dir *.exe** (or ***.bat** or ***.com**) to list files that might be the startup file. Then try running the file with the name that most resembles the program name.

Here's an example of how to start a DOS program:

1. Log on to the disk drive that has the files for the program you want to run. Change to the folder that holds the files for the program (if you need to). For example, if you have Microsoft Word 5.5 for DOS in a folder called WORD5, you change to the folder holding the program by typing **cd word5** and pressing **Enter**.

2. Type the startup command for the application, and then press **Enter**. To start Word for DOS, for example, you would type **word** and press **Enter**.

3. The application appears on-screen, usually with a brand new document open.

You've just had a crash course in DOS, and have learned to display the DOS prompt, enter DOS commands, change drives and directories, and start DOS programs. The first lesson in Part 3 explains how to add and remove programs under Windows 95.

Maximizing Your Applications

Installing and Removing Windows 95 Applications

In this lesson, you learn how to install and remove a program under Windows 95, and how to add and remove a Windows 95 component.

Installing a Program in Windows 95

With the size of the hard disks in today's computer systems, you often can install a dozen programs. If you're like me, you usually buy a new program because you have an urgent need to complete a task or have some fun, so you can't wait to get your new acquisition up and running in a hurry. Under Windows 3.11, you usually had to consult confusing documentation to find out what command you had to enter to start installing the program, and whether you had to do anything special to prepare your system for the new program.

Windows 95 makes the process of installing a new program much easier. It provides easy on-screen instructions to lead you step-by-step through the installation process, telling you to insert the necessary disks (or CD-ROM), giving you a list of install commands to choose from, and starting the installation program for you. The Windows 95 Control Panel window holds the icon that you use to install new programs.

CAUTION

Dense Disks? Software companies publish setup disks in 3.5-inch HD and CD-ROM format only. However, some 3.5-inch installation disks come in a special HD (DMF) format that lends even greater capacity than the standard HD format. Although your 3.5-inch floppy drive can read the HD (DMF) disks to install the program, it can't copy the disks or format other 3.5-inch floppies with the HD (DMF) format. The setup disks' labels will specify if the disks use the HD (DMF) format.

Follow these steps to install a Windows 95 application:

1. Click the **Start** button, point to **Settings**, and click **Control Panel**. You also can double-click the **Control Panel icon** in the Windows Explorer folder tree or in the My Computer Window.

2. The Control Panel (see Figure 1.1) has icons that allow you to set up your system and enter your preferences. Double-click the **Add/Remove Programs** icon to install a program.

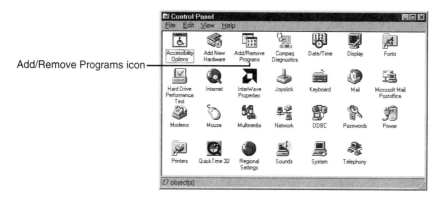

Figure 1.1 The Control Panel offers many icons for setting up your system, including the Add/Remove Programs icon.

3. The Add/Remove Programs Properties dialog box appears to enable you to begin installing a program. Click the **Install** button to begin near the top of the Install/Uninstall tab.

4. The Install Program from Floppy Disk or CD-ROM dialog box appears, telling you to insert the setup floppy disk or CD-ROM into one of the drives. Do so, and then click the **Next** button.

TIP   **Auto-Install**   If an application stored on a CD-ROM displays its own Setup screen after you insert the CD-ROM, it's often the same one you'll see after you perform the next step; so, you can just follow the program's setup prompts from there.

5. Windows 95 searches the disk for an install or setup file it can run (usually Install.exe or Setup.exe), and then displays the file's name, as shown in Figure 1.2. (If Windows 95 doesn't find the correct setup file, use the **Browse** button to navigate to it and select it.) Click the **Finish** button to start the program's own installation or setup program.

Figure 1.2 Windows 95 finds the command for starting the program installation process.

6. The initial screen of the installation or setup program appears. Most programs will lead you step-by-step through the installation. Follow the on-screen instructions.

 TIP **Choose, Please** If the installation program asks a question or allows you to make a choice, and you're not sure of the answer, just click **Yes** or **OK**. Installation programs are meant to be easy, and they usually default to the most common or safest answer.

Many Windows 95 programs offer different installation types that let you control how much hard disk space the program takes up and how many of the features are installed. You may encounter some of the following choices when you install a program, so you should be familiar with what they mean:

- **Typical.** Installs the most-used program features and consumes a moderate amount of disk space.
- **Compact (Laptop).** Installs the most essential features only, to conserve disk space.
- **Complete.** Installs all program features and consumes the most disk space.
- **Custom.** Lets you select exactly which features to install, so you can use the least or most possible amounts of disk space; recommended primarily for advanced users.
- **Run from CD-ROM.** Installs the minimum number of program files on the hard disk, and requires that you insert the program's CD-ROM before you attempt to run the program. This option is more practical with today's faster CD-ROM drives, but doesn't let you use the CD-ROM for anything else (such as listening to an audio CD) while you're running the program.

225

Uninstalling a Program in Windows 95

Just as the Add/Remove Programs Properties dialog box enables you to automatically install programs, it also gives you the power to uninstall a program or some of its components. You simply select the program from a list of installed Windows 95 programs, and then click a button. Windows runs the program's setup utility, which allows you to remove or add some or all of the program's components.

Windows 95 itself does not uninstall the programs. It simply runs the program's setup or uninstaller utility. Most Windows 95 programs will come with such a utility, but older Windows programs and DOS programs do not. To uninstall programs that do not have an uninstall utility, you'll have to use My Computer or the Windows Explorer to manually delete the program's files.

CAUTION

Auto Remove   Manually removing a program doesn't delete program files that appear in Windows system folders, and doesn't remove entries for the uninstalled program from certain Windows system files. So, to keep your Windows installation running smoothly and quickly, you should always use the Add/Remove Programs icon in Control Panel to remove a program, when possible.

Follow these steps to remove a program from Windows 95:

1. Click the **Start** button, point to **Settings**, and then click **Control Panel**. You also can double-click the **Control Panel icon** in the Windows Explorer folder tree or in the My Computer Window.

2. Double-click the **Add/Remove Programs** icon to display the Add/Remove Programs Properties dialog box.

3. At the bottom of the Add/Remove Programs Properties dialog box is a list of all the programs you can remove from your system. If you don't see the program you want to remove, you can't use this procedure to remove it. When you see the program you want to remove, click it in the list, as shown in Figure 1.3.

4. Click the **Add/Remove** button, which became active when you selected a program in the preceding step.

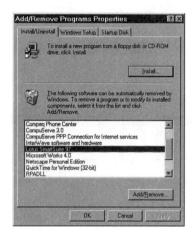

Figure 1.3 Click a program in the list to select the program for removal.

5. Windows runs the program's setup or uninstaller utility, which varies from program to program. In most cases, you can click the **Remove All** button or a button labeled **Yes** to remove all files that pertain to the program. Follow the on-screen instructions to finish removing the program.

Adding and Removing Windows 95 Components

Windows 95 also can automatically add or remove Windows 95 components on your system. When a new system comes with Windows 95, the Windows 95 installation usually includes all the components you need to take advantage of the hardware included with the system. You can remove components that you don't plan on using, or install additional components that you want to use (assuming you have sufficient disk space).

Not for Newbies If you're relatively new to using computers, I don't recommend changing your Windows 95 setup unless it's absolutely necessary. Deleting some components (such as Windows Messaging) can cause certain commands or applications to behave unexpectedly. Better safe than sorry.

CAUTION

Restart Your Engine Making a change to your Windows setup almost always requires restarting your system.

CAUTION

227

Follow these steps to update your Windows 95 installation:

1. Make sure you have your Windows 95 setup disks or CD-ROM handy. You need the setup media even when you want to remove Windows components.

2. Click the **Start** button, point to **Settings,** and click **Control Panel**. You also can double-click the **Control Panel icon** in the Windows Explorer folder tree or in the My Computer window.

3. Double-click the **Add/Remove Programs** icon.

4. Click the **Windows Setup** tab to display a list of the Windows components installed on your computer, as shown in Figure 17.4. An unselected check box means the component is not installed. A gray box indicates some parts of the component are installed. A normal check in a check box means all parts of the component are installed.

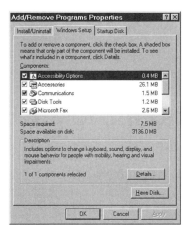

Figure 1.4 Select (check) a check box to install a new component; deselect (clear the check) a check box to remove a component.

5. To install all elements of a component, click its check box until the check box appears white with a check mark in it. To remove all parts of a component, click to remove the check mark.

6. To install selected elements of a component, click the component, and then click the **Details** button. You see all the parts that make up the selected component. Click a check box to add or remove a check mark. (If you click a component part and the Details button becomes active again, you

can click it to see even more choices that you can select.) Then, click the **OK** button.

7. Repeat steps 4-6 for each component on the list.

8. Click the **OK** button. Windows will prompt you to insert the first setup disk or setup CD-ROM if you haven't already done so. Insert the disk or CD, then follow the on-screen prompts to finish the process.

9. Windows 95 will usually prompt you to restart your system. Click **Yes**. When your system restarts, your changes will take effect.

This lesson showed you how to add and remove programs under Windows 95, and how to update your Windows 95 setup. The next lesson shows you how to start, exit, and switch between Windows 95 programs.

Starting, Exiting, and Switching Between Applications

This lesson shows you how to start and exit Windows 95 applications, and how to switch between running applications.

Start Programs with the Start Button

Windows 95 neatly tucks away most programs in the Start menu. (You may have to start programs written for DOS and Windows 3.1 at the DOS prompt or from Windows Explorer.) To start any program, you click the **Start** button and then weave your way through a series of menus and submenus with your mouse. When you see the program you want, you draw a bead on it and fire (click). The program starts, and you're ready to work.

How do programs get their names listed on the Start menu? Well, if you installed Windows 95 over your old version of Windows, or if your computer came with Windows 95 installed, the installation program added the program names automatically. The programs that are built into Windows 95 are also listed on one of the Start menu's submenus already. In addition, whenever you install a new program (see the previous lesson), Windows adds the program's name to the Start menu or one of its submenus. You also can manually add a program to the Start menu, as described in Lesson 16 of Part 2.

When you start a program, it opens in its own window in Windows 95. You can control each window's size and position on-screen.

TIP **What Program?** Many of the examples shown in figures in the rest of this part will be from Windows 95 applets, the Microsoft Office 97 applications, and other common applications.

To start a program that's installed with Windows 95, use these steps:

1. Click the **Start** button in the lower-left corner of the screen. The Start menu pops up out of the taskbar, providing options for shutting down your computer, changing settings, and more.

2. To see a list of available programs, rest the mouse pointer on (point to) **Programs** at the top of the Start menu. The Programs submenu shoots out from the Start menu. The items at the bottom of the list are programs you can run, as shown in Figure 2.1. At the top of the list are program groups (you can tell this because each item is followed by an arrow). If you move the mouse pointer over a program group, a submenu appears showing the names of the programs in that group.

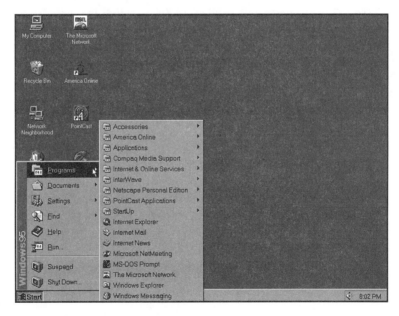

Figure 2.1 Click a program at the bottom of the Start menu to run it.

3. Rest the mouse pointer on (point to) one of the program groups at the top of the list. Each program group name is followed by an arrow, which indicates that this item opens a submenu. For example, point to **Accessories**, and the Accessories group opens, showing the names of the applets that come with Windows 95 (and from the PC manufacturer).

4. To run a program, click it. The program opens in its own window.

Starting a Program with a Desktop Shortcut Icon

In Lesson 2 of Part 2, you saw that the Windows 95 desktop includes icons called *shortcuts*. Shortcut icons point to specific programs and documents. Each shortcut icon has a small arrow in its lower-left corner. A shortcut isn't an actual program startup file or document file. Rather, it's a link to another file that lets you launch or open the file. So even though you have a single copy of the actual program startup file or document file on your hard disk, you can create multiple shortcuts to it. As a result, you can start a program from the desktop or any other folder that contains a shortcut to it.

For your purposes, all you need to know is that you can double-click any program's shortcut icon on the desktop to start the program the shortcut points to. You also can double-click any other icon on the desktop to access a Windows 95 feature, folder, or file that the icon represents.

Running a Program the Hard Way

To run a program that isn't on the Programs menu or a submenu, or doesn't have a shortcut icon on the desktop, click the **Start** button and click **Run**. Type the command required to start the program in the **Open** text box. If any folder or subfolder or the startup file name contains a space, you need to enclose the path in quotation marks, as shown in Figure 2.2, and then click **OK**. If you don't know the command required to start the program, click the **Browse** button in the Run dialog box and use the Browse dialog box to find the startup command.

Figure 2.2 Use File, Run and then enter a program's startup command if it isn't on the Start menu or lacks a desktop shortcut.

Exiting a Windows Program

Exiting a program closes any open files in the program and removes them from RAM (Random Access Memory). Then the program itself closes (is removed from RAM), and its application window is minimized back to an icon in the program group where it resides.

Before you exit from any program, you should save your work. This prevents data loss and gets you out of there faster. If you haven't saved your work, the program will prompt you to do so. Click **Yes** to save if you've saved an open file before. If you haven't saved the open file, the Save As dialog box will appear. Name the file and specify a location for it.

When you've saved your work, you have several ways to exit a file:

- Click the application window's **Close** button, or double-click the application window's **Control-menu box**.
- Click the **File** menu to open it, and then click the program's **Exit** command.
- If the program is minimized to a button on the taskbar, right-click the button to display its shortcut menu, and then click the **Close** command.
- If the application you want to exit from seems to be stalled or hung up, press **Ctrl+Alt+Delete** to display the Close Program dialog box. Click the name of the application you want to exit, and then click the **End Task** button.

Switching Between Running Programs

Do you like to watch television while you work out? Talk on a cellular phone while driving? Do two or more things at once at all possible times? If you like to juggle a lot of tasks—and if you have a powerful enough computer system with enough RAM—Windows 95 can run more than one program at once. To take advantage of that capability, you can start as many programs as your computer's RAM can hold and then switch between them to perform various operations.

As you run programs and open documents, however, the Windows desktop can become so cluttered that you might never find what you need. You can use the Windows 95 *taskbar* to dig your way out of the deepest stack of program windows.

Whenever you start a program in Windows 95, a button with the program's name is added to the taskbar at the bottom of the screen. Whenever you want to

233

return to a program, click the program's button in the taskbar, and the program immediately jumps to the front of the stack.

Follow these steps to switch between running programs:

1. Run the programs you want to use, such as Office 97 applications, My Computer, and more. When you run a program, its name is added to the taskbar.

2. To switch to a program, click its name in the taskbar, as shown in Figure 2.3. Whether the program window was minimized or behind a stack of other windows, it is moved to the front of the stack and activated.

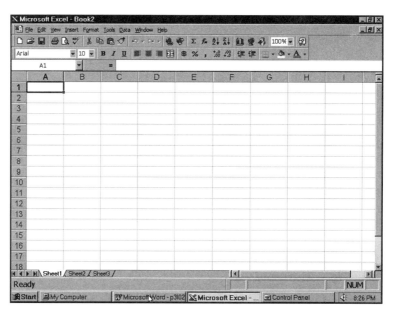

Figure 2.3 Click a program's icon on the taskbar to switch to that program.

 TIP **Quick Keys** To use the keyboard to switch to another program, press and hold the **Alt** key, and then press **Tab** without releasing the **Alt** key. A small window displays an icon for each running application. While still holding down the **Alt** key, press **Tab** repeatedly until the square outline surrounds the icon for the program you want. When that program is selected, release both keys.

This lesson shared some vital Windows 95 skills: how to start and exit Windows programs, and how to switch between running programs. The next lesson will show you how to get help in an application.

Working with Help in an Application

This lesson shows you how to work with help that's specific to an application, building on the general information you learned in Part 2, Lesson 6. See how to use tutorials, get context-sensitive help, help if you've used other applications, Internet help, and information about the program.

Using the Contents and Index

Like Windows 95 itself, Windows 95 applications offer online help. In fact, online help is fast replacing printed manuals that come with software. A couple of factors have been driving this change. First, the fact that programs can be distributed on CD-ROM means there's room to include beefy help files. And, today's faster PCs with bigger hard disks make online help a viable alternative to paper documentation; that is, it's usually faster these days to use online help than it is to find a manual and look up a topic.

In Lesson 6 of Part 2, you learned how to use Windows 95 online help, specifically how to use help Contents, the Help Index, and the Find feature. As Figure 3.1 shows, most Windows 95 applications also offer a Help Index, Contents, and Find feature. To display the Help Topics dialog box in most applications, open the **Help** menu and click the **Contents**, **Contents and Index**, **Help Topics**, or a similar command.

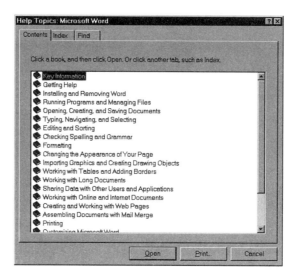

Figure 3.1 Most programs offer the same type of Help as Windows 95 itself.

Walking Through a Tutorial

Many programs, especially programs that are geared for novice users, now offer an on-screen tutorial to introduce you to key program features. Some of these tutorials feature animation, while others may actually walk you through, or demonstrate, how to perform basic operations. Others simply provide a screen-by-screen overview of what you can do with the program, like the tutorial from Microsoft Works 4.0 shown in Figure 3.2.

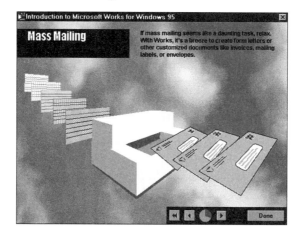

Figure 3.2 Some programs offer a tutorial to introduce you to program features.

To view an online tutorial, look for the command Introduction to [Program] or View Tutorial (or another similar command) on the Help menu.

Getting Context-Sensitive Help

You often don't need help until you encounter a situation where you don't know how to proceed. Rather than reversing the steps you took before you ran into a roadblock, you can get *context-sensitive help* to learn how to proceed. In most Windows 95 applications, you can press F1—or press Shift+F1 and click the button, selection, or area of the screen that you want help with—to display a help window providing information about the operation at hand.

 TERM   **Context-sensitive**   Fast help that pertains to the selection, command, or dialog box you're currently working with.

Quite a few manufacturers offer the Microsoft Office 97 Small Business Edition (SBE) preinstalled on new systems. If your system comes with SBE, you'll soon find another type of help in the Office applications—the *Office Assistant*. The Office Assistant is an animated character that appears in a small window on-screen. As you work, it may offer hints, or ask if you need help with a particular feature. You also can ask the Office Assistant a question, in your own words, at any time. Here's how:

1. If the Office Assistant isn't currently on-screen, click the **Office Assistant** button at the far right end of the Standard toolbar, which is usually the default, top toolbar in an Office application. You also can press **F1** or choose **Help, Microsoft [Program] Help**. If the Assistant is on-screen, just click within the Assistant window.

2. In the yellow thought balloon that appears above the Assistant, simply type your question in the **What Would You Like To Do?** text box, then click **Search**.

3. The Assistant displays a list of topics that possibly answer your question. Click the button or icon to the left of the topic that's the best match to display a Help window for that topic. For example, the Assistant listed five topics in response to the example questions shown later in Figure 3.3. I could then click the button for the topic that best matches my question: the "Save a document" topic.

When you've finished working in the Help window, click its **Close** button. You can click the Close button on the Office Assistant window to put the Office Assistant away when you don't need it.

Finding Help to Move from Other Applications

As you'll find when you're shopping for software to use, most software publishers offer reduced prices when you're switching from a competitor's program. For example, you may be switching from Lotus 1-2-3 to Microsoft Excel. Making such a transition can be tough, because you may have to learn a whole new shorthand for entering information, new functions, and new commands.

To ease such a transition, publishers often provide help specially geared to help you make the transition. For example, in Excel, you can choose **Help**, **Lotus 1-2-3 Help** to display a highly specialized dialog box. In that dialog box, you can choose a 1-2-3 command, and then have Excel either display a list of steps or demonstrate how to use the command. If you're considering buying new software, ask the salesperson whether this type of help is available.

Jumping onto the Internet for Help

In Part 4 of this book, you'll learn to set up your system to connect to the Internet. More and more, software publishers assume that users have an Internet connection. So, to supplement the online help that comes with the program, the big publishers (Microsoft and Lotus in particular) offer commands that let you jump directly from a program to Web sites offering program information and help. Here's an example from Excel 97:

1. Click the **Help** menu, and point to **Microsoft on the Web** to display a submenu of different subjects.

2. Click the subject you want to view more information about, such as **Product News**, **Frequently Asked Questions**, or **Online Support**.

3. Excel 97 launches your Internet connection and Web browser, then displays the selected page. For example, Figure 3.3 shows the Frequently Asked Questions page for Excel. Use the Web page's links and search features as needed (see Part 4 for more about working with a Web browser) to get the help you want.

Figure 3.3 You can use the Help menu to jump to a Web page for even more help.

4. Close the Web browser (click its **Close** button) and shut down your Web connection (usually you click **Yes** when prompted or **Disconnect**) when you've finished.

Learning More About Your Application

One last Help menu choice bears mention, because it can provide useful information: the About choice. When you choose **Help**, **About [Program]**, your Windows 95 program displays a window like the one in Figure 3.4. At a minimum, an About dialog box displays the program's version number (Excel 97 in Figure 3.4). You'll need this information if you ever call technical support for help.

Like the example in Figure 3.4, an About dialog box also may display system information or include a button you can click to get system information. The information you get can be as basic as your CPU, total RAM, and the amount of RAM that's currently free. Or, if you clicked the **System Info** button in Figure 3.4, you'd get a screen where you can find more detailed system information, such as available hard disk space, which programs are running, and more. Again, this system information becomes handy if you call tech support.

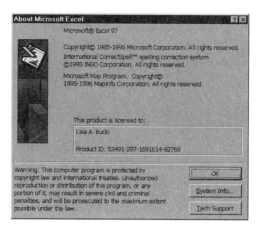

Figure 3.4   Use Help, About [Program] to verify your program version.

An About dialog box may enable you to learn *how* to call tech support. Clicking the **Tech Support** button in Figure 3.4 displays the online help screen listing tech support options.

This lesson showed you how to use help tutorials, get context-sensitive help, help if you've used other applications, Internet help, and information about the program. The next lesson shows you how to create, name, and save documents.

Creating, Naming, and Saving Documents

This lesson shows you how to handle your files in applications—creating, opening, naming, and saving them.

Starting a New File in a Windows Program

When you start a Windows 95 application, usually it will open a blank new document on the screen. You can work with that document, or you can open a different file and work with that one instead. Chances are, however, that you will create more than one new document per work session. You might write a letter, create a report, and then put together a to-do list. Every time you want to start another document, you'll need to open a new file in the program.

 TIP **Document** A *document* is a file you create in any Windows program. Documents can be (for example) spreadsheet, plain text, word processing, graphics, or database files.

In most programs, starting a new file takes no more than a simple menu command or the clicking of a button. You issue the command, and a new document window appears on-screen. In *integrated software* programs that combine several applications—for example, Microsoft Works for Windows—you also have to tell the program what *kind* of file to open.

CAUTION

Single File   Some programs can have only one document open at a time. When you start a new document in the Windows 95 WordPad accessory program, for example, it closes any document that's already open. Make sure you save your work in the open document as described later in this lesson before you start a new file.

Follow these steps to open a new document (file) in an application:

1. Open the **File** menu and click the **New** command. If your program offers a toolbar, it may have a New button or icon you can click to start a new file.

2. If the program asks you to choose a template (as shown in Figure 4.1), specify a file type. If it asks for some other information, make your selections. The new (blank) document window appears on-screen.

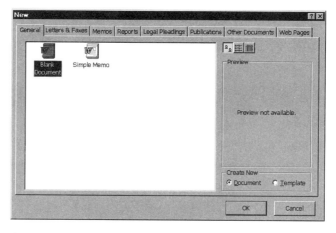

Figure 4.1   Some programs ask you to specify what kind of file to create.

Jump-Starting a File

Many programs offer automated features that help you develop new files. These helpers display dialog boxes that ask you for information and give you choices for putting a document together. In a presentation graphics (slideshow) program, for example, you could choose a look for your slide show, screen colors, and a topic. The program would then set the whole thing up and suggest an outline for you.

In Microsoft products, these automated helpers are called *wizards*. In Corel WordPerfect products, they're called *Experts*. Lotus products offer some automated help called *SmartAssistants*. Look for the command to start one of these helpers on the File menu in your application; alternatively, some applications offer the startup command in a New File dialog box. Then you follow the on-screen prompts to set up your document.

Opening a File in a Windows Program

To work on a file you previously saved to disk (which you'll learn to do in the next task), first you need to open it. This procedure loads the file from the disk where it's stored into your computer's RAM (random-access memory). With the file in RAM, you can print it, add to it, change or delete the information in it, or update it in any way you see fit.

To open a particular file, you have to know which disk and folder it's stored on and what the file's name is.

Often you may have to take a file you've created in one program and open it in a different program. Many Windows applications enable you to open files that were created in various formats. In Microsoft Works for Windows 95 (for example), you can open files from several different word processors: Microsoft Word for Windows and DOS, WordPerfect for DOS and Windows, Windows Write, and even Works files for the Macintosh.

This *file exchange* capability makes it easy for many users to share work. The quality of the file exchange varies, however, depending on how sophisticated the program is. Some exchanges let you open only the file's basic data. Other programs preserve graphics and formatting when you open a file from another application.

If the Open dialog box in your application has a Files of Type or similar option, that means you can open files in other formats. If your program doesn't have this option in the Open dialog box, look for an Import command on the File menu; it will do the same thing.

The following steps describe how you would open a file in Microsoft Word 97:

1. If the file you want to open is on a floppy disk, insert the floppy disk in the appropriate floppy disk drive.

2. Open the **File** menu and click the **Open** command. (In some programs, the command might be different—such as **Open Existing File**). If your program offers a toolbar, it may have an Open icon you can click to start a new file.

3. *(Optional)* If the file you want to open was created in another application (say, you want to open a Works word processor document in Word), click the **Files of Type** drop-down arrow to display its choices. Use the scroll bar to display the type of file you want to open, and then click that file type.

4. In the Open dialog box, click the **Look In** drop-down arrow to display the list, and then click the icon to select the disk drive holding the file you want to open. See Part 2, Lesson 5, "Using Dialog Boxes," for more about working with the Look In list and other features of a file-oriented dialog box.

5. In the list of folders and files that appears, scroll (if necessary) to display the folder that holds the file you want to open. Double-click the folder icon to select it.

6. Click the icon beside the name of the file you want to open in the list of files below the Look In list (see Figure 4.2). Then click the **Open** or **OK** button. (To open a file quickly, simply double-click it.) The file opens on-screen so you can work with it.

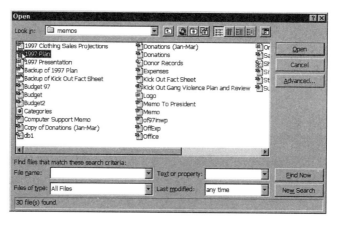

Figure 4.2 Click a file to select it so you can open it.

 TIP **Frequently Used Files** Some programs list files you've worked with recently at the bottom of the File menu. If you know you've worked with a file recently, simply open the **File** menu and click the name of the file you want to open.

TIP   **From the Desktop**   You can create an icon for a new, blank document on the desktop or in a Windows Explorer folder or My Computer window for a particular folder. Simply right-click, point to **New** in the shortcut menu, then click a program name in the submenu to define the type of document to create. Type a name for the document, and press **Enter** to finish creating the icon. Then, you can double-click the icon to launch the application and open the new document.

Note that in most Windows applications, any dialog box that lets you work with files (Open, Save, and Browse dialog boxes, for example) offers you shortcuts for working with the files. Simply right-click a file in the file list to display commands you can quickly perform on the file, as shown in Figure 4.3. Click the command you want.

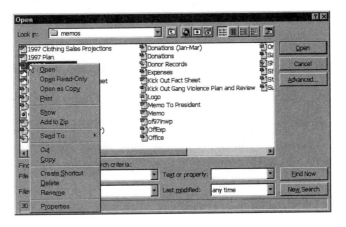

Figure 4.3   Right-click a file in a dialog box to display commands for working with the file.

Saving Your Work in a Windows Program

Saving your document in a file stores it magnetically on disk. The first time you save a file, you must give it a name and tell the computer what disk and folder to store it in. The program automatically adds a period and the extension appropriate for that program to the end of the file name. You won't have to specify the file's name again to save it; subsequent saves update the file that's already on the disk.

TIP **Sensible Saving** As a rule, you should try to save your work every five to ten minutes to protect against data loss. Some applications offer automatic saving; for more on this feature, see Lesson 14 in this part.

Follow these steps to save a file in a Windows application:

1. Open the **File** menu and click the **Save** command (or simply press **Ctrl+S**). If your program offers a **Save** button on a toolbar, click it to save the file.

2. In the Save As dialog box, click the **Save In** drop-down arrow to display the list, and then click the drive icon for the disk drive where you want to save the file.

3. In the list of files and folders that appears, scroll if necessary and then double-click the folder icon for the folder where you want to save the file.

4. To save your file in another format, click the **Save As Type** drop-down arrow to display its choices. Scroll to the format you want, and then click your choice.

5. Double-click in the **File Name** text box to highlight its contents. Then type a name for the new file, as shown in Figure 4.4. (You don't have to add the file name extension.)

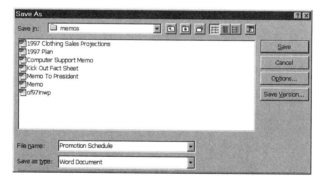

Figure 4.4 Enter a name for the file.

6. (*Optional*) If the application offers a **Create Backup Copy** option (which will create a backup file during subsequent saves), click to select that option. Then click the **Save** button.

If you continue working on the file, be sure to save it again before you close it or exit the program. To do so, open the **File** menu and click **Save** again.

Saving Your File Under a New Name

After you save a file the first time, using the Save command again simply updates the file under its existing name. If you want to create a new version of a file and still keep the original version on disk, save the file under a new name.

For example, let's say you develop a January sales report that's really effective. You want to use the same format for February, but you still need to keep the January report on disk. You can open the January file (let's say it's called January Report.xls) and save it as another file, February Report.xls. Then you could edit February Report.xls as needed.

 TIP   **Save It First**   It's important to save the file under the new name first, and then edit it. Otherwise you risk saving your new changes in the original file, where you don't want them to be.

Use these steps to save a file under a new name:

1. Click the **File** menu, and then click the **Save As** command. (Don't click the Save button in this case.)

2. If you want to save the new version of the file to a new drive and folder, specify them.

3. Double-click in the **File Name** text box to select its contents. Type a new name for the file. (You don't have to add the file name extension.) Click **Save** to finish the Save As process.

You've just learned how to perform vital file operations: creating, opening, naming, and saving. The next lesson shows you how to work with the document windows you've opened.

Working with Open Document Windows

5

You learned about window basics in Lesson 3 of Part 2. Here, you learn window techniques that apply in applications, such as selecting document windows, sizing and arranging windows, dividing and hiding windows, and closing windows.

Moving Between Windows in the Same Application

As you learned in the previous lesson, each time you open or start a new file in most Windows 95 applications, the application places that file in its own window. This may not be obvious, at first, because each opened window is usually maximized, covering the already-open files. Moving to a new window means you select a window to make it the *active* or *current window*. The title bar of the active window always appears in a color different from those of other open windows.

Active (Current) Window   The window currently in use, which contains the insertion point and indicates it's ready to accept your entries. You can tell which window is active because its title bar is highlighted.

If it's visible, click the window you want to select. When you select a new window, the one you choose typically jumps in front of all other open windows. The title bar becomes highlighted, and you can work in the window. To move to the next window using the keyboard, press **Ctrl+F6**; to move to the previous window, press **Ctrl+Shift+F6**.

You also can use the Window menu to move between windows in the same application. The names of open document windows typically appear at the bottom of this menu. Click the **Window** menu, and then click the name of the window you want to select, as shown in Figure 5.1.

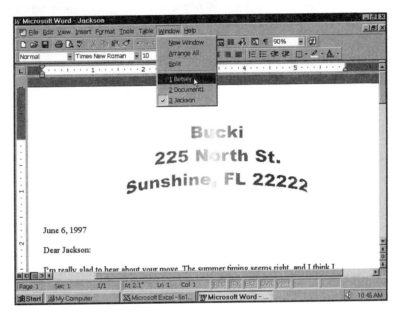

Figure 5.1   You can use the Window menu to choose which open file to work in.

Sizing and Arranging Windows

You can arrange and size multiple document windows within a program so you can see them all on-screen. This is useful when you want to copy or move information from window to window (see Lesson 7 in this part for more information).

The Window menu in most applications offers shortcut options for arranging all the windows you've opened on-screen. *Tiling* reduces the size of all the open windows and arranges them so you can see all of them at once. *Cascading* gives all the open windows an identical size, and then stacks them on-screen like overlapping cards.

Applications differ in how they enable you to tile, cascade, and otherwise arrange windows. Here are some of the methods you may encounter:

249

- The Window menu may offer Tile and Cascade commands to enable you to tile and cascade open document windows within the application window, respectively.

- The Window menu may offer only an Arrange command. Clicking that command displays a dialog box with options for arranging the open document windows. In Figure 5.2, I've right-clicked an arrangement option and have used the What's This? choice to display help about the available arrangements.

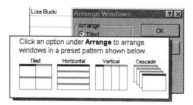

Figure 5.2 The Window, Arrange command in an application leads to several arrangement options.

- Some applications, such as Word 97, offer the Arrange All command in lieu of other formatting arrangements. Choosing **Help**, **Arrange All** places the files in a horizontal arrangement, as in Figure 5.3.

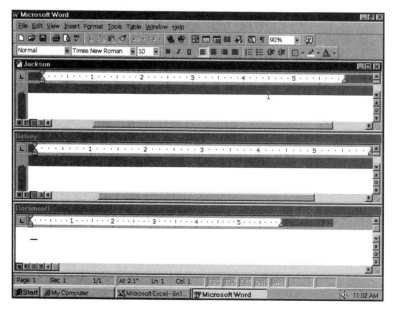

Figure 5.3 The Arrange All command in Word 97 results in this arrangement.

Controlling Windows

You can make a window that's not maximized any size you want or move it anywhere on-screen by dragging with the mouse.

The Maximize button near the right end of the title bar shows a picture of a big window. Clicking it maximizes the window, increasing the document window to the largest size available within the program window. When you maximize a window, the Maximize button changes to a Restore button, which looks like two overlapping windows. Clicking the Restore button returns the window to the size it was before you maximized it, which is called restoring the window.

 TIP **Seeing More** After you've tiled, cascaded, or otherwise arranged windows, you may want to click a window's **Maximize** button to return the desired window to full size and make it easier to work with.

The Minimize button looks like a pancake—or the window as it would be if flattened. Minimizing a document window within a program flattens the document to a narrow slice of the title bar that contains the Control-menu box, the file's name, and Restore, Maximize, and Close buttons, as shown in Figure 5.4.

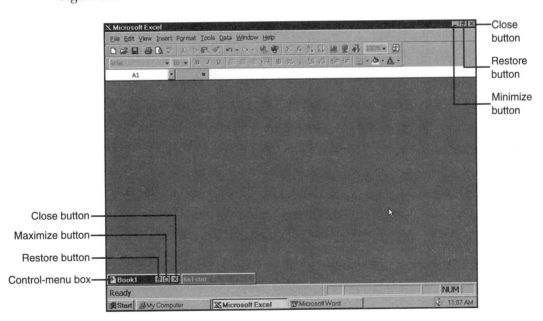

Figure 5.4 You can minimize windows within an application, as shown here for Excel.

The *Control-menu box* takes on various forms depending on the program you're running. You can click this button to display a menu for sizing, moving, and closing the window.

When the current window is not maximized, you can drag the window's title bar to move the window, or you can drag the window's border to resize the window. The lower-right corner of each window that's not maximized has a *resize area* which you can drag to quickly change the size and dimensions of the window. The window *border* is the boundary of the window; you can drag the border to resize the window in most cases.

Viewing Different Parts of a File at the Same Time

There may be times when you want to see different parts of a file simultaneously, especially if you're working with a lengthy document file or a large spreadsheet. Because many spreadsheet programs let you have multiple tabs or "pages" within each file, you may need a way to view multiple pages at the same time to check facts and results.

To deal with issues like these, many Windows applications enable you to open a second window for an open document file or split a window into panes. When you do so, each window or *pane* scrolls independently so you can indeed display different areas of the file in each window. There are generally two methods for displaying a second window of the current file:

 TIP **Pane** A portion of a document window. Heavy gray split bars usually divide panes.

- Choose **Window, New Window**. The application opens a second window for the file, usually maximized. You can use the **Window** menu to switch between the open windows for the file. When you no longer need both file windows, close one of them as described later in this lesson.
- Choose **Window, Split**. In some applications, you may then need to drag the mouse and click to position the split bar. Scroll bars appear for the panes so you can scroll each one to the view you want. To remove the panes, choose **Window, Remove Split**.

Hiding Windows

Although offered less often than some other window features, hiding a window can be useful. Spreadsheet programs offer this feature the most, primarily to enable you to hide sensitive data to prevent unwanted editing. To hide the current window, choose **Window, Hide**. To redisplay the window, choose **Window, Unhide**.

 TIP **Hiding a Window** When a window is hidden, it is still open. Its contents simply do not appear on-screen. Nor can you make the hidden window the active window.

Closing Your Document Window

When you save a file and otherwise work with a file, it remains open on-screen in its window. If you're working on several files at once and want to "clean up" your work area by putting away some of those files, simply close the current file once you've saved your work. Use one of these three methods to close a file:

- Open the **File** menu and click **Close**. If you've made changes to the file that haven't been saved, a dialog box will tell you so. Click **Yes** to save the changes and close the file.

- Click the **Close** button of the window holding the document you want to close. If you've made changes to the file and haven't saved them, a dialog box tells you so. Click **Yes** to save the changes and close the file.

- Open the Control-menu for the file and click **Close**, or press **Ctrl+W**.

You've now learned about selecting document windows, sizing and arranging windows, dividing and hiding windows, and closing windows. The next lesson helps you begin entering information in an application document.

Typing, Selecting, and Editing Information

This lesson teaches you how to enter, select, and edit information to build your document files.

Entering Text

Files hold information: text, values, formulas that perform calculations, and more. No matter what type of information you're entering or which application you're using, chances are you'll use the basic techniques described in this section for creating the data in a document.

The first step, obviously, is to create a new file. When you do so, you'll see a blinking vertical *insertion point*. This insertion point tells you the application is ready to select your entry. In spreadsheets or other applications that display a grid of cells or other fields (boxes) for holding information, you may not see an insertion point; instead, the cell will be surrounded by a heavy cell selector, telling you that the cell is ready to receive your entry.

TERM   **Insertion Point or Cell Selector**   A blinking vertical insertion point or heavy cell selector shows you where an entry will appear when you begin typing.

Once you see the insertion point or cell selector, you can simply type your information. Each character you type appears to the left of the insertion point, and the insertion point travels right, much like an old typewriter carriage. Here are a few ground rules to be aware of:

- In a word processor or other text-based application, you don't need to press Enter at the end of the line. The word processor will automatically *wrap* the text to the next line for you.

- It's not necessary to type two spaces after a sentence (as it was in the old typewriter days). Computer fonts are designed to read well with only one space after each sentence.

- Press **Enter** to finish a paragraph and start a new paragraph.

- If you're entering a formula (an expression that performs a calculation in a spreadsheet), you'll need to precede the entry with a special symbol like +, =, or @. Consult the spreadsheet program's online help to learn how to enter formulas.

- In applications that have cells or fields, you usually press **Tab** or the **right arrow** key to finish one entry and move on to the next cell or field.

- In some applications, like database programs, the fields (boxes) where you enter information may limit the lengths of some entries. If you're typing and hear repeated beeping, you've probably exceeded the allowable entry length.

- To use the numeric keypad at the right end of your keyboard to enter information, make sure the keyboard's Num Lock indicator is lighted. If it isn't, press the **Num Lock** key to activate it.

Moving Around Text-Based Screens

To edit and select information in text-based screens in applications like word processors, you need to know how to move the insertion point around in the document, between words and sentences. The simplest way to position the insertion point is to scroll to display the area where you want to position the insertion point, and then click with the mouse. Table 6.1 provides keyboard shortcuts you can use to move the insertion point.

Table 6.1 Keyboard Shortcuts for Moving in a Text-Based Program

Key	Moves the Insertion Point...
← → ↑ ↓	One character or line in the direction of the arrow.
Home	To the beginning of the current line.
End	To the end of the current line.
Pg Up	Up one screenful of information.
Pg Dn	Down one screenful of information.

Key	Moves the Insertion Point...
Ctrl+Home	To the start of the text in the document.
Ctrl+End	To the end of the text in the document.
Ctrl+← or →	One word left or right.
Ctrl+↑ or ↓	One paragraph up or down.

CAUTION

Scrolling Warning   In any application, you can use the scroll bars to view different portions of the document. But, doing so doesn't move the insertion point or cell selector.

Moving Around Grid- or Field-Based Screens

As noted previously, you press Tab or the right arrow key to finish the entry in a spreadsheet cell or on-screen field. To reselect a cell or field, you can click it with the mouse. The keyboard shortcuts in Table 6.2 also let you quickly select a particular spreadsheet cell; some of these shortcuts even work in field-based screens, such as some screens in database programs.

Table 6.2   Keyboard Shortcuts for Moving in a Grid- or Field-Based Program

Key	Selects...
← → ↑ ↓	The next cell in the direction of the arrow.
Home	The first cell of the current line (row).
End	The last cell of the current line (row).
Pg Up	A cell that's up one screenful of information, or the previous form (group of boxes or fields) in a file.
Pg Dn	A cell that's down one screenful of information, or the next form (group of boxes or fields) in a file.
Ctrl+Home	The first cell in the current spreadsheet or the first form.
Ctrl+End	The last spreadsheet cell that holds data or the last form.
Ctrl+← or →	The left or right cell entry in the current line of entries.
Ctrl+↑ or ↓	The top or bottom cell entry in the current column of entries.

TIP   **Getting It Right**   For more specific instructions on navigating your application, consult its online help.

Selecting Information

Before you can work with information in a document in any way—such as deleting it, moving it, or applying special formatting—you have to select the information. When information is selected (or highlighted), commands you choose apply to the entire selection.

To select information in a word processor document or spreadsheet, simply hold down the left mouse button while moving the mouse (drag) over the text or group of cells to highlight. Alternately, you can click to position the insertion point or cell selector at the beginning of the area to select, press and hold the Shift key, and click the end of the information to select. Figure 6.1 shows some information selected in a word processor.

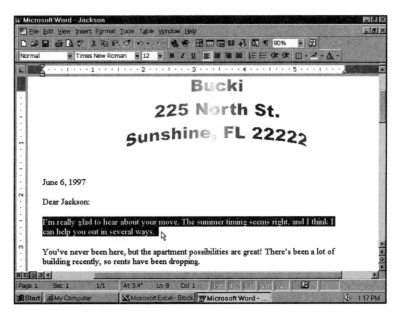

Figure 6.1   You can drag with the mouse to select text.

In a text-based program like a word processor, you can usually double-click a word to select it, or triple-click to select the whole paragraph. Pressing Shift plus an arrow key extends the selection highlight by one character or row in the direction of the arrow. In fact, using Shift in combination with any movement key (Page Up, Page Down, Home, End, and more), extends the selection from the starting point to the destination specified by the movement key. For example, pressing Shift+Page Down selects the text from the starting position of the insertion point to the destination specified by Page Down. Pressing Ctrl+Shift+Arrow extends the selection one word (← and →) or paragraph (↑ and ↓) in the direction of the arrow.

In a spreadsheet program, you can usually click a column letter or row number to select the whole row or column, as in Figure 6.2. Pressing Shift plus an arrow key extends the selection highlight by one column or row in the direction of the arrow. Pressing Ctrl+Shift+Arrow extends the selection the last column (← and →) or row (↑ and ↓) in the direction of the arrow that contains an entry.

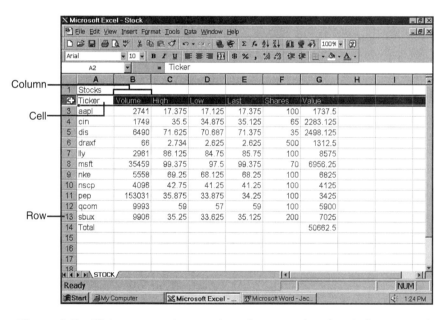

Figure 6.2 Click a row number or column letter to select the whole row or column.

TIP **Whole Highlighting** Most applications give you some way to select all the document's contents at once. Look for a command like **Edit**, **Select All** or a shortcut key like Ctrl+A or Ctrl+Numpad 5. ("Numpad 5" is the 5 key on the numeric keypad.)

TIP   **Short and Sweet**   Once you've selected some information in a word processor or spreadsheet, try right-clicking the selection. Many applications will display a menu of commands you can perform on the selection.

Making Basic Edits

Applications offer similar techniques for working with data to make it easier for you to reuse your skills. The techniques you learn in one application often apply in other applications, so you can focus on your information—not your computer skills.

So it is with editing. Here are basic keystrokes that enable you to remove information:

- **Backspace.** Deletes the character to the left of the insertion point or the whole selection.
- **Ctrl+Backspace.** Deletes the word to the left of the insertion point.
- **Delete.** Deletes the character to the right of the insertion point, or the whole selection.
- **Ctrl+Delete.** Deletes the word to the right of the insertion point.

In contrast, to insert information, begin typing at the insertion point.

TIP   **Insert versus Overtype**   Some applications offer an *insert mode*, where new information you type appears at the insertion point and pushes information to the right of the insertion point further right. In *overtype mode*, new characters you type replace characters to the right of the insertion point. Use the keyboard's Insert key to switch between insert and overtype mode. Usually, the application status bar will feature an indicator to remind you of whether the application is in insert or overtype mode.

To edit information in a spreadsheet cell, you often have to do more than select the cell. You need to activate the cell, or display the insertion point within it. To do so, you generally double-click the cell, press a special key like F2, or click in a special area called the formula bar near the top of the screen. Similarly, when you press Tab to move to a field in a form-based screen, the application highlights the whole field entry, as you can see in the Shares field of the form in Figure 6.3. When a field is completely highlighted and you start to type, your typing replaces the whole entry. To edit only part of the entry, such as transposed letters, click to position the insertion point, then make your change.

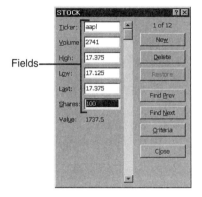

Fields—

Figure 6.3 When a whole field is selected, you can click to position the insertion point within it.

Using Undo

Edits that you make are semi-permanent in most applications. That is, you can undo your changes if you're not satisfied with them. Some applications only let you undo the action you just took, meaning you need to use the undo feature immediately before performing any further action. Other applications let you undo a dozen or more of your previous actions.

To undo the preceding action, choose **Edit**, **Undo** or press **Ctrl+Z** in most applications. You also can click an Undo button if one is offered on a toolbar. To undo one of several previous actions, you usually have to choose a drop-down list arrow on the toolbar, click the Undo button multiple times, or choose a special command that's specific to your application.

CAUTION

Can't Be Undone? Undo isn't effective for all commands in every application. So, make sure you're confident you can undo a change if needed before you make that change.

You should know enough basic editing skills—moving around, making selections, making changes, and undoing them—to survive in most applications. The next lesson explores how to move and copy information.

Moving and Copying Information

In this lesson, you learn how to copy and move information within and between documents in an application.

Revisiting Drag and Drop

Lesson 12 in Part 2 showed you how to use a feature called *drag and drop* to move or copy files or folders between the Windows Explorer and My Computer windows. Most Windows 95 applications now enable you to use drag and drop to move a selection to a new location in a document. That is, you select the *source*, "drag" it to the *destination* location, and "drop" it into place there. You'll learn the details of using this technique in the rest of this Lesson, as well as other methods for copying and moving information.

Copying Information Within a Document

Copying a selection in a file creates an exact copy of the selection's contents, and places it in the destination location you specify, leaving the original intact. Copying is one of the computer's great convenience features. Not only does it save you work, but it enables you to reduce typographical errors by reusing information you've already double-checked.

Copy versus Move When you *copy* a selection, the original data remains in its original location, and a copy of the data is placed in a second location. When you *move* the information, it no longer exists in its original location, but only in the new location.

Copying with Drag and Drop

When you use drag and drop to copy information, you'll have best results if you make sure the source information and destination location are both visible on the screen at the same time. Otherwise, if you try to drag to an off-screen location, the screen may scroll too rapidly, and you might have trouble hitting your destination location. If this is the case in your file, use the method for copying with commands, instead.

CAUTION

No Field Copying   If you're working in a field-based screen such as a database form, you usually can't copy field contents via drag and drop. You can sometimes copy via menus, though.

Use this procedure to copy information within a file via drag and drop:

1. Select the information to copy.

2. Point to the selection with a mouse. If you're copying text information in a worksheet you usually can point to any part of the highlight. If you're copying a selected group of cells in a spreadsheet, you usually need to point to the border of the selection.

3. Press and hold the **Ctrl** key, and drag the selection. When you're dragging to copy in a word processor, your Windows application displays a plus, box, and an insertion point with the mouse pointer, as shown in Figure 7.1. When you're copying in a spreadsheet, a shaded outline in the size and shape of the copied selection also follows the pointer.

4. When the insertion point or selection outline with the pointer is positioned where you want it, release the mouse button.

CAUTION

Make Way in the Destination   When you copy information in a word processor, the information is usually inserted, unless you first select text that the copied information will replace. However, in a spreadsheet program and some other types of programs, the copied information replaces the information at the destination location. So, you have to be careful not to copy over information you need.

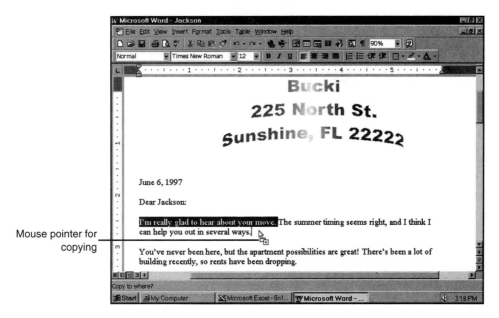

Mouse pointer for copying

Figure 7.1 A plus sign by the mouse pointer indicates you're copying the selection that you're dragging.

Copying with Commands

When the source and destination information is widely separated in a file, it may be your best bet to use commands to copy, as follows:

1. Select the information to copy.

2. Open the **Edit** menu or right-click the selection and choose **Copy** (**Ctrl+C**). Or click the **Copy** button if one is available on the application's toolbar.

3. Position the insertion point at the destination location in a text-based program. For a spreadsheet program, click to select the upper-left cell in the destination location.

4. Open the **Edit** menu or right-click the destination location and choose **Paste** (**Ctrl+V**). Or, click the **Paste** button if one is available on the application's toolbar. Windows pastes the copied selection in the location you've selected.

TIP **Where'd My Copied Graphic Go?** When you copy all or part of a graphic and try to paste it in the same file, very often the copied information will appear right over the original or in the upper-left corner of the file when you paste it. A flashing dashed outline will let you know that you can then drag the copied information to its destination location.

Moving Information Within a Document

Moving a selection removes it from its original location and places it in the new destination location you specify. As with copying information, you can move most selections by dragging them to different places with the mouse.

TIP **Spaces, Please** When you move or copy full sentences and paragraphs, you may create irregular spacing between sentences or paragraphs. So, when you select the original information, be sure to select a leading or trailing space if needed, or a blank line before or after a paragraph. If you're copying or moving to a blank word processor document, press the **Spacebar** or **Enter** key a couple of times to make your target larger.

Moving via Drag and Drop

With the mouse, follow these steps to complete a move:

1. Select the information to move.

2. Point to the selection with your mouse. If you're moving text information in a worksheet you usually can point to any part of the highlight. If you're moving a selected group of cells in a spreadsheet, you usually need to point to the border of the selection.

3. Drag the selection. When you're dragging to move in a word processor, your Windows application displays a box and an insertion point with the mouse pointer. When you're moving in a spreadsheet, a shaded outline in the size and shape of the selection follows the pointer, as in Figure 7.2.

4. When the insertion point or selection outline with the pointer is positioned where you want it, release the mouse button.

	A	B	C	D	E	F	G	H	I
1	Stocks								
2	Ticker	Volume	High	Low	Last	Shares	Value		
3	aapl	2741	17.375	17.125	17.375	100	1737.5		
4	cin	1749	35.5	34.875	35.125	65	2283.125		
5	dis	6490	71.625	70.687	71.375	35	2498.125		
6	draxf	66	2.734	2.625	2.625	500	1312.5		
7	lly	2961	86.125	84.75	85.75	100	8575		
8	msft	35459	99.375	97.5	99.375	70	6956.25		
9	nke	5558	69.25	68.125	68.25	100	6825		
10	nscp	4096	42.75	41.25	41.25	100	4125		
11	pep	153031	35.875	33.875	34.25	100	3425		
12	qcom	9993	59	57	59	100	5900		
13	sbux	9906	35.25	33.625	35.125	200	7025		
14	Total	50662.5							

Figure 7.2 When you move or copy a spreadsheet selection, you'll see an outline for the selection with the mouse pointer.

Moving with Commands

When the source and destination information is widely separated in a file, it's again more safe to use commands to move a selection, as follows:

1. Select the information to move.

2. Open the **Edit** menu or right-click the selection, and choose **Cut** (**Ctrl+X**). Or click the **Cut** button if one is available on the application's toolbar.

3. Click to position the insertion point at the destination location in a text-based program. For a spreadsheet program, click to select the upper-left cell in the destination location.

4. Open the **Edit** menu or right-click the destination location and choose **Paste** (**Ctrl+V**). Or, click the **Paste** button if one is available on the application's toolbar. Windows pastes the selection you cut into its new location.

Wrong Move or Copy? If you move or copy the wrong files or folders, you can choose **Edit**, **Undo Copy (or Move)** or click the **Undo** button on the toolbar.

CAUTION

265

TIP   **Paste Again** Once you've used Edit, Copy or Edit, Cut (or the equivalent
shortcuts), the information is placed on a storage area called the *Windows
Clipboard*. So, you can paste multiple copies of the original information, until
you cut or copy something else. Each time you cut or copy information, it
replaces any information that was previously stored on the Clipboard.

Copying and Moving Between Files

Windows 95 doesn't limit you to copying within a single file. In most applications, you can copy and move a selection between two document files in the
application.

Here's how to copy and move between files with drag and drop:

1. Open the source and destination files in the application, and arrange their
windows so that you can see both the source information in its original file
and the destination location in the second file. (For more on arranging
document windows, see Lesson 5 in this part.)

2. Select the source information to move or copy.

3. Point to the selection with a mouse. If you're copying text information in
a worksheet you usually can point to any part of the highlight. If you're
copying a selected group of cells in a spreadsheet, you usually need to
point to the border of the selection.

4. Drag the selection over the second document, pressing and holding the
Ctrl key first to copy. Figure 7.3 shows a copy operation between documents in progress.

5. When the insertion point or selection outline with the pointer is positioned
where you want it, release the mouse button.

Using commands to copy or move information between files is just as easy:

1. Open the source and destination files.

2. Select the information to move.

3. Open the **Edit** menu or right-click the selection; choose **Copy** (**Ctrl+C**) to
copy or **Cut** (**Ctrl+X**) to move. Or click the **Copy** or **Cut** button if one is
available on the application's toolbar.

4. Open the **Window** menu, and click the name of the destination file to make
it the active window (bring it to the forefront on-screen).

5. Click to position the insertion point at the destination location in a text-based program. For a spreadsheet program, click to select the upper-left cell in the destination location.

6. Open the **Edit** menu or right-click the destination location and choose **Paste (Ctrl+V)**. Or, click the **Paste** button if one is available on the application's toolbar. Windows pastes the selection into its new location.

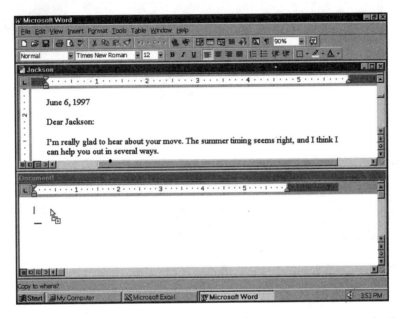

Figure 7.3 You can use drag and drop to copy (shown here) or move a selection between open document windows.

TIP **Application Go-Between** You can copy or cut information, switch to a document in another application, and then paste the information. This will enable you to transfer data in most instances, although you may encounter special circumstances when pasting graphics, or the destination application may alter the formatting of the pasted information.

In this lesson, you learned how to copy and move information using drag and drop and menu commands, toolbar buttons, or shortcut menus. In the next lesson, you'll learn how to apply attractive formatting to a selection.

Formatting a Selection

This lesson shows you how to apply attractive fonts, sizing, colors, and more to make selected information more attractive.

Taking a Quick Look Back at Documents

Prior to personal computers, typewriters offered a few different letter sizes and styles. If your typewriter's letter style didn't suit your needs, handwriting or professional typesetting were your other options for producing documents with a different type or size of lettering.

Personal computers introduced easier and more varied formatting for documents. Today's software and computers enable you to apply multiple letter sizes and styles, special elements like borders, fills and shading, and more. Even better, you can change a document's look and see the results—without ever printing it out—so you can try many different formatting combinations to find the right look for a document.

Formatting (Documents) In Lesson 14 of Part 2 you learned how to format disks. With regard to documents, formatting refers to adjusting the document appearance via changing how characters look, adjusting margins, using graphical elements, and more.

This Lesson and the next two introduce you to common formatting options offered in many programs.

Using Quick and Dirty Formatting

One of the early downsides of formatting computer documents was the "ransom note effect." Users, excited by the formatting possibilities, used so many different types of lettering and sizes that their documents looked like pieced-together ransom notes.

Some of today's applications offer an automatic way to format a selection with nice lettering, borders, and more. This useful feature helps prevent ransom note documents, and also can be useful if you question your taste in selecting formatting, don't want to learn a lot of formatting commands, or don't want to make a lot of selections.

While the command you use to apply automatic formatting varies from program to program, the overall process works like this:

1. Select the material to format.

2. Choose the command that applies automatic formatting. Look for such a command on the application's Format or Text menu. In Office 97 applications, you choose Format, AutoFormat.

3. The program will display a dialog box like the one in Figure 8.1. Click various formats in the list that's presented to see a preview of each one.

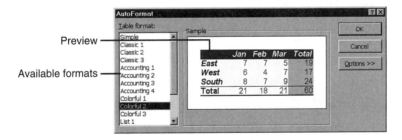

Figure 8.1 Fancy formatting can be one command away.

4. When you've selected the format you want, click **OK** to select the new format and close the dialog box. Or, click **Apply** to apply the format but leave the dialog box open so you can choose a different format, if needed.

Applying Text Formats

When you enter data into an application, it appears with default formatting set up by the application. You may want to change the formatting for a word, phrase, cell entry, title, and so on to emphasize it and make it easier to read. Here are some of the most common formatting changes you can make for a selection:

- **Font.** Without getting too technical, the font generally means the shape and design of the characters. The available font selections depend on how many fonts have been installed with Windows 95. (Many applications install extra fonts automatically, and some printers even come with fonts.) You generally can choose anything from letters with fancy curlicues or script to plain, dignified lettering like the type used in this book.

- **Size.** Size settings refer to the size of the letters. Sizing is usually measured in points, with each point equal to 1/72 inch. Sizes of 11-13 are usually good for body information, with 14 and above usually being best for headings.

- **Attributes (Font Style).** Attributes include such treatments as bold and italics. Generally, you use attributes to emphasize text (such as bolding and important word) or to follow common punctuation conventions (such as italicizing the name of a book).

- **Color.** Most programs let you apply various colors to letters, borders, and more. This is great for information you'll be showing on-screen or printing with a color printer.

Color Alert   Be careful when using colored text if you have a black and white printer. Some colors may not be readable when printed. And some printers may only print well if characters are plain black.

CAUTION

- **Special effects.** These include things like strikethrough, underlining, and subscript, used in special circumstances like emphasizing words or creating mathematical expressions. Some desktop design programs provide even fancier effects, like shadows and 3-D, that are good when used sparingly in headlines.

- **Alignment (Justification).** You can control how information lines up. In a word processor, you control how text is positioned relative to the left and right margins. In a spreadsheet, you control how information aligns within cells. In presentation and other graphics programs, you control how information aligns within a frame or boundary. Alignments usually include left, right, and center. You may see a justify choice, which spreads text between margins. Special alignments such as aligning information vertically or rotating it may also be available.

- **Number and Date.** For applications like spreadsheets and databases, you usually can format how values and dates display. For example, you can choose whether a number you've entered has one decimal zero or two, and whether a date displays as 30-Mar-98 or 3/30/98.

Usually, to format information, you select it first. Then you display a dialog box or window containing the formatting choices. To do so, you choose a command like **Format, Font; Format, Cells;** or **Text, Font & Color.** (You may find the alignment settings under a different command such as **Format, Alignment** or with the paragraph formatting settings.) Often, you can right-click a selection and click the appropriate command, as well. Make your selections from the dialog box, then click **OK** to apply them and close the dialog box.

In addition, many applications enable you to choose formatting directly from the toolbar or status bar. Figure 8.2 shows example tools from the Word 97 toolbar. Just select the text to format, then use a drop-down list to make a choice or click a button to toggle a format on and off. For example, select text and click the **Bold** button to make it bold. Click the **Bold** button again to remove the boldfacing.

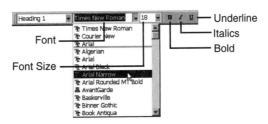

Figure 8.2 Use toolbar and status bar choices to apply font formatting.

Adjusting Paragraphs

Not all of the settings you find in a program apply strictly to the characters you enter. Other settings are intended to adjust larger chunks of text. Such settings— like tabs and indention and spacing—most often apply to paragraphs in a word processing program.

Using Tabs and Indention

Tab stops, available most often in word processors, enable you to line up information in neat rows and columns. Some programs have tabs stops set by default at every .5 inch, so that when you press Tab, the insertion point jumps to the next tab stop to the right, or up to .5 inch per stop. You can adjust tab settings in a selection to accommodate longer entries.

TIP   **Table It**   Many word processors and presentation programs, in particular, offer an even better way to create rows and columns of data. You can create a *table* (a spreadsheet-like grid of rows and columns) to align information. Look for a **Table** command or icon that you can use to create a table.

To adjust tab settings for a selection or the paragraph holding the insertion point, look with the paragraph settings (a command like Format, Paragraph) or right-click the selection and choose a command like Set Tabs on Ruler. The dialog box that appears usually will enable you to enter the measurement (in inches by default) where a new tab should be inserted. You can select the type of tab stop, too—one where text aligns to the left, right, center, or at a decimal point. You also may see other settings, like adding a *leader*, a row of repeated characters that fills any spaces without text between tab stops. A leader helps the reader's eye stay on the same line when traveling between text separated by tabs. So, if you're planning to have a lot of room between tab stops, consider a leader to make the information more readable.

Indention is extra spacing you insert to the left or right of a paragraph, for the first line or all the lines in a paragraph. You can even indent both sides of the paragraph within the margins. You'll most often see indention used to start the first line of a paragraph of text; instead of pressing Tab to create indents, though, you can use indention settings. This helps because if you ever add and delete text, stray tab stops can be annoying. You may also see an option for creating a *hanging indent,* where the first line is aligned normally and the lines below are indented. (Figure 8.3 illustrates different types of tab stops and indention.) You'll often find indention settings with other paragraph formatting commands (Format, Paragraph).

All Negative?   Entering indention settings can require a little practice, because you can enter both positive and negative measurements. Just remember that positive numbers move the text in from the margins, and **CAUTION**   negative numbers move text out toward the margins.

You also can use an application's ruler to set tabs and indents. To set a tab, you first select a tab type by clicking a selector or right-clicking to display a menu of choices. Then, you click the ruler to place the tab. To set indents, you usually drag an indention marker. Figure 8.3 shows the ruler, along with some indentions set in text.

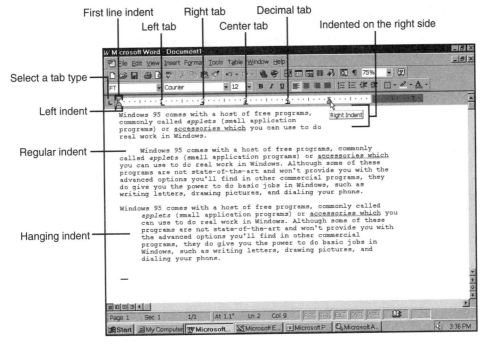

Figure 8.3 The ruler enables you to set tabs and indents.

Spacing Information

Spacing can make a big difference in how readable material is, whether printed or not. Some fonts can look really dense on-screen in a paragraph with normal, single-line spacing. If you want to print a document that others will add written comments on, double-spacing (inserting a line of space between each line) provides more room. In other instances, you can set an exact row height, at a particular point size. For example, if you're using text that's 12 pts. high, you might want to set the line spacing at 14 pts. to lend a little extra spacing between lines without using double-spacing. Again, a command like **Format**, **Paragraph** generally displays a dialog box that enables you to choose a line spacing option or enter a line spacing point size.

TIP   **Spreadsheet Rows**   In spreadsheet programs, you can adjust the height of rows to add extra space between lines. Leave the font size small, but increase the row height. You can often change row height by dragging the top row border. Or, look for a Row Height command.

Copying and Reusing Formatting

Let's say you apply several different types of formatting and you're pleased with the resulting look. You want to use the same formatting on another area, but don't want to go through all the steps. Or, you want to use the formatting in other documents. Many programs offer ways to reuse formatting you like.

Copying Formatting

Programs increasingly offer a way to copy the formatting you like to other selections within a document. For example, in the Office 97 applications, this feature is called the Format Painter. In Lotus SmartSuite 97 applications, this feature is called Fast Format. To use such a feature, you select the information that has the formatting you want, click a special toolbar button so that the mouse changes to a special "painter" pointer, then drag over the selection to which you want to apply the copied formatting. Figure 8.4 shows the Format Painter pointer in Excel 97.

Saving Formatting in Styles

Applying a number of different types of formatting to a selection can be time-consuming. Let's say you have a document that has 20 headings. If you wanted to change the font, font size, line spacing, and perhaps bolding of every heading, you'd have to perform 80 or so actions altogether! To cut down on such tedious, repetitive work, you can use styles if your program offers them. A style holds a group of formatting settings, so applying the style to selected text simulta-neously applies all those formatting settings. For example, a heading style in a word processor might offer the font, font size, line spacing and bolding you want. By simply applying the style to the 20 headings in the example document mentioned earlier, you get the formatting you want but drastically reduce the amount of work you have to do!

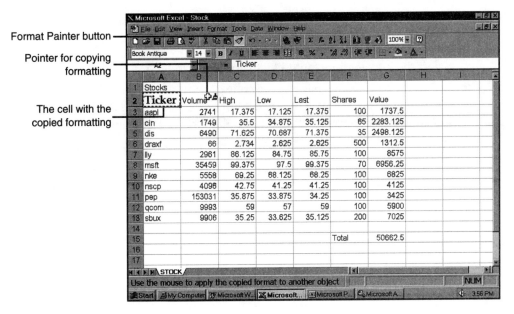

Format Painter button

Pointer for copying formatting

The cell with the copied formatting

Figure 8.4 When you copy formatting, you drag a special pointer over the selection to format.

When you want to use a particular collection of formatting settings over and over, you can save them as a style. (Some applications even enable you to use styles in other documents, by adding the style to a *template*. You'll learn about templates in the next task.) In some cases, you create styles by example. You select the text with the style formatting, then use the program's command for saving the style. In other cases, you display a dialog box, create the style settings, and then save the style. Consult your program's online help to learn how to save a style.

 TIP **Styling** The easiest way to create a style in many programs is to apply the formatting you want to some text, then select the text. Choose the **Format**, **Style** command (or the equivalent command in your program), then click **New**. Type a name for the style in the appropriate text box of the dialog box that appears, then click **OK** or **Add**. The style is usually saved in the template used by the current document, so to apply the style in another document, that document must use the template that holds the desired style.

Applying a style—whether it's one provided by the program or one that you've saved yourself—takes simple steps, as follows:

1. Select the information you'd like to apply the style to.

2. If the toolbar or status bar offers a style drop-down list for selecting styles, use it to choose the style you want. Otherwise, open the dialog box for selecting styles (**Format**, **Style** or a similar command on a menu like **Text**), then choose the style you want in the dialog box.

This lesson gave you the general steps for using automatic formatting, choosing different formatting for characters, making changes to paragraphs, and copying and saving formatting. The next lesson explains how to apply formatting that affects the whole document.

Formatting the Whole Document

This lesson provides an overview of adjusting document settings like paper size, margins, headers and footers, page breaks, and more.

Working with Paper Sizes and Margins

Although standard letter-sized (8.5 x 11) paper is what most of us use, some situations and professions require other sizes of paper—most notably legal professionals which tend to use legal-sized paper. In addition to setting up a document for a particular paper size you can adjust a document's margins and orientation. Changing paper size and margins enables you to squeeze more or less information onto a page. Changing orientation helps you accommodate the width of your information; if you have many columns of data in a database printout, for example, you need a wide page orientation.

Page Margins and Orientation   The margin is the empty border area around the information on each page. Orientation determines whether the page is taller than it is wide (portrait orientation) or wider than it is tall (land-scape orientation).

In most cases, these settings are part of the page setup (along with other settings). To access these settings, choose the **Page** or **Page Setup** command from the **File** menu or another menu; other applications use a similar command. The available page or paper sizes usually appear in a drop-down list, as shown in

Figure 9.1; these sizes are often affected by the current printer selection. To set margins, a program usually offers text boxes for you to enter top, bottom, left, and right margin settings, generally in inches. To choose the proper orientation, click the option button for it.

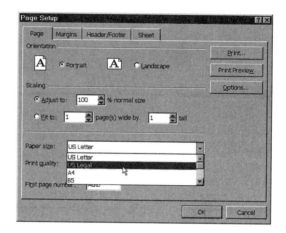

Figure 9.1 Choose a page size from a drop-down list.

CAUTION

Minimum Margins Most printers limit how small you can make margins, due to the mechanics of how the printer transfers images to the paper. The usual minimum is .25 inch. If you set margins that are smaller than the minimum, the edges of your information will be "cut off" of the printout. In some cases, you'll see a warning if you try to set margins that are too small for your printer.

Adding Headers and Footers

When you look at a long document like this book, at the top or bottom of each page you'll see the page number and usually some other information like the document name, chapter name, section name, or even the name of the person who created the document. If document information like the document name and page number appears at the top of each page, it's called a header. Footer information appears at the bottom of each page.

Looking at a Header/Footer Example

Header and footer settings and commands vary widely among applications, so consult your program's online help to learn the specifics that apply to you. For example, some applications let you set up a header or footer in a special header/footer dialog box or the Page Setup dialog box. Others use a different approach, like the next example. These steps provide an example of how to add a header or footer in Microsoft Word 97:

1. If you want the header or footer to start on a particular page of the document, click that page to place the insertion point on it. (Some applications like Word even let you specify a different header/footer for odd and even pages; in such a case, select an odd page to create an odd header/footer and an even page to create an even header/footer.)

2. Open the **View** menu and choose **Header and Footer**. The Header and Footer toolbar appears, and the document switches to a view that shows you how the printed document will look.

3. Use the **Switch Between Header and Footer** toolbar button to choose whether you want to enter header or footer information. Clicking the button toggles between the header and footer.

4. The insertion point appears in the header or footer area by default. Type any title or information you want. You can use the tab key and set tabs if you wish. To place a page number at the location of the insertion point, click the **Insert Page Number** button. You can use the **Insert Date** button to insert the current date in the header/footer, or the **Insert Time** button to insert the current time. Other toolbar buttons enable you to insert additional types of information. You can even press **Enter** to add additional lines to the header or footer.

5. You can select the header/footer text and format it as you wish, choosing a new font, size, and so on. Figure 9.2 shows an example document header, with formatting.

6. If you want to add both a header and footer, click the **Switch Between Header and Footer** button on the toolbar and repeat steps 4 and 5.

7. Click the **Close** button to finish creating the header or footer.

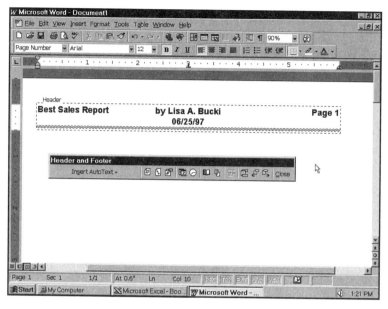

Figure 9.2 Here's how a header looks as you create it.

 TIP **Header/Footer, Please** In general, if your document is more than one page in length, is some type of business document (as opposed to a personal letter or schedule), and you plan to print it and distribute it to others, you should include a header or footer. This will help your reader in case pages become separated or if you send multiple, updated versions of the same document. If you'll be sending multiple versions of a document to others for review, you also can include version information in the header or footer. For example, you can included "Draft 1," "Draft 2," "Draft 3," and "Final" in the header or footer to distinguish the different versions.

Numbering Pages Only

If you don't want to go to the trouble of creating a header or footer for a document, you can simply number the pages near the top or bottom and specify a number style. This gives simple, plain-vanilla page numbering. At the top or bottom of each page, the program inserts a page number, aligned where you specified. There is no additional information. For example, you might simply include a page number at the bottom center position of each document.

Page number settings usually appear within a Page Setup dialog box, although in Word 97 you use the **Insert, Page Numbers** command to display a Page Numbers dialog box for adding and aligning page numbers. You often can specify whether the page numbers appear at the top or bottom of the page, and whether they align left, center, or right. Further, you can choose different numbering styles such as regular Arabic numerals, Roman numerals, letters, and others, depending on the application.

TIP **Other Numbers** You also may find options where you can change the number used for the first page of the document (if you want it to start with page 10 rather than page 1) or number the lines in a document, as is done in many legal documents.

Adjusting Page Breaks

If you do nothing but enter text and data, most applications will automatically break the document up into pages—if not on-screen with page break lines, then definitely when you print. That doesn't necessarily mean you'll agree with the automatic (soft) page breaks or that they'll suit your needs. For example, you may want to have a title page with a word processor or spreadsheet printout.

You can override the page breaks created by the application and insert your own manual, or hard, page breaks to divide pages where you prefer. Here are some ways that you may be able to insert page breaks in your applications:

- In word processors, position the insertion point where you want the new page to begin, and press **Ctrl+Enter**. Some applications may use a different keystroke; consult your application's online documentation if Ctrl+Enter doesn't work.

- Position the insertion point in a word processor, or select the cell in a spreadsheet that you want to become the upper-left corner of the new page. Click to open the **Insert** menu and click **Break** or **Page Break**. Figure 9.3 shows a page break inserted in an Excel 97 document.

TIP **Other Breaks** You often use the Insert, Break command (or the equivalent) in word processors to create column breaks (divide information between columns) and section breaks (new parts of a document that can have different headers/footers and other formatting).

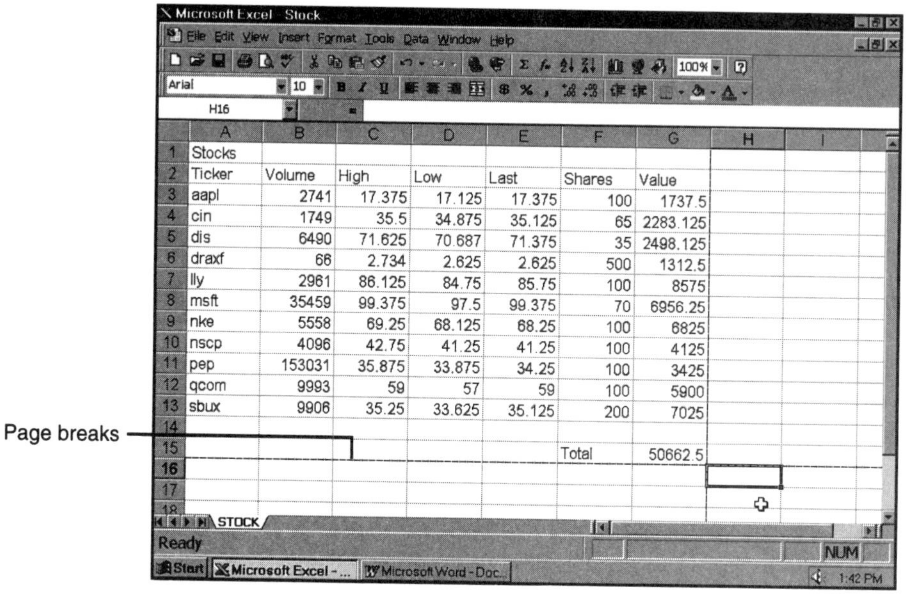

Figure 9.3 Select the cell you want to be the upper-left corner of a new page before you insert a page break.

- In a presentation graphics program, insert a new slide or page with the appropriate toolbar button or command (such as **Insert**, **Slide**).

- In a database program, you need to create a *report* to control how displayed and printed information breaks up into pages. For example, in a database that holds names and addresses, each page of a report might hold the name and address for one contact in your list. Because creating a report is a fairly detailed process, consult the online help for your database to learn how to tackle that task.

- When designing graphic images, you can't add subsequent pages. Each image must appear on a single page.

Understanding and Using Templates

In the previous lesson, you learned that you can save a few particular formatting choices as a style that you can apply to other selections in a document. A *template* does the same for a document. A template can contain not only particular saved styles that you can apply to text selections, but also various page settings such as page size, orientation, header/footer, page breaks, and graphical elements like those described in the next lesson. So, after you select a template, you can concentrate on adding information to the document, and fine-tune the formatting. Much of the formatting already has been done for you.

Most applications—especially word processors and presentation graphics programs—now ship with a number of templates. For example, Word 97 offers templates for faxes, memos, and more. Before you invest a lot of time in creating a document with fancy or specialized formatting, review the available templates to see if any meet your needs.

Any document based on the template adopts its formatting from the template. The template styles are available in the document. For example, a template may have different styles for various headings or titles, one or two styles for body text (indented and not indented), bulleted and numbered lists, and so on; you can apply any such styles to selected paragraphs. Templates go by various names in programs from various publishers. For example, while they're called *templates* in Word 97, Lotus WordPro 97 calls them SmartMasters. You may find two opportunities to apply a template to a file:

- **When you create the new file.** When you choose the **File**, **New** command, word processor and presentation graphics programs, in particular, present the available templates so you can choose one to apply to your file. In the dialog box that presents the template options, you usually can click a template to get a preview of its look, as in the example from PowerPoint 97 in Figure 9.4. When you find the template you want, click **OK** to apply it to your file.

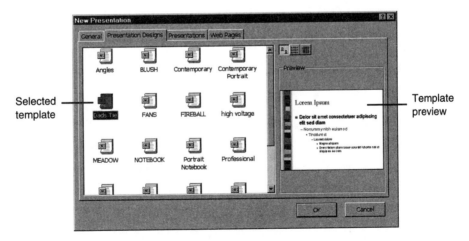

Selected template

Template preview

Figure 9.4 Click a template to select it and see its preview.

CAUTION **Template Default?** When you click the New (or equivalent) toolbar button to create a new file, you usually don't get to choose a template. Instead, the application uses a default template to ensure that the New button provides the most streamlined way to create a new file.

TIP **More than a Pretty File** Some presentation graphics programs even offer templates, wizards, or SmartMasters that suggest the content for different types of presentations (like a sales presentation) in addition to providing attractive formatting.

- **After you've entered file information.** Often, you can change the global formatting by applying a template at some time after you create a file. The commands for choosing a new template vary significantly, so look in online help for a Templates (or SmartMasters) command. Then, as when choosing a template for a new file, click a template to preview it, then click **OK** to select it.

At this point, you've seen an overview of how to set up the overall look of your document by specifying paper size and margins, headers and footers, page breaks, and document templates. The next lesson provides a look at how you can add graphical elements to a document to improve it.

Working with Graphical Elements

This lesson shows you how to improve the appearance of a document by adding graphical elements like bulleted and numbered lists, borders, shading, and clip art.

Creating Bulleted and Numbered Lists

In early applications, adding bullets or numbers to set off a list was a tedious process. To create a bullet, you often had to type a special code (which you had to remember, of course), and then set up the bulleted paragraph with hanging indents. Setting up a numbered list was similar, with an important drawback. If you wanted to insert or delete a new item within the list, you had to renumber all the items manually.

Because bulleted and numbered lists provide such a concise, clear way to communicate, they're used often. Computer users urged software publishers to automate list features, and the publishers complied. Leading word processing and presentation graphics programs all provide easy methods for creating a numbered or bulleted list. Here's a numbered list reviewing how to create numbered and bulleted lists:

1. Position the insertion point at the far left end of the first line where you want the first bulleted or numbered list item to appear.

2. Click the toolbar button (or other button) in the application for creating numbered or bulleted lists. The application inserts the first bullet or number, and adds the formatting for hanging indention.

Note that presentation graphics programs offer various slide designs, such as a slide with a bulleted list. Simply click in the area of the slide that holds the bulleted list, then use steps 3 and 4 to add list items.

3. Type the text for the first bulleted or numbered item.

4. Press **Enter**. The application starts a new bulleted or numbered item, as shown in Figure 10.1.

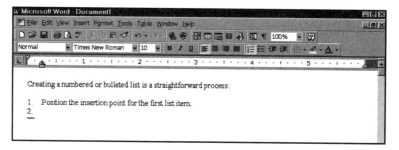

Figure 10.1 Once you've turned on bullets or numbering, just press Enter to create each new list item.

5. Repeat steps 3 and 4 to add as many items to the list as you want.

6. After you finish the last item and press Enter, you'll be left with a blank line with a bullet or number. To turn off the bullets or numbering, click the button for creating numbered or bulleted lists. The bullet or number disappears, so you can begin typing regular paragraph text.

It's easy to remove bullets or numbers, too. Just click in the list item (or select a number of items) you want to remove the bullet or number from, then click the button for creating bulleted or numbered lists to toggle the list features off. If you want to apply bullets or numbers to a group of several contiguous paragraphs, select the paragraphs. Then, click the button for creating bulleted or numbered lists.

TIP **Better Bullets or Numbers** You can select items in bulleted or numbered lists, then use a command (like **Bullets and Numbering** on either the **Format** or **Text** menu) to display a dialog box with other bullet or number styles. You can even choose other small graphics files to use as bullets, in some applications.

Working with Borders

Borders are lines that help you set off information. Most fully-featured applications enable you to use borders with paragraphs, list items, titles, groups of cells, graphical elements you want to box, and more. You generally have several options in terms of placing the border: above, below, and around the selection, or even as a grid to delineate a group of spreadsheet cells or a table in a work processor, database printout, or presentation graphics program. In addition, you can specify the style and even the color of the border.

Today's software makes it easy to add a border. Select the text or range of cells that you'd like to place a border around, then choose the program's command for adding borders. Following are the commands for adding borders from various programs; see your program's help to find the command you need if you don't find one of the commands on this list:

- Format, Borders
- Text, Borders and Shading
- Format, Colors and Lines

You'll see a dialog box resembling the one in Figure 10.2. You simply click the border style, width, and color options you want, then click to indicate where you want the border placed around the selection. Click **OK** to apply your choices.

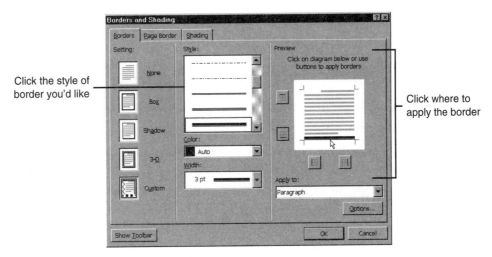

Click the style of border you'd like

Click where to apply the border

Figure 10.2 You can add a stylish border to set off information.

TIP **Border Button** Check your application for a toolbar button or other shortcut for creating borders. Office 97 applications, for example, offer a button you click to display a special Borders toolbar.

Adding Shading

Like borders, shading or fills enable you to emphasize or highlight information, as shown in Figure 10.3. You usually can choose not only a color for the background, but also its shading intensity—from 100 percent of the color to lighter shadings. Some applications even enable you to use a pattern or graphic image as the fill.

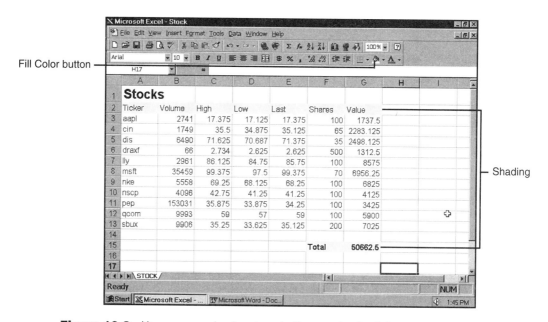

Figure 10.3 You can use shading to set off or emphasize information.

Select the text or range of cells that you'd like to place a fill (shading) behind, then choose the program's command for adding shading (**Format**, **Borders** and **Shading** or a similar command). You may need to click a tab in the dialog box that appears to display the shading options. Click the fill style and color options you want, then click **OK** to apply your choices. Some programs may offer a Fill or Fill Color button that you can click to apply the shading.

CAUTION

Color Me Readable Keep contrast in mind when you're adding a background fill to a selection. Black text with a dark blue background won't be readable on-screen or in a printout, whether black and white or color. Dark text with a lighter background is most readable. Also be aware that laser printers with lower resolutions may not print light fill areas very well.

Inserting Clip Art

Graphic images can make a document more lively and interesting. Color printers also make them more practical to use today, because your printed documents will look as great as your on-screen ones. Presentations, in particular, are good candidates for clip art.

TERM

Clip Art Graphic images provided with a program. They can be used to enhance documents.

Inserting a clip art image generally takes a few steps:

1. Choose your program's command for adding clip art (such as **Insert**, **Picture**, **Clip Art**). Alternately, click the toolbar button for inserting clip art if one is offered in your program. A dialog box will appear, listing the available clip art images.

2. Scroll through the clip art choices, as shown in Figure 10.4.

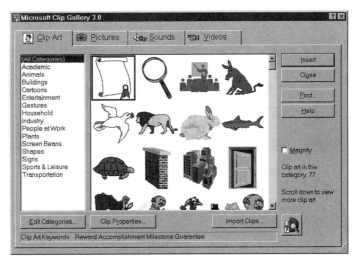

Figure 10.4 A dialog box enables you to review a clip art image before inserting it.

289

3. Click **Insert, Open,** or **OK** to close the dialog box.

4. The mouse pointer now usually includes a plus sign. Drag diagonally to draw a box indicating where you want the clip art to appear. When you release the mouse button, the clip art appears in the document. If the program doesn't need for you to draw a box for the clip art, it will instead insert the clip art picture immediately at its default size.

CAUTION

New View   Some applications require that you be working in a particular *view* on-screen to be able to insert clip art or graphics that you draw. If you try to insert the clip art or drawing in the wrong view, the application will prompt you to change to the correct one.

Inserting Other Graphics

With all the online resources available today (see the next part to learn more), it's easy for you to gather images in a number of graphic formats to add to your documents. As long as you make sure that an image isn't protected by copyright (or otherwise get permission to use it), you can download and insert the image in your documents.

There are a number of common formats for graphic images, including .pcx, .gif, and .jpg. Check your program's online help to ensure it lets you use an image of the type you have, then use these steps to insert the image:

1. Choose your program's command for inserting an image (such as **Insert**, **Picture**; **Insert**, **Picture**, **From File**; or **File**, **Import Picture**). A dialog box will appear.

2. Use the **File of Type** or a similar drop-down list to select the format of the graphics file you want to insert.

3. Navigate to the folder holding the image you want to insert.

4. Scroll through the image choices. If you click a choice, you'll sometimes see a preview of the graphic in the dialog box.

5. Click **Insert, Open,** or **OK** to close the dialog box.

6. The mouse pointer often now includes a plus sign. Drag diagonally to draw a box indicating where you want the graphic to appear. When you release the mouse button, the graphic appears in the document. If the program doesn't need for you to draw a box for the graphic, it will instead insert the picture immediately at its default size.

TIP **A Better Look** When you add a graphic object like a border or clip art to a document, right-click the object to display commands for working with the object, including commands for changing the object's border, color, and other formatting options.

This lesson showed you how to add bulleted and numbered lists, borders, shading, and graphic images to make your document more attractive and highlight key information. The next lesson shows you how to view your documents in different ways.

Getting a Better View of Your Work

This lesson shows you how to control which tools appear on-screen and how the application shows your document.

Showing and Hiding Screen Elements

The great number of tools an application offers can make your work significantly faster. The command you need is usually just a quick click away. In other instances, an application may display so many tools that you're distracted from entering and using your information.

Applications frequently offer a View menu to enable you to choose what tools appear on-screen and how the document itself looks. Here are the kinds of items you can normally view or hide via the View menu and other methods:

- **Toolbars or icon bars.** Choosing **Toolbar** or similar command from the **View** menu displays a submenu (see Figure 11.1) or dialog box listing the available toolbars. To remove a toolbar from or return it to display, you click it in the submenu; use the check boxes beside toolbars in the toolbar dialog box (clearing checks beside toolbars you no longer want to display) and click **OK**. You also can often right-click toolbars or click a drop-down arrow on an icon bar to display a list of the bars, then click the name of the bar to remove it from or add it to the screen.

- **Rulers.** While rulers are great for formatting text, they're not of much value when you're doing straight text entry or drawing a graphic image. Choose a command like **View**, **Ruler** to toggle ruler display on and off.

Figure 11.1   Click a toolbar in the submenu to hide or display it.

- **Palettes.** Programs that let you draw or create graphics often display a palette or window of choices such as colors or line styles that you can use in the graphic. When such palettes are available, the **View** menu often includes a command to enable you to choose which palettes appear. Other palettes appear automatically when you choose a particular drawing or painting tool. To close a palette, you often simply click its **close** button.

- **Comments or Notes.** By default, most comments or notes remain hidden until you point to the selection to which the note was added, at which point the comment or note pops up on-screen. The **View** menu may offer a command to enable to you display and hide all document comments. Use the **View, Notes**; **View, Comments**; or your program's equivalent command to toggle comment display on and off. Word 97 and WordPro 97, among other programs, also offer a special toolbar or icon bar with buttons for working with comments.

Comments or Notes   These offer extra user-supplied information about some point in a document; for example, you can add a comment to a spreadsheet cell to explain the cell's calculation. Comments or notes can be hidden and then displayed only when needed.

Selecting a Special View

Applications usually offer you several ways to see the information in a document. For example, if you're working strictly with a document's text, you don't necessarily need to see the document's graphics. Each way of displaying a document is called a *view*. Most applications offer at least a couple of views; simply choose the view you want from the choices available on the **View** menu (or the equivalent command in your program).

General

The default view in most applications is its *Normal* view. In this view, you see the document's text in a bland format, and may even see symbols representing non-printable codes, like paragraph marks. Graphics often don't appear in this view.

The next most common view is a *Page Layout* view. In this view, you see a more accurate representation of how your finished document looks. Columns, graphics, and other bells and whistles appear in place. Usually, text is large enough in this view to enable you to proceed with editing.

Another common view is the *Print Preview* view, which shows full pages of the document so that you'll know how it will look when printed. (In the next lesson, you'll learn about printing your document.)

Many word processing and presentation graphics programs also offer an *Outline* view. In a word processor, Outline view collapses the document to display its headings. In a presentation graphics program, Outline view displays slide contents (titles and text) in a text-only format, so you can see how the information progresses in the slideshow. In both types of programs, you can drag information around to make major structural changes or use tools to adjust the outline level (heading, subheading, second level subheading, and so on) of a selection.

Full Screen Views

To enable you to see and read the most information on-screen at once, look for a view called the *Full Screen* or *Clean Screen* view. Such a view removes almost all the program window features and tools from the screen, sometimes including even the title bar and menu bar. In a drawing or painting program that you use to create and work with graphic images, a Full Screen or Image Only view shows the finished image on-screen, with nothing but a plain background surrounding it.

Figure 11.2 shows an example of the Full Screen view in Excel 97. To switch to this view, you choose the applicable command from the menu bar. To return to the previous view, you generally press **Esc** or another key combination, or click a button that appears, as in Figure 11.2.

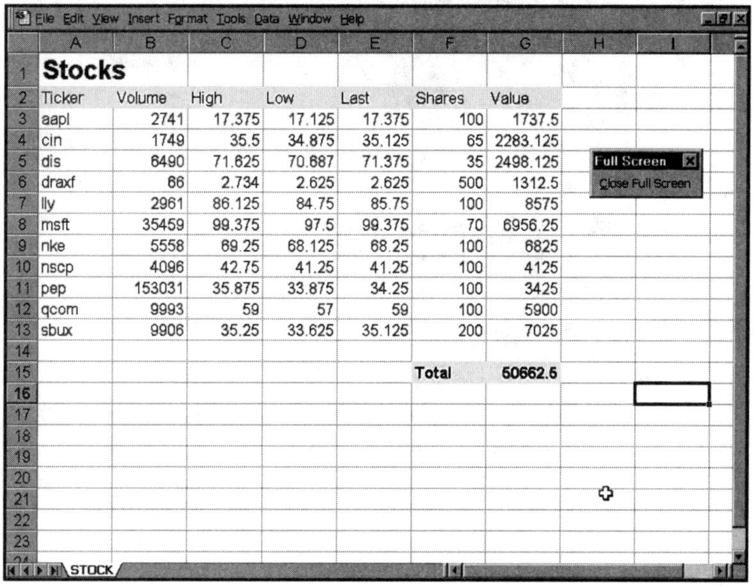

Figure 11.2   A Full Screen or Clean Screen view enables you to focus on text or data.

Specialized Views

The special nature of how some programs manage information require those programs to offer still other views. Check your program's View menu for options like these:

- Presentation graphics programs usually offer commands for running the presentation (slideshow) on-screen and for viewing multiple slides on-screen so you can sort (reorder) them.

- Page breaks have long been tough to manage in spreadsheet programs. Excel 97, for one, now offers a Page Break preview, so you can see exactly how information will be broken into pages when printed, and even drag to adjust page breaks.

- Database programs like Access 97 normally offer at least a few database-specific views. *Design* views often enable you to specify what fields (types of information will appear in the database) or how reports or forms will look. A *Table* view shows the database information in a spreadsheet-like grid of rows and columns, for quick data entry. A *Report* view enables you to create a condensed listing of the database, including and excluding fields, and sorting information. A *Form* view enables you see one or more records on-screen in an attractive layout, as in Figure 11.3.

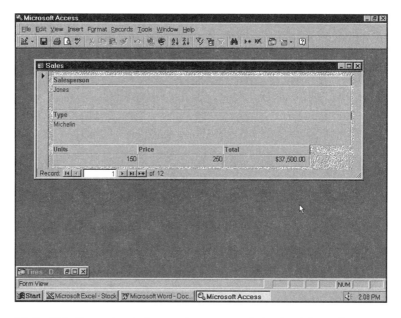

Figure 11.3 This Form view in Access is one way of viewing information.

 TIP **Give Your Report** When a form is designed to display one record (collection of related fields) at a time, much like a Rolodex, it's ideal for entering data. You can create such a form to enter address book entries, customer orders, or similar types of records. In contrast, use forms that display multiple records per page for reporting purposes, rather than data entry.

- Other special views you might see vary depending on the type of application and the offerings of software publishers. For example, word processors may offer a view to summarize information in a special way or manage the components (sections) that make up a lengthy document.

Presentation graphics programs may offer a view to let you alter the template used in a presentation or the layout of the current slide.

Zooming In and Out

The Normal view in most programs displays information at actual (100 percent) size. This makes the information easier to read, and gives you an idea of its printed size. There may be times when you want to see the on-screen images at a slightly larger or smaller size. For example, you might want to zoom in on (enlarge) text with a small font to proofread it more easily. Or, you might want to zoom out on (shrink) an area of a document to get another view of how a graphic looks in place.

The different view sizes you can choose are expressed as a percentage of a document's default (100 percent) size. The available range will depend on your application, but generally range from 10 to 200 percent or more.

Applications usually provide a couple of ways to select a zoom percentage for the current document:

- Choose the **Zoom** command from the **View** menu (or the equivalent command in your application). In the dialog box that appears, click an option button to select a zoom percentage, or enter a more precise percentage in the text box offered for that purpose. Click **OK** to close the dialog box and apply your settings.

- Use the **Zoom** drop-down list on the toolbar to choose a zoom percentage, as in Figure 11.4. Or, click in the text box for the **Zoom** drop-down list, type a specific percentage, and press **Enter**.

 TIP   **Zoom It**   Many applications enable you to zoom in on a selection. For example, if you selected a group of cells, then chose the Selection choice in the Zoom drop-down list in Figure 11.4, Excel would zoom in to a close up of the selection. In many graphics programs, you click a magnifying glass (zoom) button or tool, then click the image or document to zoom in. Right-click to zoom back out.

When you want to, you can change how your application and document look on-screen by using the viewing choices covered in this lesson. The next lesson explains how to print a document and control print jobs.

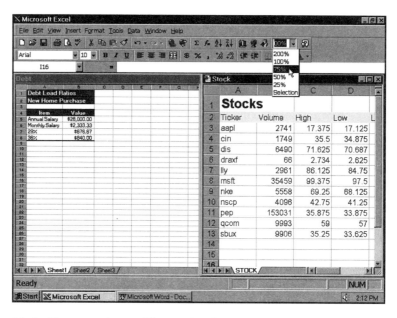

Figure 11.4 You can select a different view for the current document using the Zoom drop-down list. Notice that both windows shown here feature a different zoom setting.

Printing and Controlling Your Printer

This lesson shows you how to print a file and how to control printing once you've issued the print command.

Printing in a Windows Program

Unless you've made a complete transition to paperless publishing, chances are that you have some sort of printer connected to your computer. (If you haven't set up your printer yet, see Lesson 1 in Part 5, which explains how to set up a printer under Windows 95.)

Documents exist to be looked at. They carry a message from you to a friend, colleague, boss, client, student, or teacher—or anyone you want to communicate with. The reality is that you can't call every one of these people to come look at your computer screen or e-mail a document to them in all instances.

Instead, you'll need to print out your document. This process requires you to tell your computer to send the information you've created and saved to your system's printer so it can be put on paper.

Previewing the Printed Document

If you create a document, often you do a lot of *formatting*—which can include adjusting major settings like the page margins and page breaks; at some point you could lose sight of what the final document will look like. In the old days, you had to print out a preliminary copy of the file and then go back to fix the formatting (either to fit the page or to look more attractive on the page).

Today, most software publishers have built a feature into their products that shows you what the printed document will look like. In some applications, you can even print (or make changes to margins and the like) while a document is in this *Print Preview mode* (shown in Figure 12.1).

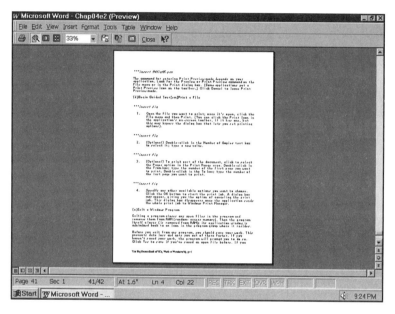

Figure 12.1 An application's Preview mode shows what your printed document will look like.

The command for entering Print Preview mode depends on your application. Look for the **Preview** or **Print Preview** command on the **File** menu or in the Print dialog box. (Some applications also put a **Print Preview** button on the toolbar.) Click **Close** or a similar command to leave Print Preview mode.

Printing a File

Windows 95 includes built-in printer management features that control every print job and help eliminate problems. It acts as a go-between to let your Windows 95 application programs communicate with your printer. Once your printer is set up to work correctly with Windows 95, printing from any Windows application should be easy.

The following steps explain, in general, how to print a file. The available options vary from one application to the next (depending on your application's features), but generally you can specify how many copies to print and whether you want to print all or part of a document.

Follow these steps to print a document:

1. Open the file you want to print. Make any last-minute changes, if necessary, and save the file.

2. Open the **File** menu and click **Print**. (You can click the **Print** button in the application's on-screen toolbar, if it has one, but that may bypass the dialog box in which you can set printing options.) The Print dialog box for the application appears, as shown in Figure 12.2.

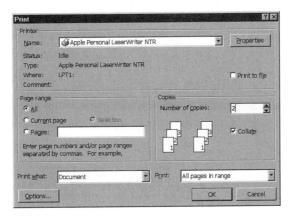

Figure 12.2 An application's Print dialog box presents available printing options.

3. Select the print options you'd like to use. For example, click in the **Number of Copies** text box to select it, and then type a new value. Or, to print only a part of the document, click to select the **Pages** option in the **Page Range** area. Then click in the **Pages** text box and type the range of pages you want to print. You can separate contiguous pages to print with a colon or hyphen, as in 3:5 or 3–5. To enter non-contiguous pages to print, separate the page numbers with commas, as in 3,5.

4. After you've finished specifying all the options, click the **OK** or **Print** button to start the print job. A dialog box may appear, giving you the option of canceling the print job. This dialog box disappears once the application sends the whole print job to the Windows 95 print management application.

TIP   **Fast Fax Facts**   If you've set up multiple printers or fax modems (you have to "print" to a fax modem to send a fax) under Windows 95, most applications usually will let you select the printer to use in the Print dialog box. In the Print dialog box for Word 97, shown in Figure 12.2, you use the **Name** drop-down list to select the printer you want. The **Properties** button lets you control the various settings offered by the selected printer, such as the paper size or graphics resolution. To learn more about printer properties and how to set up a printer under Windows 95, see Lesson 1, "Adding and Setting Up a Printer in Windows 95," in Part 5.

Pausing, Resuming, and Canceling Printing

Windows allows you to print documents (from Windows programs) in the background while you are working in other programs. Windows does this by printing the documents to a temporary file on your hard disk and then *spooling* the documents to your printer. When you print a document from a Windows program, Windows stores the document in a queue (a waiting line) and then feeds the document to the printer.

The following steps illustrate how to manage the documents that Windows is in the process of printing. You learn how to start and stop your printer (in the event of a mishap), how to resume after you've corrected a problem, and how to cancel printing altogether, with these steps:

1. When you start printing, a printer icon appears next to the time in the taskbar, as shown in Figure 12.3. Double-click the **printer icon** to view a list of documents in the print queue.

2. The print queue window appears, showing the status of the documents in the print queue. You can stop all printing by opening the **Printer** menu and clicking **Pause Printing**.

3. To pause the printing of a single document, select the document by clicking it in the list, open the **Document** menu, and click **Pause Printing** (see Figure 12.4.) Your printer may continue printing one or two pages, because Windows cannot control what has already been sent to the printer.

4. To continue printing, open the **Printer** or **Document** menu and click **Pause Printing** again to remove the check mark.

5. You can cancel all print jobs (and stop printing) by opening the **Printer** menu and selecting **Purge Print Jobs**. This removes all documents from the print queue.

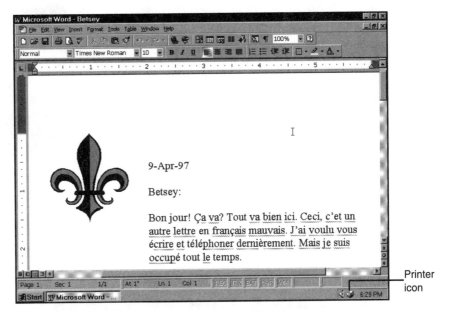

Figure 12.3 The printer icon appears in the taskbar.

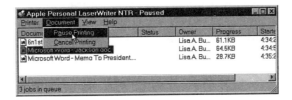

Figure 12.4 You can pause the printing of a document.

6. To remove one or more particular documents from the print queue, click the first document, press and hold **Ctrl**, and click additional documents. Then open the **Document** menu and select **Cancel Printing**.

7. You can rearrange documents in the print queue by dragging the document names up or down in the list.

CAUTION

Not Your Print Job If the printer you're printing to is a network printer (that is, a printer attached to a computer network in your office), keep in mind that some of the documents in the print queue might have been printed by other users. You don't want to pause or purge another user's print job.

This lesson showed you how to print a document and to control how print jobs flow to the printer. Read the next lesson to learn how to fax or e-mail a file.

Faxing or E-Mailing a File

In this lesson you learn to use built-in Windows 95 features to create an address book and fax or e-mail a document to a colleague— either within an application that supports messaging or from the Windows 95 desktop.

Understanding Windows Messaging

The Inbox icon on your Windows 95 desktop enables you to work with Windows Messaging features—the basis for transferring and managing faxes and e-mail messages (although some e-mail programs like Internet Mail manage their own messages).

 Windows Messaging This component of Windows 95 OSR 2 (OEM Service Release 2, the latest version on Windows 95 that started shipping on all new PCs starting in the Fall of 1996) enables you to send and receive e-mail and provides an inbox for Microsoft Fax and some other messaging programs you specify (like CompuServe mail). Under the original release of Windows 95, Microsoft Exchange served the same function as Windows Messaging.

Setting Up Windows Messaging

Before you can e-mail a message or use Microsoft Fax to send a fax, you may need to set up Windows Messaging. To check to make sure Messaging is completely set up, double-click the **Inbox icon** on the desktop. If the Windows Messaging window opens, Messaging is set up.

Otherwise, a series of wizard screens will prompt you for the information needed for Messaging to manage information. Make your choices in each screen, then click **Next**. For example, one screen will ask you what information services to set up. At the very least, you'll want to check **Microsoft Mail** and **Microsoft Fax**.

Additional screens may help you set up a *communications profile*, asking you for information about your modem, prompting you to set up a place to receive faxes and messages (your Personal Folder, which serves as a master postbox), asking if you want to use your Personal Address Book to store addresses or another compatible address book, and more. This process may vary slightly, depending on how much setup work your system's manufacturer did. Consult online help if you have any questions.

CAUTION

It Doesn't Work   If you get an error message when you try to send a fax or e-mail message, Windows Messaging may not be set up correctly. If you suspect this problem, right-click the **Inbox icon** and click **Properties**. Check to make sure your modem is selected, and to ensure your Personal Folders are set up (see the Services tab) and ready to receive mail and faxes (see the Delivery tab). As a last resort, you can remove and reinstall Windows Messaging and Microsoft Fax. Lesson 1 of this part explains how to add and remove Windows 95 components.

CAUTION

Outlook?   If your system has the Standard or Professional version of Office 97 installed, you may see the Outlook icon on the desktop instead of Inbox. Outlook takes over the Windows Messaging chores and offers an Address Book and another list called Contacts, an inbox, and even more features. Consult the Outlook online help to learn more about working with Outlook.

Adding an Address Book Entry

An *address book* or address list in a mailing and faxing program enables you to store contact information about possible message and fax recipients. You enter the contact information into the address book once, then simply choose the recipient's name later to send an e-mail message or fax. This saves you the trouble of typing contact information repeatedly, which is not only tedious but also could lead to typos.

These steps provide an example of how to set up a contact in the Windows Messaging Personal Address Book:

1. Double-click the **Inbox icon** on the desktop. The Inbox-Windows Messaging dialog box appears.

2. Click the **Address Book** button on the toolbar or choose **Tools, Address Book**. The Address Book window appears.

3. Click the **New Entry** button on the toolbar or choose **File, New Entry**. The New Entry dialog box appears.

4. Choose an entry type such as Fax or Internet Mail from the list. Use **Other Address** for other e-mail addresses or if you're not sure of your choice. Make sure Personal Address Book appears as the **In The** drop-down list choice. Click **OK**.

5. A dialog box prompting you for information about the new Address Book entry appears. The dialog box and its fields will vary depending on the type of entry you selected in step 4. Complete the entry information, as shown in Figure 13.1, then click **OK**.

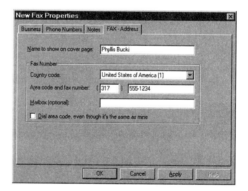

Figure 13.1   Here is information for an Address Book Fax entry.

6. Close the Address Book window by clicking its **Close** button in the upper-right corner.

306

Sending a Fax

You can send a fax in two different ways: from within an application or directly from Microsoft Fax, which comes with Windows 95. When an application offers the option for you to fax a document, choose that command, which provides the fastest faxing method. Here's an overview of how to do so:

1. Open the document that you want to fax. Make any last-minute changes, and save the document.

2. Choose **File**, **Send To**, **Fax Recipient**. The Fax Wizard appears to lead you through the steps of setting up and sending the Fax. (If the Fax Wizard doesn't appear when you fax from an application, you'll probably see Microsoft Fax Wizard steps that more closely resemble the next set of numbered steps in this section.)

3. Click **Next** to proceed to the next step of the wizard. Specify which open document to send (if any), whether or not to include a cover sheet, or just to send a cover sheet with a note.

4. Click **Next**. Specify whether to use Microsoft Fax or a different program to send the fax, as shown in Figure 13.2, or whether you want to print the document for faxing, instead.

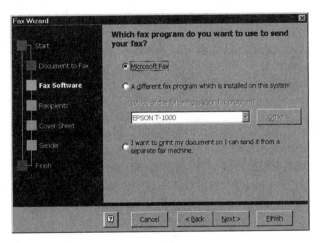

Figure 13.2 The Fax Wizard lets you choose another faxing program if you have programs other than Microsoft Fax installed on your system.

5. Click **Next** to specify the fax recipients. You can type the Name and Fax number entries directly in the appropriate text boxes. Or click the **Address Book** button, and choose a communications profile, if prompted. In the Select name dialog box, choose the address book or contacts list to use in the top drop-down list, then double-click a fax recipient in the list that appears. Redisplay the address book as needed to add other recipients.

6. Click **Next**. Choose a cover sheet style (Professional, Contemporary, or Elegant) by clicking the corresponding option button.

7. Click **Next**. Edit the Sender information in the next screen that appears.

8. Click **Finish**. The cover sheet appears on-screen.

9. Select the field reading **[Click here and type any comments]**, type your coversheet information, and click the **Send Fax Now** button.

10. Microsoft Fax dials the fax number and sends the fax document. It displays a message box telling you the fax has been sent. Click **OK** to close the message box.

If your program doesn't offer a File menu command for sending a fax, you can still fax from within the program or directly from Microsoft Fax. You can fax from the Print dialog box of virtually all applications if Microsoft Fax is set up on your system. Open the list of printers in the Print dialog box, choose Microsoft Fax (or other fax software that's installed on your system), and click OK. A set of Compose New Fax dialog boxes walks you through the process. The Compose New Fax dialog boxes for "printing" a fax are with one exception identical to the Compose New Fax dialog boxes that appear when you send a fax by choosing the Microsoft Fax command from the desktop. So, the following steps cover both methods for sending a fax:

1. Within the program, open the file to fax and choose **File**, **Print**. In the Print dialog box, open the **Name** drop-down list and click **Microsoft Fax**. Then click **OK**. To fax from Microsoft Fax itself instead, click the **Start** button, point to **Programs**, point to **Accessories**, point to **Fax**, and click **Compose New Fax**.

2. At the first Compose New Fax dialog box that appears, choose different dialing properties, if needed, then click **Next**.

3. In the next Compose New Fax dialog box that appears, you can enter **To** and **Fax #** entries by hand, then click the **Add to List** button after each entry. Or, click the **Address Book** button, select an address book, double-click each recipient to fax to, then click **OK**.

4. Click **Next**. Choose whether or not you want to send a cover page, and what style it should be. Click the **Options** button to set fax options such as setting a specific time to send the fax or whether the fax should be editable (if it's being received by a fax modem rather than a paper fax).

5. Click **Next**. If you opted to send a cover sheet in the preceding step, type its **Subject** and your **Note**. Otherwise, if you're faxing from within an application (you used File, Print in step1), go to step 7. If you're faxing from Microsoft Fax, go on to the next step, step 6.

6. Click **Next**. If you're faxing from within Microsoft Fax, this next Compose New Fax dialog box prompts you to specify what **Files to Send**. (When you're faxing by "printing" from within an application, you don't see this screen, because the open file is faxed by default.) Use the **Add File** button and the dialog box it displays to add one or more files to the list.

7. Click **Next**. The final Compose New Fax dialog box tells you you've finished setting up the fax.

8. Click **Finish**. The Microsoft Fax Status window appears as shown in Figure 13.3. It informs you as it formats the fax, dials the fax number, sends, and disconnects, then the window closes.

Figure 13.3 Microsoft Fax shows you that it's sending your fax.

Sending an E-Mail

The process for sending a file via an e-mail message with Windows Messaging is just as easy as sending a fax, once you have Windows Messaging set up (see "Setting Up Windows Messaging," earlier in this lesson). Whereas when you send a fax, it's sent to another user's fax machine or fax modem, when you send an e-mail with Windows messaging, it's sent to another user's e-mail address on a network (or the Internet).

Transport Problems If you're trying to use Windows Messaging to send mail to an Internet e-mail address, you may get an error message saying a transport provider was not available to send the message. That means that you need to install the Internet Mail service for dealing with Internet messages.

CAUTION

309

Unfortunately, the Internet Mail transport service isn't provided on all Windows 95 OSR 2 installations. To check to see if it's available on your system, start Windows Messaging. Choose **Tools, Services**, then click **Add**. If Internet Mail appears in the list that appears, click it, then click **OK** to install it. You'll then see a dialog box prompting you for various settings; if you're confused about any of them, check with your Internet Service Provider or network administrator. (Alternately, some systems might offer a different Internet transport. On my system, I installed the Netscape Internet Transport that was provided.) This can get a bit tricky, even for more advanced users. If you don't have Internet Mail or feel intimidated, you can use Internet Mail e-mail program to work with Internet e-mail, instead. To learn how, see Lessons 2 and 8 in Part 4 of this book.

1. In your application, open the file that you want to send as your e-mail attachment. Make any last-minute changes and save the file.

2. Choose **File, Send To, Mail Recipient; File, Send**; or the equivalent command in your application.

3. If you're prompted to choose a communications profile, do so and click **OK**.

 TIP   **Desktop Messages**   You also can start Windows Messaging and create a new message from the desktop. To do so, double-click the **Inbox** icon on the desktop. If you're prompted for a profile, specify it. Then, choose **Compose, New Message** or click the **New Message** button on the toolbar. The New Message window appears on-screen, and you can use it as described in the rest of the steps.

The New Message window appears on-screen. If you use a mailing program other than Windows Messaging for mailing (such as Microsoft Outlook or Lotus cc:Mail), you may see the new message window for that program rather than Windows Messaging.

4. Specify whom to send the message **To** (recipients) using the addressing method used for your company e-mail system (check with your system administrator if you need help) and type a **Subject**.

5. You can click in the message area beside the file attachment and enter additional message text, as in Figure 13.4.

6. Click the **Send** button or choose **File, Send** to send the message.

Recipient — 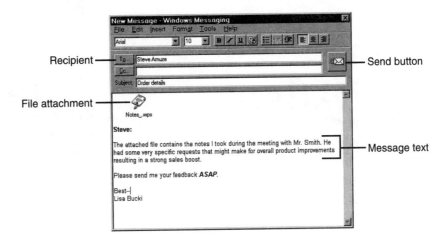 — Send button

File attachment —

Message text —

Figure 13.4   When you send a message with Windows Messaging, you can even attach a file.

This lesson showed you how to e-mail and fax your documents. Use the next lesson to learn about program options.

Setting Application Options

Learn how to use application (program) options such as default view options, user information, editing, and saving options to make the application more closely suit your working style.

Finding Your Options

Every program offers options or preferences that dictate how the program appears and behaves. For example, you may not want to see a status bar, or may prefer not to enable drag-and-drop editing. Once you set the options or preferences you want, they remain set until you change them. So, you don't have to repeatedly hide that status bar or turn a particular feature off for each work session.

As with all the other commands that you saw in Lessons 6 through 11 of this part, the actual command you use to set options as well as the various options varies from program to program (and software publisher to software publisher). To find the preferences in your application, look for a command like **File**, **User Setup**, **Preferences**; or **Tools**, **Options**.

The Options or Preferences dialog boxes in most applications today offer multiple pages or tabs of information to divide the choices into manageable categories. Click the tab for the page of options you want, and change the settings as needed. Adjust settings on other tabs as needed, and click **OK** to enable your new settings. The rest of this lesson covers typical categories and settings.

Setting View Options

Logically, options in the view category cover what elements appear on-screen and how those elements look. Figure 14.1 shows example view options from the Word 97 application. Typically, you can choose whether to display the status bar, scroll bars, or other optional elements. You also may have control over items such as gridlines and column headings in a spreadsheet. Still other programs may enable you to specify a draft view or control whether a startup dialog box appears.

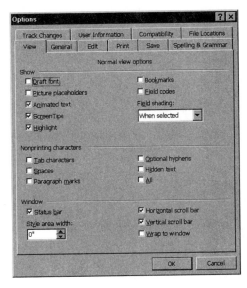

Figure 14.1   Control your program view with options like these.

Updating User Information

Most programs offer a separate tab or some area for you to specify information about yourself, usually including your name, initials, and mailing address. Here's how that information can be used in a program, which provides good reasons for keeping the information up-to-date:

- **User name.** When you save a file, the program saves properties, or information about the file. When you create and save a file, the application uses the user name information to identify you as the file's creator.

File Properties Applications track properties for each file including the file type, name of the author (user name), creation date, size, and more. You can usually enter key words to make it easier to search for the file, as well as comments about the file. To view the current file's properties and edit property settings when allowable, choose **File**, **Properties**.

- **Initials.** Even though the program tracks your files by your user name, it also may need your initials to label comments, notes, annotations, or revisions you make in a file, if the program automates such features.
- **Address.** Address information is particularly useful in word processors, where you create documents like fax cover sheets, return addresses on envelopes, and reports that may include your address. Some templates and other document creation tools will automatically insert the address information you enter in your program's Preferences or Options dialog box.

Using Editing Options

Editing options give the program information that makes it easier for you to enter and edit data. Figure 14.2 shows an example—the editing options in Excel 97. You can turn editing options on and off as you prefer. For example, if your mouse is acting a little sticky, you can turn off drag-and-drop editing (the **Allow Cell Drag and Drop** check box in Figure 14.2). You can specify settings like a default number of decimal points for values you type in spreadsheet programs, whether information you type replaces the current selection in a word processor, and more. In some programs, you can set the number of Undo levels or whether the application will display a dialog box asking you to verify certain edits.

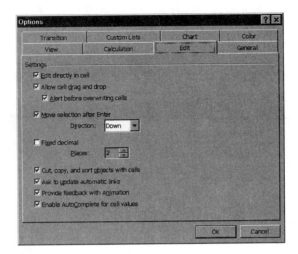

Figure 14.2 If you hate drag and drop or another editing feature, you can turn it off in an options or preferences page like this.

Saving Options

Most programs offer several options with regard to saving, the most important feature in a program. (If you couldn't save, all your computing efforts would be wasted.) Figure 14.3 shows some example saving options from Word 97.

The most important saving options offer file protection features. Look for a check box that, when enabled, has the program make a backup copy of every file you save. Then, even if the main file is lost or corrupted, you can open the backup file to recover at least part of your work. It's a good idea to turn on this option. The backup files that are created have a different file name extension— such as .bak—than the normal document.

TIP **Clean Up Time** Even though backup files are good, it's probably unnecessary to keep them for files that are several months old. So, delete old backup files. Also, keep in mind that keeping a backup of each file doubles the amount of disk space used to store your files. This is further reason to prune out old backup files.

Another feature that applications commonly offer is automatic saving (called saving AutoRecover info in Microsoft applications). When you enable this feature, you can specify a time interval for saving. Then, each time that

315

designated interval passes, the application will automatically save the file (as long as you've previously saved and named it). While this feature causes the application to "pause" as it saves, it still offers worthwhile protection. You should set up autosave to save your file every five to ten minutes.

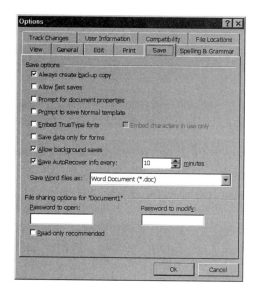

Figure 14.3 To add saving protection, turn on automatic saving (saving AutoRecovery info) and specify that the application should create a backup file when you save.

You may also find options for assigning a password to saved files. (You have to change these settings for each file to assign unique passwords.) Simply type your password in the text box that's provided.

TIP **It's Still Your Job** Don't be lulled into a false sense of security if you have saving options turned on. When an application creates a backup file, that backup file only contains your changes up until the backup. If you work for 25 more minutes without saving and then a power loss zaps your main file, your backup is 25 minutes old and you've lost that much work.

This last lesson in the part introduced you to common program options you can adjust to work more effectively, including viewing, editing, and saving options, as well as user information. The next lesson leads off Part 4 by giving you an overview of the Internet, the subject of the part as a whole.

Using the Internet

A Brief Internet Tour

In this lesson, you learn what the Internet has to offer once you connect to it using your modem.

Go Online: An Overview

No person is an island. Although you can use your computer in isolation if you prefer, adding a modem to your system enables you to connect with other users. You may have heard a lot of buzz lately about "going online" or "the Information Superhighway." If your computer has a modem (and you have a telephone line that you can connect it to), then the amazing world of electronic online communication is wide open to you.

In the last few years, millions of people have jumped online for the first time to search for information and graphics, get up-to-date reports on the news and stocks, buy and sell things, and chat or exchange messages with other users. This section introduces you to the *Internet*, which gives you the broadest possible online options today.

 Internet A collection of computers world wide that are connected for storing, sharing, and routing various kinds of information. Once you've connected to the Internet using your computer and modem, you can exchange e-mail, browse for information, retrieve files, and more.

The lessons in this part are akin to dipping your toe into water—a *large* body of water. You're not going to learn everything you'll need to know to be proficient using the Net (short for Internet). Dozens of large books cover the Internet or various aspects of the Internet. What you will find in this part, however, are the basics of getting connected and moving around.

How the Internet Is Organized

Think of each Internet *site* as a "library" of information from various sources. Not every library offers the same lineup of books and magazines. For example, while your neighborhood library may offer a lot to you, it may not have the Standard & Poor's stock information you need. You may have to go to another, larger library to find that information.

Internet Site or Server   The individual systems connected to the Net are called *servers* or *sites*, because these computers are actually servers for local networks.

Similarly, each Internet site offers a unique set of information or services; connecting to the site only gives you access to its unique information or features. Over time, several different server types and services have evolved as standards on the Internet.

E-mail, Internet Relay Chat (IRC), and newsgroups are services users can access to exchange relatively private, instant, and public messages, respectively. File Transfer Protocol (FTP) and the World Wide Web (Web) are repositories for many different kinds of information such as files you can download or reference information—and each uses a different method for storage, organization, and access of that information.

Most newer users are interested primarily in working with the Web, e-mail, and newsgroups, so that's what I'll focus on in this part of the book. You use a different kind of software to work with each type of service. For example, you use an e-mail program to manage e-mail. You'll learn about software for using the Web, e-mail, and newsgroups in later lessons.

Things to Do Online

You need to understand how the Internet is organized to know how to navigate once you're connected. But knowing the lay of the land doesn't tell you what you can do once you're there. In case curiosity alone isn't enough to entice you to explore the Internet, consider these ways that you could exploit the Net once you're there:

- **Read news.** Numerous Web sites offer hourly updates about current events, as well as specialized areas for business, weather, sports, and other information, as shown in the example in Figure 1.1. You can subscribe to electronic magazines and various news services.

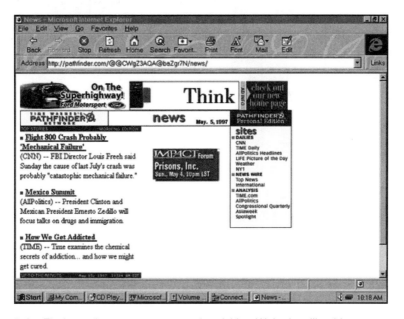

Figure 1.1 Find out about current events by visiting Web sites like this one.

- **Read and post general messages**. You can find these in *newsgroups*, online areas where users go to share information about special topics like having a home business. You can read existing messages, respond to existing discussions, or post new messages of your own.
- **Exchange electronic mail (e-mail)**. Send a letter to one or more users, without licking a single stamp (see Figure 1.2).
- **Exchange files**. You can *upload* files (send them to another computer) for other users, or *download* files (get them from another computer) that you want. You may swap original documents, shareware or freeware programs, graphic files, sound files, and more in this way. You can send files to other users via e-mail, or often download a file directly from a Web site.

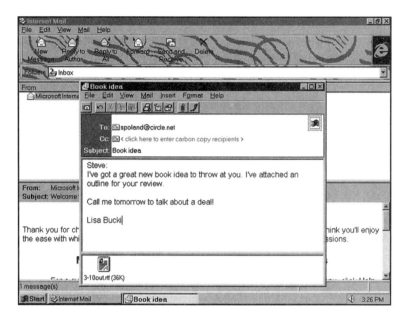

Figure 1.2   Send an e-mail message directly to a friend, relative, or colleague.

- **Talk live online with other users**. Some sites offer live chat areas where users can go to meet others from around the world to talk about a specific topic. You'll increasingly find chat areas on the Internet, but you may need to install special software to join. A special type of chat service on the Internet called Internet Relay Chat (IRC) enables you to join a topic or "channel" for chatting. You can download shareware and freeware IRC software for chatting via IRC. When you're chatting, type in your message, and it appears instantly for all the other users in the chat area, who can reply immediately.

- **Buy stuff, and more**. Visit a variety of stores on the Web (see Figure 1.3) and spend, spend, spend. You can also make your travel reservations or purchase other services online.

CAUTION

Plastic Alert   It's most convenient to pay by credit card when you make a purchase from a Web site. This is relatively safe when you're purchasing from a large retailer. In other instances where security is lacking, hackers may be able to steal your credit card number as it's transmitted. If you have any doubts, don't send your credit card number, Social Security Number, or any other private information via the Web.

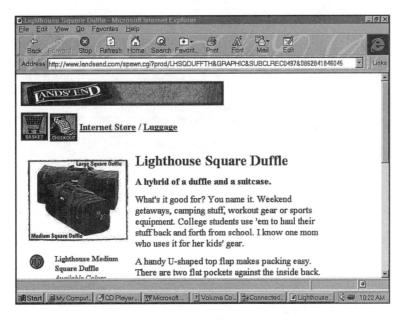

Figure 1.3 Web sites are springing up to sell you just about anything!

- **Work smarter, not harder.** You can find a variety of databases and reference books online so you can find facts when you need them—whether for a school project, a client proposal, or to settle a bet.

- **Play a little**. Many Web sites offer game areas where you can play online by yourself or against online opponents, win contests, and download games for your personal use.

How to Find an ISP to Log On

New computer systems or modems purchased today generally come with software and offers to join major online services (like America Online) or find an Internet service provider (ISP) so you can sign up for an Internet account. ISPs generally charge a flat monthly fee of $20-$25 for Internet access. Once you have an Internet account and the right software, you can access the Web, e-mail, newsgroups, and other Internet services. Often, new computer systems already have Microsoft Windows 95 Internet software installed.

If your modem or PC didn't come with a kit for setting up an Internet account, another option to get connected is to buy an Internet startup kit from your local computer store. You can install the software and dial in with your modem to set up your account with a particular service provider.

To find an ISP on your own, you can ask a computer store salesperson or your friends who are already wired about Internet providers. You may find local providers in the Yellow Pages under "Computers" or "Internet." Another way is to visit your local bookstore and check out books that offer Internet sign-up kits or Internet magazines (which are littered with ads and offers from companies that want to get you connected). Finally, major long distance companies like MCI (Network MCI) and AT&T (AT&T WorldNet) offer Internet access; these can be convenient, as your Internet account will be billed along with your long distance.

A typical ISP account starts at about $20 per month for either unlimited access (meaning you can be online for as many hours per month as you'd like) or for a generous allotment of hours—120 per month or so. Make sure you understand how many hours per month the monthly fee covers, because beyond that amount, you'll start paying per-hour charges that can accumulate quickly. If you will be using your account for business reasons or research purposes, or several family members will be using the account, the best bargain is probably an unlimited access account.

 TIP   **Find Me an ISP**   You also can let the Windows 95 Internet Connection Wizard help you find an ISP, as the next lesson explains. Make sure you ask for a PPP account. (The ISP will know what you mean.)

When you get an account with an ISP, be sure to ask for a PPP (Point-to-Point Protocol) connection. This kind of account works more smoothly under Windows 95, and is the standard today. Make sure the access phone number you get for dialing in to your account is a local call. If you travel a lot, you'll want a provider that has a toll-free access number, too.

In this lesson, you learned the basics about what the Internet offers and why it's so popular. The next lesson explains how to use the Internet Connection Wizard to connect to your ISP and the Internet.

Getting Started with the Internet Connection Wizard

This lesson shows you how to set up Windows 95 to dial into and connect with the Internet, and provides the steps for launching and closing that Internet connection.

Introducing the Internet Connection Wizard

Windows 95 can help you establish a Dial-Up Networking TCP/IP connection for dialing up and connecting to the Internet. Dial-Up Networking enables your system to save a set of dialing instructions (phone number and so on) so you can quickly connect to another computer. What you need to know about TCP/IP is that it connects you to your Internet Service Provider (ISP) in such a way that you can then run Windows-based graphical software, like an e-mail program, to work with the Internet, by pointing and clicking.

ISP An Internet Service Provider is a company with a computer server that has a high-speed connection to the Internet. When you get an account with the ISP, you can connect to the Internet by using your modem to connect to the ISP's system. The ISP gives you an e-mail address, stores and manages your e-mail, and more.

In the initial release of Windows 95, setting up a TCP/IP connection was usually a manual process. Later, Microsoft introduced the *Internet Connection Wizard*, which walks you through the setup process, step by step. The Internet Connection Wizard is installed by default on new systems with the latest Windows 95

OEM Service Release 2 (OSR 2) version, along other TCP/IP and connection software. The next two sections show you how to use the Internet Connection Wizard to establish your connection and how to connect when you need to. The Internet Connection Wizard can also help you find an ISP if you don't already have one.

 TIP   **Missing Wizard**   If you don't have the Internet Connection Wizard on your system or it doesn't appear the first time you double-click the desktop's Internet icon, you'll need to install the latest version of Internet Explorer, version 3.02. You can have a friend download it for you from **http://www.microsoft.com/ msdownload/ieplatform/iewin95.htm**. Then install it as described in Lesson 1 of Part III, which explains how to install new programs under Windows 95.

Setting Up If You Already Have an ISP

You've signed up for an account with an ISP, but you're not sure how to connect to it. One option is to use the setup software that your ISP provided. ISP setup software usually works fine, but it's not bulletproof. And, it doesn't always take advantage of Internet capabilities that are already available in Windows 95.

You will need a few pieces of information from your Internet Service Provider to set up the connection. Before you begin the wizard to set up your connection, gather this information:

- **ISP phone number**. This is the number your modem must dial to connect. Your ISP might have different phone numbers for different connection speeds: 14,400bps, 28,800bps, and so on. If your ISP provides different dial-up numbers for different modem speeds, make sure you get the number for the fastest connection your modem can handle. Otherwise, you won't be able to connect at the best speed possible.

- **User name and password**. Your ISP provides these when you create your account.

- **IP (Internet Protocol) addresses**. These are special numbers used to identify your ISP's servers on the Internet. IP addresses always have four sets of one to three numbers each, separated by periods. For example, 207.79.160.1 is an IP address. You need to know whether your ISP automatically (dynamically) assigns an ISP to your system when you log in. You also need to know the IP address for your ISP's Domain Name Service (DNS) server.

- **Login method**. If your ISP offers the PAP or CHAP protocols for logging in (you don't really need to know what these acronyms mean), you can set up your connection so it remembers your user name and password and provides them automatically when you connect.

Once you have the information you need, follow these steps to set up your connection:

1. Click **Start**, point to **Programs**, and point to **Accessories**. On the Accessories menu, point to **Internet Tools**, and click **Get on the Internet** (or **Internet Setup Wizard**). Alternatively, you can double-click the **Internet** icon on the desktop if you haven't previously used the Internet Connection Wizard (if you have, this icon launches Internet Explorer instead).

2. The first Internet Connection Wizard (ICW) dialog box appears. Click **Next**.

3. In the next ICW dialog box, select how to set up your computer. Because these steps assume you already have an account with an ISP, click **Manual**, then click **Next**.

4. In the ICW Welcome dialog box, click **Next**.

5. Assuming you're a home user and will be connecting to the Internet with a modem, leave **Connect Using My Phone Line** selected in the next ICW dialog box, then click **Next**.

6. In the next ICW dialog box, click **No, I Don't Want to Use Windows Messaging**. This is because you're going to use Internet Mail, which comes with Windows 95 OSR 2, instead. Click **Next**.

A Modem Detour   After step 6, the Internet Connection Wizard may prompt you to select your modem. If it does so, choose your modem and click Next to continue with the Internet Connection Wizard.

CAUTION

7. ICW tells you it's going to begin installing files. Click **Next**. If Windows 95 prompts you to insert your installation CD or disks, do so.

8. ICW begins prompting you for information about your ISP. The first screen asks you for the **Name of Service Provider**. Enter it, then click **Next**.

9. In the next ICW dialog box, shown in Figure 2.1, enter the phone number for your ISP, including the area code. If your ISP doesn't offer PAP or CHAP login, click to check the **Bring Up Terminal Window After Dialing** check box. (This displays a window when you connect so you can enter your username and password.) Click **Next**.

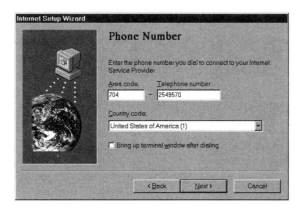

Figure 2.1   Enter the phone number your modem will use to dial the ISP.

10. In the next window, enter your **User Name** and **Password**. These are both supplied by the ISP; you can't just choose any user name or password. Click **Next**.

11. Most users can normally just click **Next** at the IP Address window that appears next. However, if your ISP doesn't dynamically assign an IP address, click the **Always Use the Following** option button and enter an IP address before clicking Next. Again, if your ISP requires you to enter a specific IP address, the ISP will provide you the correct IP when you establish your account.

12. Next, enter the **DNS Server** IP addresses for your ISP, as shown in Figure 4.2. These settings are not optional, and your ISP provides the correct addresses. Click **Next**.

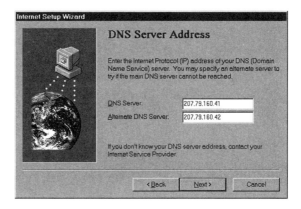

Figure 2.2   Enter the DNS server addresses your ISP provides.

13. At the ICW dialog box that tells you the connection is complete, click **Finish**.

14. At the dialog box that prompts you to restart your computer, click **Yes**. The computer restarts and updates your system's settings.

Getting Help Finding an ISP

If you don't yet have an ISP account and prefer some help in that direction, the Internet Connection Wizard can provide some suggestions. Grab the credit card that you want your new Internet account to bill to, then follow these steps:

1. Click **Start**, point to **Programs**, and point to **Accessories**. On the Accessories menu, point to **Internet Tools**, and click **Get on the Internet** (or **Internet Setup Wizard**). Alternatively, you can double-click the **Internet** icon on the desktop, if you haven't previously used the Internet Connection Wizard (if you have, this icon launches Internet Explorer instead).

2. The first Internet Connection Wizard (ICW) dialog box appears. Click **Next**. In the next ICW dialog box, select how to set up your computer.

3. If you don't already have an account with an ISP, click **Automatic** and click **Next** to continue.

4. At the Begin Automatic Setup screen, click **Next**.

5. The Location Information screen prompts you to enter your area code and the first three digits in your phone number. Do so, then click **Next**.

6. The Internet Connection Wizard downloads a list of ISPs in your area (based on the phone number information you provided in the last step) from the Microsoft Internet Referral Server. When the download finishes, the list of ISPs appears on-screen, as shown in Figure 2.3. Click the **Sign Me Up** button next to the service provider you want.

7. The Wizard dials the ISP. An Account Registration screen appears. Follow its instructions to create your account, then follow the remaining Internet Connection Wizard instructions that appear after you finish signing up. If the Internet Connection Wizard doesn't restart after the ISP sign up, follow the steps in the preceding section to create your Internet connection.

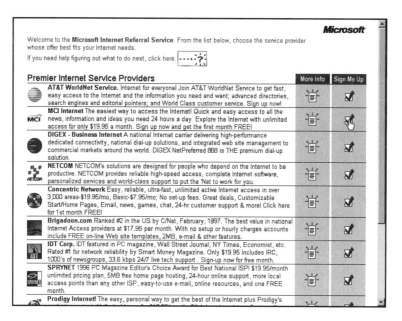

Figure 2.3 Choose an ISP with which you'd like to set up an account.

Launching and Closing Your Internet Connection

You can't stay continuously connected to your ISP. First, most of us don't leave our computers on 24 hours a day, so you can't be connected while the computer's off and the modem isn't powered. Also, even though an ISP account may be "unlimited access," that doesn't mean you can remain connected continuously. Your ISP can see whether you're actively using your connection, or whether the connection is sitting idle; if it is idle, the ISP will disconnect you to enable another customer to log on because ISPs have a finite number of modems.

To connect to the Internet when you need to and then disconnect when you've finished working, follow these steps:

1. If you see Internet icon on the desktop (meaning that Internet Explorer is installed), you can simply double-click that icon to display the Connect To dialog box (see step 4). After you connect, Internet Explorer launches.

2. If you don't want to launch Explorer but do want to connect, click **Start**, point to **Programs**, and point to **Accessories**. On the Accessories menu, click **Dial-Up Networking**.

3. In the Dial-up Networking window, double-click the icon for your Internet connection. (It has the name you entered for your ISP in the Internet Connection Wizard.)

4. In the Connect To dialog box (Figure 2.4), click **Connect**. The modem dials, and Windows sends your logon information to the ISP. (If specified by your connection, a terminal window displays; when you're prompted, enter your user name and press Enter, then enter your password and click **Continue**.)

TIP **Password Preservation**   If the Internet connection you create can't remember your ISP password, it may be because you need to set up a passwords file under Windows 95. To do so, choose **Start**, **Settings**, **Control Panel**. Double-click the **Passwords** icon, then click the **Change Windows Password** button. Type a new password in the **New Password** and **Confirm New Password** text boxes of the Change Windows Password dialog box, then click **OK** twice. Your Internet connection should then be able to save your logon password. If you get tired of typing the Windows password each time you start Windows, repeat the password process to display the Change Windows Password dialog box. Type the existing password in the Old Password text box, then leave the New Password and Confirm New Password text boxes blank. Click **OK** twice. The password file will still exist, but you won't have to type a password to log on to Windows.

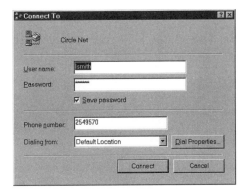

Figure 2.4   Click Connect to connect to your ISP.

5. The Connection Established dialog box appears, providing information about your connection. Click **Close**.

6. To close your connection, double-click the connection icon at the right end of the taskbar, then click the **Disconnect** button. Windows logs off from your ISP and hangs up the modem.

 TIP **Connection Shortcut** Drag the icon for your Internet connection from the Dial-Up Networking window to the desktop to create a shortcut for it. Then, you can simply double-click the shortcut to connect.

This lesson showed you the easiest way to set up your system to connect to an Internet Service Provider (ISP), how to find an ISP, and how to connect to and disconnect from the ISP and therefore the Internet. The next lesson shows you how to start and close your Web browser.

Launch and Exit Your Web Browser

To learn to launch and close a Web browser program or adjust its settings, follow the steps in this lesson.

Looking at Browsers

Web browser software enables you to access information on World Wide Web (usually known as just plain Web) sites in the Internet. Web sites are the equivalent of a graphical user interface for Internet information. Not only can you read the text provided on the Web, but you also can click icons and special links to jump from topic to topic. The Web also offers graphics that illustrate or simply decorate the information.

The Web browser software you may have depends in some part on the system you bought and how you chose to find an ISP. If you bought an Internet startup kit, it provided some type of Web browser software. Most ISPs provide Web browser software with their service. Most new computer systems come with at least one Web browser software program installed (my newest system, purchased in April 1997, had two Web browsers).

The top two Web browser programs are Netscape Navigator from Netscape (which is part of the larger package of Netscape Communicator, and is now in version 4.01) and Microsoft's Internet Explorer (now in version 3.02, which offers minor updates to versions 3.0 and 3.01; a new 4.0 version is expected in fall 1997). You also may encounter the Mosaic browser. Mosaic actually comes in different versions published by different sources. Variations include SPRY Mosaic, Air Mosaic, NCSA Mosaic, and Spyglass Enhanced Mosaic. Other browsers include NetCruiser and NetManage Chameleon.

To make it easy to follow the Web browser lessons in this part, I'll be using Internet Explorer to demonstrate steps. Internet Explorer 3.0x comes with all new PCs that have Windows 95 OSR 2 installed, so many new users will in fact have access to this software.

TIP   **Not My Software**   Even though the lessons in this part may not show the Internet Web browser, e-mail, and news reader software you use, the general steps and principles apply no matter what software you're using. At the very least, these lessons will give you an idea of where to look for a command you need.

Launching and Exiting Internet Explorer

By default, the Internet Explorer software (and Internet Mail and Internet News, other Internet software installed with Windows 95 OSR 2) is set up to automatically dial the Internet when you start the software. This saves you the trouble of launching the Internet connection (which you created with the Internet Connection Wizard) before launching the software. Similarly, when you shut down Explorer, it will ask whether you'd like to shut down your Internet connection.

The following steps assume Internet Explorer is set up to launch and close your Internet connection. If it doesn't presently work this way, see the final section in this lesson, "Browser Settings You Need to Know About," to learn how to turn on automatic connection.

TIP   **Online Action**   Once you're connected (even if you launched the connection before starting a program), you can start one or all of the Internet software programs simultaneously. Each can then work with information on the Internet. For example, you can run both your Web browser and your e-mail program. (But, if you have a slower system or have several other applications running as well, your system might slow down or give you out of memory errors.)

Launching Explorer and Connecting to the Web

Follow these steps to connect to the Internet and start Internet Explorer (assuming you've set up your Internet connection as described in the last lesson):

1. Click **Start**, point to **Programs**, and click **Internet Explorer**. Or, double-click the **Internet** icon on the desktop. (If you're using another Web browser, look for its startup command or folder on the Programs menu, or a startup shortcut for it on the Windows 95 desktop.)

2. In the Connect To dialog box, click **Connect**. The modem dials, and Windows sends your logon information to the ISP. (Enter your logon information in the terminal window, if it appears.)

3. After the logon finishes, Internet Explorer opens automatically and takes you to the Microsoft Web site, as shown in Figure 3.1. This is the default *start page* for Internet Explorer.

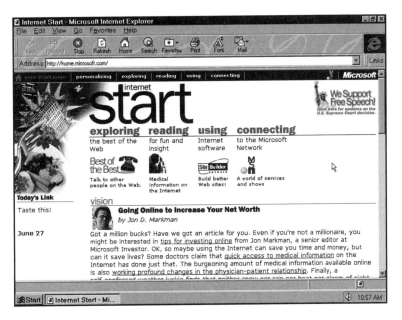

Figure 3.1 Internet Explorer launches and connects you to Microsoft's home page.

Start Page This is the Web information your Web browser displays initially, each time it connects to the Internet. The start page (called a home page in some browsers) serves as a jumping off point for your Web browsing. The start page is often the Web page of the publisher of your browser software, or the main Web site of your ISP.

335

TIP   Other Starts   To open Internet Explorer from either Internet Mail or Internet News, choose **File, Start Page**.

Shutting Down Explorer and Your Web Connection

When you're finished using Explorer or your Web browser, follow these steps to close Explorer and disconnect from the Web:

1. Open the **File** menu and select **Close**. (The command might be **File, Exit** in your browser.) You also can click the application window **Close** button.

2. At the Disconnect dialog box that asks whether to close your Internet connection (see Figure 3.2), click **Yes**. Windows logs you off and hangs up the modem.

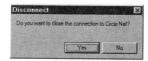

Figure 3.2   To hang up the modem, click Yes at this dialog box.

Browser Settings You Need to Know About

Like other Windows 95 applications, Web browser programs offer a variety of options for controlling how the browser, and the Web information it displays, looks and acts. In fact, the current version of Internet Explorer offers six tabs of program options.

To access the options for Internet Explorer, right-click the **Internet** icon on the desktop, then click **Properties**. Or, if Explorer is already open, choose **View, Options**. The Options dialog box for Explorer appears. (In your browser, look for an Options menu, or an Options or Preferences command to find the setup settings you can adjust.) Without describing each and every option (that would take a few lessons), here's a look at each of the six tabs of options:

- **General**. This tab offers settings for controlling how Multimedia objects, Colors, and Links are treated in the Web information you see. You can turn off Multimedia features so information downloads to your computer and displays more quickly, or choose the colors for the Web text, background, and links that you click (see the next lesson to learn about links). The Toolbar options enable you to specify which parts of the Explorer toolbar appear on-screen.

- **Connection**. This tab, shown in Figure 4.3, helps you set up Internet Explorer so that it will dial the Internet automatically when you open it, among other things. Make sure to check **Connect to the Internet as Needed**, then choose your ISP in the drop-down list below if you want Explorer to automatically dial the Internet. (Note that this setting controls automatic connection for Internet Mail and Internet News, as well). Clear the top check box to dial your ISP manually.

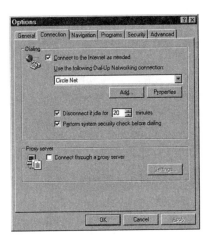

Figure 4.3 Make sure Connect to the Internet as Needed is checked if you want Explorer and other Internet software to dial your ISP.

- **Navigation**. The top area of this page lets you specify what Web page (information) Explorer uses as the Start Page, the Search Page (used for searching the Web), and other pages. Click your choice from the **Page** drop-down list, then enter the **Address** for the page. You'll learn more about pages and Web addresses in the next lesson. You also can keep a History list of pages you've visited using the settings at the bottom of the tab. If you're doing a lot of research and may need to jump back to a page, you may want to keep a history list for up to 20 days (the pages you've visited in the last 20 days). Otherwise, I recommend reducing the days tracked in the history to 3-5, because history links do tend to eat up disk space.

- **Programs**. This tab enables you to specify programs to use for reading e-mail and newsgroups when you choose to launch an e-mail or news program from within Explorer. For example, choose **Internet Mail** as the Mail choice if you want Explorer to launch Internet Mail if you open the **Go** menu or click the **Mail** button, and then click **Read Mail**. Similarly, you can choose Viewers to tell Explorer what program on your system to use to view different kinds of files encountered on the Web.

- **Security**. This tab enables you to set up a number of security options, including: Settings that help you restrict what children can view when using your computer to browse the Web; tools called *certificates* that help your computer check the security features used by Web sites and display warnings if you may be sending information to a suspect site; and settings that control whether certain active (animated and programming) content, which may contain viruses, can download on your computer.

- **Advanced**. This tab offers still more security settings and other advanced settings. You can specify which warnings Internet Explorer displays. For example, click to check **Warn Before Sending Over an Open Connection** if you want Explorer to ask you to verify any information you send over the Web. You can determine which folder on your system holds temporary Internet files (files such as pages and graphics that download to your system so you can redisplay pages more quickly) and how much space to use for those files. You can even clear the folder. A few other miscellaneous options appear at the bottom of the tab.

CAUTION

Feeling Insecure?   Web security gets a lot of coverage in the computing, business, and general media. It's true that there are unscrupulous folks out there, as in any business. Most Web browsers now offer multiple security features to prompt you before, say, you send information like a credit card number over the Web. I can't cover all the security issues and options here, so consult the online help system for your Web browser. However, companies doing business on the Internet are continuously making safety improvements, particularly in the area of credit card transactions. So, you can feel more safe using the Internet for purchases today than you could even a year ago.

This lesson showed you how to launch and close the Web browser that comes with Windows 95 OSR 2—Internet Explorer—and how to access Explorer settings. The next lesson explains how to move around the Web with Explorer.

Jumping to a Web Page

This lesson explains how to use your Web browser to display information on the Web via links, Web addresses called URLs, and browser buttons.

Understanding Web Navigation

The Web is made up of special sites along the Internet that support a technology that enables you to perform *Web browsing*—using links and special addresses to move to and view. On the Web, information is stored in what are called "pages." Each page is actually a file in html format; when you display a page, you are actually displaying a specific html file stored on a Web server computer.

HTML The acronym for HyperText Markup Language, HTML formatting enables a Web document not only to display graphics but also to include links to other pages. Clicking a link displays the page that the link points to. Html files have either the .html or .htm file name extension.

When a Web page appears on-screen, you can use scroll bars to scroll through and read its contents. You can print the page's information, or even use the **File**, **Save** or **Save As** command to save the page to your hard disk.

The Web wouldn't be too useful if it only let you display a single page. In fact, the easy steps for moving among pages, much as you browse the pages of a magazine, lead to the name Web *browser*. You can navigate from one place to another by selecting a *link* that appears on a Web page. A link might be a picture or some highlighted or underlined text that appears on-screen. You just click the picture, highlighted text, or underlined text, and your Web browser links (or jumps) you to the requested spot on the Internet. With a Web browser such as Netscape Navigator or Internet Explorer, surfing the Web is as simple and easy as using Windows.

From your start page, which appears when you launch your Web browser and connect to the Internet, you can go to other pages on the Web in one of several ways:

- By clicking a *link*.
- By entering the *Web address* of the page you want to view.
- By using browser buttons to move between pages you've viewed during your current browsing session.
- By selecting a previously saved address from a list.

Links are by far the easiest way to explore the World Wide Web. Links are graphic pictures or specially highlighted text that automatically jump you to a different Web page when you click them. In this lesson, you'll learn how to use links, Web addresses, and browser buttons to explore the Web. Lesson 5 will explain how to select previously saved addresses.

TIP   **AOL and CSi**   Even if you're connecting to the Web via America Online (AOL) or CompuServe Interactive (CSi), you'll be able to use many of the browsing techniques described in this lesson. Current versions of the AOL and CSi software have built-in Web browsers with some funky features, but they still let you work with links and Web addresses.

Using Links to Browse

When you browse, you'll see that many pages contain specially highlighted text called links. The highlighted text represents a topic; to find more information about that topic, click the link. Text links on a Web page are marked in blue by default. That is, if you see some text that's blue and has an underline, that text is a link to another Web page. When you use a particular link and then return to the page holding the link, your Web browser changes the link's text color to purple so you can easily tell which links you've already explored. Of course, like many things on the Web, even this small convention is changing. So you might run into pages that use colors other than blue and purple (like red, pink, or anything else) to mark unused and used links. In addition to text links, you'll find graphical pictures that are links. When you click some of these graphic links, a border around the graphic changes color to tell you you've visited the link. But, other pictures don't have a changing border, so it is harder to tell if you've used one of those links.

TIP **Address Preview** When you move the mouse pointer over a link, the address (or a shortcut representing the address) of the Web page will display when clicked, appears in the status bar at the bottom of your Web browser screen. This gives you some idea of where you'll be going if you decide to click the link at some point.

Follow these same basic steps for using links no matter which Web browser you're using:

1. Start your Web browser so that it connects to the Internet. If you need help connecting to the Internet or starting your Web browser, see the previous task.

2. When you move the mouse over a link, the pointer changes to a hand. The address of or shortcut for the Web page it links to appears in the Web browser status bar, as shown in Figure 4.1.

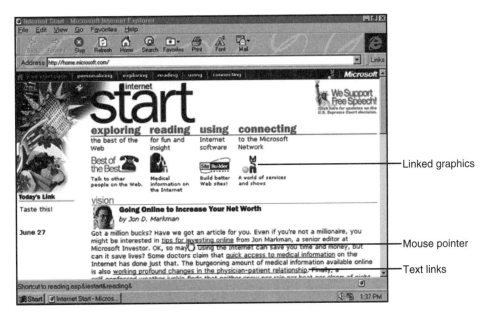

Figure 4.1 Internet Explorer launches and connects you to Microsoft's home page.

3. To jump to (display) a linked Web page, click the link.

4. Some links are graphic images instead of text. To verify that a graphic represents a link, point to the graphic. The mouse pointer changes to a

pointing hand, you see a Web address or shortcut in the status bar, and may even see a pop-up label for the link. To connect to the linked Web page, just click the graphic.

5. Continue clicking text and graphical links to jump to other Web pages that you can read and print.

Handling a Failed Link

Sometimes when you try to connect to a Web page, it doesn't display completely (it fails to load). Normally, when you click a link or enter an address to jump to in Internet Explorer, a comet spins around the big E icon in the upper-right corner of the screen to cue you that the connection is active and information is downloading to your system. (Other browsers use other animated icons.) If the animated icon stops moving before all the graphics have displayed on-screen—leaving unsightly placeholder boxes—it means that the connection has failed and the page won't finish loading.

If that happens, you have two options to get things moving again:

- Click the **Refresh** button at the top of the Explorer window. This button might read "Reload" or something else in another browser.

- If the page fails to load after you click Refresh, click **Stop** to discontinue loading the Web page. Click the **Back** button to redisplay the link if needed, then try clicking the link again.

 TIP **Error!** If you click a link and get a plain gray page with black text telling you the linked page couldn't be found, click the **Back** button as described in the last section of this lesson to back up.

Using a Web Address to Display a Specific Web Page

Each Web page has its own Web address or *URL* (*Uniform Resource Locator*). You'll see and hear about Web addresses in any number of TV, print, radio, and billboard advertisements. A typical URL looks like this:

http://pages.nyu.edu/~liaos/indigo.html

You can jump directly to the Web page you want by simply typing its address (if you know it) into your Web browser. Every address or URL (pronounced "earl") has two parts: a content identifier and a location.

- **Content Identifier.** The content identifier (or content-ID for short), tells you what protocol (computer communications method) must be used to display the page. For Web pages, the content-ID is http:// because Web pages are transferred and displayed using HyperText Transfer Protocol (HTTP). So, most of the addresses you'll enter into your Web browser will begin with http://. Web browsers also support other protocols such as ftp://, gopher://, telnet://, and news://. These protocols connect you to other parts of the Internet besides the Web. For example, you might connect to an ftp site to download (receive) a file. (If you're sure that the address is an address for a Web page, you can often leave off the content identifier and just type the location portion of the address, described next, to jump to the Web page.)

- **Location.** The second part of every URL identifies the location of the page and looks suspiciously like a folder or directory path—which is exactly what it is. As noted earlier in the lesson, every Web page is actually a file that exists on some Internet computer. These directory paths follow the UNIX format, using forward slashes (/) in place of the backslashes (\) you're used to seeing in Windows. The paths can also contain periods (.). The address

  http://www.conline.com/txmall/garden.html

  indicates that the file garden.html is located on the Internet computer known as www.conline.com in the txmall directory.

CAUTION

No Page, Please   In some cases, you don't have to include an actual Web page in a URL—you stop at a particular directory. That doesn't mean the address won't work or is wrong. It just means that when you specify that directory, a default page (usually something like index.html) will display.

TIP   **URL Management**   Once you enter an address into your Web browser, you can save it so that you can revisit it later, as described in the next lesson. If you don't know the address of a particular Web page or even which pages you might want to view, you can search for applicable pages using a Web search tool such as Yahoo! (see Lesson 7). You can also get addresses for hot Web sites from any computing or Internet magazine; even newspapers, business magazines, and lifestyle and hobby magazines offer Web addresses.

Follow these steps to jump directly to the URL of your choice:

1. Type the address (URL) of the page you want to go to in the **Address** text box near the top of the browser window (see Figure 4.2). This box may have a different name in your browser, such as **Go To/Location** in Netscape Navigator. Make sure that you use forward slashes (/) to separate the parts of the address.

Figure 4.2 Enter an URL in the text box near the top of your browser window; this is the URL for Que's Web page.

2. Press **Enter**. Your Web browser sends a request to the computer where that page is located. The other computer transmits the page, which your browser displays on-screen.

 TIP **Stop the Start Page** If you're like me and don't like to wait for the start page to load because you're anxious to jump to a specific page, click the **Stop** button, then enter the address to jump to.

Using Navigation Buttons

Because it can take from several seconds to several minutes for a Web page to download to your PC for display, the Web pages you view are stored on your hard disk temporarily. That way if you ever need to see a Web page again during your current Internet browsing session, you can redisplay it from the hard disk, and it pops back up in about a second—no need to wait for the page to be copied (downloaded) to your computer again.

Although you'll learn more ways to revisit pages in the next lesson, the easiest method to use is to click the appropriate button on your browser's toolbar. By convention, these are called the Back and Forward buttons (see Figure 4.3). Using a Web browser's Back and Forward buttons is a lot like flipping through pages in a book. To return to a previously viewed page, you move backward in the "book." After moving backward, you can move forward through your previously viewed Web pages.

The Forward and
Back buttons

Figure 4.3 Use the Back and Forward buttons at the left end of the toolbar to redisplay pages you've recently viewed.

Here's how to work with these browser buttons:

- To return to the Web page you just viewed, click the **Back** button. The **Forward** button becomes enabled.
- To return to the page you were on before you clicked the Back button, click the **Forward** button.
- If you've previously viewed several pages, you can click the **Back** button as many times as you need to return to a previously viewed page.
- As with the Back button, you can click the **Forward** button as many times as necessary to return to the page you'd like.

CAUTION

Grayed Out   If the Forward (or Backward) button is gray, one of two situations has occurred. First, it's possible that you haven't jumped around enough for one of the buttons to be active. For example, you have to click the Back button at least once to be able to use the Forward button. The second possibility is that you have moved to the end (or the beginning) of the succession of pages you've viewed. For example, if you've clicked Back so many times that your start page appears on-screen, you can't back up any further and the Back button becomes grayed.

345

You just learned basic browsing skills—using a link, using a Web address, and using browser buttons—for displaying pages on the Web. The next lesson shows you how to save links to your favorite pages.

Track and Visit Your Favorite Pages

This lesson shows you how to navigate even more quickly by jumping to a page you've recently viewed or creating a command to jump to a favorite page.

Jumping to a Previously Viewed Web Page

As you change from one page to another on the Web, you create a kind of working history of where you've been. Your Web browser saves this history for you, making it easy for you to return to any previously viewed page. In fact, as you saw near the end of Lesson 3 in this part, you can control how many days of history your Web browser tracks. So even if you visited a page several days ago, you can check and see if it's still in the history rather than looking up its Web address (URL) all over again.

While the last lesson showed you how to use the Back and Forward buttons to jump between previously viewed pages, those buttons only move you one page at a time. So, for example, going back five pages means that you have to click the Back button five times.

Your Browser As in the last two lessons, this lesson uses Microsoft's Internet Explorer to illustrate browser techniques. The terminology, commands, and steps in your browser will be slightly different.

CAUTION

It's much easier to jump directly to a particular previously viewed page. You can use one of these three methods to do so, with the third method providing the most detailed access to pages you've visited previously:

- After you enter an address in the Address or Go to/Location text box near the top of your browser screen, your Web browser keeps it in a list of recently typed addresses. To return to a previously entered address (even one from an earlier session), click the **Address** drop-down arrow and select an address from the list, as shown in Figure 5.1. (This drop-down list may be called **Netsite/Location** or another name in your browser.)

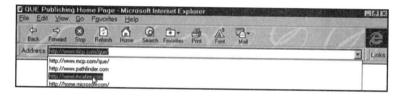

Figure 5.1 Use the Address drop-down list (or your browser's equivalent), to revisit an URL you've previously typed.

- You can jump directly to a previously viewed page by opening the **Go** menu and selecting the page you want to visit from those listed at the bottom of the menu. This is a nice way to revisit pages if you prefer to recall the page by topic or title rather than by URL.

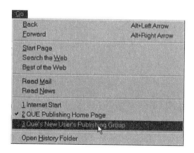

Figure 5.2 The Go menu (or your browser's equivalent) tracks previously visited pages by name.

- If you don't find the page you want using one of the last two methods, open the **Go** menu and click **Open** History folder. (In another browser like Netscape, you might choose a command like **Communicator, History** instead). The History window box appears. In the History dialog box, double-click the page you want to view, as shown in Figure 5.3. Your browser displays the page you selected. Click the **Close** button or choose **File**, **Close** to shut down the History window.

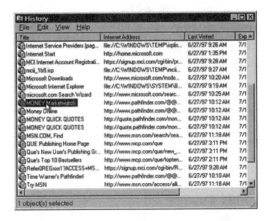

Figure 5.3 To retrace your steps, double-click a page in the History window.

Jumping to a Favorite Web Page

Web addresses (URLs) are often long and complex, which makes it difficult to enter them correctly. When you finish typing an address into your Web browser, you may not want to lose it. But there's no need to worry about that because every Web browser provides a means of saving the addresses of Web pages you like to visit.

Web addresses you save are called *favorites* or *bookmarks*. You add the URLs of your choice to the Favorites list. Then, to return to a favorite page you've marked, you select the proper favorite (or bookmark) from a list. Favorites provide a more permanent means of returning to previously visited pages. Unlike the History entries, which clear out from the list after a designated time period, each favorite you add remains on the Favorites list until you delete it at a later time.

This section explains how you can organize, create, and use Favorites in your browser.

Creating Folders to Organize the Favorites You'll Create

It's easy to collect a lot of favorites, which might leave you confused as to what some of the links lead to or be cumbersome if more than one person uses your computer to surf the Web. For that reason, a lot of Web browsers allow you to organize your favorites or bookmarks in folders. I recommend that you at least add a folder for each person using your computer before any of you starts saving favorites, so you'll build the Favorites list in an orderly way.

Follow these steps to create a folder to organize favorites:

1. Click the **Favorites** button or open the **Favorites** menu, and select **Organize Favorites**. (You might use another command like **Bookmarks**, **Organize** bookmarks in a browser other than Explorer, and the steps might vary slightly from these).

2. The Organize Favorites dialog box that appears looks like other file management dialog boxes you've seen in Windows 95. In fact, you use it to organize folders with techniques similar to the ones you saw in the Windows Explorer folder tree. In the Organize Favorites dialog box, click the **Create New Folder** button.

3. A new folder appears, with its default name highlighted, as shown in Figure 5.4. Type a name for the folder and press **Enter**.

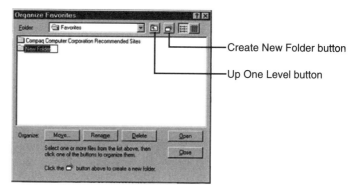

Figure 5.4   Type a name for the new folder.

4. To display the favorites in a folder, double-click the folder name. The favorites in the folder you selected appear.

5. You can click any favorite in a folder, then use the **Delete** button to delete it.

6. To move one level up the Folder list, click the **Up One Level** button.

7. To add an existing favorite to a folder, drag the favorite into the folder if both are visible. If you can't see the folder, right-click the favorite and click **Copy**. Navigate to and double-click the folder where you want the favorite to appear, then right-click in a blank area of the Folder list and click **Paste**.

8. When you're through, click the **Close** button to close the Organize Favorites dialog box.

TIP **Many Favorites** You can select multiple favorites at one time in the Organize Favorites dialog box by pressing **Ctrl** and clicking each one. Then drag the group to the folder in which you want to place the favorites, or right-click to display commands you can use on the whole group.

CAUTION **Bad Favorite** Occasionally, the address of a Web page changes. Many companies store their Web pages with an ISP. Because there's a big market in Web space rental these days, some companies tend to move from one ISP to another, causing their Web page addresses to change. So a bookmark that you can count on one week to take you to a favorite site may not be valid the next week. You can click an invalid favorite in the Organize Favorites dialog box, then click the Delete button to remove it.

Saving the URL for a Favorite Page

Now that you've created a folder to neatly house your favorites, follow these steps to add a favorite to your list:

1. First, display a Web a page whose address you want to save in your Favorites list.

2. Click the **Favorites** button or open the **Favorites** menu and select **Add To Favorites**. (The command in Navigator is **Bookmarks, Add Bookmark**.) The Add to Favorites dialog box appears.

3. (Optional) Change the name of the Web page by typing the new name in the **Name** text box.

4. To save the page to the main Favorites list, click **OK** and you're done. Otherwise, if you want to add the favorite to a folder you've created, click **Create In** button. The Add to Favorites dialog box expands. Click the folder in which you want to save your bookmark, as shown in Figure 5.5, and then click **OK**. The new favorite is added to the Favorites list.

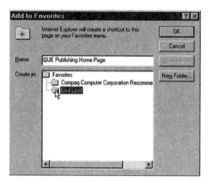

Figure 5.5   Click a folder to tell your browser to add the new favorite to it.

 TIP   Need a Folder?   You also can click the New Folder button shown in Figure 5.5 to create a new folder for the new favorite.

Selecting a Favorite Page

Favorites are useful because they're a breeze to access. To display a Web page that you've added to your Favorites list, follow these steps:

1. Click the **Favorites** button or open the **Favorites** menu.
2. If the favorite you want is stored in a folder, point to the folder name to display its submenu of favorites.
3. Click the favorite you want. The favorite Web page loads in your browser.

This lesson showed you how to save time by jumping to a page that's stored in history or by creating and using a list of favorite pages. The next lesson explains how to look at and download information from the Web.

Downloading Files and Pages

6

This lesson shows you how to download useful files and how to save Web pages and other items to your computer.

Downloading Files from the Internet

People thought TV was the greatest thing going for years—until the VCR came along. Suddenly, you didn't have to wait for a rerun of your favorite sitcom or spend big bucks on movie tickets. You could record all the shows and movies you wished, and play them back over and over. Similarly, it's great to have access to all the information on the Web, but it's even better to be able to capture some of the information on your system to be able to use and refer to again without having to travel the Web again.

Your Web browser makes downloading files a simple process. Prior to the invention of the Web (and Web browsers), you needed to use something called an FTP program if you wanted to download (receive) a file from an Internet site. But because a Web browser understands FTP protocols, you can use it to download files instead. A Web browser makes downloading files as simple as point and click: Just point to a link that's connected to a file on an FTP site, and then click to begin the downloading process. Select an existing folder into which you want the file placed or create a new folder, and the downloading begins.

 FTP FTP stands for *File Transfer Protocol*, and simply identifies a communication method computers use to exchange files on the Internet.

CAUTION

Access Denied   A Web browser can only link to "open" systems—FTP sites that allow anonymous logins. If you need to access an FTP site that allows only restricted access, you're going to need an actual FTP program.

The most common types of files you'll download from the Web are documents (such as Word .doc files and plain .txt text files) holding information a Web page publisher wants to distribute, or program files that are either free or shareware game and utility programs (for which you pay a fee on the honor system), fixes and updates for your existing software, driver files for hardware, demo programs so you can review features of a program before buying it, file compression (zip) programs for compressing files so they take up less disk space, or templates or other add-ons you can use with one of your existing application programs. You'll also find entertainment-oriented downloads—images, files, and sounds for jazzing up your Windows desktop and documents you create.

Downloading a File via a Web Link

One way to download a file from the Web is to find a Web page with the link to the file. You'll find links to document files you can download all over the Web. Likewise, a number of large software companies, smaller software publishers, and individual programmers offer links to downloadable programs. Que itself provides a software library with downloadable programs featured on the CD-ROMs bundled with some Que books.

Other Web sites specialize in offering files for download. Table 6.1 gives a list of popular software sites.

Table 6.1   Popular sites where you can download software.

Site name	URL	What it has...
Stroud's	**http://cws.iworld.com**	Internet software
TUCOWS	**http://www.tucows.com**	Internet software
Tools of the Net	**http://TOOLS.ofthe.NET**	Internet software
Windows 95 Internet		
Headquarters	**http://windows95.com**	Windows 95 software
shareware.com	**http://shareware.com**	PC software
The WinSite Archive	**http://www.winsite.com**	Windows software

Once you find a Web page with a direct link to a file, all you have to do is click the link to begin downloading it. Most software sites work in a similar manner: Typically, you select the category of software in which you're interested, and then you select the software program you want from those listed. The file you select is then downloaded to your system. Review the following steps to learn how to download a file to your system (the steps may vary slightly depending what browser you're using and what type of file you're downloading):

TIP   **File It First**   You may want to create a single folder on your hard disk for all the files you get off the Internet. That way, you can keep all your downloaded files in a safe place until you've had a chance to use an antivirus program to verify that the files you've received are virus-free before you attempt to install and use them on your system. (If you don't have an antivirus program, you should get one before extensively downloading files. Web browsers don't offer security features that check files.) See Lesson 15 in Part 6 for more about viruses.

1. Display the Web site that has links to downloadable files.

2. If the site offers various categories of files to download, click the link to the category you want. (You may even have to navigate through a few category levels). Most sites provide at least some information about each downloadable file, such as the size of the file so you can estimate download time (see Figure 6.1).

3. Click the link that's offered for downloading the file. Sometimes you'll click the file name itself, but in other cases you click a download link (like the **Download Now** link in Figure 6.1) or button.

4. A dialog box asks whether you want to open the file on-screen or save it. Make sure the **Save It To Disk** option is selected, then click OK.

5. In the Save As dialog box, use the Save In list to select the drive and folder where you want to save the file. (This works just like the Save As dialog box in other programs.) Click **Save**.

6. The File Download dialog box (see Figure 6.2) keeps you aware of the download progress. (For small files, the File Download dialog box may precede the Save In dialog box, so that when you click the Save button, the download operation is finished.) After the file is downloaded to your PC, you're returned to your Web browser. You can click **Cancel** if you want to cancel the download, especially if it's moving very slowly or hangs up. When the download finishes, the File Download dialog box closes.

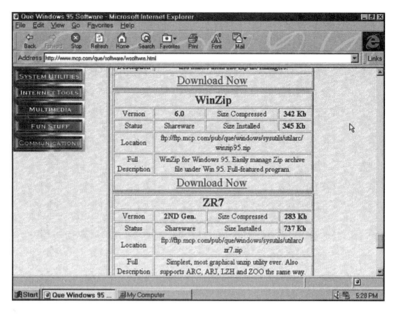

Figure 6.1   Here are descriptions of downloadable files from Que and links for downloading them.

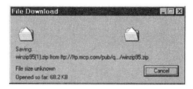

Figure 6.2   You'll see the download progress.

Downloading a File Directly from an FTP Site

If you happen to know the address of the FTP site that contains the file you're looking for, you can connect to the FTP site directly, locate your file, and then download it. Use these steps to download a file directly from an FTP site using Internet Explorer:

1. If you know the FTP site that a particular file is on, you can go directly to that site. For example, type **ftp://ftp.mcp.com** in the **Address** text box and press **Enter** to go to Macmillan's FTP site. (Even though you can leave off the http:// to connect to a Web site, you must start all FTP site

addresses with ftp://. Also, FTP addresses are generally case-sensitive, so if a resource like a magazine article uses unusual capitalization for an FTP address, follow that capitalization exactly.)

2. Your browser displays the root directory of this FTP server. To move from directory to directory, simply click the folder you want to open. For example, click the **pub** directory.

3. You'll see a listing of all the subdirectories in the pub directory, as shown in Figure 6.3. To display the files in one of those directories, click it. To move back up the directory tree, click the **Up to Higher Level Directory** link.

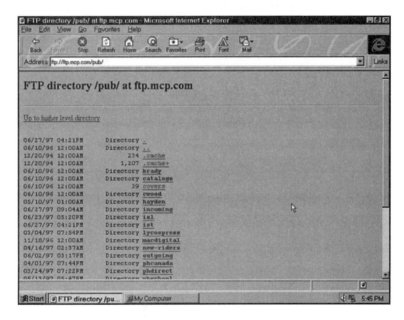

Figure 6.3 These are the folders within the pub directory of ftp://ftp.mcp.com.

4. Continue to browse directories until you find the file you want. To download the file, just click its name.

5. A dialog box asks whether you want to open the file on-screen or save it. Make sure the **Save It to Disk** option is selected, then click **OK**.

6. In the Save As dialog box, use the Save In list to select the drive and folder where you want to save the file. Click **Save**.

7. The File Download dialog box keeps you aware of the download progress. (For small files, the File Download dialog box may precede the Save In dialog box, so that when you click the Save button, the download operation is finished.) After the file is downloaded to your PC, you're returned to your Web browser. You can click **Cancel** if you want to cancel the download, especially if it's moving very slowly or hangs up. When the download finishes, the File Download dialog box closes.

 TIP **Slow Going** If your file downloads seem very slow, it could be because you're downloading during a period of heavy Internet traffic or heavy traffic to the site you want to connect with. Early morning or very late at night is usually a great time to download because you're likely to encounter less traffic.

Saving Web Page Information

While being online can be a great deal of fun, you may not always be able to spend the time you'd like with a Web document. Or, you may find a Web page that you know you'd like to print later, or a graphic that you'd like to print. This section explains how to save and reuse Web pages and their contents.

Keeping It Legal

An important note is always in order when talking about the Internet. Everything that you find online is someone else's property or creation, and is protected by copyright laws. If it's posted, you can assume the author wants you to read or view it. But that doesn't necessarily mean you can reuse the information in any way that you wish.

In general, you're expected to pay the shareware licensing fees for any shareware software you download, if you use that software regularly. In terms of Web page text and downloaded documents, you're not allowed to republish the information or otherwise profit from it as if it were your own. You can quote or cite information (a practice known as fair use). With regard to images, you need to use them for personal purposes only. If you're at all in doubt about how you're using information or an image, get permission to reuse the material from the document's author/publisher or the subject of the photo.

Saving a Graphic

As noted, you can download graphics for personal purposes. Most graphics on Web pages are in the .gif or .jpg formats. So before you download a graphics file, make sure the program you want to use to edit the graphic or the program for the document where you want to insert the graphic image can handle those types of file formats. Use these steps to download a graphic:

1. Right-click the graphic on the Web page, then click **Save Picture as**.
2. In the Save As dialog box, use the Save In list to select the drive and folder where you want to save the file. Click **Save**.
3. For small files, the file will simply save. In other cases, the File Download dialog box will appear to show you the download progress. Click **Cancel to** cancel the download, if needed.

An alternate method of grabbing a small graphic is to right-click it, then click **Copy** in the menu that appears. Open a new file in a graphics application, then choose **Edit**, **Paste**. Figure 6.4 shows a graphic copied from a Que Web page. You can then save the graphic in any format that your graphics program allows.

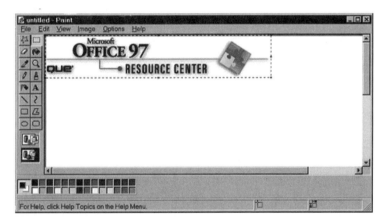

Figure 6.4 Here's a graphic copied from a Web page, used in Window's Paint program.

CAUTION

Online Time Some sounds and video clips can be played online and saved to your system. The clip must download completely to your system (which can be a lengthy wait for video clips) before you can play all of it. Your Web browser will use a plug-in program like QuickTime for Windows (which comes preinstalled with Windows 95 OSR 2) to play the file while you're online. After the clip downloads, right-click its on-screen placeholder, click the Save Movie (or Save Sound) command, then use the Save As dialog box to save it.

Saving a Page

You can save an entire Web page you're viewing to be able to view and access its text later (although this method doesn't usually capture the page graphics). Display the Web page you'd like to save, then click **File**, **Save As File**. Use the Save As dialog box to save the file. To open the Web page later, navigate to the folder where you saved it in either My Computer or Windows Explorer. Double-click the icon for the file. The page will reload in your Web browser, generally without graphics.

To copy any of the Web page information, drag to select it, then choose **Edit**, **Copy**. Open a new document in the application of your choice, then choose **Edit**, **Paste**.

TIP **Word 97 and HTML** Word 97 also enables you to open HTML pages. So, once you've save a Web .htm page to your hard disk, you can open it in Word if you prefer to view it there (or even edit and print its contents) rather than in your Web browser.

In this lesson you learned to transfer information from the Web to your computer by downloading files, and saving graphics and Web pages. Turn to the next lesson to learn to search the Web for information.

Searching for Information

This lesson explains how to use your Web browser to search for information on the Internet.

Introducing Search Tools

The World Wide Web is a big place. Sometimes it's almost impossible to find the information you want. Web search tools can help you narrow your search by providing you with a list of pages that may contain the information you're searching for.

Common search tools (and their addresses) include:

InfoSeek	**http://infoseek.com/**
Yahoo!	**http://yahoo.com/**
Lycos	**http://lycos.com/**
Alta Vista	**http://altavista.digital.com/**
Excite	**http://www.excite.com/**

When you jump to a Web search page, you're typically presented with a *form*. A form works like a dialog box (see the example in Figure 7.1); in the text box, enter the subject of your search, select additional options by clicking them, and then start the search by clicking a Search or Submit button. Sometimes you can narrow your search by selecting a category such as news or recreation first. When the search is complete, you're presented with a list of Web pages that match your search criteria. To jump to a page, click its link.

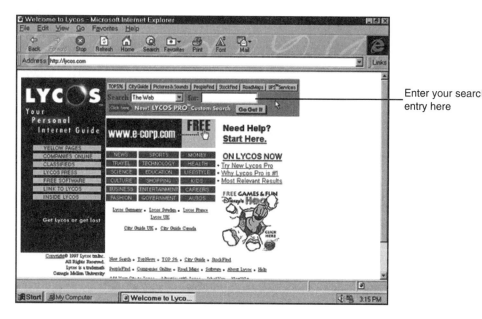

Enter your search entry here

Figure 7.1   Here's the Lycos search page; as with other search pages, type the topic to search for in the text box provided on the page.

TIP   **Search a Site**   Most large Web sites also provide search tools for searching for information on the site. For example, on some news and online magazine Web sites, you can search for articles by topic. Many sites also provide links you can click to jump to one of the search tool pages listed above.

Understanding How Web Search Tools Work

When you use a Web search tool to locate a particular Web page, you're not actually searching the Web—that would take too long. Instead, you're searching through a list of Web pages collected and organized by the Web search tool you're using. To compile their lists, each Web search tool regularly explores the Web in search of new Web pages. When it finds a new page, the search tool scans its contents and adds the page's location to its master list. The list of cataloged pages then resembles the table of contents for a book; the search tool can quickly scan through the list's topics to find ones that match yours. Anyone who publishes a Web page also can register his or her page with the various search tools to ensure its contents are listed.

When you enter your search criteria, the Web search tool simply scans its master list and produces the addresses of the Web pages whose contents match what you're looking for. The Web pages are listed in order of probability. Therefore, the pages whose contents most closely match your search criteria are displayed at the top of the list.

Each Web search tool has a different method for searching the Web, so each one produces its own unique listing of Web pages. If you don't find what you want using one Web search tool, you should try your search again using one of the other tools.

TIP   **Bring Me the News**   Web search tools sometimes also search news groups for the information you're looking for, so search results may include links to newsgroup discussions.

Improving Search Results

Some Web search tools, such as Yahoo! , allow you to narrow your search by selecting the category in which your topic belongs. For example, you might select Arts and Humanities if you're searching for a Web page containing information on the hottest new Jazz artists. Then, the search tool might show a list of subcategories or topics like the one shown in Figure 7.2.

You can narrow your search further by using unique search criteria. For example, if you're looking for information on how to fertilize your lawn and you type **gardening**, you'll get quite a list. However, if you enter **organic fertilizers** or **organic lawn care** instead, you'll narrow your list considerably. To increase your chances of finding the page you want as quickly as possible, try to use search words that are unique and specific.

One problem with entering more than one search word is that most Web search tools are set up to look for pages that contain *any* of the search words. So entering something like **deep sea fish** will produce a list of pages that contain the word "deep," or "sea," or "fish." Pages that contain two or more of the search words will be displayed at the top, but you'll still end up with a long list of Web pages to search through.

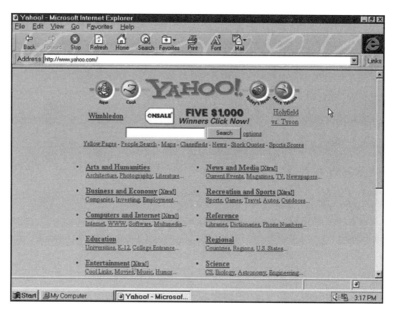

Figure 7.2   Some search tools offer search categories.

Fortunately, you can usually tell the Web search tool to include only those pages that contain all of your search words instead of pages that contain any of them by simply typing quotation marks around your search words like this: "**deep sea fish**". You can also use plus signs or the word AND to indicate that you want to locate only those pages that contain your search words, as in **infant AND car AND seat** or **+infant+car+seat**. You can use a minus sign or the word NOT to exclude pages that contain certain words, as in **pets NOT cats** or **pets– cats**. Finally, the word OR tells the search tool to display pages that contain either of your search words, as in **Indiana OR Ohio**.

Performing the Search

The following steps explain how to access and use a search tool:

1. You can enter the address of the search tool, such as **http://www.excite. com**, to jump directly to that page. (See Lesson 4 in this part to learn how to go to a page.) Some browsers also offer a Search button. If you click the Search button, you'll get a list of the search tools. For example, if you click Explorer's Search button, you'll get the Microsoft default search page.

Click the option button for the search tool you want (see Figure 7.3), enter the entry to search for, then click **Search**. In other browser search pages, you might just click a link to jump to the search tool you want.

Type your
search entry

Search tools

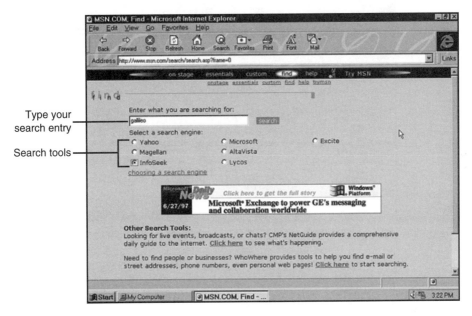

Figure 7.3 Explorer takes you to the Microsoft search page. Click a search tool, then click Search.

2. The search tool appears. It may provide a list of categories that enable you to narrow down the search list to a likely area. If you like, click a category to select it.

3. A list of subcategories is displayed. From here, you can click a subcategory, and continue clicking links until you see a list of Web pages that fit the category you selected. To jump to a particular Web page, click its link.

4. Another way to search for a Web page is to enter a series of search words, as discussed earlier. You can begin a search on a search tool's main page or on one of the subcategory pages. Simply type your search words into the appropriate text box, and then press **Enter** or click the **Search** button.

5. A list of Web pages that match the search criteria appears. The pages that most closely match what you're looking for appear at the top of the list, as shown in Figure 7.4. To jump to a Web page, click its link.

Match ratings ———

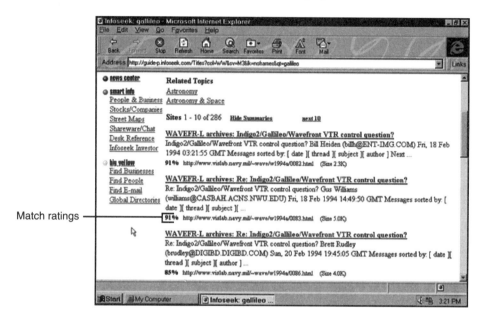

Figure 7.4 The search tool returns a list of pages that cover your topic. Click a page link to display that page.

Now that you've learned to use Web search tools to find information on the Web, the next lesson moves on to e-mail—launching and exiting your e-mail program.

Launch and Exit Your E-Mail Program

This lesson prepares you to exchange e-mail over the Internet, showing you how to set up, launch, and exit your e-mail program.

Setting Up Your E-Mail Software

As you learned in Lesson 1 of this part, e-mailing refers to sending and receiving messages electronically. You can e-mail messages and files with messages attached if you're connected to a company network, an online service, or the Internet. To create, send, receive, and store e-mail messages, you need special e-mailing software. There are numerous programs on the market for handling Internet e-mail, including Microsoft's Internet Mail, Netscape Communicator, Pegasus, Eudora, and more. Your Internet Service Provider (ISP) will usually provide e-mail software. Your computer may have come with e-mail software already installed. And, you also can download freeware and shareware mail software (like Pegasus and Eudora) from the Web.

TIP   **Internet Mail**   The lessons in this book focus on using Internet Mail, which comes with Windows 95 OSR 2 and is, therefore, installed on most new systems. The steps may not be exactly the same in your mail program, but the general principles will apply.

No matter what Internet e-mail software you use, you need to make sure the software is properly set up to communicate with the mail server (the computer location that handles e-mail) at your ISP.

To set up your e-mail software, you'll need:

- **Your ISP's mail server addresses.** There are usually two servers: the POP or IMAP server that manages incoming mail, and the SMTP server for outgoing mail. The address for each of these servers is usually something like **mailhost.bubba.net,** although you may have to enter two different addresses like **pop3.bubba.net** and **smtp.bubba.net**.

- **Your e-mail address.** Usually, you combine your user name, an @ symbol, and the *domain name* (address) for the service provider. For example, an e-mail address might look like **jblow@bubba.net**.

- **Your account password.** Your ISP will provide this.

CAUTION

Two Users, One Account   If you only have a mailbox attached to another user's Internet account, such as your spouse's or a small business account, then in some cases you use the user name and password for that person or account. Other ISPs might provide a separate user name or password. Check with your ISP to ensure you get the right user name and password for your extra mailbox.

Once you've gathered this information, follow these steps to set up Internet Mail:

1. Click **Start**, point to **Programs**, and click **Internet Mail**. Because Internet Mail knows it needs connection settings if you haven't previously set it up, it will begin prompting you for information. (If Mail starts without prompting you for setup information, choose **Mail, Read Mail**.)

2. Click **Next** at the first Internet Mail Configuration dialog box.

3. In the next dialog box, shown in Figure 8.1, enter the sender **Name** that you want to use for your e-mail. This can be a name or nickname. Enter your **Email Address** in the bottom text box. Click **Next**.

4. Enter the addresses for your mail servers in the text boxes of the next dialog box, as shown in Figure 8.2. Click **Next**.

5. In the **Email Account** text box, enter your user name. Then, enter the **Password** (it appears as asterisks). Click **Next**.

6. Unless you're connecting to the Internet via a network, in the next dialog box click **I Use a Modem to Access My Email**, then choose your ISP connection from the drop-down list. Click **Next**.

7. Another dialog box appears to tell you the setup is finished. Click **Finish**. Internet Mail starts and is ready to go.

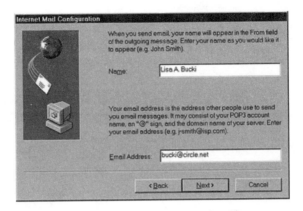

Figure 8.1 Enter your name or nickname and e-mail address.

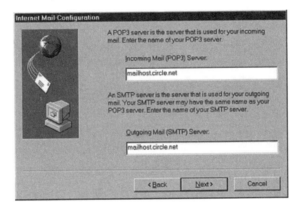

Figure 8.2 Enter addresses to help your computer communicate with your ISP's mail server.

Starting and Exiting Your E-Mail Program

Internet e-mail programs are designed to enable you to work offline. This is because you don't want to waste valuable online time typing a long message, and because some systems may work a bit more slowly when they're logged on to the Internet. So normally, starting Internet Mail and other e-mail programs doesn't launch your Internet connection. The connection will launch when you try to send or read messages, as described in the next two lessons.

TIP   **Online Mailing**   You can launch your Internet connection before launching your e-mail program, if you prefer, or start your e-mail program when you're connected and browsing the Web.

To start Internet Mail, click **Start**, point to **Programs**, and click **Internet Mail**. The Mail program starts. Figure 8.3 shows Internet Mail. To load another e-mail program, look for its command or a folder for it on the Programs submenu.

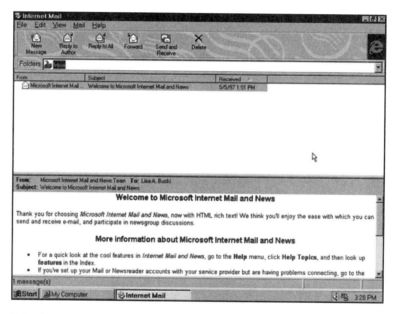

Figure 8.3   Internet Mail looks a lot like Internet Explorer.

TIP   **Mailing from the Browser**   Most Web browsers offer a command to enable you to launch your e-mail program, saving you a step or two. In Internet Explorer, click the **Mail** button or **Go** menu, then click **Read Mail**.

To exit Internet Mail, open the **File** menu and choose **Close**. (In your e-mail program, the command might be **File**, **Exit**.) If you launched your Internet connection from within Mail (by reading or sending messages), a dialog box will ask whether you'd like to disconnect from the Internet. Click **Yes**.

This lesson showed you how to prepare your Internet e-mail program to send and receive messages, and how to start and exit your e-mail program. The next lesson shows you how to create and send an e-mail message.

Create and Send
an E-Mail
Message

This lesson explains how to create and send e-mail messages.

Working with E-Mail Addresses

You can send e-mail to anyone who's connected to the Internet—even if that person is connected to the Internet indirectly (such as through CompuServe or America Online). All you need to know is his or her e-mail address. An Internet address looks something like this:

jnoname@que.mcp.com

The first part of the address is the person's *username* (the name by which he is known to his home system). Most usernames consist of the person's first initial and last name run together, although the username can be anything, including a nickname or a code name. An at symbol (@) always comes after the username. The part of the e-mail address that follows the @ sign is a *location* on the Internet. In this case, it's the address of Que, which is a part of Macmillan Computer Publishing—hence the location name que.mcp. The .com part of the location tells you that que.mcp is a commercial (business) venture. Other endings you'll see include .edu (educational), .net (an Internet server), .org (non-profit organizations), .gov (government), and .mil (military).

CAUTION

On Your Case   When addressing e-mail, be careful to use upper- and lowercase letters *exactly* as they are given to you. Some mail servers require that you use the exact case. So, if someone tells you that his address is SRPoland@BusineSS.com, you must type the address exactly that way. He will not receive his mail if you send it to srpoland@business.com because that is a completely different address.

If you're sending e-mail to a person who connects to the Internet through an online service such as CompuServe, you will need to adjust the address itself for use on the Internet. For example, when sending e-mail from one member to another through CompuServe, you might enter an address such as 71520,3121. To send a message to that same person through the Internet, you must change the address to 71520.3121@compuserve.com. The following list shows you the format of e-mail addresses for the most popular online services:

Online Service	Sample Address
CompuServe	71354.1234@compuserve.com
America Online	joeblow@aol.com
Prodigy	joeblow@prodigy.com
The Microsoft Network	joeblow@msn.com

Most e-mail programs include an address book in which you can save the e-mail addresses of the people to whom you most often send messages. That way, you don't have to worry about making a typing mistake when addressing a message to one of your friends or colleagues. To create an Address Book entry in the Internet Mail Address Book, for example, choose **File**, **Address Book**. Click the **New Contact** button, and enter the person's name, nickname, and e-mail address as shown in Figure 9.1. You can enter information on the other tabs in the Properties dialog box, too. Click **OK** to finish the new entry, and click **File**, **Close** to close the Address book.

You should use the online help system for your Internet e-mail software to learn as much as you can about its address book capabilities, because address books can really save you time. For example, many address books enable you to create a *recipient group* or *recipient list*, or a list of addresses. For example, say you lead a weekly meeting attended by 10 people, and you're responsible for e-mailing the meeting summaries to all the attendants. You could add each person's e-mail address to a recipient group. Then, rather than sending 10 separate messages or adding 10 separate addresses to the message, you could just select the recipient group to send the message all 10 attendants.

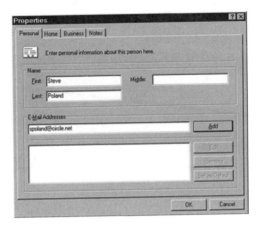

Figure 9.1   Create an Address Book entry for anyone you'll mail to frequently.

Creating and Queuing Messages

If you use one of the leading e-mail programs, like Internet Mail, you don't have to connect to the Internet in order to create an e-mail message. In fact, it can be more cost effective (if you have limited connect time or pay for your Internet access by the hour) to create your e-mail messages offline if your software allows it and then connect to the Internet and send your messages.

If you have several e-mail messages to send at one time, you can create each one while you're offline and save them to send later. When you're ready to send the messages, you connect to the Internet and send all the messages in your Outbox at once. This process is available in most e-mail programs, including Internet Mail.

Outbox   The Outbox is a folder where your e-mail program holds messages until you connect to the Internet to send or transmit them.

In addition to being able to send multiple messages at one time, you can also include files with your e-mail messages. This is called *attaching* a file to a message. Although you can include any file with a message, you may want to "shrink" or compress the file first, in order to make it as small as possible for transmission. Doing so reduces the chance of the file not arriving intact.

373

You use a file compression program (see Lesson 5 in Part 6) to compress the file; your recipient must have software to be able to uncompress the file, too. (If you receive a file with a .zip file extension, for example, you'll need a program like WinZip to unzip it.)

Keep in mind, however, that you don't want to attach a file that's larger than 1 or 2 megabytes to a message. Larger files not only take too long to transmit, but also may cause your ISP to reject your message because it's too large.

Follow these steps in Internet Mail to create a message and place it in the Outbox (your e-mail program will use similar steps):

1. Click the **New Message** button, or choose **Mail**, **New Message**.

2. The New Message window appears. Enter the recipient's address in the **To:** text box. If you're sending to more than one person, separate additional addresses with semi-colons as in:
   joenoname@BigCo.com;jsmith@sales.com.
   To send a message to someone whose address you've saved in your Address Book, click the **Address Book** button on the Internet Mail toolbar, click the recipient name, then click **File**, **Send Mail**.

 TIP   **Another Address Book**   Internet Mail also enables you to use addresses you've stored in your Windows Messaging or Microsoft Outlook address books. Click the **Address Card** button that appears in the To: text box in the New Message Window. Select the name of the person to whom you want to send your message, click **To ->**, and click **OK**.

3. Click the **Subject:** text box and type a subject line.

4. Click in the large text area at the bottom of the window, then type your message. Messages, by default, are sent as text only. Figure 9.2 shows a message with the To:, Subject:, and message text entries completed.

5. To attach a file to send with your message, click the **Insert File** button or choose **Insert**, **File Attachment**. In the Insert Attachment dialog box, select your file, and click **Attach**. The attached file appears as an icon at the bottom of the message window.

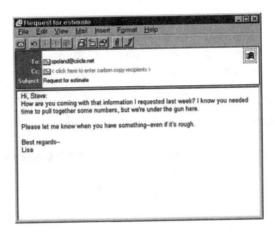

Figure 9.2   A message looks something like this before you send it.

CAUTION

Attachment Safety   Before you attach a file to a message, save your latest changes to the file in its source application, then close the file. This ensures the recipient will get your latest changes, and that you won't encounter any error messages when you try to send the message. Also, before you send the message, do not move the file attachment to another disk or folder; doing so would create an error when you try to send the message. This is true because when you attach a file to a message, the e-mail program doesn't create a separate copy of the file on your system. Instead, the e-mail program creates a pointer or reference to the attachment. Then, when you send the message, the e-mail program follows the pointer, copies the file it finds, and sends the file copy to the recipient. If you moved the file before sending, the pointer would refer to the wrong file location.

6. Click the **Send** button or choose **File**, **Send Message** to send your message.

7. If you see a warning telling you that the message will be placed in your Outbox (to be sent later), click **OK**.

8. Repeat steps 1-7 to add other messages to the Outbox.

TIP   **I Don't Want To Connect**   If your system asks you whether you want to connect to the Internet after step 6, simply click **Cancel** to instead send the message to your Outbox. In this situation, different options may be set for your Internet Mail installation. You can use **Mail**, **Options** to view and change various options.

Sending Messages from the Outbox

Before you send messages from your Outbox to your recipients, you can view the Outbox contents and even reopen messages. To view what's in your Outbox, click the **Folders** drop-down list near the top of the Mail window, then click **Outbox**, as shown in Figure 9.3. (You can then choose **Inbox** from the same list to redisplay the Inbox, which holds received messages.)

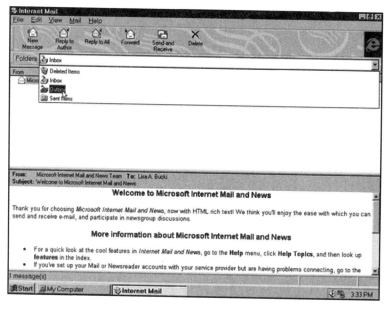

Figure 9.3 Choose the Outbox folder to review outgoing messages.

Click a message in the **Outbox** to view its contents in the lower pane, or double-click it to open it and make changes. Right-click a message to display a shortcut menu with commands for working with the message, such as the Delete command for deleting the message before you send it.

To subsequently send the messages that are in the Outbox, no matter what folder is currently displayed, follow these steps:

1. Click the **Send and Receive** button or choose **Mail, Send and Receive**.

2. If you're not currently connected to the Internet, the Connect to dialog box appears. Click **OK** to dial your Internet connection. When your system connects, Internet mail will inform you as it sends your message(s).

3. When the messages finish sending, open the **File** menu and choose **Close**. (In your e-mail program, the command might be **File**, **Exit**.)

4. A dialog box will ask whether you'd like to disconnect from the Internet. Click **Yes**.

This lesson gave you the steps for creating an Address Book entry, creating an e-mail message, and sending e-mail messages from the Outbox. The next lesson shows you how to work with incoming messages.

Receiving, Replying To, and Managing E-Mail Messages

This lesson explains how to get, respond to, and file e-mail messages.

Retrieve and View E-Mail Messages

The process of retrieving an e-mail message is like going to your mailbox and checking for mail. If there's mail in your mailbox, you take it out, open it, and read it. The e-mail program does the same thing: It goes to your electronic mailbox (which is located on your Internet Service Provider's computer), checks for mail, and brings back anything it finds.

Retrieved messages are placed in a folder that's usually named Inbox. If the Inbox isn't the currently-displayed folder in Internet mail, click to open the Folders drop-down list, then click Inbox. Once a message is in the Inbox, you can open and read it, print it, and more.

 TERM   **Inbox**   The Inbox is a folder where your e-mail program holds received messages.

You can initiate the mail checking and receiving process whenever you want, using these steps in Internet Mail and a similar process in your e-mail program:

1. If needed, start Internet Mail.

2. Click the **Send and Receive** button or choose **Mail**, **Send and Receive** to check for new mail.

3. If you're not currently connected to the Internet, the Connect To dialog box appears. Click **OK** to dial your Internet connection. When your system connects, Internet mail will inform you as it receives your message(s).

4. After messages are received, they appear at the top of the Inbox listing in bold text.

5. You can disconnect from the Internet if you want to work offline with the received messages.

Opening an E-Mail Message

Once you retrieve your mail, you "open" it to read it. To view the contents of a message, click its listing (header) in the Inbox list. The e-mail message appears in the Preview Pane, as shown in Figure 10.1. If necessary, scroll down to read the complete message. After you've viewed a message, its header changes from bold to regular text.

TIP   **Where's the Preview?**   If the Preview Pane is not currently displayed, open the **View** menu, select **Preview Pane**, and select **Split Horizontally** or **Split Vertically**.

If the message contains an attached file, a paper clip icon appears at the left end of the message header. To save this file to your PC's hard disk, press and hold the **Ctrl** key as you click the icon, and then select the file name from the list that appears. In the Save As dialog box, select a folder in which to save the file, and then click **Save**. (You can rename the file prior to saving it by typing a new name in the **File Name** text box.) You can then open the file in the application you use to work with files of its type (such as Word 97 for a .doc file).

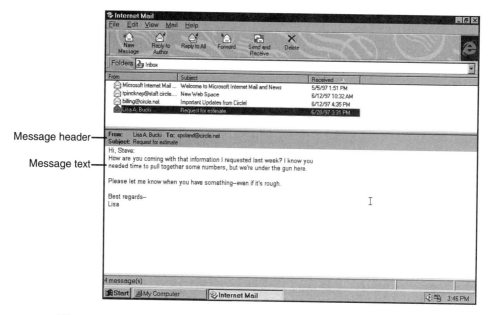

Message header

Message text

Figure 10.1 Click a message to read it.

If you clicked the paper clip icon (instead of holding down the Ctrl key and clicking), Internet Mail attempts to open the appropriate program so you can view the file's contents. First, however, you'll see a warning message. Click **Open It**, and then click **OK** to continue. Once the proper program associated with this file type has been identified, the file's contents are displayed.

CAUTION

Before You Open It... Don't open a file attachment without virus scanning it if the file isn't from someone you know and trust. Even if the attachment is from a reliable source, it's a good practice to scan the file for viruses before opening it. See Lesson 15 in Part 6 to learn more about viruses and virus scanning software.

You can print an open message if you want and save it in your hard disk. To print a message, click its header in the Inbox, then choose **File** (or right-click the header), and click **Print**. You also can select text within an open message and copy it, then paste it into a document in another application such as a word processor. Most e-mail programs offer an Edit menu with Copy, Cut, and Paste commands that work just like those in other applications (see Lesson 7 in Part 3 for a refresher on moving and copying information).

Replying to an E-Mail Message

You can reply to or forward any message you receive. When you reply to a message, the e-mail program automatically fills in the address of the originator as the recipient address for your new message. You can also send your reply to anyone who received the original message. In any case, all you have to do is type your message reply, and it will be sent to either the originator or the originator and all its recipients—whichever option you select.

When you reply to a message, the text of the original message is included for reference. You can customize your e-mail program so that the original text is never included, or you can simply delete the original message text if you don't want to include it in a particular reply.

Follow these steps to reply to an e-mail message:

1. In your Inbox, click the message to which you want to reply.

2. Click either the **Reply to Author** or the **Reply to All** button, or the command of one of those names on the **Mail** menu.

3. Internet Mail updates the header information, filling in the To: and Subject: lines. In the message area, the text from the original message appears, preceded by arrows (>), as shown in Figure 10.2. If you want to delete any of these original lines, just select them and press **Delete**.

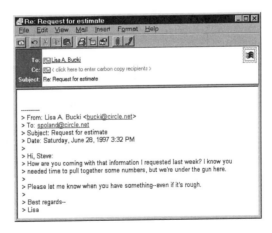

Figure 10.2 Arrows point to lines of text from the original message in a reply.

4. Type your message above the copied text from the original message. Or you can type your reply between the lines of the original message to respond point by point to the questions in the message, making it easy for the reply recipient to review your responses. To intersperse your responses within a message, place the insertion point at the end of an original line and press **Enter** to create a blank line on which you can type.

5. Click **Send** or choose **File, Send Message** to send your reply. If you see a warning telling you that the message will be placed in your Outbox (to be sent later), click **OK**.

6. To send the message later, click the **Send and Receive** button to send the message, as described in the last section of the previous lesson.

Forwarding a Message

When you forward a message, your e-mail program sends a copy of the original message to the person you indicate. You can forward a message to more than one person if you want. When you forward a message, the original message is treated as an attachment. You can add a message of explanation about the attachment to a forwarded message if necessary. Follow these steps to forward a message:

1. Click the message you want to forward.

2. Click the **Forward** button, or choose **Mail**, **Forward**.

3. The original message appears in the text window, preceded by arrows (>). In the **To:** text box, type the address(es) of the person(s) to whom you want to forward this message, or add recipients using the Address Book, as described in the last Lesson.

4. Type any additional message above the text for the forwarded message, or insert information within the existing message by clicking to place the insertion point and then typing your comments.

5. Click the **Send** button or choose **File**, **Send Message** to forward the message. If you see a warning telling you that the message will be placed in your Outbox (to be sent later), click **OK**.

6. To send the message later, click the **Send and Receive** button to send the message, as described in the last section of the previous lesson.

Filing Your Message

Just as you can create folders on a disk to organize your files and programs, you can create folders in most e-mail programs. For example, you could create a folder for each of your current projects, and file messages relating to each project in the appropriate project folder.

Creating a Folder

To create a custom folder in Internet Mail (the process will be similar in your e-mail program), follow these steps:

1. Click **File**, point to **Folder**, and click **Create**.
2. Type a folder name in the Create New Folder dialog box that appears, as shown in Figure 10.3.

Figure 10.3   You can create folders to hold your mail messages.

3. Click **OK** or press **Enter**.

Transferring a Message to a Folder

Moving a message from the Inbox to a particular folder is as easy as these steps:

1. Click the message to move in the Inbox.
2. Click **Mail**, point to **Move To**, then click the name of the folder you want to move the message to, as shown in Figure 10.4. Internet Mail moves the message.

To view the messages you've stored in a folder, click to open the Folders drop-down list, and click the name of the folder to view.

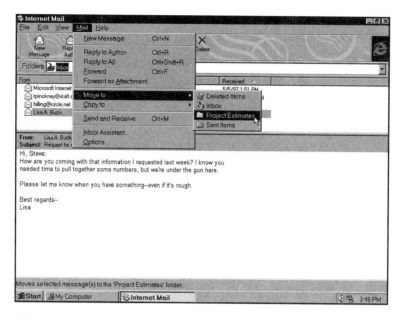

Figure 10.4 You can move the current message to another folder.

This lesson showed you how to get your messages, reply to them, and file them in custom folders. The next lesson introduces you to opening and closing your Internet News reader.

Launch and Exit Your News Reader

This lesson explains how to set up, start, and exit your Internet news reader.

Setting Up Your News Reader

A news reader program reads messages in public forums called newsgroups. There are thousands of newsgroups covering thousands of topics. Some news groups offer discussions about issues relating to a particular state or country. You'll find newsgroups that are technology-oriented, hobby-oriented, business-oriented, career-oriented, and more. Some newsgroups have classified listings, while others simply have messages about pop culture or underground culture topics. Most users will find dozens of newsgroups that are interesting!

Special newsgroup server computers on the Internet hold and manage the newsgroup messages. Before your computer can connect to and access news group information, you have to set up your news reader software so that it connects with your ISP's mail server computer.

 TIP **Internet News** The lessons in this book focus on using Internet News, which comes with Windows 95 OSR 2 and is therefore installed on most new systems. Even if the steps may not match your news reader program exactly, the general principles will apply.

To read newsgroups with Internet Mail, you'll need your ISP's news server address, which is usually something like **newshost.bubba.net**. This server computer holds the newsgroup information. Also verify whether your ISP requires that you use your user name and password to log on to the mail server, and have that information handy. Then, follow these steps to set up Internet News (your news reader will use a similar process):

1. Click **Start**, point to **Programs**, and click **Internet News**.

2. Click **Next** at the first Internet News Configuration dialog box.

3. In the next dialog box, enter the sender **Name,** that you want to use to identify yourself in any articles (messages) you post in a newsgroup. This can be a name or nickname. Enter your **Email Address** in the bottom text box. Click **Next**.

4. Enter your ISP's **News Server** address, as shown in Figure 11.1. If your ISP's news server requires you to log on with your user name and password, click to check **My News Server Requires Me to Logon**, then enter your **Account** (user name) and **Password** below. Click **Next**.

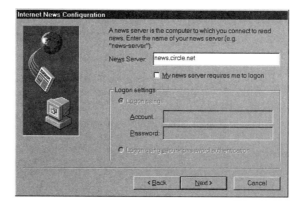

Figure 11.1 Identify your ISP's news server address for Internet News.

5. Unless you're connecting to the Internet via a network, in the next dialog box click **I Use a Modem to Access My Newsgroups**, then choose your ISP connection from the drop-down list. Click **Next**.

6. Another dialog box appears to tell you the setup is finished. Click **Finish**. A Connect to dialog box may prompt you to specify whether you want to dial your Internet connection. This is the same dialog box you'll see when you start Internet News, as described next.

Starting Your News Reader

After you set up your news reader like Internet News, you can start it later, connect to the Internet, and use it to read news. The first time you start your news reader and connect to the Internet, the list of newsgroups downloads to your news reader. Sit tight for this process. At last count, there were close to 30,000 newsgroups, so the download takes a while.

Subsequently, when you start your news reader, the message headers for any newsgroups you've subscribed to (joined) are updated, a process that's far less time consuming.

 TERM **Newsgroup** A newsgroup is, in essence, a topic area that holds messages or articles about the topic. Newsgroup names, in typical Internet fashion, follow certain conventions—groups of characters separated by periods and hyphens. The beginning of a newsgroup name gives you a clue as to the seriousness of its subject. A name like biz.marketplace.computers is business-oriented. The group alt.games talks about games.

Follow these steps to launch Internet News and connect to your ISP's news server on the Internet:

1. Click **Start**, point to **Programs**, and click **Internet News**.
2. The Connect To dialog box appears. Click **OK** to dial your Internet connection and logon.

Once you've connected, Internet News downloads the newsgroup listing or the new message headers in the groups you've already subscribed to from the news server. When it finishes downloading groups for the first time, the Newsgroups window appears. You'll learn to use it in the next lesson. Otherwise, you see the Internet News window, as shown in Figure 11.2.

 TIP **Get Your News Here** If you're short on time, but want to check for newsgroup news about a particular topic, you can use the Deja News search tool. Deja News is a Web page (http://www.dejanews.com) that enables you to search newsgroups for the topic of your choice. Simply type the topic you're looking for in the Web page text box, then click Find for a list of links to related newsgroup articles. For more on using your Web browser, see Lessons 3 through 7 in this part. Lesson 7, in particular, explains how to use Web search tools, which work just like Deja News.

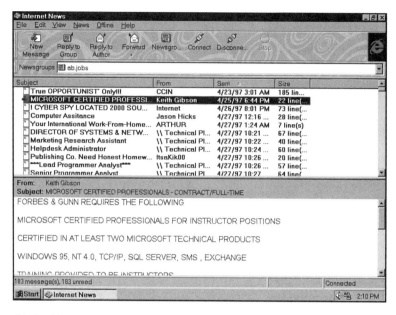

Figure 11.2   Here's how your Internet News screen will look, once you've chosen some newsgroups to use.

Disconnecting and Closing Internet News

As you'll learn in Lesson 13 of this part, to work with the newsgroup articles (messages), you need to read or reply to them while you're online, or download selected articles to your computer so you can read them later. If you want to disconnect from the mail server and the Internet without closing Internet News, click the **Disconnect** button or choose **File**, **Disconnect**.

TIP   **Reconnect Me**   Of course, to redial your Internet connection and reconnect to the news server from within Internet News, click the Connect button or choose File, Connect.

To exit Internet News and disconnect, open the **File** menu and choose **Close**. At the dialog box asking whether to close your Internet connection, click **Yes**. Windows logs you off and hangs up the modem.

This lesson introduced you to your news reader software, helping you set it up, start it and connect to the Internet, and disconnect and close it. The next lesson explains how to select the newsgroups you'll want to read regularly.

Subscribing, Unsubscribing, and Working with Newsgroups

This lesson explains how to get a current list of newsgroups, subscribe to groups, unsubscribe, and go to a group without subscribing.

Updating the Group List

As you learned in the last lesson, there are tens of thousands of newsgroups, and the newsgroup list automatically downloads to your news reader the first time you connect to your ISPs newsgroup server. The total number of groups has exploded—only a few years ago there were four or five thousand groups. So, while you don't want to download the group list to your computer every time you read news, from time-to-time you will want to take the time to refresh your newsgroup list.

Down Time   If you try to download the newsgroup list during periods when your ISP is very busy with connected users, it'll take even longer than usual. So, shoot for a low-traffic period such as very late at night or early in the morning to accomplish the update as quickly as possible.

CAUTION

Follow these steps in Internet News to update the newsgroup list:

1. Start Internet News and connect to the Internet.

2. Click the **Newsgroups** button or choose **News, Newsgroups**. You'll see the Newsgroups window, as shown in Figure 12.1.

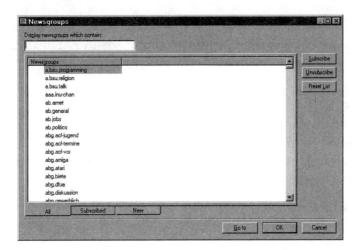

Figure 12.1 Use the Newsgroups window to work with newsgroups.

3. Click the **Reset List** button. The newsgroup list downloads to your computer, and Internet News shows you the progress, as in Figure 12.2. When the download concludes, you can work in the Newsgroups window or click its **Cancel** button to close it.

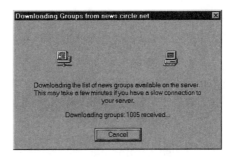

Figure 12.2 Because there are so many newsgroups to download, you'll see this message box for a while.

Subscribing and Unsubscribing to Groups

Subscribing to (joining) a newsgroup is similar to subscribing to a newspaper or magazine. When you connect to your Internet news server, the headers (descriptive lines) for messages in the subscribed group(s) automatically transfer to your news reader program, giving you a quick way to browse through topics of interest. This is much faster than the alternative—browsing through the thousands of newsgroups each and every time you want to read news.

If you've found that a particular newsgroup isn't for you, you can unsubscribe from it. This tells the news reader that you no longer want to download article headers from the group when you connect, reducing the connection download time. Because you can go to a particular newsgroup at any time without subscribing (see the next section in this lesson), it pays to keep your subscription list lean and mean.

To select the newsgroups you'd like to subscribe to or remove others from the list, follow these steps:

1. Start Internet News. Connect to the Internet.
2. Click the **Newsgroups** button or choose **News**, **Newsgroups**. You'll see the Newsgroups window.
3. Update the newsgroup listing, if needed, as described in the last section.
4. On the All tab, click a group in the **Newsgroups** list, then click **Subscribe** to subscribe to it. Internet News adds the name of the subscribed group in the Subscribed tab.

 TIP   **Fast Find**   You can narrow the Newsgroups list so it displays groups matching your topic of interest, making it easier to find the groups you want to subscribe to. For example, if you type **art** in the **Display Newsgroups Which Contain** text box at the top of the Newsgroups dialog box, the list will display only newsgroups which contain "art" in their names.

5. Click the **Subscribed** tab to see the list of newsgroups you've subscribed to. It will look something like Figure 12.3.
6. To remove a group from the subscribed Newsgroups list, click its name, then click Unsubscribe.
7. When you've finished, adding and deleting groups, click **OK** to return to the main Internet News screen.

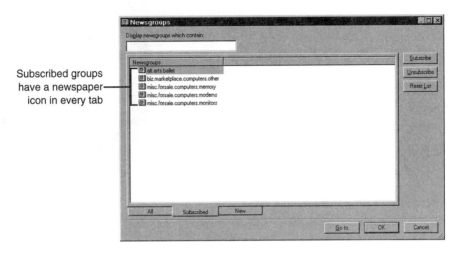

Subscribed groups have a newspaper icon in every tab

Figure 12.3 Here's the list of newsgroups you've joined.

Displaying a Group You Haven't Subscribed To

There may be special cases when you want to display the message headers for a group you haven't subscribed to. For example, you may have a question about an application, and may want to see if a newsgroup contains the answer. Follow these steps to take a look at the messages in any group:

1. Start Internet News. Connect to the Internet.

2. Click the **Newsgroups** button or choose **News**, **Newsgroups**. You'll see the Newsgroups window.

3. Update the newsgroup listing, if need, as described in the last section.

4. On the All tab, click a group in the **Newsgroups** list, then click **Go To**.

5. If Internet News asks whether you want to subscribe to the newsgroup, click **Yes** or **No**, as appropriate. The main Internet News window reappears, with the newsgroup you selected displayed as the Newsgroups list choice. The articles for the newsgroup are listed in the top pane of the Internet News window.

This lesson showed you how to update the list of newsgroups, subscribe to and unsubscribe from groups, or display the articles in any group. The next lesson shows you how to read articles.

Reading and Posting Articles

This lesson explains how to read an article, reply to a topic, post a new article, and transfer article contents to your computer.

Reading and Replying to an Article

After you've chosen your newsgroups, the next steps is to read an article (message). Once you've displayed an article's contents, you can reply to the article. Follow these steps to read and reply to an article:

1. Start Internet News. Connect to the Internet when prompted.

2. Subscribe to new newsgroups if needed. (Or, select a newsgroup as described in the last section of the previous lesson, then skip to Step 4.)

3. Click to open the **Newsgroups** drop-down list, then click the name of the newsgroup with the articles you want to view, as shown in Figure 13.1. The headers (subjects and information) for the articles appear in the top page of the Internet News window.

4. Scroll through the article display. When you see an article whose contents you'd like to read, click its header. Its text appears in the bottom pane, as shown in Figure 13.2.

5. To reply to the current article, open the News menu and choose **Reply to Newsgroup** for a public response, **Reply to Author** to send a confidential e-mail, or **Reply to Newsgroup and Author** to do both.

6. The window that appears is addressed for you. Simply type your text and click the **Post Message** button or choose **File**, **Post Message**.

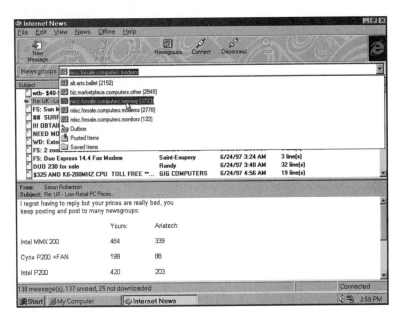

Figure 13.1 Choose a newsgroup to list its articles.

Message replies start with "Re:"

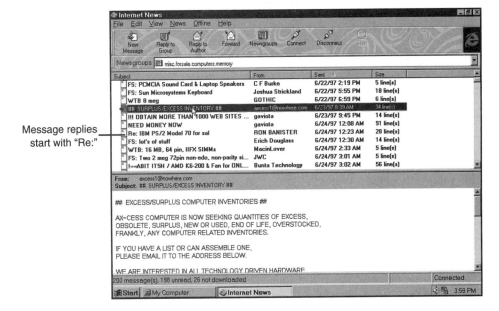

Figure 13.2 Click an article to view its text in the bottom pane.

7. A Post News message box tells you that your message has been sent but may not appear immediately. (The message gets posted in the newsgroup when the server computer is able to post it there; if the server isn't busy, it'll usually only take a few minutes or so, but it can take dramatically longer. As long as you're still in viewing the same newsgroup and Internet News is using the default setting that tells it to check for new messages every 10 minutes or so, you'll eventually see the message pop up. Otherwise, you'll need to come back later to the newsgroup to check for it, or use the **View**, **Refresh** command to make sure the new message gets downloaded to your system.) Click **OK**.

8. Repeat steps 3 through 7 to continue working, then close and disconnect when you've finished.

Posting a New Article

Rather than replying to an existing article or message, you can simply post your own using these steps:

1. Start Internet News. Connect to the Internet when prompted.

2. Click to open the **Newsgroups** drop-down list, then click the name of the newsgroup to which you'd like to post the article. The headers (subjects and information) for the articles appear in the top page of the Internet News window.

3. Click the **New Message** button or choose **Mail, New Message to Newsgroup**. The New Message window appears.

4. Click in the **Subject:** line and type your subject.

5. Click in the message text area and type your message.

6. Click the **Post Message** button or choose **File, Post Message**.

7. A Post News message box tells you that your message has been sent but may not appear immediately. (The message gets posted in the newsgroup when the server computer is able to post it there; if the server isn't busy, it'll usually only take a few minutes or so, but it can take dramatically longer. As long as you're still in viewing the same newsgroup and Internet News is using the default setting that tells it to check for new messages every 10 minutes or so, you'll eventually see the message pop up. Otherwise, you'll need to come back later to the newsgroup to check for it, or use the **View**, **Refresh** command to make sure the new message gets downloaded to your system.) Click **OK**.

TIP **Messages Offline** If you want to create your message while offline, choose the appropriate newsgroup from the Newsgroups drop-down list. Click the **New Message** button or choose **Mail, New Message to Newsgroup**. Create your message in the New Message window. Click the **Post Message** button or choose **File, Post Message**. Then, to transfer the message later, reconnect and choose **Offline, Post and Download**.

TIP **Be a Good Net Neighbor** Because of the public nature of newsgroups, it's particularly important to follow a few common courtesy rules (called "Netiquette" in online lingo) in your postings. For example, typing in all upper-case letters is considered SCREAMING, and is in bad taste. You shouldn't be unnecessarily rude in response to any posting. Likewise, posting sales messages, posting messages that don't relate to the subject of the group, quoting all of a message when you respond to it, and similar actions are considered rude. If you have any questions about newsgroup etiquette, review the postings in the news.newusers.questions newsgroup, or post a question of your own.

Downloading Articles for Later Use

As noted earlier, you may not want to stay continuously connected while you're reading articles. You can instead download articles to your system, then disconnect and read them. Use these steps to download articles to your computer:

1. Start Internet News. Connect to the Internet when prompted.

2. Subscribe to new newsgroups if needed. (Or, select a newsgroup as described in the last section of the previous lesson, then skip to step 4.)

3. Click to open the **Newsgroups** drop-down list, then click the name of the newsgroup with the articles you want to download.

4. Choose **Offline, Mark All for Download**.

5. Choose **Offline, Post and Download**. Internet News transfers the articles to your system, even if you didn't look at any of them while online.

6. Click the **Disconnect** button, or **File, Disconnect** to close your Internet connection but leave Internet News open.

7. To read a downloaded message, click its header in the top page of the Internet News window.

This lesson explained how to read and reply to messages in a newsgroup, concluding this part's overview of what you can do on the Internet. The next part teaches you how to upgrade your system, starting with adding a new printer.

Choosing and Installing Peripherals

Adding and Setting Up a Printer in Windows 95

If you need to add a new printer to your system, follow the steps in this part for connecting it and setting up Windows 95 to run it.

Reviewing Printer Background Information

Printers come in all sorts of shapes and sizes, and they use different technologies to produce a finished page. The most popular printer types are dot-matrix, inkjet, and laser:

- *Dot-matrix* printers are all but extinct. They produce text in a manner similar to a typewriter: by pressing the character to be printed against an inked ribbon, which in turn, leaves its image on a piece of paper. Dot-matrix printers produce the fuzziest results.

- *Laser* printers use a pencil-point laser beam to create a reproduction of the entire page, in a manner similar to a photocopy machine. Laser printers are the most expensive printers, but their print quality is unrivaled.

- As you might have guessed, the output quality of *inkjet* printers (which produce text by spurting a jet of ink onto a piece of paper) is somewhere between that of dot-matrix and laser printers. You can purchase a color inkjet printer for about the same price as a noncolor laser printer. However, to get color-capability, you'll give up some of the print quality you'd get with a laser printer.

Fortunately, the type of printer—and whether or not it prints in color—doesn't matter at all when you're connecting the thing to your computer. All printers hook up to computers with a single cable, and the installation is typically simple and straightforward. You plug one end of the cable into the printer and the other end into the computer.

That said, you may run into complications when you try to get your computer to communicate with your printer. Different printers respond to different instructions. In fact, printers use a unique language, and they require your computer to speak that language as well.

Differences in language are handled not by your applications (the word processor, electronic spreadsheet, and so forth), but by a small program known as a *printer driver*. There is a printer driver for every model of printer on the market. When you install a new printer, hooking the thing up to your computer is only one part of the job; the other part is installing the printer driver under Windows 95 so your software can recognize the new printer you have installed.

Printer Driver   A printer driver is a special software file that help Windows and your applications communicate with the printer. The printer driver also tells Windows 95 and your applications what options and capabilities your printer offers.

Connecting the Printer Hardware

Most printers connect via a parallel cable using one of your computer's *parallel* connections, which is by far the most common way (and on many printers, the only way) to attach a printer to a computer. If your printer uses a *serial* connection, the task of attaching the printer to the computer is considerably more difficult. You will need to consult the manual that comes with the printer to find out what kind of connection you need. You may also need to ask a knowledgeable friend or associate for help.

Cable Woes   Whether you buy your printer when you buy your system or later, you'll need to make sure the printer cable is included with your purchase. If not, don't forget to buy a printer cable, which will cost anywhere from $5 to $15. Typical cable lengths include 6', 10', 15', and 25'. Get the shortest cable you can practically use based on your workstation setup.

So, follow these steps to connect your computer to your system's parallel port:

1. Unpack the printer from the box and remove all shipping materials. Insert the ribbon, ink cartridge, or toner cartridge (depending on the type of printer you have), according to the instructions packed with the printer.

2. Find the printer cable and connect one end to the printer. The printer cable uses different connectors on each end; only one of these will attach only to the printer. It will look like Figure 1.1.

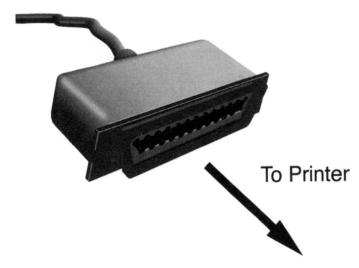

Figure 1.1 The end of the cable with a large ridge along the connector connects to the printer.

3. With your computer off, connect the other end of the printer cable to the computer. Most likely, your computer will have only one connector of the correct size and shape to accept the printer cable. (The end of the printer cable that plugs into the computer will have 25 pins.) Use this connector.

4. Most printers have a built-in self-test, often activated by pressing and holding one of the control buttons on the front panel of the printer (usually the **On Line** button) while turning the printer on; check the manual that came with your printer for more information. Insert a few sheets of paper into the printer and perform the self-test now. If the printer manual recommends other tests to perform, perform those tests as directed in the manual.

403

Installing a Printer to Run Under Windows 95

When you print in Windows 95, your program sends its data to the Windows printer driver, which then communicates with the printer. Follow these steps to install a new printer driver in Windows 95.

You will need your Windows 95 Setup disks or CD-ROM to complete the printer setup. Or, if your printer came with an installation or setup disk, the driver you need will be on that disk. Once you have the disk, follow these steps to install a new printer driver so your computer can print to the computer you just hooked up:

1. Turn your computer back on. If your new printer is a Plug and Play printer, Windows will automatically recognize the new printer, and prompt you to insert the install or setup disk that came with the printer. Follow the on-screen prompts to finish installing the printer driver. If Windows 95 doesn't automatically recognize the new printer, follow the rest of the steps in this process.

2. Double-click the **My Computer** icon, then double-click the **Printers** icon in the My Computer window. Instead, you can click the **Start** button, point to **Settings**, and click **Printers**.

3. The Printers window appears, showing icons for all the printers installed on your computer. Double-click the **Add Printer** icon.

4. The Add Printer Wizard appears, which will lead you through the process of installing a printer driver. Click the **Next** button.

5. The wizard asks if you want to install a local printer (connected directly to your system) or a network printer (which will be available to other computers on the network). Make sure **Local Printer** is selected, and then click the **Next** button.

6. The wizard next asks you to specify the manufacturer and model of your printer. Click the brand name of the printer in the **Manufacturers** list, and then click the make and model of your printer in the **Printers** list, as shown in Figure 1.2. (If your printer came with an install or setup disk, you can insert the disk in drive A, click **Have Disk**, then click **OK**. If needed, select the appropriate model in the **Printers** list.) Click the **Next** button.

7. A list of printer ports appears. Most printers connect to the parallel printer port (LPT1). If in doubt, pick **LPT1,** as shown in Figure 1.3. Click the **Next** button.

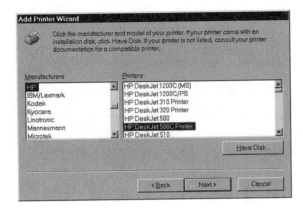

Figure 1.2   Choose your printer manufacturer and model in this dialog box.

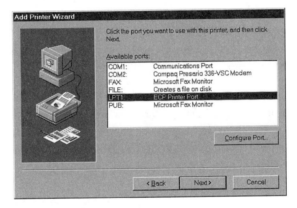

Figure 1.3   Specify the port you connected your printer to, usually LPT1.

8. The wizard asks if you want to use this printer as the default printer for your Windows programs. To have this printer act as your full-time printer for all your Windows programs, click **Yes** and click the **Next** button. If you select **No**, you'll have to select this printer in your program's printer setup each time you want to use it.

9. Click the **Finish** button. If the files for the selected printer are on your hard disk, the wizard installs the printer and adds an icon for it in the Printers window. If the files are not available, the wizard prompts you to insert a Windows disk or the manufacturer's disk.

10. If prompted to insert a disk, insert the disk and click **OK**.

TIP **Another Default**   To pick a different printer as the default, right-click its icon in the Printers window and click **Set As Default**.

CAUTION

Printing from a DOS App   If you use DOS, you'll need to set up your new printer within each of your applications, using the application's installation disk (check each program's manual for instructions). During setup, the program will install the appropriate printer driver for use with that program only.

Connecting More than One Printer

If you want to connect more than one printer to a computer, or two computers to a single printer (such as your desktop and laptop), you can buy a parallel switch for about $20. You'll need two extra cables, too. Simply connect the port on the switch labeled "printer" to the parallel port on the back of the PC with a parallel cable. Then, plug a cable into each printer, and plug each cable into a port on the back of the switch. (One will be labeled A, and the other B, usually.)

Then, install the printer driver for each printer under Windows 95. To choose which printer to print to, flip the switch on the switch box to A or B, as needed. Then, in the Print dialog box for the application you're printing from, choose the printer to print to, as shown in the example in Figure 1.4. Click the **Print** or **OK** button.

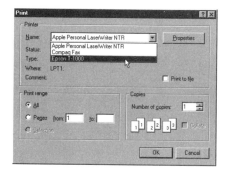

Figure 1.4   Choose which printer to print to in the application's Print dialog box.

This lesson showed you how to attach a printer to your system and set up Windows 95 to print to the printer. The next lesson provides you with the steps you need to install a new mouse or keyboard.

Installing a New Mouse or Keyboard

2

This lesson reviews how to attach a mouse or keyboard to your system, how to install drivers for the new hardware, and how to adjust mouse and keyboard settings.

Adding a Keyboard

In Lesson 12 of Part I, you learned how to connect a keyboard to your new computer system. A keyboard provides your primary means of inputting information and giving the printer instructions. As such, a new computer system will already be set up to work with the keyboard that comes with it.

You may want to replace your keyboard at some point, though. Keyboards do stop working eventually, or develop problems with particular keys. In addition, you might want to opt for an ergonomic keyboard to make extensive keyboard time more comfortable for your wrists and fingers. Other keyboards offer special features, such as programmable keys. You simply may want to upgrade your keyboard to have more keyboard capabilities. This section explains how to add that new keyboard to your system.

CAUTION

Connections Keyboard receptacles are round and accept come in a couple of different sizes (with either five or six pins). Check out the plug for your existing keyboard, and make sure you buy a keyboard with the same style plug.

Attaching the Keyboard

The keyboard plugs into a round receptacle on the back of the computer. The keyboard connector that plugs into this receptacle has five or six pins and a square. A notch in the plug rim by the square helps you line up the plug. So, to connect the new keyboard:

1. Turn off the computer.

2. Unplug the old keyboard from its receptacle. If no keyboard is plugged in, the keyboard receptacle should be clearly marked.

3. Plug in the new keyboard.

 TIP   **Laptop Add-Ons**   Most laptops offer a port so you can plug in an external keyboard or mouse. You may want to do so if you're using the laptop at your desk and want a more comfortable keyboard or mouse.

Setting Up the Keyboard

Even though your system will recognize the new keyboard, it may not be able to take advantage of all the keyboard's features. To ensure that Windows 95 can work smoothly with the keyboard and take advantage of all its settings, you need to set up the keyboard under Windows 95, which basically installs the driver file for running the keyboard. Windows 95 offers drivers for numerous keyboards; or look for a disk that came with your keyboard, which will offer the appropriate driver.

To install the keyboard under Windows 95, follow these steps:

1. Turn your system back on, and don't start any programs. If your new keyboard is a Plug and Play keyboard, Windows will automatically recognize the new keyboard, and prompt you to insert the install or setup disk that came with the keyboard. Follow the on-screen prompts to finish installing the keyboard driver. If Windows 95 doesn't automatically recognize the new keyboard, follow the rest of the steps in this process.

 TIP   **Find the Keyboard**   If you turn your computer on and no lights blink or appear on the keyboard, the keyboard has not been found by the system. If this happens, make sure you've plugged the keyboard into the right receptacle. You might have accidentally plugged it into the mouse port, for example.

2. Click the **Start** button, point to **Settings**, and then click **Control Panel**.

3. Double-click the **Keyboard** icon. The Keyboard Properties dialog box appears.

4. Click the **General** tab. This tab enables you to choose the keyboard you're using.

5. Click the **Change** button beside the Keyboard Type text box.

6. Click the **Show All Devices** Option button in the Select Device dialog box to display more keyboards in the Models list, as shown in Figure 2.1.

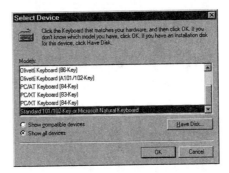

Figure 2.1   Select the keyboard you're adding to your system.

7. Scroll through the Models list, and click your keyboard. (If your keyboard came with an install or setup disk from the manufacturer, click the **Have Disk** button, insert the disk in drive A, and click **OK**; then select the keyboard model.) If Windows asks you to verify the keyboard change, do so.

 TIP **File type?**   Many hardware driver files (installation information) have an .inf extension rather than .exe. That's why you have to add them using a Properties dialog box rather than by simply running the setup file.

8. Click **OK**. Windows 95 may prompt you for a Windows 95 Setup disk or CD-ROM. Insert it and click **OK**. The driver is set up on your system.

9. After the driver installs, you may be prompted to restart your system. Click **Yes** so the new keyboard driver will take effect.

Changing Keyboard Settings

All keyboards offer basic settings you can change under Windows 95. The most important is probably the repeat rate. If you hold down a key, it starts to repeat, and it should repeat at a rate that is comfortable.

Follow these steps to adjust the most typical keyboard settings:

1. Click the **Start** button, point to **Settings**, and then click **Control Panel**.

2. Double-click the **Keyboard** icon. The Keyboard Properties tab appears, with the Speed tab displayed, as shown in Figure 2.2.

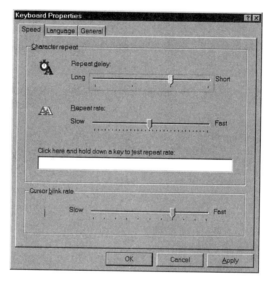

Figure 2.2   Select the settings for your keyboard.

3. To change how long you have to hold down a key before it starts repeating, drag the **Repeat Delay** slider to the left (so you have to hold down the key longer) or to the right (so the character will start repeating more quickly).

4. To change how fast the character repeats when it starts repeating, drag the **Repeat Rate** slider to the left (to repeat slowly) or to the right (for a quicker pace).

5. To change the speed at which the insertion point blinks, drag the **Cursor Blink Rate** slider to the left or right.

6. Click the **OK** button. Your changes are saved, and your keyboard will start acting as you instructed.

TIP   **Parlez-Vous?**   You can set up your keyboard's keys to type characters from a different language using the Language tab of the Keyboard Properties dialog box.

Adding a Mouse

The other key tool for telling your computer what to do is your mouse. While the keyboard provides for convenient data entry, many users find the mouse makes entering commands easiest. And, you'll definitely want a mouse to use with drawing and graphics programs.

Most computers come with a mouse, which should last a few years at least, like other computer components. Yet, you may encounter situations like these where you need to replace the mouse:

- Your current mouse dies. Hey, it happens. If the mouse that came with your system was on the cheap side, it may not stand up to the wear and tear you give it.
- You want more ergonomic (hand- and wrist-friendly) features, or don't like the size, shape, or responsiveness of your current mouse.
- You want to replace the mouse with a trackball.

You can replace a mouse with relative ease, as described in this section.

Attaching the Mouse

The most important consideration in adding or replacing a mouse is how a new mouse connects to your computer. Check out what kind of mouse you have now. Some mouse connectors are round, with five or six pins and a box, like a keyboard connection (a mouse that connects this way is called a BUS mouse). The outlet should be clearly marked; if it's not marked, look for it near the port for your keyboard. If your system has a round mouse receptacle, look for a mouse or trackball that uses this type of connector, if possible.

Another kind of mouse or trackball might use one of your PC's serial ports to attach to your computer. If the new mouse you want to add hooks up to your computer by way of a serial port, your computer must have one available, and it must be the correct size to accept the connector on the end of the mouse cable. A serial port has nine pins; a parallel port (usually used for printers) has 25 holes instead.

More than likely, unless you have attached an external modem to your computer, the serial port on your PC is available and waiting to be hooked up to a mouse. In the event that a serial port is not available, you'll have to add one. This entails opening your computer and installing an adapter card that has one or more serial ports on it. (See Lesson 4 in this part, "Installing an Adapter Card.")

 TERM   **Serial Port**   It's called a "serial" port because the data goes in and out of the connector one bit at a time in series (one after the other). The cable of the typical serial mouse is equipped with a 9-pin "D" connector. If the serial port on your PC is a 25-pin "D" connector, you will need an adapter, available from your dealer.

Once you've purchased the new mouse or trackball and have verified that you have the right type of connector for it, follow these steps to connect it:

1. Turn off your computer.

2. Locate the 9-pin "D" connector or circular mouse port on the back of your computer, as shown in Figure 2.3. (Laptops usually have the mouse and keyboard ports on the side of the system.) Most mouse connectors and serial ports are clearly marked.

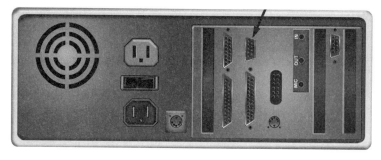

Figure 2.3   If your mouse attaches to a serial port, find it on the back of your system.

3. Plug the end of the mouse cable into the serial or mouse port on the back of the computer.

Setting Up the Mouse

In addition to connecting the mouse to your PC, you will need to install a *mouse driver*, just as you install drivers for keyboards (as described earlier in this lesson) and other hardware components. This software enables your PC to "talk" to your mouse. (The driver program comes on a disk included with your mouse.)

Although you may find that your computer recognizes your new mouse when you start up, you should follow these steps to install the mouse driver to ensure the new mouse (or trackball) works correctly:

1. Turn on your computer. Windows 95 starts. If your new mouse is a Plug and Play mouse, Windows will automatically recognize the new mouse, and prompt you to insert the install or setup disk that came with the mouse. Follow the on-screen prompts to finish installing the mouse driver. If Windows 95 doesn't automatically recognize the new mouse, follow the rest of the steps in this process.

2. Click the **Start** button, point to **Settings**, and click **Control Panel**.

3. Double-click the **Mouse** icon to view the current mouse settings. The Mouse Properties dialog box shows the current settings for the mouse.

4. Click the **General** tab.

5. The Name text box displays the type of mouse Windows thinks is installed (probably your old mouse). Click the **Change** button to pick a different mouse type if the current name is wrong.

6. The Select Device dialog box that appears lets you pick a mouse type. If needed, click the **Show All Devices** option to display more models, as shown in Figure 2.4.

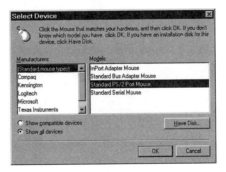

Figure 2.4   Choose the mouse model here.

7. Click the manufacturer's name and the model. (If the mouse came with a disk that has its own Windows 95 driver, click the **Have Disk** button, insert the disk in drive A, and click **OK**; then select the keyboard model.) Click **OK**.

8. The required mouse driver may not be on the hard drive. Windows might need to copy it from one of the Windows Setup disks or the Setup CD-ROM. If prompted for a disk, insert the specified disk and click **OK**.

9. After it installs the mouse driver, Windows will ask if you want to restart the PC. Click **Yes**.

Changing Mouse Settings

As with your keyboard, Windows 95 enables you to control the behavior of the mouse. You can change the look of the mouse pointer, change the speed at which it travels across the screen, and even switch the functions of the left and right mouse buttons for all you lefties. Follow these steps to adjust your mouse settings:

1. Click the **Start** button, point to **Settings**, and click **Control Panel**.

2. Double-click the **Mouse** icon to display the Mouse Properties dialog box. The Buttons tab appears in front, as in Figure 2.5.

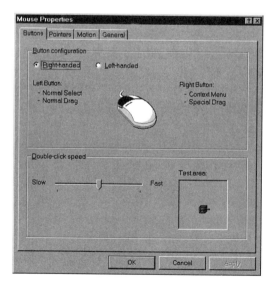

Figure 2.5 Here are the settings for adjusting how your mouse buttons work.

3. Under **Button Configuration**, click **Right-Handed** or **Left-Handed**. Left-handed swaps the functions of the left and right mouse buttons so that the left button brings up shortcut menus and the right button selects items.

4. To change the speed at which you must click twice for Windows to acknowledge a double-click, drag the **Double-Click Speed** slider to the left or right. (You can double-click the jack-in-the box animation to test the speed.)

5. Click the **Pointers** tab. Then open the **Scheme** drop-down list and click the desired mouse pointer scheme. The list of mouse pointers changes to display the various mouse pointers in this scheme. (You can change the look of an individual pointer by clicking it, clicking the **Browse** button, and selecting a different pointer.)

6. Click the **Motion** tab to set the speed at which the mouse pointer travels across the screen. Drag the **Pointer Speed** slider to the left or right to change the speed of the pointer.

7. To have the mouse leave a trail as it travels across the screen, click **Show Pointer Trails**, and then use the slider to set the length of the pointer tail. (Roll your mouse around to test the effects of your change.)

8. Click the **OK** button to save your new mouse settings.

 TIP **Joystick** To calibrate a joystick attached to your system, double-click the Joystick icon in the Control Panel.

This lesson showed you how to install a new keyboard or mouse for your system. The next lesson covers general preparation tasks for more complex hardware upgrades.

Cracking the
Case and Other
General Stuff

This lesson covers general procedures for upgrading your hardware including precautionary steps, tools, basics for opening the system unit, working with device drivers, and editing key system files.

Backing Up Files

Adding new hardware (particularly internal hardware) to a system can have unpredictable results. Before you ever open up your system unit to make a change, you need to make sure valuable information from your hard disk is protected.

First, follow the steps listed in Lesson 1 of Part 6 to create an updated startup disk. Make sure, at a minimum, that you copy your Autoexec.bat and Config.sys files to the startup disk. Then if your system won't reboot after the upgrade, you can boot from the startup disk to begin diagnosing the problem. In addition, follow the procedure outlined in Lesson 14 of Part 6 to back up important data files. The precautionary measure will enable you to retrieve those files should they somehow become damaged on the disk.

Tools

The most essential tools for any upgrade are a small, flat-head screwdriver and a small Phillips-head screwdriver. You can buy these in the right sizes from any computer store. These tools are enough to enable you to remove and replace virtually all connecting screws. You might find a few additional tools useful, though:

- A nut driver for removing and replacing the screws on the back of the case.
- Needle-nosed pliers for adjusting jumpers and other tight operations.
- A soft artist's brush for brushing dust out of the system.
- A can of compressed air (available at computer stores) for blowing debris out of the system.
- Masking tape and a felt-tip pen for labeling connections.
- An anti-static wristband (Figure 3.1), which you connect to your wrist and a metal part of the computer case to discharge static electricity.

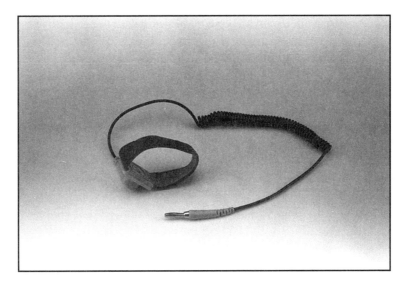

Figure 3.1 Attach the band to your wrist and the other end to a metal part of the case to discharge static.

Avoid Zaps Avoid touching any edge connections (the metallic parts that insert into slots) for adapter cards, memory modules, or any type of circuit card. Static electricity from your body could zap the component through the connection you touched.

CAUTION

Opening and Closing the Case

Many upgrades you'll perform will involve removing the cover from the system unit to insert, remove, connect, and disconnect components. You might be intimidated the first time you "crack the case," but it's actually the easiest part of most upgrades. So, use these steps to open your system unit so that you can access its internal components for upgrades:

1. Shut down the computer and all its components. Also unplug the system unit or simply unplug the surge protector that your other components are plugged into.

2. Unplug the monitor from the back of the system unit and move the monitor out of the way, to a safe place. If needed, disconnect other components from the back of the system unit, too.

3. Remove the screws on the back of the system that hold the system unit's cover on. If you have a flat, desktop case, there will be a screw in each corner, one in the middle top, and perhaps one in the middle bottom. Tower/minitower cases have two or three screws on each side. (Don't remove screws that are more toward the center of the back panel; these hold the system fan and power supply in place.)

CAUTION

Pop-off Case   If the back of your system unit has only four screws grouped closely together, your case may have a pop-off front panel. To remove such a panel, you don't have to remove any screws. Feel along the bottom front of the case for a handhold to use to gently pull off the front panel.

4. After you've removed the screws on the back of the case, slide the cover carefully forward and off the base of the system unit (see Figure 3.2). Some covers slide nearly all the way forward or backward, then lift up for removal. For others, slide the cover an inch or two forward and lift. Set the cover aside.

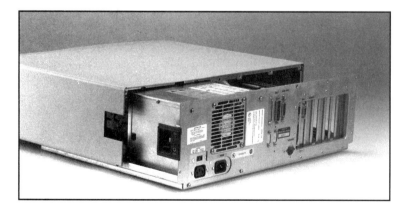

Figure 3.2   Slide this case nearly all the way forward, then lift it off.

5. Touch a metal part of the case before you do anything else to ground yourself. Or, if you've purchased an anti-static wristband, connect it and put it on now. You need to ground yourself or discharge static electricity, so that electricity doesn't build up and short out a delicate internal component (such as an entire chip) when you touch it. Also, avoid touching the large power supply box within the system for several minutes, because it can hold a charge for some time.

6. Take some precautionary steps to ensure you'll be able to put everything back together. Put the case screws in a safe place, and do the same with any other screws or parts you remove. Before you disconnect any internal wire or cable, apply a piece of masking tape to it (like a flag) and label it with the name of the socket it connects to on the motherboard (if the motherboard is labeled) or elsewhere.

 TIP **Screw Holders** Small, zip-style sandwich bags make a great holder for screws and parts. Place the screws or parts in the baggie, zip it closed, and label it with a pen and a piece of masking tape.

After you've finished working inside the case, you need to replace it, using the following steps:

1. Double-check all connections you've made inside the system unit, and make sure adapter cards are inserted firmly. Tuck all cables and wires safely within the case.

2. If you removed an adapter card, leaving a hole where its connectors used to be at the back of the system, install an adapter cover to cover the gap (your system comes with all the extra slots covered, you should save any adapter covers you remove). If you don't replace the adapter cover, your system will tend to suck in dust and debris.

3. Slide the cover back on and carefully ease it into place, making sure you're not pinching any cables.

4. Replace the screws that held the cover on at the back of the case.

5. Reconnect all the system connections (such as the monitor), and plug the system back in.

Installing and Removing Device Drivers

Adding the new hardware during an upgrade doesn't finish the job. You need to install the *hardware driver* software that helps Windows 95 recognize and communicate with the device. With Windows 95, this process is fairly automated, but does vary slightly depending on whether or not the device you buy is plug and play.

Adding Drivers for Plug and Play (PnP) Devices

Plug and Play devices are semi-intelligent, meaning that Windows 95 can "ask" the device what it is and basically take care of the setup process without any intervention on your part. You simply turn off the computer, install the adapter card and connect the device, and turn on your computer. Windows 95 will automatically tell you that it's found the new device and is installing it. It may prompt you for the install disk that came with the device. Insert it and follow the on-screen prompts, restarting the computer if Windows prompts you to do so. After you restart the second time you're ready to roll.

But in order for Plug and Play to work, your computer (and the device you want to install) must meet the following requirements:

- Your computer must have PCI or VLB expansion slots (or some other type of expansion slot that is capable of handling Plug and Play expansion boards).

- Your computer must have a BIOS (a chip that contains a set of instructions that tells the various computer components how to work together) that supports Plug and Play.

- Your operating system must support Plug and Play standards, which Windows 95 does.

- The device you are connecting to your computer must be Plug and Play compatible.

If your system (or new device) does not meet all of the requirements on the Plug and Play list, you won't be able to simply plug it in and relax. If you install the device and turn on your PC, and Windows 95 still does not recognize it, simply run the Add New Hardware Wizard, described next, to install the new device on your computer.

Add New Hardware

When you installed Windows 95, the setup program searched for hardware devices (sound card, modem, printer, mouse, and so on) already installed in your computer and set up these devices to work in Windows. However, if later on you add a sound card, game card, or other device that's not Plug and Play, you must tell Windows to set up that new hardware.

Fortunately, Windows 95 offers a wizard that leads you through the process of installing new devices and helps you resolve any problems that might occur. Just follow these steps to run the Add New Hardware Wizard to install the driver for a new device:

1. Install the adapter card and start your system. Close any programs that automatically load when Windows starts.

2. Click the **Start** button, point to **Settings**, and then click **Control Panel**.

3. Double-click the **Add New Hardware** icon.

4. The Add New Hardware Wizard appears, telling you what the wizard will do. Click the **Next>** button.

5. The wizard asks if you want it to search for new hardware on your system. Make sure **Yes (Recommended)** is selected, and then click the **Next>** button.

6. The wizard indicates that it is about to search your system for any new devices. Click the **Next>** button.

7. The wizard displays a progress meter as it searches your computer for any new hardware that's installed. This can take several minutes.

8. Wait until the detection process is complete (several minutes), and then click the **Finish** button. The wizard installs the new device, and you can go on to step 12.

9. If the wizard is unable to detect your new device, you'll see a message box telling you that. Click **Next>** and follow the rest of the steps.

10. Select the type of device you want to install from those listed. Click **Next>.**

11. Select the manufacturer and model number of the device you want to install. If your device is not listed and you have an Install disk, click **Have Disk,** select the install program, and click **OK.** You're returned to the Add New Hardware Wizard. Click **Next>.** You may see additional setup screens for particular devices; if so, select the appropriate on-screen options and click **Next>** to move to the next screen. Eventually, the wizard will install your new device.

12. The wizard will prompt you to restart your computer. If it doesn't, click the **Start** button, click **Shut Down**, click **Restart the Computer?** and then click **Yes**.

Checking for Device Conflicts

If you start your system and install the driver software and your new device doesn't work at all or works erratically, it may be suffering from a device conflict. A device conflict happens when two devices try to access the same *Interrupt Request* (or IRQ, a direct communications line to the CPU); *Direct Memory Access* (or DMA, a direct communications line to the RAM); or *base address* (a.k.a. I/O address or Input/Output Range, another line of communication to the system). You can resolve some device conflicts by changing settings in Windows. In other cases, you'll need to try removing and reinstalling the driver software, or even changing settings on the adapter card (covered in the next lesson).

Follow these steps to identify a hardware conflict and to try to change device settings within Windows 95:

1. Click the **Start** button, point to **Settings**, and then click **Control Panel**.

2. Double-click the **System** icon. The System Properties dialog box appears.

3. Click the **Device Manager** tab. The tab lists all the types of devices connected to your system and installed under Windows 95.

4. Click the plus sign beside the type of device you want to check for a conflict. For example, click the plus beside **Modem** to see the modems installed on your system, as in Figure 3.3. If the device you're looking for has a conflict with another device, a yellow circle with an exclamation point will appear over the device's name.

5. To try to fix a conflict, click the device, then click the **Properties** button. If the Properties dialog box that appears has a Resources tab, you may be able to change its settings to remove the conflict. Otherwise, try removing and reinstalling the software driver (described next); if that doesn't work, you'll need to open the system back up and change the settings on the adapter (as described in the next lesson), and then reinstall the driver.

6. Click the **Resources** tab. The resources (Interrrupt, I/O, and DMA) the device is using are listed in the Resource Settings list in the dialog box, as shown in Figure 3.4.

Figure 3.3 Click a plus to display the devices in a category. A yellow circle with an exclamation point indicates a conflict.

Figure 3.4 Check and change device resource settings here.

7. Clear the check beside **Use Automatic Settings**.

8. Then, click the setting to adjust in the Resource Settings list, and click **Change Setting**. A dialog box for the setting appears, like the example shown in Figure 3.5.

Figure 3.5 This example shows where to change the Interrupt Request (IRQ).

9. Adjust the settings to ones you believe are not in use by other devices, and click **OK.** (Watch the Conflicting Device List at the bottom of the Resources tab to make sure you're eliminating the conflict with the new settings, or to verify that the new settings haven't created a conflict. The list will read No Conflicts when all the conflicts have been eliminated.)

10. Repeat steps 8 and 9 to change other settings if needed, then click **OK** to close the Properties dialog box for the device. Restart your system when prompted, so your new settings will take effect.

Removing and Reinstalling the Driver

If you try to resolve a conflict in the Device Manager tab of the System Properties dialog box (usually just called the Device Manager) and it won't let you or doesn't work, you should try to remove and reinstall the driver.

 TIP **Upgrade Component Doesn't Work** If you remove an older device and replace it with a new one, such as replacing an old modem with a newer faster one, the new device may not work. This could be because the driver for the old device is conflicting with the driver for the new device. Try using steps 1-7 that follow to remove the old device driver, and see if that solves the problem.

Here's how:

1. If you think you need to change the settings on the adapter card (see the next lesson), do so. You'll have to open your system unit, as described earlier in this lesson, to access the adapter card.

424

2. Click the **Start** button, point to **Settings**, and then click **Control Panel**.

3. Double-click the **System** icon.

4. Click the **Device Manager** tab.

5. Click the **plus sign** beside the type of device you want to remove.

6. Click the device driver to remove, then click the **Remove** button.

TIP   **Disable the Device Instead**   To disable the device driver instead of removing it, click **Properties** instead of Remove (step 6). On the General tab, clear the check beside **Original Configuration (Current)**.

7. When prompted, verify the deletion and restart your system. If you're not prompted to restart the system, do so anyway.

8. Follow the prompts to reinstall the driver for a Plug and Play device, or start the Add New Hardware Wizard as described earlier in this lesson.

TIP   **No Plug and Play**   Sometimes Plug and Play devices will stop working if you make a change to your Windows 95 installation. To get the device to work again, remove its driver in Device Manager as just described and restart your system. On startup, Windows 95 should then recognize the device and lead you through the process of reinstalling the driver from the install or setup disk that came with the Plug and Play device.

Editing Key System Files with Sysedit

Out of the hundreds, possibly thousands, of files on your computer, only a handful specifically instruct it on how to operate. Two files in particular, Config.sys and Autoexec.bat, are loaded after you turn on your computer. These contain commands to load drivers, define settings, and generally prepare your computer for everyday use. When you install the drivers for hardware devices as described in several other lessons in this part, the setup process will automatically modify these *startup files*, if needed. Sometimes, though, you may need to modify these startup files manually to make your system run more efficiently.

When properly configured, these files tell your computer how to operate at peak performance, and load the drivers for some hardware devices. If you're having trouble with a hardware device, it's documentation may advise you to try to make changes to Autoexec.bat, Config.sys, Windows.ini, and System.ini. These files are text-based, but finding and opening them can be a drag. Fortunately, Windows 95 offers an automatic tool for editing system files called Sysedit.

Follow these steps to use Sysedit to open and edit system files:

1. Click the **Start** button and select **Run**.
2. Type **SYSEDIT** in the Run dialog box and click **OK**.
3. Immediately, the System Configuration Editor loads and displays several files: System.ini, Win.ini, Config.sys, and Autoexce.bat, as shown in Figure 3.6. In addition, the Mail.ini and Protocol.ini files may be opened.

Figure 3.6   Edit system files here.

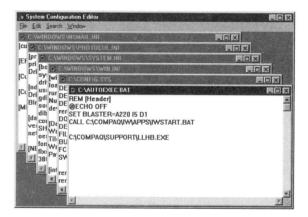

4. Although four or more files are displayed, you don't need to edit each one. Simply edit the file(s) you want. When you finish editing each file, save the file by choosing the **File**, **Save** command.

Disabling a Line   You can disable a command (line) in one of these critical system files. This is a good strategy, because it leaves the text of the line intact, so you don't have to remember the exact syntax (command, switches, and parameters) contained in the line. To disable a line, type **REM** in front of it and press the **Spacebar**. To reinstate the line, when needed, simply delete the REM and the space.

TIP

5. To exit SYSEDIT, open the **File** menu and choose **Exit**.
6. Any changes you made to the startup files won't take effect until you

restart your computer. To do so, choose **Start, Shut Down**. Click **Restart the Computer?** then click **Yes**.

This lesson covered key guidelines for performing an upgrade: preparatory steps and tools, opening the system unit and reassembling it, installing and removing device drivers, and editing system files. The next lesson explains how to install adapter cards, the basis of many upgrades.

Installing an
Adapter Card

*This lesson covers how to accomplish a crucial upgrade task—
installing an adapter card inside your computer.*

What Adapter Cards Are and Where They Go

Your PC is set up to enable you to add components. New components, commonly called *expansion cards* or *adapter cards,* are inserted inside the computer in special connectors known as *expansion slots* or *bus slots.* For some components, such as an internal modem or sound card, the adapter card itself is the device. In other cases, you install the adapter card then connect a device to it; the adapter card in such a case serves as an interface between the device and the motherboard. For example, disk drives and CD-ROM drives usually connect to an adapter card.

 TIP **Already Spoken For** When you buy your computer, one or more expansion slots are probably already taken up by adapter cards. So-called *base unit* adapter cards typically control the disk drives in your computer, as well as the hard disk, the monitor, and the parallel and serial ports.

New computers today typically offer 3-5 expansion slots for new devices, even if you buy a system that's fully-equipped with sound, a modem, and other extras. Today, there are two types of expansion slots and corresponding adapter cards in use: ISA and PCI (see Figure 4.1).

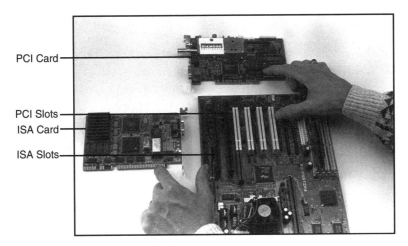

PCI Card

PCI Slots
ISA Card

ISA Slots

Figure 4.1 This motherboard shows the two "flavors" of adapter cards, and their corresponding slots.

To add an adapter card, you don't need to know the differences between how the two card types operate. You'll just need to keep in mind or check out these items:

- PCI slots are smaller than ISA slots, giving you an easy way to tell them apart.
- If you're not sure what type of slots your system has available, open the system unit (see the last lesson) and check.
- Make sure the adapter card (or the device's adapter card) you buy is of a type that you have an open slot for.

Although there are hundreds of different kinds of adapter cards, most computer users are involved with only a handful. These include sound cards, CD-ROM interface cards, and internal modems. Your disk drives attach to adapter cards. Removable and tape backup drives do, as well.

Remember, while installing a new adapter card is an essential part of many upgrades, the new card can cause problems with your system. Keep a careful record of all the changes you make to your system as you install the card. Then, if your system doesn't work properly, reverse the process and remove the card. However, if you follow the advice in this lesson, you should be able to install adapter cards from well-known device manufacturers.

Setting Jumpers and DIP Switches

Before you install some adapter cards into your system (or if you install the card and find it conflicts with another device as described in the last lesson), you need to adjust settings on the adapter card itself. Check the card's instructions to learn the specifics. The most common settings you need to change specify the *Interrupt Request (IRQ) address* and *DMA channel* the device will use to communicate with the CPU and with RAM. You also may need to set a *base address* (also called the *IO address*) for the device. The documentation will recommend what settings to use for the card.

TIP   **Finding IRQ Settings**   To find the IRQ settings for current devices, choose **Start**, **Settings**, **Control Panel**. Double-click the **System** icon, click the **Device Manager** tab, and double-click the **Computer** icon. Or, go to a DOS prompt, type **MSD**, and press **Enter**. Select **IRQ Status**, and look for a free address. Press **Esc**, use **File**, **Exit**, and return to Windows (Type **EXIT** and press **Enter** if needed).

To change the settings on the card, you change its DIP switches and jumpers. The DIP switches are a little bank of switches, shown in Figure 4.2, each of which can be set to an on or off position. Jumpers are plug-like receptacles that create a connection between two pins on the adapter. Usually, the adapter card will have one or two banks of eight pins each or so. To change the jumper setting, you pull the jumper off the two pins it's currently plugged onto, and move it to other pins, in either a vertical (connecting pins above and below each other) or horizontal (connecting pins that are side by side) position. You may want to use needle-nosed pliers to work with jumpers, as shown in Figure 4.3.

Figure 4.2   A card's DIP switches.

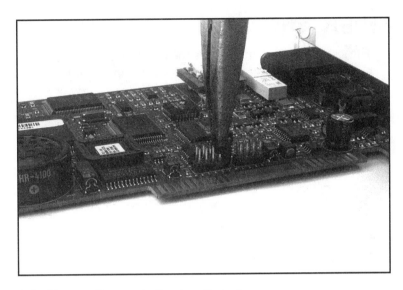

Figure 4.3 Use needle-nosed pliers to adjust a jumper.

Many cards come with the DIP switches and jumpers set to default settings that'll work on most systems. If you know you need to specify other settings, consult the card's manual to learn what DIP switch settings and jumper configurations to use. You'll usually see diagrams of specific DIP switches and jumper settings. (First, though, make a note of the default settings, then write down any changes you make.)

Keep these potential setting changes in mind when installing or troubleshooting conflicts for adapter cards:

- When installing a sound card, you will need to specify the *interrupt* (also called an "IRQ") and *base address* for the card. The address and interrupt you use cannot be shared with any other device in your computer. You may also need to specify the DMA channel.

- When installing a mouse card (for a so-called "port" mouse rather than for a serial mouse), you will need to specify the interrupt. The interrupt you use cannot be shared with any other device in your computer.

- When installing an internal modem (with or without a fax capability), you will need to specify the interrupt and serial port designator (such as COM1 or COM2) used for the card. Normally the interrupt and serial port designator you use cannot be shared with any other device in your computer.

Installing the Card

The steps here only summarize the technical setup of adapter cards. Because each card is different, you *must* have the manual for your card by your side when installing it. If you don't have a manual handy or if you don't understand it, don't even think about installing the card. Get help instead.

Follow these steps to install an adapter card in your system:

1. Shut down the system and follow the steps from the last lesson for removing the cover from the system unit and preparing for the upgrade.

2. Change the adapter card DIP switches and jumpers if needed.

3. Locate an empty expansion slot inside your computer. On most PCs, some slots have two connectors, and others have one. In addition, the connectors may vary in length. Look at the bottom of the adapter card, and use an expansion slot that matches the connector on the card. (In a pinch, you can install an adapter card that needs only one connector in an expansion slot with two connectors.)

4. Using a small Phillips-head screwdriver, remove the back plate at the back of the system unit for the expansion slot you want to use. Store the removed plate in a safe place. Keep the screw handy because you'll need it in a moment.

5. Insert the adapter card into the slot by first aligning the card over the slot, then carefully pushing straight down, as shown in Figure 4.4. A little bit of resistance is normal, but don't apply too much pressure, or you may break something. Instead, try rocking the card slightly to work it into the slot.

6. Using the screw you removed in step 4, secure the adapter card to the back of computer's case. Don't over-tighten.

7. If the card connects to some accessories (like a mouse, modem, or an internal drive), attach them now. Later lessons will cover some of the devices. Also consult the manual that came with the device.

 TIP   **Ribbon Connector**   Many internal devices connect to an adapter card via a wide, flat band of joined wires called a ribbon connector. The connection itself is notched to plug into the adapter in a particular way, so that pin 1 on the card lines up with the hole for pin 1 on the cable connector. A red line down one edge of the ribbon connector cable tells you that that side of the connector leads to the pin 1 socket. Pin 1 is also usually labeled on the adapter card.

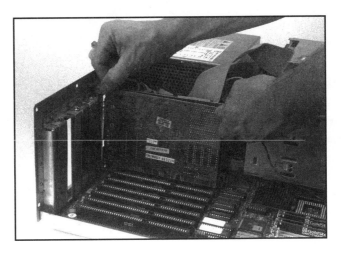

Figure 4.4   Gently push the card into the slot.

8. Before replacing the case and closing the computer, you should test the operation of the adapter card. Attach the monitor, plug your computer back in and turn it on. Install the driver software, either when prompted for a Plug and Play device, or by using the Add New Hardware Wizard, as described in the last chapter.

9. If the operation of the adapter card checks out, turn your computer back off. Put the computer back together by replacing the cover and screws as described in the last lesson. Your computer is now ready for regular use.

TIP   **Tilt It Out**   If you need to remove an adapter card, first disconnect any cables attached to it. Remove the screw that secures it to the back of the system unit, then pull gently up on the bracket on the back of the card (where the screw was) to tilt the card's back end out of the slot first. Then, ease out the rest of the card.

Adding SCSI Adapters and Devices

One type of adapter card that bears special mentions are SCSI adapter cards (also called a *SCSI controller card* or *host adapter*). This type of card installs in your system like any other, using the steps just described. You should, though, consult the documentation for your SCSI controller and devices to learn more about configuring and working with them. SCSI devices are growing in popularity (SCSI Zip and Jaz drives are available, for example), so you have occasion to want to add SCSI capability to your system.

Advantages

So why talk about SCSI? Because even though it's a bit more expensive to add a SCSI controller and even though SCSI devices that connect to the controller are themselves more expensive, you can connect up to seven devices to a SCSI controller once it's installed, with minimal additional setup. SCSI devices are faster than other comparable devices, which is in particular important for hard disks and removable disks, where disk speed affects your perception of how fast your system is overall. Finally, each SCSI adapter enables you to connect both internal devices and external devices (Figure 4.5), giving you a lot of flexibility in adding further hardware.

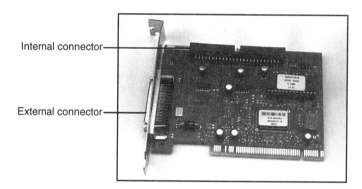

Internal connector

External connector

Figure 4.5 A SCSI controller lets you connect external and internal devices.

Like other computing standards, SCSI standards are evolving all the time. Currently, you'll see both SCSI and Ultra Wide SCSI controllers and devices on the market, with Ultra Wide being the latest and fastest standard. The two SCSI standards use different types of connectors, so in general, if you have a standard SCSI controller, buy standard SCSI devices, and don't pay the extra money for an even faster SCSI device. (You can, though, get connectors to connect one type of SCSI device to the other type of controller, if you really need or want to.)

Termination and IDs

All the devices you connect to a SCSI controller form a single chain, even if you've connected both internal and external devices to the same SCSI controller.

To chain the devices, you plug the first device into the internal or external connection, plug the next device into the first device, and so on. To build the chain in both directions, you plug the first device into each connector, plug the second device into the first device in each direction and so on. So, each chain can include the controller itself, plus a total of seven internal and/or external devices. For example, you could have two external and three internal devices connected, for a total of six (including the controller) in the chain.

With SCSI, each end of the chain must be terminated. So, in the example just listed, the second external device and third internal device would need to be terminated, because they're at opposite ends of the chain. If you have only internal or external devices connected (that is, the chain only runs in one direction from the controller), you need to terminate the last device in the chain and the SCSI controller itself. The controller usually automatically handles its own termination as needed. To turn termination on and off for other devices, you usually change a jumper, DIP switch, or a special switch on the back of the device. In other cases, you'll need to plug a termination resistor into the second SCSI port (each device has two) on the back of the device. Consult the manual for your SCSI controller and individual devices to learn more about setting termination.

Each device in a SCSI chain also must have a SCSI ID—set from 0-7. Generally, any device in any location of the chain can have any number, with the these two exceptions: if a hard disk on the chain is your system's boot disk, its SCSI ID must be set to 0; the SCSI controller itself (host adapter) should generally be set to 7. Again, SCSI IDs are often set via DIP switches and jumpers, so check the documentation for your controller and devices.

Adding a Parallel Port

Another little thought-of adapter card upgrade that could be helpful to you is to add a second parallel port to your system. I explained how to use two printers with your system via a switch box at the end of this part's Lesson 1. While that's great for printers, it won't work for other devices that connect to a parallel port such as a Zip drive or tape backup drive. And, even though you can plug a printer into the back of one of those devices and have both the printer and the device work, you can't plug any other type of parallel device into the back of another. For example, you can't plug your tape backup drive into the printer port on your SyQuest driver. The driver software for non-printer parallel devices must sense that the device is attached directly to the port. Otherwise, the device won't be detected.

The best way to attach two such parallel devices, then, is to add another parallel (LPT) port. These ports cost about $25, making them a good bargain for the convenience they offer.

Installing a parallel port resembles installing other adapter cards (but check the manual for the port you buy for specific instructions):

1. Use Device Manger or MSD (as noted earlier in this lesson) to find IRQ and base address settings for existing devices on your system, because you must specify a free address for the port.

2. Use the DIP switches or jumpers on the card to configure it for the right IRQ and base address. On most systems, LPT1 uses IRQ 7 and the base address 0378. You can then use IRQ 5 (or 7, if 5 is in use and 7 is available) and base address 0278 for the second parallel port you add, LPT2; these are the defaults for a second parallel port.

3. Open the system and put the card into place.

4. Install the 25-hole parallel connector at the back of the system unit using a mounting bracket, as in Figure 4.6.

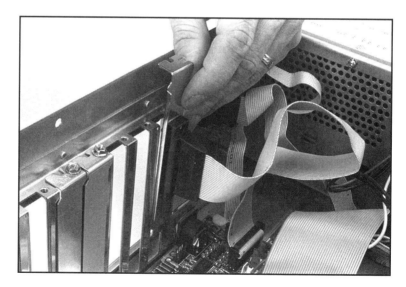

Figure 4.6   Install the port connector at the back of the system using a mounting bracket.

5. Plug the other end of the connector's cable into the appropriate spot on the adapter card.

6. Put the system's cover back on and restart.

7. Run the PC's setup program (also called the BIOS setup). You usually start this program by pressing **Del** or **F2** as the system boots. An on-screen message may flash the appropriate command as your system boots. Check your system's documentation to learn how to start this setup program, if you don't know how.

8. Make sure the new parallel port (usually LPT2) is set up as an EPP or ECP port as specified by the port's manual.

9. Save your settings, exit the setup program, and reboot. The new port should be recognized by your system and Windows 95.

This lesson explained how to add an adapter card to your system. Because most hardware devices either are or connect to an adapter card, this is a key upgrade to master. The next lesson explains how to add a modem to your system.

Adding and Setting Up a Fax/Modem

Use the steps in this lesson to learn how to install a modem.

Installing an Internal Modem

The process of installing an internal modem is just like installing an adapter card, as described in the last lesson. Most modems are ISA cards, so you'll need an ISA slot free in your system.

The one significant difference in the internal modem installation process is setting up the card before installing it, if needed. (Consult the modem's manual—you don't need to change the settings on all modems.) You have to think in terms of the COM port selection, as much as the IRQ. That's because COM ports share IRQs, even though they have different base addresses:

Port	Address	IRQ
COM1	3F8-3FF	4
COM2	2F8-2FF	3
COM3	3E8-3EF	4
COM4	2E8-2EF	3

Basically, if you have a high-traffic device like a mouse attached to one of your COM ports, you'll want to use the modem's jumpers and DIP switches to set it to a COM port that uses another IRQ. If your mouse is on COM1, set the modem up for COM4. When the mouse is on COM2, put the modem on COM3. If your system won't let you use COM3 or 4 and your mouse is on COM1, set up the modem for COM2.

After you install the internal modem, plug one end of the phone line that comes with it into the "Line" jack on the back of the modem and the other into your phone jack. Then start the system, install the modem driver software, and check the modem as needed.

TIP **Plug and Play** I installed a new Plug and Play modem a few months ago, and it was seamless. I didn't even have to change any jumpers or DIP switches. I just plugged the card in, attached the phone line, booted, and was prompted for the setup disk to install the driver. Plug and Play modems from the big manufacturers (U.S. Robotics, for example) are becoming easier and more reliable to set up.

Installing an External Modem

An *external* modem sits in its own case outside your computer and connects to your PC by a cable. Therefore, external modems are generally easier to install; however, they also tend to be a little more expensive.

In order for you to connect the external modem, your computer must have a serial port available (a serial port has either 9 or 25 pins, as in Figure 5.1). If there is no such serial port, you'll need to add one. This entails opening your computer and installing an additional adapter card that has one or more serial ports on it. (Adding more serial ports is more complicated than adding parallel ports.)

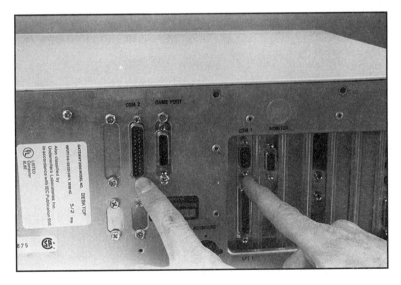

Figure 5.1 Find a COM (serial port) to connect the modem to.

Follow these steps to connect an external modem:

1. With your computer turned off, locate the serial 9-pin or 25-pin connector on the back of your computer. It is shaped like a "D" and has pins on it.

2. Plug one end of the modem cable into the serial port (see Figure 5.2). If the cable doesn't match your connector, you'll need to get an adapter (9-pin-to-25-pin, or vice versa), available at your computer dealer.

Figure 5.2   Plug the modem into the COM port.

3. Plug the other end of the modem cable into the 9- (or 25-) pin connector on back of the modem.

4. Plug one end of the phone wire into the modem's Line or Telco jack and the other end into a nearby telephone jack. If you have only one phone line in your office, connect the phone line coming from your telephone into the modem's phone jack. This will allow you to use your phone whenever you're not using your modem, and vice versa.

5. Start your system and set up the modem software.

Installing the Modem Driver Under Windows 95

In addition to installing the modem itself, you'll need to install the software driver that runs it; this software comes with the modem, on its install or setup disk.

If the modem is Plug and Play, after you install the modem card and restart your system, Windows 95 will automatically start the process for setting up the driver.

Otherwise, you can use the Add Hardware Wizard (Lesson 3 in this part) or the following steps to install the Modem driver:

1. Click the **Start** button, point to **Settings**, and click **Control Panel**.

2. Double-click the **Modems** icon.

3. The Modems Properties dialog box appears, showing a list of the modems that Windows thinks are installed on your computer. Click the **Add** button.

4. The Install New Modem dialog box appears. If you know the manufacturer and model name of your modem, you can select it from a list by choosing the **Don't run the Hardware Installation Wizard** option. In this case, though, you can let Windows attempt to determine your modem's type itself by *not* selecting this option. Click the **Next>** button.

5. Take one of the following steps:

    If Windows picked a modem type and you agree with it, click the **Next>** button, and then click the **Finish** button. You're done.

    If Windows picked a modem type that does not match your modem (or if it picked Standard), click the **Change** button and proceed to step 6.

    If you select the **Don't Detect My Modem** option so you can pick your modem type from a list, proceed to step 6.

6. Click the brand name of the modem in the **Manufacturers** list, and then click the model in the **Models** list, as in Figure 5.3. (If the precise model is not listed, pick a model that looks close. If the modem came with a disk, insert the disk, click **Have Disk**, and follow the instructions.)

7. Click **OK**.

8. You're returned to the Verify Modem dialog box, where the name of the selected modem is displayed. Click the **Next>** button.

9. If your modem has any special setup requirements, you may see additional screens. Eventually, Windows will indicate that the installation is over. Click the **Finish** button, and you're returned to the Modem Properties dialog box. Click the **Close** button to save your change.

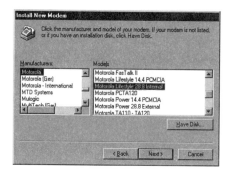

Figure 5.3   Select your modem model.

Other Modem Software

As you learned in lessons in the preceding two parts, Windows 95 comes with software that enables you to use your fax/modem for faxing, communications, and connecting to the Internet.

Your modem may come with special software for communicating or faxing, such a WinFax Pro. If you want to install the modem software, install it just as you would any other Windows 95 program (see Lesson 1 in Part 3).

This lesson explained how to install and set up an internal or external modem. The next lesson explains how to add a sound card and connect your speakers to it.

Installing a
Sound Card and
Speakers

This lesson shows you how to add a sound card to your system, and attach its speakers.

Installing the Card

More and more computers come with sound capability. So, chances are, you won't need much of the information in this lesson until your sound card goes on the fritz and you need to replace it.

As the name implies, sound cards are simply adapter cards that handle sound within your computer. The steps for installing the sound card itself are generally the same as those outlined in Lesson 4 of this Part, but should check your sound card to learn the specifics. Check for an available IRQ, configure the card for it by setting DIP switches and jumpers, open the system unit and install the card (see Figure 6.1).

In addition to installing the card though, you need to connect an audio channel cable from the sound card to the connection labeled Audio on the back of the CD-ROM drive for your system. (If you're upgrading an older system that doesn't have a CD-ROM drive, you don't have to attach the audio channel cable to anything.) This enables the sound card to play sounds from audio and multimedia CDs. Figure 6.2 illustrates how to make this connection. The manual that comes with your sound card can give you details about finding the right connection on the card.

Figure 6.1   Install a sound card in the system unit just as you'd install any other adapter card.

If you bought a multimedia kit that includes a CD-ROM drive and lets you run the CD-ROM drive from a controller on the sound card rather than a separate controller, connect the ribbon cable from the controller on the sound card to the back of the CD-ROM drive. (This kind of setup is often harder to configure than running the CD-ROM from your system's regular Enhanced IDE [EIDE] controller that manages hard disk drives.) Keep in mind that you will still need a separate IRQ and other settings available for the CD-ROM drive, too.

After you've made all the connections, reassemble the system. Boot, and have Windows 95 lead you through the driver setup for a Plug and Play card, or start the Add New Hardware Wizard (Lesson 3 of this part) and install it yourself. If you're planning to play DOS games with sound and your sound card also comes with DOS setup software, you'll need to run that software as explained in your sound card's manual.

 TIP   **Sound and Data**   Some upgrade kits now feature cards that function both as a sound card and as a voice-capable modem. Creative Labs offers two: the Sound Blaster 32 Value PnP (about $140) and the Phone Blaster 33.6 PnP (about $240).

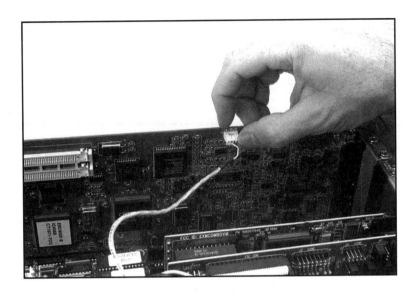

Figure 6.2 Connect the audio channel cable to the sound card (top) and the back of the CD-ROM drive (bottom).

Attach Speakers and a Microphone to a Sound Card

For a sound card to make sound, you have to attach some speakers to it. This is a simple job: Just insert the plug for the speakers into the appropriate jack on back of the sound card. If you want to record sound, you'll need a microphone, too. Simply plug the microphone into its jack on the sound card.

Before continuing, however, let's pause to consider the speakers you'll need for computer sound. The speakers that come with many sound-card-equipped computers don't provide amplification of their own. The strength of the sound depends entirely on the sound card, and some cards put out louder sound than others.

If you find the sound isn't loud enough for your tastes, first try to turn up the volume on the sound card (many sound cards have volume controls) or the "master volume" control on the sound software running on your computer. In Windows 95, this master volume control is often found on the taskbar in the form of a Volume icon (it looks kind of like a speaker). If these steps don't improve the sound volume, you may want to consider replacing the speakers with better amplified types. Amplified speakers come with (surprise!) their own amplifiers. Their sound tends to be much louder (and of better quality) than what you get from unamplified speakers.

 TIP   **Not Just Any Speakers**   Be sure to buy "shielded" speakers designed specifically for computer use. Don't use just any old speakers (like the ones on your stereo) unless your sound card uses RCA style plugs and specifies that stereo speakers are okay to use. You have to be careful with some stereo speakers, though. They contain powerful magnets that can damage a disk.

Follow these steps to attach new speakers and a mic to your sound card:

1. With your computer turned off, locate the **Speaker** jack on the sound card in the back of your computer. Plug the speaker plug into this jack (if your sound card uses RCA style plugs, there will be two jacks, one each for the left and right speakers.) Most sound cards have several jacks that look alike, and you can damage the speakers and sound card if you plug the speakers into the wrong jacks.

2. Locate the microphone jack on the back of the sound card (sometimes labeled "mic" or "micr"), and plug your microphone into it. Again, be sure you use the correct jack in order to avoid damaging your sound card.

3. If your sound card has a volume control on it, set the control initially to about half to three quarters (if the control is numbered, set it between 5 and 7).

4. You can now test your new speakers by starting any program that uses sound. While listening, adjust the volume control (if applicable) on the sound card.

5. To record sound (for a test, for use as an annotation, or within Windows), start **Sound Recorder.** In Windows 95, click **Start**, select **Programs**, select **Accessories**, and then select **Multimedia**. Click **Sound Recorder**, which appears as shown in Figure 6.3

Figure 6.3   Use the Windows 95 Sound Recorder Accessory to record sounds using your microphone and sound card.

6. Click the **Record** button (its the last one on the right). Speak or play music into the microphone. When you're done recording, click **Stop** (it's the fourth button).

7. Click **Play** (the middle button) to play your recording. To save it, open the **File** menu and select **Save**. Then enter a file name for the recording and click **OK**. The file is saved in .WAV format, which all Windows programs support.

This lesson explained how to add a sound card to your system and attach and test your speakers and microphone. The next lesson covers adding a CD-ROM drive.

Installing a Hard Drive, CD-ROM Drive, or Tape Backup Drive

This lesson explains how to add an (E)IDE-type or SCSI hard, CD-ROM, or tape backup drive to your system.

What Hard Disks, CD-ROMs, and Tape Backup Drives Have in Common

To provide consistency in the computing industry and ease of manufacturing and installation for components, drive manufacturers use consistent types of controllers (interfaces) for the major types of data drives. Most drives today connect via either an enhanced IDE (EIDE) controller or a SCSI controller. The steps for attaching each type of device to a particular type of controller are roughly the same. That is, you use roughly the same steps to attach a hard disk as you do for a CD-ROM. As such, this lesson provides overview steps for attaching a new drive to either an EIDE or SCSI controller. As always, you'll need to consult the manual that comes with the drive you buy to verify the correct steps and settings for your particular case.

Installing an Internal, EIDE-type Drive

Most internal hard, CD-ROM, and tape backup drives attach to what's called an IDE connector. Most motherboards today now actually support what's called Enhanced IDE (EIDE), and IDE and EIDE connectors are the same. This section describes how to install an IDE or EIDE drive.

Drive Bay

You'll need an empty disk drive bay into which you install the drive. There are two types of drive bays, and you should make sure you have the right type available on your system.

An external drive bay enables you to install a CD-ROM or tape drive, where you need to insert and remove media from the drive. *External drive bays* have pop-off face plates, so that the face of the new drive is flush with the front of the computer once the drive is installed and the system unit cover is replaced. External drive bays are usually at the far right end of desktop system units (below existing floppy and CD-ROM drives) or toward the top of a tower unit. *Internal drive bays* are for hard disks, and are usually in a location where the cover for the system unit will hide them from view.

Bays have different widths, too—3.5" and 5.25". The bay needs to be wide enough to accommodate the drive. If the bay is wider than the drive, attach mounting brackets to the drive (see Figure 7.1). All drives slide into the bay via slide rails, which attach to either the drive itself or the mounting brackets.

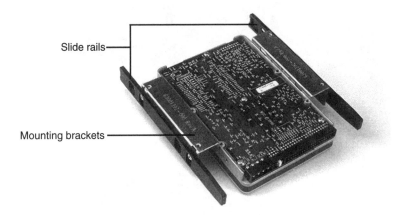

Slide rails

Mounting brackets

Figure 7.1 Mounting brackets help this 3.5-inch drive fit in a 5.25-inch bay, and the slide rails help it to slide into place.

CAUTION

Missing Brackets and Rails The brackets and rails you need don't always come with the drive. Also, different computers require different types of slide rails. You may have to make an unexpected run to your local computer store or call your computer's manufacturer to get these nitty-gritty pieces.

Primary and Secondary IDE Controllers

The EIDE controller on today's systems is usually embedded on the motherboard. Each EIDE controller actually has two IDE connections, the Primary IDE and Secondary IDE, as shown in Figure 7.1. (In earlier days, IDE controllers were housed on adapter cards, and to add another drive you had to add another card.) The cable that connects drives to an IDE is a 40-pin ribbon cable, like the ones shown in Figure 7.2. Each cable has a connection at one end that you plug into the controller, and two connections that each plug into a drive.

Figure 7.2   Find the two IDE connections on your motherboard.

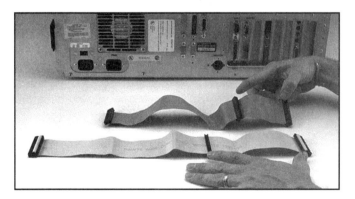

Figure 7.3   40-pin ribbon cables attach to the IDE connections on your motherboard's EIDE controller.

Your C drive will be connected to the Primary IDE connector. When you add a second hard disk to the system, it's best to add it to the 40-pin ribbon cable attached to the Primary IDE. Tape drives use the secondary IDE controller only, and the factory settings for CD-ROM drives also assume that you'll connect the drive to the Secondary IDE unless you specify otherwise. To connect either a tape drive or CD-ROM drive to the Secondary IDE, you'll need to make sure you get an additional 40-pin ribbon cable.

CAUTION

Too Many Devices The procedures described in this lesson assume you have a basic system setup with one hard disk attached to the primary IDE controller, and that the additional hard disk will be the second hard drive attached to your system via the primary IDE controller. I also assume that a CD-ROM or tape backup drive you add will be the only drive connected to your secondary IDE controller. If you have additional drives already installed on your system, your setup will be more complicated, and you'll need to consult your drive and computer system's manual (and perhaps a computer geek friend who owes you favors) before continuing.

Master versus Slave

Because you can attach two drives to each IDE connector, and because the system needs to know which drive to boot from, it has to have a way to distinguish between the drives attached to each connector. So, you must identify each drive as a *master* or a *slave*. The master drive on the primary IDE is the boot drive. Here's how to configure the various drives when you add them to your system:

- **Second hard disk.** When your C: drive (boot disk) is the only hard disk on your system, it may not specifically be configured as the master. So, when you add your second hard disk to the 40-inch ribbon cable attached to the Primary IDE, set the existing C: drive as a master and the new drive as a slave. Your system will automatically label the new hard disk as D:, as a result.

- **A CD-ROM drive.** Many CD-ROM manufacturers assume the CD-ROM will be installed as the master drive on the Secondary IDE connection, so unless you install it otherwise (such as if you add a tape backup drive and have to set up the CD-ROM drive as a slave), you usually won't need to reconfigure it. Usually, if your system has a CD-ROM drive labeled drive D: and you install a second hard disk, the CD-ROM will automatically be renamed as drive E:.

- **A tape backup drive**. When you connect an IDE tape backup drive to your motherboard's on-board EIDE controller, most manufacturers require you to use the secondary IDE and assume it will be the master. (Some tape backups come with their own IDE controller cards that you install and attach the drive to, and others do let you connect to the Primary IDE or set the drive up as a slave.)

To set a drive as master or slave, you generally adjust some jumpers on it. Check your manual to find out where the jumpers are and look at jumper diagrams if needed. Figure 7.4 shows master and slave jumper settings on two example hard disks.

Figure 7.4 The top EIDE hard drive is set as a master and the bottom one is set to slave. Notice the labels—MA for master and SL for slave.

Installing the Drive in the System

Once you're ready to go, follow these steps to install the drive in the system unit:

1. Back up your data, shut down and unplug your system, and safely remove the cover as described in Lesson 3 of this part.

2. If you're installing to an external drive bay, remove its face plate from the front of the system unit, as needed.

3. Set the drive to master or slave as needed.

4. Add any brackets and slide rails to the drive.

5. Attach a 4-pin power connector see (see Figure 7.5) to the back of the drive.

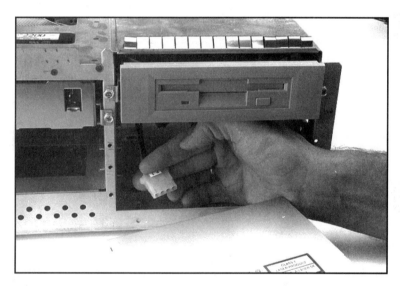

Figure 7.5   A four-pin power connector must be attached to each drive. (You can buy a Y-splitter to add more power connections if needed.)

CAUTION   **Power Shortage**   There is a limit to how many drives you can insert into your system and how many of them the power supply can handle. If you install four drives (all that your IDE connector can handle) and then want to install a drive like a tape backup or SCSI drive that attaches to another controller card, make sure your system's power supply can handle the load. Contact your system's manufacturer to verify the power supply's capacity, if needed. You don't want to overload (and therefore break) the power supply, which can be costly to replace.

6. Attach the second connection from the 40-pin ribbon cable connected to the Primary IDE to the second hard disk. Or, attach a second 40-pin ribbon cable to the Secondary IDE, and attach one of its connections to the CD-ROM or tape backup you're installing. Note that the connections on the ribbon cable are notched so you can line them up correctly. Also note that the red line along one side of the ribbon leads to the pin 1 connection, which is also labeled on the motherboard.

 TIP **Connection OK** As long as your jumpers are set correctly to designate a master or slave drive, it doesn't matter which connection on the 40-pin ribbon cable you connect each drive to.

7. Align the drive, and slide it into position in the drive bay, as in Figure 7.6. Note that in some cases, you might need to slide the drive partially into place before making the connections described in steps 5 and 6. Some drives may also require you to add a screw or two to hold it in place.

Figure 7.6 Slide the drive into place.

8. Put the cover back on the system, then try booting. If your system doesn't immediately recognize the drive, read on for additional steps.

454

Running System Setup

For some drives, you'll need to run the PC's setup program (also called the BIOS setup) to set drive settings or help your computer recognize the drive. You usually start this program by pressing **Del** or **F2** as the system boots. An on-screen message may flash the appropriate command as your system boots. Check your system's documentation to learn how to start this setup program, if you don't know how.

For a hard disk, you may have to set the Cyls (number of cylinders in the drive), Heads (number of read/write heads in the drive), and S/T (number of sectors per track) drive parameters. For a CD-ROM drive, you might have to specify IRQ settings. For drives connected to the Secondary IDE, you may have to enable that IDE on the motherboard. Consult the help in your system setup to learn how to access various settings, and the manual for your drive to learn what settings may need to be changed.

After adjusting system settings, exit the setup program and reboot.

Other Setup Software

At this point, Windows 95 should recognize the drive (especially if it's Plug and Play). In some cases, you may need to install driver software (but not for hard disks). Some CD-ROM drives and tape backup drives may require that you install additional software to enable the system to recognize the drive when you boot in command prompt (MS-DOS) mode, as described in Lesson 3 of Part VI. If the drive comes with an install disk, that's a good tipoff that you'll need to install Windows drivers and perhaps other software for it. Consult the drive's manual for specifics. For tape backup drives, you need to install the tape backup software, unless you plan to use Microsoft Backup.

 TIP **CD-ROM Woes** Sometimes, non-IDE CD-ROMs need to be set to a particular IRQ setting, too. If your system can't find your CD-ROM drive, consult its manual regarding IRQ settings, and try the steps for resolving device conflicts in Lesson 3 of this part.

Formatting and Partitioning a New Hard Disk, If Needed

New hard disk drives may need another bit of attention. You may need to format and partition the drive. Some drives come with special utilities for performing these drive setup functions. Others require that you boot in MS-DOS (command prompt) mode and (see Lesson 3 in Part VI) and use the FDISK and FORMAT commands to partition and format the drive. Consult your manual to learn how to proceed for your particular drive. (Because Windows 95 OSR 2 supports the FAT32 file system, which eliminates the need to partition large disk drives, you won't have to partition the large disk drive under OSR 2.)

Installing a SCSI Drive

In Lesson 4 of this part, you learned about SCSI adapter cards and how they enable you to attach multiple, more speedy devices to your system. The process for attaching a SCSI hard disk, CD-ROM drive, or tape backup drive to a SCSI controller are the same as those described in that lesson:

1. Shut down your system.

2. Determine where in the chain you'll be putting the new drive.

3. Set the termination and SCSI ID for the drive. (If you need to adjust the termination on another device as a result, do so.)

4. If the device is external, simply connect it where needed within the external chain of devices and connect its power cable to the drive and the surge suppressor. If the device is internal, crack the case, connect it to the SCSI chain, attach a power source and slide rails, slide it into place, and reassemble the system.

5. Boot the system, and install any drivers (Windows 95 and DOS) for running the drive, as well as any software for using the drive (like backup programs for tape backup drives).

CAUTION **Boot SCSI** If you want to boot from a SCSI hard disk, you cannot have an (E)IDE hard disk attached to your system—unless your SCSI adapter card supports SCSI boot. If your SCSI adapter does not support SCSI boot, you'll have to remove the (E)IDE hard disk to boot from the SCSI disk.

This lesson provided the key steps for installing EIDE and SCSI drives. The next lesson explains how to add a Zip or other removable drive to your parallel port.

Adding a Zip or Other Removable Drive to a Parallel Port

This lesson explains how to add a removable drive that connects to a parallel port.

Easy-Add Drives

With today's larger hard disks, it's becoming more and more difficult for the average user to back up important data to floppy disks. Some users opt for a good tape backup system, but more and more users are choosing Zip drives or other types of drives that use removable cartridges.

Zip drives from Iomega (and their larger capacity cousins, Jaz drives) operate like floppy disk drives: You insert a formatted disk or disk cartridge and then copy onto the disk in the usual manner. The main advantage here is storage capacity. A Zip disk can store up to 100M of data (about as much as the small hard drives of a few years ago), and a Jaz disk can store about 1G.

Another company, SyQuest, offers 230M EZFlyer removable drives and SyJet 1.5G removable drives. (SyQuest previously offered 44M, 88M, 135M, 200M, and 270M removable drives.) There are still other companies that offer removable drives, but by far, the Zip drive has become most popular.

TIP   A Bigger, Better Floppy   Even though Zip drives are wildly popular, there's also a bigger, better floppy drive on the market. LS-120 floppy drives are destined to replace the now-standard 3.5-inch 1.44M floppy drives. LS-120 drives use 120M disks and read and write information up to five times faster than standard floppy disks. In addition, an LS-120 drive can read from and write to today's 3.5-inch disks (both 720K and 1.44M), something a Zip drive can't do. Further, LS-120 disks tend to be cheaper than Zip disks. Some newer machines are shipping with an LS-120 drive already installed. Due to cost-effective disk pricing and compatibility with 3.5-inch disks, LS-120 drives might someday replace today's floppy drives, according to many experts.

The large capacities of most removable drives make them a good choice for a backup system because you won't need to change your disks as often (if at all) in order to back up your important data. In addition, a removable drive can act as a removable hard disk: A program can be installed on a disk, along with the documents you might create while using the program. Storing programs that you don't use very often on removable disks is convenient because the programs won't take up valuable space on your hard disk.

Slow Programs   Keep in mind that a program stored on a Zip disk (as opposed to the hard disk) will run a bit slower, but probably not enough to be very noticeable.

CAUTION

Removable disks are useful for many other purposes, as well. With a removable drive like a Zip drive, you can do any of the following things:

- Copy large amounts of data from one computer to another (provided the second computer also has a drive of the same type attached).
- Store large multimedia files, such as scanned photos and sound files.
- Transport data between home and work much more easily (as long as you have the same type and format of removable drive attached to both systems).
- Store financial and other confidential data on a removable disk that you can keep in a safe overnight.

Connecting and Setting Up

Installing a removable drive is relatively simple. First, you connect the drive to your PC, and then you run a Setup program to tell your PC that the drive exists.

By far, the easiest type of drive to install is a parallel one, which piggybacks onto the same port your printer uses. Follow these general steps to add a removable drive to your system:

1. Turn your computer off. Turn your printer off as well.

2. Using the cable that came with your drive, connect the end marked for the drive ("ZIP" in the case of Zip drive) to the back of the drive.

3. Connect the other end of the cable to a parallel port on the back of your PC. (If your PC has only one parallel port, disconnect your printer so you can plug in the parallel drive. You'll reconnect the printer in step 4.)

4. If you disconnected your printer in step 3, connect your printer cable to the second port on the back of the drive, as shown in the example in Figure 8.1.

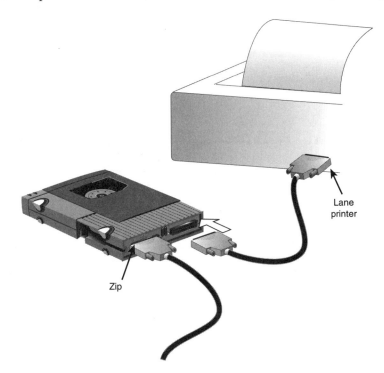

Lane printer

Zip

Figure 8.1   Connect one cable from the drive to the parallel port on your system, then another from the port on the drive to your printer.

5. Connect the removable drive to a power supply. A green light on the front of the drive indicates that it is On and receiving power.

6. Insert a disk cartridge into the removable drive (the Zip tools disk that came with the drive in the case of a Zip drive, or the startup cartridge for your drive), and boot your system.

7. Insert the drive's Install disk into your floppy disk drive.

8. If you use Windows 95, open Explorer, click the drive containing the Install disk, and then double-click the startup file for the drive's setup program. Install runs automatically.

9. Install the software for the drive that comes on the cartridge that comes with the drive. (For example, for a Zip drive cartridge, install the Zip tools software by clicking the **Zip drive** in Explorer, opening the **W95stuff** folder, and double-clicking **Setup95**.) The removable drive software is installed in Windows 95, and your drive is now ready to use.

 TIP   **Parallel Tape Backups**   Use roughly the same steps as those just listed to install and set up a tape backup drive that attaches to a parallel port.

 TIP   **Two Parallel Devices**   To connect more than one parallel device (other than printers), you need to add a second parallel port. See Lesson 4 in this part to learn more.

Other Removable Drive Flavors

Removable drives actually are available in external SCSI formats, too. You connect those drives to a SCSI adapter. If your system doesn't have a SCSI adapter, you'll need to install one, then attach the drive to it. (The SCSI adapter, of course, is an additional expense.) Lesson 4 of this Part explains how to install SCSI adapter cards and set up a SCSI device.

 TIP   **Internal Removable Drives**   Some new systems come with internal IDE Zip drives. Internal IDE Zip drives should soon be available as system add-ons. Other types of removable drives are available in internal formats in addition to external formats. For example, SyQuest SyJet drives are available in an internal IDE format.

This lesson explained how to connect a drive such as a Zip drive to a parallel port. The next lesson explains how to deal with video card upgrades.

Upgrading System Video

This lesson helps you make changes to have better display performance on your system.

Selecting the Right Components

Lesson 5 in Part 1 walked you through the most important considerations in selecting a monitor and video card for a new system. A later upgrade of your video card and monitor (if you find you're not satisfied with it) actually not only makes graphical information look better, but also improves the apparent speed of your system. No matter how fast the processor, if the information isn't drawn to the screen quickly, the system will seem sluggish.

As you learned earlier, the video card really controls the speed and resolution of the display, because it generates the images and provides them to the monitor. So, simply adding a new monitor to your system (even if it's larger) may not be a satisfactory upgrade. Conversely, the monitor must support the speed, resolution, and other features of the video card. So, even if you upgrade to a really souped-up video card, if the monitor can't keep up you won't see the benefits.

CAUTION

Buy Both   The bottom line is that a video upgrade will usually entail buying both a new monitor and a new video card, unless you're replacing a dead video card with a similar model.

Video cards start in the $200 range and can easily cost more than $1000 (or a couple thousand dollars) for professional-level cards used for graphics and digital video capture and editing. At the basic level, you'll be concerned with resolution, 3-D, and video RAM, as discussed in Part 1. If you start looking at higher-end cards and monitors, you'll also need to make decisions about these features:

- **Refresh rate**. This refers to how many times (per second) the video display adapter (video card) paints the image to the screen. 70-72Hz is the minimum, but a higher refresh rate is not only better but necessary for higher-resolution displays.

- **Multisynch**. This refers to a monitor that can support a range of vertical and horizontal frequencies generated by the video card. For example, to display at 1024×768 dpi, the monitor must support a vertical frequency of 60Hz and a horizontal frequency of 58khz. Just make sure the monitor supports the frequencies used.

- **Flat screen**. Less curvature in the monitor means a truer image and less glare.

Installing the Card

The overall process for installing a video card resembles the steps you saw in Lesson 4 of this part. However, there's an important first step to take before you crack the case: removing the driver for your current monitor in Windows 95 and switching to the standard VGA driver, which works with any monitor.

If you fail to do this and restart your system, it may not start at all because Windows will be looking for your old video card. Because display is so important to proper operation, display conflicts can keep the system from booting.

So, before you crack the case to install the video adapter card, follow these steps:

1. Choose **Start**, point to **Settings**, and click **Control Panel**.
2. Double-click the **Display** icon. In the Properties dialog box that appears, click the **Settings** tab.
3. Click **Advanced Properties**.
4. Click **Change** on the Adapter tab, then click the **Show All Devices** option button.
5. Scroll up to the top of the Manufacturers list and click **(Standard display types)**. Click **Standard Display Adapter** in the Models list, if needed, as shown in Figure 9.1.

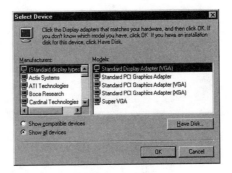

Figure 9.1 Select the Standard Display Adapter (VGA) before replacing your old video card.

6. Click **OK** to close the Select Device dialog box, then click **Close** to close the Advanced Display Properties dialog box.

7. Click **Close** to close the Display Properties dialog box.

8. When the **System Settings Change** dialog box appears to prompt you to restart your computer, click **Yes**.

Original Windows 95 If you don't have Windows 95 OSR 2 on your system, click Change Display Type in step 3 above and follow the dialog boxes.

CAUTION

Once you've changed to the plain VGA video driver, shut down your system. You can configure any jumpers as needed for your card, although this is usually not necessary if your card is Plug and Play. (Consult the manual with your card.) Disconnect the power source and the monitor, remove the case, and remove the screw holding the current video card in place. Gently rock the card out of its slot.

Insert the new card (as shown in Figure 9.2) into the appropriate slot for it (usually PCI these days), and secure it to the back of the case with a screw. (Make sure the card is firmly seated in the slot.) Before you put the system unit back together, test the video and monitor. Connect the monitor to the back of the video card. Plug the monitor and the system unit into a power source. Start the system, and look for the copyright notice for the video card. If you see it, the system is recognizing the card, and it should work.

Figure 9.2   Install a video card in a system by inserting it into an available slot.

Shut down your system, reassemble it, and restart. Install the drivers for the display (which come on the video card's install disk) under Windows 95. If you're not prompted to install the drivers when Windows loads, use the Add New Hardware wizard to install the device drivers, as described in Lesson 3 of this part.

In addition, you may need to install DOS-based software for the video card, including a setup program for the card or utilities for adjusting the resolution. Consult the manual for the video card to see what additional software you may need to display, and what additional steps you may need to take to calibrate or customize the display.

Adding More Display RAM

Most video cards come with at least 2M of onboard memory (RAM). Sometimes, the card will have room for even more. If you consult your computer's manual or contact the manufacturer of your system's video card and find that it has available memory slots, adding memory to improve display speed can be a more cost-effective option than replacing the video card altogether. If you use a lot of multimedia CDs or often work with graphics but are on a limited budget, moving up to 4M of RAM on your video display adapter could be your best bet.

The next lesson provides specific steps for installing RAM on a card, which is a straightforward process. The major consideration is purchasing the right memory for your card. Video adapter cards today use a veritable alphabet soup of different RAM types: EDO RAM, DRAM, VRAM, MDRAM, and more. Consult your manual or contact the card manufacturer to find out specifically what kind of RAM upgrade you need to buy. In fact, it might be your best bet to buy the RAM from the card manufacturer, if possible.

This lesson explained important considerations for upgrading your system's video, and gave you the steps for doing so safely. The next lesson helps you upgrade your system's RAM.

Upgrading Memory

Use the guidance in this lesson to add to the RAM on your system.

Increasing Available Memory Without New Hardware

Memory (*random-access memory* or *RAM*) within your computer is a precious thing because it's in memory that your computer performs its work. Information stored in memory is temporary; it's placed there long enough for the computer to do something with it, and then the data is copied back to the hard disk for permanent storage. In this way, the memory in your computer is like your office desk: You place documents, magazines, or books on your desktop to work with them, and when you're through, you put them back where they belong.

In addition to the documents you may be working on, programs you start (such as Microsoft Word or Lotus 1-2-3) are also placed in memory so the computer can process their commands. It's always a good idea to use your computer's memory efficiently so you can get your computer to do all the things you need it to do. For example, suppose you attempt to run a program (particularly a DOS-based program such as a game), and it refuses to run. You'll probably see a message that says **Insufficient memory**. In reality, you actually have enough RAM installed in your computer to run the program, but your computer may not be using that memory very efficiently.

In addition, if your PC does not have a lot of memory (8M or less, for example), you can tell Windows to use part of your hard disk as a kind of fake memory called *virtual memory*. Then when RAM becomes full and Windows needs to place some information in memory, it simply copies it to virtual memory (on the hard disk). Although using your hard disk for temporary storage is not terribly fast, it'll work in a pinch.

If you have Windows 95, it will create virtual memory (an area of the hard disk used for memory) for you. However, you can adjust the minimum and maximum size and the location of the virtual memory as needed. For example, you may want to move your virtual memory from a compressed drive to a noncompressed drive because it will make Windows faster.

CAUTION

To Change, or Not? Even though Windows 95 lets you make changes to the virtual memory settings, sometimes those settings will actually cause your system to run more slowly or give more out-of-memory errors. If that's the case, follow the steps as follows again and choose **Let Windows Manage My Virtual Memory Settings (Recommended)** in step 5. Then, after you restart your system, try moving files off the drive that Windows uses for virtual memory to free up more space for virtual memory.

Follow these steps to increase the amount of virtual memory under Windows 95 or change the hard disk location of virtual memory:

1. Click **Start**, select **Settings**, and then select **Control Panel.**

2. Double-click the **System** icon.

3. In the System Properties dialog box, click the **Performance** tab.

4. Click the **Virtual Memory** button, and the Virtual Memory dialog box appears (see Figure 10.1).

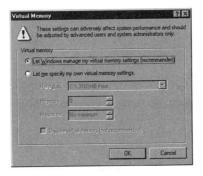

Figure 10.1 Use this dialog box to change virtual memory.

5. To use space on a different drive (such as a noncompressed drive) as virtual memory, select the **Let Me Specify My Own Virtual Memory Settings** option, and then select the drive you want to use from the **Hard**

Disk drop-down list. Let Windows specify the Minimum and Maximum size for the virtual memory, and click **OK**.

6. Restart your system if you're prompted, so the new memory settings will take effect.

Upgrading System Memory

Memory is one of the most important components of your computer. In order to run a program or make changes to a file, that program or file must first be placed into memory. Once the file is in memory, the computer can read the data and perform tasks with it.

When you run many programs at one time (which is easy to do with Windows), you can quickly use up your computer's available memory. Sometimes running only one complex program with a large file can use up all your available memory. When Windows runs out of memory, it starts copying the oldest data out of memory to a temporary holding area on the hard drive. From there, if the data is later needed back in memory, Windows copies the data back. As you can imagine, this whole process of copying data in and out of memory slows down your computer a considerable amount. The only solution is to run fewer programs at the same time, to use smaller data files, or to add more memory.

When installing memory, you need to consider many things. For example, memory comes in several flavors: DIP, SIMM, and DIMM. DIP memory chips are inserted individually, making them more difficult to install. SIMM and DIMM memory chips are contained on a small board and inserted into special sockets (slots) on the motherboard, making them simple to install.

RAM is a crucial system component. If it isn't installed properly or isn't the right type for your system, your system probably won't boot. If your PC uses DIP chips, or if you're not comfortable performing the upgrade yourself, you may want a computer technician to upgrade the system memory for you.

Some other things to think about:

- Every PC has a limit to the amount of physical memory you can install. Check your owner's manual to determine the amount of memory you can add, if any.
- Memory comes in different speeds, such as 70 nanoseconds (70 ns) or 60ns. You have to match the speed of the memory chips your PC already has (unless you opt to replace the existing memory chips).

- Memory also comes in various capacities, such as 16M or 32M. All the memory chips in the same bank of memory must have the same capacity. With SIMMs and DIMMs, this isn't a problem because all the chips on a SIMM memory module automatically have the same capacity. But when installing DIP chips, you'll need to get nine chips of the same capacity to fill a bank of memory.

- SIMMs come in two different sizes (see Figure 10.2), while DIMMs come in one larger size. Be sure to get the right size SIMMs for your system.

Figure 10.2   SIMM modules come in 30-pin and 72-pin sizes. Note the notches in the lower-left module corners; these notches help you line up the SIMM.

- SIMMs are installed in banks of two, and you must install SIMMs of matching capacity in each bank. For example, you have to install two 4M SIMMs in a bank, or two 16M SIMMs in a bank. You also must fill bank 0 first.

- Memory modules come in different speeds and error-checking. You need to purchase the speed of memory that your system needs (usually 60 to 70 ns or nanoseconds) and error-checking (parity or non-parity).

- Finally, most motherboards have very particular requirements for RAM. For example, many newer systems require that you use SIMMs that are 16M or larger. The motherboard also might require that you use a particular type of RAM like EDO RAM (see Lesson 2 in Part I for more on RAM). Before you purchase any RAM, consult your system's manual or contact the manufacturer to verify what kind of RAM to buy.

469

Where do you start? First, open your computer (after unplugging it, of course) and locate the memory modules currently installed. Write down the number that appears on the top of the chips and make a note of the number of blank memory rows still available. Take this information to your local computer store, and they should be able to help you purchase compatible memory modules for your PC. Then, follow these steps to install your RAM:

1. Back up your important system data, shut down and unplug your system, and remove the cover as described in Lesson 3 of this part.

2. Find the SIMM sockets on the motherboard, as in Figure 10.3.

Figure 10.3 Find the SIMM sockets on the motherboard. Line up the notch on the SIMM with the appropriate end of the socket, then insert it at an angle.

3. Hold the SIMM by its top edge. Make sure that the notch at one end of the SIMM matches up with the notch on the SIMM socket. Position the SIMM over the socket, and gently insert it at an angle, also shown in Figure 10.3.

4. After inserting the SIMM, press it gently backwards until the tabs on either side pop up to lock it in place.

TIP **You've Got the Angle** Some SIMMs are inserted at a 90-degree angle and then pressed forward into the 10 o'clock position.

5. Put your PC back together and turn it on. Most PCs will automatically recognize the new memory. If yours does not, you will need to update the system setup. You usually start this program by pressing **Del** or **F2** as the system boots. An on-screen message may flash the appropriate command as your system boots. Check your system's documentation to learn how to start this setup program, if you don't know how. Change and save the settings, exit the setup program, and reboot. If the system beeps at you when you restart, the SIMMs probably aren't inserted correctly. Shut down and open the system unit to check the installation.

TIP **Memory Check** Go to the DOS prompt (refer to Lesson 17 in Part II), type **MEM**, and press **Enter.** Your system will give you a report about the memory it finds. This will help you verify that the system can find the new RAM you installed.

TIP **Mother of All RAM** Older motherboards require that you set jumpers and DIP switches to enable the board to recognize all the RAM.

Upgrading Memory on an Adapter Card

Sound cards and video cards also have memory sockets, so you can update the memory on these boards to increase their speed. Memory on video cards, in particular, can increase the apparent speed of your system, because graphics-intensive programs can take some time to draw to the monitor if your video card is low on memory.

The type of memory needed depends on the brand and model of your card. Usually, you'll simply add a particularly type of SIMM module onto the card. Check with the card's manufacturer or your reputable computer dealer to buy the right memory for your card.

To install the new RAM, shut down your system safely as described in Lesson 3 of this project and remove the card as noted in Lesson 4 of this part. Install the SIMM in the slot for it as described above for installing SIMMs on the motherboard. Figure 10.4 shows an example of how to install a SIMM module on an adapter card. Reinsert the card into your system, hook up its connections, and reboot. You don't have to do anything further to configure your system to recognize the memory on the card.

Figure 10.4   You also can install a SIMM on a sound or video card.

This lesson showed you how to complete the last hardware addition described in this book—how to increase system RAM and upgrade the RAM for the system and adapter cards. The first lesson in the Troubleshooting part, next, covers how to create a startup disk that can be booted in case of emergency.

Troubleshooting

Creating and Using a Startup Disk

This lesson explains how to create and use the most important troubleshooting tool you can have—a startup disk for your system.

Using a Startup Disk

At startup, your PC refers to several important files on the hard disk drive for instructions that enable it to start and tell it exactly how it should start. If something should happen to these files, your computer might be rendered completely unusable—at least until the files on the hard drive could be replaced or repaired. An ugly catch-22 situation can occur, however: You need to have the computer working to replace the system files, but the computer won't start without the system files!

There is a way to restart your computer even if the system files on it are damaged—or have somehow been erased. To work this magic, you create a *startup disk*.

Startup Disk   A startup disk is a floppy disk (not a removable disk) that contains the basic system files your computer needs to start. You start the computer with this disk, and then you can usually access the computer's hard disk drive and copy an undamaged version of your config-uration files to it. You can use a floppy as a startup disk, because by default, if a system can't boot from the C: drive, it can then only boot from the first floppy drive, A:.

The processes for installing or removing hardware or software, or taking steps to improve your system's performance can lead to accidentally deleted or corrupted files. Creating a startup disk just in case something happens to the system files is simply good (and cheap) insurance. Plus, if you ever need serious help from Windows 95 Technical Support, you may need to have a startup disk available so that the tech support representative can help you get your system up and running.

You should create (or update) your startup disk before installing new software (Lesson 1 of Part 3) or hardware (Part 5), or performing any of the "optimization" procedures outlined in Lessons 5, 6, 8, and 14 in this part. Table 1.1 outlines the files a startup disk offers.

CAUTION

More Than a System Disk In Lesson 14 of Part 2, you learned that you can copy basic system files to a disk you format. While that process does create a bootable disk that you can use to start your system, a startup disk offers more files, including some programs that can help you diagnose and repair problems. So, a bootable disk with system files isn't adequate for safety. You really need to create a startup disk.

Table 1.1 Files Copied to a Startup Disk

File...	Used to...
Attrib.exe	Change the attributes (read-only, hidden, archive, system) of system files so you can replace them.
Chkdsk.exe	Check a disk for errors.
Command.com	Boot the system (it's the basic command interpreter).
Debug.exe	Test and edit files, especially program files.
Drvspace.bin	Track information on a system that has a volume compressed with Drivespace (see Lesson 5 in this part).
Edit.com	Edit text files such as system files.
Fdisk.exe	Work with a hard disk's partitions (if partition information is deleted, your system can't boot).
Format.com	Format hard or floppy disks.
Io.sys	Boot Windows 95.
Msdos.sys	Give Windows 95 startup information for booting.
Regedit.exe	Edit the Windows 95 Registry (covered later in this lesson).

File...	Used to...
Scandisk.exe	Perform a more detailed diagnostic scan on a disk and fix errors.
Scandisk.ini	Store Scandisk settings.
Sys.com	Copy system files to another disk (such as from the startup disk to the hard disk).
Uninst.exe	Remove some Windows 95 components.

Creating a Startup Disk

To create a startup disk, you need a new blank floppy disk of the size used by the A: drive. If the A: drive is a 5.25-inch disk drive, that should be the size you use to create the startup disk. If the A: drive is a 3.5-inch disk drive, that should be the size you use. In addition, use an HD (high density disk), whether you use a 5.25-inch or 3.5-inch drive to ensure there's enough space available for your startup files. You will also need your Windows 95 Setup disks or CD-ROM.

Follow these steps to make your blank floppy disk into a startup disk in Windows 95:

1. Click the **Start** button, point to **Settings**, and click **Control Panel**.

2. The Control Panel window appears. Double-click the **Add/Remove Programs** icon.

3. Click the **Startup Disk** tab to display it, as shown in Figure 1.1.

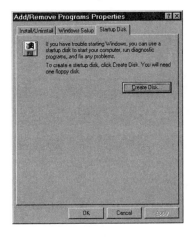

Figure 1.1 Use this tab in the Add/Remove Programs Properties dialog box to create a startup disk.

4. Click **Create Disk**. Insert the first Windows 95 Setup disk or the Setup CD-ROM into the drive, if Windows prompts you to insert the disk, then click **OK**.

5. If Windows displays an Add/Remove Programs Properties dialog box asking you to specify the location of a startup file, specify the path to the Windows 95 folder on your Setup CD-ROM (usually D:\WIN95, where D: is the driver letter for your CD-ROM drive) in the **Copy Files From** text box, then click **OK**. (You may be prompted for different disks if you installed Windows 95 from floppy disks.)

6. Windows copies the required files and then prompts you to insert a labeled disk (a blank floppy) into drive A:, as shown in Figure 1.2. Label a blank floppy disk "Windows Startup" and insert it in floppy drive A.

Figure 1.2 Insert a disk to hold the startup files when you're prompted to do so.

7. Click **OK**. Windows formats the floppy disk and copies the startup files to it.

8. Click **OK** to close the Add/Remove Programs Properties dialog box.

Enhancing a Startup Disk

A few other files can customize your startup disk to work more specifically with your system's applications and hardware. (Believe it or not, if you don't add the files as described here, you may be able to boot from your startup disk, but you may not be able to access your CD-ROM drive—a big problem if you need to reinstall Windows 95 from a CD-ROM disc.) Use Windows Explorer or My Computer to copy the Config.sys and Autoexec.bat files from C:\ to your startup disk. Also copy Win.ini and System.ini from C:\Windows (or the folder where Windows 95 is installed on your system) to the startup disk.

TIP   **Keep It Current**   You should update your startup disk regularly (or make multiple startup disks) to ensure that the Config.sys, Autoexec.bat, and other system files are the latest versions. It is especially important to do this before you install any new hardware or software or perform a maintenance task.

Booting with Your Startup Disk

To use your startup disk when you need it, shut down your computer. Insert the startup disk into your A: drive. Turn on the computer and monitor. The system boots to the Windows 95 DOS prompt. From there, you can run one of the utility programs on the startup disk or work with files on the hard disk.

Saving Emergency Recovery Information

The last section discussed the fact that certain system files (like Config.sys and Autoexec.bat) provide needed information to help your system work with the specific software and hardware that's installed. There are even more system files that you should back up in case of emergency, including User.dat and System.dat. These are files that make up the Windows 95 System Registry.

TIP   **Registry or System Registry**   In Windows 95, the Registry stores important information about preferences, installed Windows 95 components, and applications installed on your system. The Registry provides even more detail to Windows than .ini files. That detail, though, makes Registry files a bit large.

If something should happen to your system after you install a new program, you can use your copies of the original system files and system registry files to put your system back to the way it was, where you can better determine what to do next. You can't just copy the same files from a friend's computer and expect your computer to work properly. You need to keep a copy of the system files from your system in case anything happens to the original file—and believe me, many unexpected things can happen. Often, the problem has nothing to do with what you do on your computer day-to-day. But the loss of these important files can render your computer useless. So, you should copy all your system files to a backup folder or disk. From this folder or disk, you can copy system files back to the appropriate locations on your hard disk.

The Windows 95 Setup CD-ROM offers a little-known utility to backup even more system files: the Emergency Recovery Utility (ERU). You can use this utility to create backup copies of several important system files (which you can later copy to the appropriate location if one of the original files becomes corrupted).

Follow these steps to use ERU to back up system files:

1. Insert the Windows 95 Setup CD into your CD-ROM drive.
2. Use Windows Explorer or My Computer to open the \Other\Misc\Eru folder on the CD.
3. Double-click the Eru.exe file to start the utility.
4. In the Emergency Recovery Utility welcome screen, click **Next**.
5. In the dialog box that asks you where to place the backup files, click **Other Directory**, then click **Next**.
6. You can edit the Directory text box entry, or click **Next** to accept the default recommendation (see Figure 1.3).

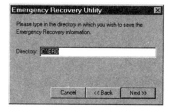

Figure 1.3   Specify where to save emergency recovery information.

7. The Emergency Recovery Utility dialog box appears, listing the files it will copy (see Figure 1.4). Click **Next**. ERU copies the files to the specified folder.

 TIP   **Floppies, Please**   All the files that ERU backs up won't fit onto a single floppy. So, you can run ERU two or three times to back up selected files to different floppies, specifying the A: drive in step 5, and clicking the Custom button in the Emergency Recovery Utility dialog box (step 7) to choose which files to copy to the disk.

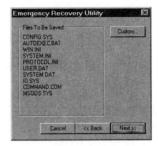

Figure 1.4 Here are the files that the ERU backs up.

Restoring the Registry

As noted in the last section, the Windows 95 system registry is really composed of two files that Windows 95 reads when it starts:

- **System.dat** tracks the type of files you use and the programs that create them, as well as the various Windows 95 components.

- **User.dat** keeps track of user preferences. Although it's not affected by program installations, you should back up the file from time to time because it will prevent you from going through numerous steps to set up your system all over again.

If you find your computer does not work properly following the installation of a new program, you can use the copies of the system registry files to return your system configuration choices to the way they were. (If needed, you may first want to make a copy of the altered System.dat and User.dat in a separate folder so you can compare the old and new versions of the files.)

If your computer simply doesn't work correctly, use these steps to restore the copies of System.dat and User.dat that you created with the Emergency Recovery Utility (ERU), as described in the last section:

1. Start Windows 95.
2. Use Windows Explorer or My Computer to navigate to the folder where you stored the system backup copies you made with ERU.
3. Select System.dat and User.dat.
4. Choose **Edit, Copy**.
5. Display the C:\Windows folder (or the folder on your system where Windows 95 is installed).

481

6. Choose **Edit, Paste**.

7. Restart your computer so Windows 95 can read the new files.

If your system won't boot and you get a message that your registry has been corrupted, follow these steps to restore it:

1. Reboot your system using your startup disk. Or, press **F8** during startup and choose **Command Prompt Only** from the menu that appears.

2. If you booted from the startup disk, type **C:** and then press **Enter** to log on to the hard disk.

3. Change to the Windows 95 folder. Type **cd windows** (or substitute the name of your Windows folder) and then press **Enter**.

4. Type these command lines and press **Enter** after each one:

> **attrib -h -r -s system.dat**
> **attrib -h -r -s system.da0**
> **attrib -h -r -s user.dat**
> **attrib -h -r -s user.da0**

5. Back up the current registry files one more time. Type these commands and press **Enter** after each one:

> **copy system.dat system.bak**
> **copy user.dat user.bak**

6. Now, restore the registry files. Type each of these commands and then press **Enter**:

> **copy system.da0 system.dat**
> **copy user.da0 user.dat**

7. Press **Ctrl+Alt+Del** to restart your system.

TIP **More Registry Backups** You can backup the registry from within the Registry Editor, a program for working with the registry. Choose **Start**, **Run**. Type **regedit** in the Open text box of the Run dialog box. Click **OK** to start the Registry Editor. Choose **Registry**, **Export Registry File**, select a location for the file, and click **Save**. The file is saved with a .reg extension. To use the .reg backup, start the Registry Editor and open it with the **File**, **Import Registry File** command or double-click the .reg backup file in My Computer or Windows Explorer.

This lesson explained how to create a startup disk and backup other system files so you can restart your system and restore key files. The next lesson explains how to attack other startup problems when they occur.

Fixing Startup Problems

*If you're having a problem when you start your computer, this
lesson suggests possible fixes to get it back up and running.*

Checking the Power If You Have No Startup or No Display

If you flip the power switch or press the button on your computer and you don't
hear some grinding or see any lights come on, the PC isn't getting power. Make
sure the power cord is securely plugged into the surge suppressor and into the
back of the PC. If you plug your PC into a power strip, make sure the surge
suppressor is plugged in and turned on.

If all the connections are okay, unplug your computer from the wall outlet and
plug in a device (such as a lamp) that you know works. If the lamp doesn't work
in that outlet, you may have tripped a circuit breaker or blown a fuse; fix that
problem, and your computer should start. If the lamp works but the computer
doesn't, your computer may have a faulty power cord or power supply; seek
professional help from a computer repair shop.

 Power Supply This is a component inside the computer that accepts the
power that flows into the computer and distributes that power. It's different from
the surge suppressor, which is the device you plug your computer components
into (before plugging the surge suppressor itself into an electrical outlet) to
protect the system against power surges.

If the computer monitor doesn't display anything, something is wrong with the
monitor or one of its connections. Try the following solutions:

- First try performing a full cold boot. Shut down the power to your system and monitor, then power the system back up to see if the display returns.
- Make sure the monitor is plugged into a surge suppresser, and that it is on. Your monitor should have a power indicator that lights when the power is on.
- If the power is on but you still have no picture, crank up the brightness control on your monitor. Then readjust the brightness once you get a picture.
- Turn everything off and check the connection between the monitor and the system unit. (This connection wiggles free at times.)

Dealing with Repeated Beeps

If you hear a series of loud beeps when you start up the computer, several things might be wrong:

- There might be a problem with the motherboard (system board) or the power supply.
- There might be a problem with a memory (RAM) chip, or you may not have upgraded some new RAM properly (Lesson 13 in Part 5 explains how to add RAM to your system).
- The keyboard may not be connected properly, or you accidentally pressed several keys during startup.
- The monitor may not be connected properly, or your graphics adapter card may be failing.
- You may have left a disk in one of the floppy drives, or the drive itself may not be responding.

TIP   **Key Accident**   If you do accidentally press some wrong keys during startup, your system will usually display a message on-screen telling you to press another key, such as F1, to resume startup.

Typically, some type of error message accompanies the beeping noise. Start with the simple things first: Check your connections, make sure there's nothing in the floppy disk drive, and then reboot. If you just installed a new component or have replaced an existing component, check its installation. Restart the PC. If you get the same beeping noise, try uninstalling the upgrade you made and restarting again. If the beeping continues, something may be critically wrong, in which case you should have your PC checked out by a professional.

Dealing with Bootup Error Message

It's easier to solve a problem when the computer tells you what's wrong. This section covers error messages you may see on startup, and possible solutions for each error.

"Non-system disk or disk error."

You usually get this message if you happened to leave a non-bootable floppy disk in drive A. Take the disk out of drive A and press any key to boot from your hard disk. If you have an old computer and you boot it from a floppy disk, this message is telling you to insert a bootable floppy disk into drive A and press any key.

"General Failure Error Reading Drive C"

This message indicates a situation that's as ominous as it sounds. When you start your computer, the BIOS can't read the hard disk's boot sector, which stores the master boot record information your system must be able to read to boot. This problem could've been caused by a power jolt that zapped the boot sector or perhaps even a virus. Follow these steps to try to fix the problem:

1. Insert your startup disk (see Lesson 1 of this part) in drive A: and press **Ctrl+Alt+Delete** to restart the computer. You'll use the Fdisk.exe program on the disk to try to fix the problem.

2. Type **fdisk /mbr** and press **Enter**.

3. After only a moment, the prompt returns. Remove the startup disk from drive A: and press **Ctrl+Alt+Delete** to restart the system.

TIP   **FDISK Menu**   If you forget to include a switch with the FDISK command, you'll see a menu on-screen. FDISK can wipe out everything on your hard disk, so you shouldn't use these menu options unless you really know what you're doing. Press **Esc** to close the menu and return to the DOS prompt.

If you follow the just-listed steps and your computer still doesn't boot, you have a serious hard disk problem. Take your system to a repair shop, where you can get help in replacing your hard disk and perhaps retrieving information from the old disk.

CMOS Error Messages

CMOS, pronounced "SEE-moss," is a battery-powered device that stores important information—including the date and time, the number of disk drives the computer has, the type of hard disk it's using, and how much memory is installed. When you see an error like "CMOS display type mismatch," something's wrong with your computer setup stored in the CMOS. At this point, you need to display your PC's setup options. Watch the computer screen during startup to see which key to press—most likely, it's the F1, F2 or Delete key. Press the appropriate key to access your computer's setup options. (On older PCs, try restarting your PC and pressing **Ctrl+Alt+S** or **Ctrl+Alt+Enter**.)

Check the options and change any settings you know are wrong. For example, if you know the video setting or date and time are wrong, change them. Don't change any settings you are unsure of. Basically, you press **Tab** or the **down arrow key** to move from item to item. Typically, you use the left or right arrow key to change the value of a particular setting. When you're finished, press **Esc** or select **Yes** to save the settings, and then try to reboot. In most newer computers (manufactured in the last three years), you can simply access the setup options and then save (without changing anything). This makes the computer recheck its memory and fix any memory problems automatically.

If you keep getting a particular CMOS error message or get a "CMOS battery state low" message, it may be a sign that the battery that keeps your CMOS alive is losing its charge. Seek professional help at this point to replace the CMOS battery.

"Bad or missing command interpreter"

If you start your computer and you get a message that says you have a **Bad or missing command interpreter**, your DOS *command interpreter* (a file called Command.com) is either missing or messed up. The command interpreter is your PC's captain; it loads when you boot your computer, and it interprets commands sent to the central processor or CPU. If Command.com doesn't load on startup, you can't use your computer.

To fix the problem, follow these steps:

1. Insert your startup disk (see Lesson 1 of this part) in drive A: and press **Ctrl+Alt+Delete** to restart the computer.
2. At the DOS prompt type **copy command.com c:** and press **Enter**.
3. Remove the startup disk from drive A: and press **Ctrl+Alt+Delete** to restart the system.

Dealing with FAT and Other Disk Errors

Sometimes you will see an error message telling you that a disk error (caused by improperly shutting down, for example) or a FAT error is preventing proper startup. In this case, try using Scandisk to fix the problem:

1. Insert your startup disk (see Lesson 1 of this part) in drive A: and press **Ctrl+Alt+Delete** to restart the computer.

2. Type **scandisk c:** and press **Enter**.

3. If Scandisk prompts you to specify any options, do so and then follow the on-screen instructions to continue. ScanDisk will sometimes prompt you to save Undo information, so you can undo any changes ScanDisk makes. Have a blank, formatted floppy disk on hand to save the undo information. You want to save this information because Scandisk sometimes alters critical system files that you may need to restore to their original state; you should always take the greatest level of precautions available when dealing with any key system files.

4. Scan disk will take several minutes to run. When it finishes, remove the startup disk from drive A: and press **Ctrl+Alt+Delete** to restart the system.

If Scandisk doesn't solve the problem, get professional repair help. In some instances, a program like Norton Utilities can be used to fix the problem.

This lesson provided help for getting your system to boot when it won't. The next lesson covers special methods for restarting your system when needed.

Restarting Your System When It Locks Up

This lesson shows you various ways to restart your system, including startup methods to help you troubleshoot a problem.

Restarting from Windows 95 When It Locks Up

Even though Windows 95 stops working much less frequently than its predecessors did, you still may encounter instances where it simply freezes up or the mouse stops working. (For example, when I disconnect from the Internet on one of my computers, the system sometimes simply freezes.) Lesson 1 in Part 2 explained how to restart (warm boot) using the mouse after you've installed new software or have performed some other action. Those steps won't work if the system or mouse is locked up, so follow these steps instead:

1. Make sure it's not a particular application that's locked up. The next lesson provides help about this subject.

2. Most new systems offer power management features and can go into "sleep" mode to save power if the computer sits idle for several minutes. Sleep mode enables you to conserve power while leaving your system on—reducing wear from powering up the system and leaving it on to receive faxes and voice mail messages. Move the mouse or press a few keys to see if you can get the computer to wake back up.

3. Press **Ctrl+Alt+Delete**. The Close Program dialog box appears. (If the Close Program dialog box doesn't appear, follow the steps for cold booting your system, described in the next section.)

4. Press **Ctrl+Alt+Delete** again. The system will restart.

TIP   **Locked**   Several things can cause your computer to lock up, including problems with the computer's video. To help diagnose video problems, check out Lesson 11 in this part.

TIP   **DOS Prompt Reboot**   To restart your system from the DOS prompt, if you booted using your startup disk or booted to DOS prompt mode as described later in this lesson, press **Ctrl+Alt+Delete** once.

Cold-Booting Your System

Sometimes warm-booting your system doesn't work. You press Ctrl+Alt+Delete and nothing happens. The mouse also probably doesn't work, so you can't click the Start button to choose the Shut Down command. This usually means your computer has locked up in such a way that it can't accept keyboard and mouse commands.

When warm-booting doesn't work, you have to *cold-boot* your system. Cold-booting means you use the hardware to reset the computer, depriving it of power or making it "cold." There are two different ways to cold-boot. One involves your system's Reset button (if it has one). The second method greatly resembles starting your system, as described in Lesson 1 of Part 2. Don't use the second method unless the Reset button doesn't work or your system doesn't have a Reset button.

To cold boot with the reset button, follow these steps:

1. Remove any disks that are in floppy disk drives. If you don't, your computer will try to read from the floppy disk instead of your hard drive when it restarts.

2. Press and release the **Reset** button on the front or side of the computer. Your computer will beep at you, and whatever was on-screen will be wiped off. The computer will go through its startup process all over. In some cases, Scandisk will run to clear up any disk errors that may have been preventing the system's proper operation.

To cold boot using the power switch, use these steps:

1. Remove any disks that are in floppy disk drives. If you don't, your computer will try to read from the floppy disk instead of your hard drive when it restarts.

489

2. Turn the system unit's power switch to the **Off** position. Listen to your computer, so you can hear it power down.

3. When it's silent (the power-down process has finished), wait about two minutes and turn the power switch back to the **On** position. Again, ScanDisk may run automatically to clean up any disk errors.

Restarting Windows 95 in Safe Mode

If you install a new program or a hardware device (such as a new video card), and you have problems starting Windows 95, you can start it in *safe mode*. Windows often gives you the option of starting in safe mode whenever you restart after the system locks up or when you don't shut down correctly. When Windows starts in safe mode, it runs with a plain-vanilla setup that's almost sure to prod Windows into action. In safe mode, Windows 95 will not load any fancy display settings, and you won't be able to use your CD-ROM drive or printer.

 TIP **No Settings** Safe mode in essence skips the loading of Autoexec.bat and Config.sys, so none of the commands or drivers specified in those files are active.

The purpose of safe mode is to get Windows up and running so you can correct any problems that are preventing it from starting in its usual way. For example, you could remove the driver for a modem you just installed and then restart to see if you can then get your system to reboot.

Here's what you do to start Windows 95 in safe mode:

1. Restart the system using **Ctrl+Alt+Delete** (once or twice, as needed) or turn the system and monitor on if they were shut down.

2. When you see the message **Starting Windows 95**, press and release the **F8** key. A list of startup options appears.

 CAUTION **Manufacturer Startups** Some manufacturers, like Compaq, alter the startup sequence, so you may have to experiment to find out when exactly to press F8. On a Compaq system, where the first startup screen reads "Compaq," wait until the blinking cursor jumps to the upper right-corner, then press F8.

3. Press 3 to select **Safe mode**, and then press **Enter**. Windows starts in safe mode, and a dialog box appears telling you that.

4. Click the **OK** button to close the dialog box. The Windows desktop appears, and it shows "Safe Mode" in the corners to make it clear that you're in safe mode and not simply having display or other problems, as shown in Figure 3.1.

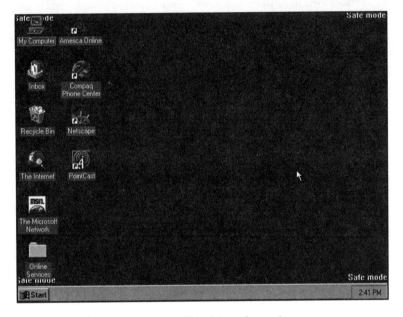

Figure 3.1   Here's how your screen will look in safe mode.

TIP   **Safe at the Prompt**   You also can opt to go to the Windows 95 DOS prompt in a safe mode. Restart or start your system. When you see the Starting Windows 95 message, press and release the **F8** key. Press **7** to choose **Safe mode command prompt only**.

If you're having problems and Windows 95 won't start up in safe mode, you may have a more drastic startup problem. Consult the last lesson to learn about some methods that might help.

Restarting with Step-by-Step Confirmation

Whenever you boot your computer, the startup commands and instructions (those in Autoexec.bat and Config.sys) often scroll by too fast for you to read them. While that's normally not a problem, under troubleshooting circumstances you may prefer to see the startup commands. In fact, by watching each startup command and driver instruction load, you can see precisely which commands and drivers are causing problems because an error message will appear after it loads.

Follow these steps to step through the commands, and gather information about the possible cause of a system problem:

1. Restart (with **Ctrl+Alt+Delete** once or twice, as needed) or start up the computer.

2. When you see the **Starting Windows 95** message, press and release the **F8** key.

3. Press the number for the **Step-by-Step confirmation** choice (usually 4 or 5), and then press **Enter**.

4. Windows runs the startup commands one at a time, asking you to confirm each line by pressing **Y**. After you press Y for each command, watch to see if any error message appears after that command loads. If an error does appear, right down the error message and the command line that caused it.

After you step through all the commands, Windows will load (or will fail if you've been having problems). At this point, you have a couple of ways in which you can precede. You can restart the computer and choose Step-by-Step confirmation again, this time pressing **N** to skip the commands you think are causing problems; if those commands were the problem, Windows will start, although the features and hardware loaded by the commands you bypassed won't work.

Alternately, you can start Windows 95 in Safe Mode and use the SYSEDIT utility (see Lesson 3, Part 5) to remark out (insert REM and a space to the left of) command lines you don't want to load in Autoexec.bat and Config.sys. Save the edited files, exit SYSEDIT, and restart your computer. Windows should load without executing the offending commands.

Getting Back to the Desktop from the Command Prompt

You can also run Windows 95 in command prompt mode (at the DOS command prompt) if needed. In fact, some DOS-based games and utilities require you to go to command prompt (DOS) mode before they'll run. There are two ways to get to DOS mode:

- From the desktop, choose **Start**, **Shut Down** to display the Shut Down Windows dialog box, choose the **Restart the computer in MS-DOS mode** option as shown in Figure 3.2, then click **Yes**. Your computer will restart, and you'll be left at the DOS prompt. From there, you can perform any regular DOS function, such as running a DOS-based game.

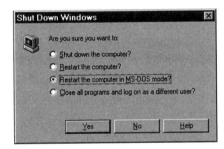

Figure 3.2   Choose this option to restart in command prompt (DOS) mode.

- Start the computer or use Ctrl+Alt+Delete (once or twice as needed) to reboot. When you see the **Starting Windows 95** message, press and release the **F8** key. Press the number beside the **Command prompt only** choice (usually 5 or 6), and then press **Enter**. The startup commands load and the command prompt appears.

To return to Windows 95, all you need to do is reboot by pressing **Ctrl+Alt+Delete** and let the computer do its thing. Sometimes this does not return you to Windows; instead, you may appear to be stuck in DOS. To solve the problem, you need to remove the line DOS=SINGLE from your Config.sys using SYSEDIT, as described in Part 5, Lesson 3.

How did the line get there? Well, that's anyone's guess. But typically, when installing a DOS utility, game, or other program, Windows 95 inserts the line on behalf of the setup program, intending to take it out again when the installation is through. That, however, does not always happen, so you have to do it yourself to return your system to normal. After editing the Config.sys and removing the line, restart your PC and you should see the Windows 95 desktop.

Accessing Your CD-ROM Drive at the DOS Prompt

On many machines, especially newer ones, Windows 95 loads a *virtual device driver* to control your CD-ROM drive. The advantage of a virtual device driver is that it doesn't take up any conventional memory, so that leaves more room for your DOS program to run. However, virtual device drivers don't work when you try to run a program in MS-DOS mode, because the only drivers that do work are the ones loaded by Config.sys.

If you want to reboot to DOS and access your CD-ROM drive, follow these steps to "turn on" a CD-ROM drive. First, make sure that your Config.sys file contains the command to load your CD-ROM device driver. The command may look something like this (but consult your system or CD-ROM manual for exact specifications and the exact name and location of the CD-ROM driver file):

DEVICE=C:\CDSYS\SLCD.SYS /D:MSCD001 /B:340

Then add the following line to the Dosstart.bat file you'll find in the \Windows folder (if it's not there, create one using Notepad):

C:\WINDOWS\COMMAND\MSCDEX.EXE /D:MSCD001 /M:4

In this case, the values that follow the /D: and the /M: may be different for your particular CD-ROM drive, but all systems will use the Mscdex.exe command. Be sure to check the manual for your CD-ROM drive for details.

CAUTION

CD-ROM Commands The Config.sys command for loading your CD-ROM can vary dramatically form the ones shown above. And the switches and parameters used with Mscdex.exe may vary dramatically. For example, some systems might require the switch and parameter /D:MSC000 or /D:TSD0001 instead of /D:MSC001. If you've having problems, consult the documentation for your system or contact technical support to learn how to load the CD-ROM drive at the DOS prompt, if it doesn't do so automatically.

This lesson explained different ways to restart and start your system, with troubleshooting in mind. If you're having trouble with an individual application locking up, see the next lesson.

Closing an Application that Is Locked Up

This lesson shows you how to get out of trouble when an application stops working.

Shutting Down an Application

When things stop working, certainly one option to get you back to work is to reboot your system, as discussed in detail in the last lesson. However, Windows 95 provides another option. Under Windows 95, you can shut down individual applications that have stopped working rather than restarting the whole system. This can save you a great deal of time and aggravation, especially if you have a slightly older system that boots slowly under Windows 95.

Before you shut down an application, however, you should try a few tests to find out whether the program's really locked up:

- Jiggle the mouse or press a couple of keys to make sure your system isn't in sleep mode.
- Wait about 15 seconds and try resuming your work. You might be typing or entering commands faster than your computer can interpret them at the current time; if so, wait for it to catch up. You also need to make sure the computer isn't saving data, which can take a while for large files. Waiting a bit and checking to make sure none of the drive lights are on are good safety measures.
- Press **F1** for Help. If you're trying to perform an operation that's impossible, Help will explain what's going on.
- Sometimes you can select something with the mouse without realizing it, which might keep you from performing a later operation. Try clicking in various places on-screen.

- Press the **Spacebar** or try some other keystrokes to see whether the keyboard simply has a stuck key.

If you decide you need to shut down an application under Windows 95, follow these steps:

1. Press **Ctrl+Alt+Del** to cancel a program that's giving you trouble.

2. In the Close Program dialog box that appears, you'll see [Not Responding] beside the name of the program if it's irretrievably stalled.

3. Click the name of the program that's labeled as not responding or the one that you think isn't responding, then click **End Task**; otherwise, click **Cancel** and wait a few moments for the program to respond.

CAUTION

Vital Programs Some programs and program components load behind the scenes, so that the only way to unload them from RAM is to use the Close Programs dialog box. Be careful, though. You generally don't want to shut down Explorer or systray, which affect how Windows 95 runs.

TIP

Stuck Programs If you've used a program's **File**, **Exit** command but you suspect the program hasn't completely unloaded (perhaps because you got an out of memory message when you tried to run another program), display the Close Program box by pressing **Ctrl+Alt+Delete**. Even if the suspect program unloaded from the screen, it still may be listed as [Not Responding] because it's "stuck" in RAM. Click the program, then click **End Task**.

Dealing with a Program that Won't Start

Sometimes you can't even get a program going. You might click its Start menu command or double-click a shortcut icon for it in My Computer, in Explorer, or on the desktop, and get a message that one of the application's files is missing.

The first thing to do in such a case is to double-check the shortcut using these steps:

1. In Explorer, My Computer, or on the desktop, right-click the program's icon and select **Properties**. To check a Start menu shortcut, right-click a blank area of the taskbar, then click **Properties**. In the Taskbar Properties dialog box, click the **Start Menu Programs** tab, and click **Advanced**. In the window that appears, open the folder holding the command shortcut you want, then right-click the shortcut in the right side of the window and click **Properties,** as shown in Figure 4.1.

Figure 4.1 Select the Start menu shortcut to verify that it points to the right startup command.

2. In the Properties window that appears, click the **Shortcut** tab to display its options, shown in Figure 4.2.

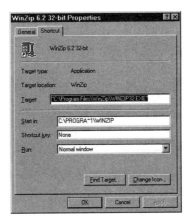

Figure 4.2 Check the path for the shortcut.

3. Make sure that the correct path and command appears in the **Target** text box, and the correct program path in the **Start In** text box. If either entry is incorrect, change it as needed.

497

4. Click **OK** to close the dialog box and finalize the change.

 TIP   **Find that Startup**   To verify the location of the startup command listed in the Target text box of the Shortcut tab of a file's Properties dialog box (see step 3 in the preceding procedure), click the **Find Target** button.

If that doesn't solve the problem, try removing and then reinstalling the application as described in Lesson 1 of Part 3. Sometimes essential files can get damaged or deleted when Windows crashes (or if you turn off your computer before exiting Windows). If the problem persists, call the technical support number for your program; you can usually find it in the documentation.

Working with Problems with DOS Programs

When you run some DOS programs under Windows 95, you can encounter some particular problems with applications, including having a program hang. This section covers the most common problems and how to handle them.

Dealing with a Slow DOS Program

Windows allows you to *shell out* to DOS (see Lesson 17 in Part 2), in order to type in some DOS command or to run a DOS program. However, because your computer is still running Windows in the background, the commands you type or the programs you run may respond a bit more slowly. If the program runs too slowly, you can try to restart Windows 95 in command prompt (DOS) mode as described in the last lesson, and then run your DOS application.

If you really want to run the program from the Windows 95 desktop, try djusting the program startup file's property settings:

1. Right-click the program's startup file in Explorer or My Computer and select **Properties**.

2. Click the **Program** tab, and then click **Advanced** to display the Advanced Program Settings dialog box (see Figure 4.3).

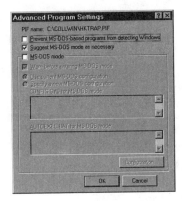

Figure 4.3   You can specify that a DOS program will run in a particular mode under Windows 95.

3. Select the **MS-DOS Mode** check box, which tells Windows to give the game its exclusive attention (you'll have to shut down other Windows programs before running the game). You may also want to select the **Fast ROM Emulation** option on the **Screen** tab to speed up the screen display.

4. Click **OK** to finish changing the settings, then click **OK** again to close the Properties dialog box for the file. Then try running the file again.

What to Do When a DOS Program Crashes

The causes of system crashes are difficult to track because any conflict between two applications or devices can cause the problem. Try the following fixes:

- If the program doesn't even show its face, you probably selected the wrong video driver when you installed the program. Run the setup program again and try a different video driver.

- Do you have other applications running? If you do, try closing them and then running your application. Also, check your Autoexec.bat file to see if it is running any applications on startup (such as a screen saver or anti-virus program). These *memory-resident programs* often cause problems. Add the REM command before these commands to prevent them from running (see Lesson 3 in Part 5 for more), and then reboot your computer.

- If you're trying to run this program from within Windows, you may have better luck exiting Windows and booting to the command prompt (DOS) mode, as described in the last lesson.

- You could possibly run your program within Windows 95, provided you optimize it. To do that, right-click the program's startup file in Explorer or My Computer and select **Properties**. You can change a lot of settings with the Properties dialog box that appears; however, most problems can be cleared up by changing the settings on the Memory, Screen, and Misc tabs. See the Windows Help system for additional information.

- If the program freezes when you move the mouse, the mouse driver is usually at fault. Try reinstalling the mouse driver that came with your mouse.

  If you just installed another device (such as a sound card), it may have an interrupt setting (IRQ) that conflicts with the mouse interrupt. Try running the device's setup program again (or using the Device Manager, as covered in Lesson 3 of Part 5) and choosing a different IRQ setting.

  If that doesn't fix the problem, call the mouse manufacturer and ask for an updated mouse driver.

- As a precaution and to free up disk space, delete any unused files from the Windows TEMP directory; for more information, see the next lesson.

- Try reinstalling the application. Sometimes a corrupted file can make an application crash. By replacing the corrupted file with a fresh copy, you might be able to prevent future crashes.

- Run ScanDisk, which is covered in Lesson 6 of this part. Sometimes *lost file clusters* (parts of files that get scattered over a disk) can cause strange problems. ScanDisk sweeps these clusters off the disk.

What to Do When a DOS Window Won't Maximize

In Windows 95, the size of the window in which your DOS program runs depends on its screen resolution. For this reason, you may not be able to completely maximize a DOS window (to fill the screen) when you click the Maximize button.

To run a DOS program full-screen, right-click the program's startup file in Explorer or My Computer and select **Properties**. Click the **Screen** tab and select the **Full-screen** option, as shown in Figure 4.4. Click **OK** to save your changes, and **OK** again to close the Properties dialog box.

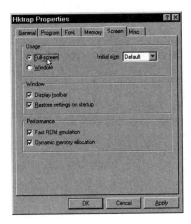

Figure 4.4   Choose this option to load a DOS application in a maximized window.

 TIP   **Copy Text from a DOS Program**   If you want to copy text from a DOS application to another application, you must run your DOS program in a window. If you're currently running the program full-screen, press **Alt+Enter** to switch to a window. To select the text you want, open the **Control** menu, select **Edit**, and then select **Mark**. Drag over the text you want to select, and then press **Enter** to copy it to the Clipboard. You cannot cut or move text, only copy. To move text, copy it to your other document and then return to your DOS program and delete the copied text.

Switching from a DOS App to a Windows App

When running a DOS program full-screen in Windows 95, you may encounter a problem if you want to switch from it to another program, because the taskbar is not visible. Press **Alt+Esc**, and you'll see the taskbar. Click the program to which you want to switch.

This lesson explained how to shut down an application that's locked up under Windows 95, and how to deal with some Windows and DOS application problems. The next lesson shows you how to squeeze more space out of a disk.

Finding More Disk Space When You've Run Out

This lesson shows you how to remove unneeded files and how to use the DriveSpace utility to make more room on a disk.

Deleting Unneeded Files

With the large hard disks available today, it's hard to imagine ever running out of room—but believe me, it happens all the time. Just as you eventually must rummage through closets, the garage, and your attic to throw away the junk you've accumulated in your house over the years, you must eventually remove old, junky files from your hard disk to make room for new ones.

 TIP **Helping the Disk Even More** After removing unwanted files from your hard disk, you can improve the disk's efficiency by rearranging how the files are stored. This process is called *defragmenting*, and you can learn more about it in Lesson 8 of this part.

Deleting Old Programs and Data

You'll find two general types of files on a computer: program files and data files. *Program files* are the files that came with the programs installed on your computer. If you are no longer using a certain program, you should consider removing its files. This will give you more space for programs you like. Lesson 1 in

Part 3 gives detailed instructions for removing Windows 95 programs, so I won't cover that information again here.

Data files are the files you create by using the programs on your computer. A typical data file is a document you write (like a letter or a school report) with a word processor such as Microsoft Word or WordPerfect. You might also have data files on your system that you didn't create, but that you downloaded from the Internet or an online service such as America Online. These files might include graphics, sound files, documents, and the like. Files you download can add up quickly.

On most computer systems, data files don't take up as much room as program files (especially if the programs are designed to be used with Microsoft Windows). However, you should still be in the habit of removing unnecessary data files from time to time. After a typical pruning of outdated data files, you may find you have 5–10 percent more hard disk space.

If You're a Packrat...   Before you jump in and start deleting files from your hard disk, you may want to copy them to a floppy or removable disk for safekeeping in case you should ever need them again.

CAUTION

Just Don't Do It   If you have any question about what a file is or does, don't delete it! You don't want to mistakenly delete a program file you may later need.

CAUTION

Follow these steps to delete old files:

1. Click the **Start** menu, select **Programs**, and then select **Windows Explorer**. (You can also complete this task using My Computer if you prefer; see Lesson 9 in Part 2 to learn more about using My Computer.)

2. Use the folder tree to select the folder that contains the file(s) you want to delete. The contents of the selected folder appear in the contents list at the right side of the Explorer Window.

3. In the contents list, locate the file you want to delete and click it. To select several adjacent files, press and hold the **Shift** key and click the first and last files in the group. To select nonadjacent files, press and hold the **Ctrl** key and click each one.

4. With the file(s) you want to delete selected, press the **Delete** key.

5. If the Confirm File Delete dialog box appears, click **Yes** to complete the deletion process.

TIP **Folder Be Gone** If you want to delete a folder and all the files it contains, select the folder in the folder tree or contents list of Windows Explorer or in a My Computer window and press **Delete**. Click **Yes** to confirm the deletion.

Clearing Out Internet Files

Part 4 explained how to use the Windows 95 OSR 2 Internet Explorer browser program to look for and download information on the World Wide Web (or Web). There, I mentioned that Explorer downloads Web pages and their elements to your system as you go to enable you to redisplay recently-visited pages more quickly. This is a good thing for Web browsing but a bad thing for hard disk space—those Web page files stay on your hard disk and take up several megabytes of space.

Use these steps to clear Internet files from your system in Internet Explorer (if you use a different browser, the steps will be similar):

1. Right-click the **The Internet** icon on the desktop and choose **Properties**. Or, if Explorer is already open, choose **View**, **Options**. The Properties or Options dialog box appears, depending on which selection method you used; these dialog boxes offer the same choices even though they have different names.

2. Click the **Advanced tab** to display its options.

3. In the Temporary Internet Files section of the dialog box, click the **Settings** button to display the Settings dialog box in Figure 5.1.

4. Click the **Empty Folder** button.

5. In the message box that prompts you to verify the deletion, click **Yes**. The Settings dialog box reappears.

6. (Optional) If you want to decrease the amount of disk space used for temporary Internet files, drag the **Amount of Disk Space to Use** slider to the left. You'll have to experiment with this setting over time to find the right balance between disk space used and the performance of your Web browser.

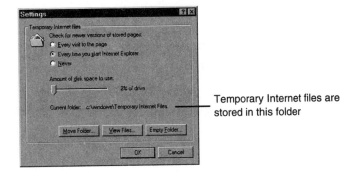

Temporary Internet files are stored in this folder

Figure 5.1   You can clear out temporary Internet files with this dialog box.

7. Click **OK** to close the Settings dialog box, and **OK** again to close the Properties or Options dialog box.

Deleting .tmp Files

Windows 95 and its applications create temporary files (with a .tmp extension) as you work to hold information until you save it to a file. Normally, when you save and close a file, its corresponding .tmp file closes. But, if an application hangs or you need to shut down an application or Windows itself for any reason without closing your files, the .tmp files can be left hanging around on your disk. These .tmp files are more of a nuisance than a serious problem—they eat up disk space and can slow your system down a bit.

The first place to look for .tmp files to delete is in the \Windows\Temp folder, which holds the .tmp files for the Windows system (Figure 5.2). Open this folder in Explorer or My Computer, select the .tmp files, and press **Delete**. Click **Yes** in the message box that appears to verify the deletion.

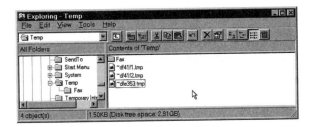

Figure 5.2   Also delete .tmp files, like these in the \Windows\Temp folder.

Also look in your program folders for .tmp files. To make a really clean sweep, use the File Find feature in Explorer (described in Lesson 13 of Part 2) and enter *.tmp in the **Named** text box to find all the .tmp files. Then delete them from the search results list.

Using a Compression Utility to Downsize Files

Many shareware and free programs you might download from the Internet and other online services or find on software sampler disks and CD-ROMs are stored in a single large file called a Zip file. A Zip file is actually a "container" for a lot of other files, and is also called an *archive*.

The individual files in a Zip file are *compressed* (reduced in size), so that the Zip file itself takes up less disk space than the total of all its individual files. For example, even though a program's files may take up a total of several megabytes of hard disk space, they might take up only one megabyte when "compressed" into a Zip file. The Zip technique is not the only one used to compress files into a single chunk, but it is by far the most common.

One advantage of the smaller Zip file is this: A one megabyte Zip file can easily fit on a standard floppy disk, whereas the individual files for a larger program might not. In addition, it takes less time to download a Zip file from the Internet (or wherever) than it does to download all the individual files for a particular program.

Using Zip files, you also can archive your older documents so that they take up less room on your hard disk—yet are easily accessible.

Zip files are generally easy to identify; their names have .zip extensions. If you see a file named Program.zip, for example, you can be pretty sure it is a Zip file.

Getting WinZip

WinZip is a shareware program—meaning that you can get the program from a variety of sources for free, but you need to register it and pay a reasonable shareware fee to continue using it. The current version of WinZip is version 6.2 (32-bit) for Windows 95. It's frequently distributed on sampler disks, or can be downloaded from **http://www.winzip.com** or a number of other online sources.

Zip files can be made to be *self-extracting,* which means that the recipient of such a file does not need to have WinZip (or any other Zip utility) to decompress the files in it. A self-extracting Zip file ends in .EXE, so it looks like a program file. But when you double-click the file in Windows Explorer or My Computer, the individual files contained in it are automatically decompressed and copied to the current directory. If you download a copy of WinZip, you'll find that it is self-extracting. To install it, simply place the file in a new folder and double-click it. After WinZip has decompressed, a setup program automatically starts. Follow the on-screen instructions to complete your WinZip installation.

Creating a Zip File with WinZip

The following steps show you how to compress files to create your own Zip file, using the "classic" WinZip interface. If you prefer, you can use the Wizard interface instead. The Wizard walks you through the process of unzipping your files with a series of dialog boxes. The Wizard, however, cannot be used to create Zip files. To start the Wizard, click the Wizard button on the WinZip toolbar.

1. Start WinZip by clicking the **Start** button and selecting **Winzip**. The default WinZip installation automatically puts a shortcut for WinZip at the top of the Start menu.

2. If you have not yet registered your copy of WinZip, you'll need to click **I Agree** to continue. It's good form to register, though.

3. To create a new archive, click the **New** button.

4. In the New Archive dialog box, navigate to the folder in which you want to create your Zip file, and type a name in the **File Name** text box. Make sure the **Add Dialog** check box is checked, and click **OK**. The Add dialog box appears.

5. Press and hold the **Ctrl** key, and then click each file you want to add (see Figure 5.3). When all the files are selected, click **Add**.

6. The files you selected are added to the archive, which is displayed in the main WinZip Window. Click the **Add** button and repeat step 5 to add files from other folders to the archive.

7. When you finish working in WinZip, click the **Close** (X) button, or open the **File** menu and select **Exit**.

Figure 5.3   Files selected to add to a Zip file.

TIP   **Zip Shortcut**   When you install WinZip, you can have it add a command to the Windows 95 shortcut menus in Explorer and My Computer. Then, to create a new archive, you simply select the files you want to archive, and right-click. From the shortcut menu, select **Add to Zip**.

Extracting a File from a Zip File with WinZip

Before you can use the files in a Zip archive, you must *decompress* ("extract" or "unshrink") them. This requires a WinZip or another decompression program. Use these steps to extract a file from a Zip file in WinZip:

1. Start WinZip by clicking the **Start** button and selecting **WinZip**.

2. If you have not yet registered your copy of WinZip, you'll need to click **I Agree** to continue. But you should register. The WinZip program window opens.

3. To open a Zip file you want to decompress, click the **Open** button.

4. In the Open Archive dialog box, select the Zip file you want to open and click **Open**.

5. WinZip lists the contents of the Zip file. Select the files to extract. Press and hold the **Ctrl** key and click individual files to extract (see Figure 5.4), or use **Actions**, **Select All** (**Ctrl+/**) to select all files.

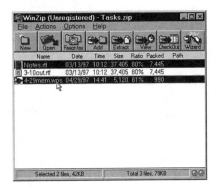

Figure 5.4   Select files to extract (decompress) from the Zip file.

6. To extract (decompress) the selected file(s), click **Extract**.

7. The Extract To drop-down list contains the names of folders to which you've extracted files before. Choose one of the folders from the **Extract To** list, or select any folder you want to use from the **Folders/Drives** list. Then click **Extract**.

8. The extracting process may take some time, especially if you're decompressing a long list of files. Meanwhile, you can watch the progress bar at the bottom of the window. The red light lets you know that WinZip is still working; you can start a new task after you see the green light. When you're ready to leave WinZip, click its **Close** (X) button, or open the **File** menu and select **Exit** to return to the Windows desktop.

9. If you switch back to Explorer or My Computer, you can see that the files in your Zip file were decompressed and placed in the folder you selected.

TIP   **Quick Unzip**   When installing WinZip, you can set up an association so Windows knows that files ending in .zip are associated with WinZip. If you do that, all you need to do to open an archive is double-click the name of the Zip file within Windows Explorer or My Computer.

Creating a Compressed Drive with DriveSpace

Windows 95 offers another solution to the disk space dilemma—its DriveSpace utility. With DriveSpace, you can effectively double the capacity of a floppy or removable disk. Obviously, the disk doesn't physically change—rather, the method used to store files changes, almost as if you were zipping up all the files on the drive with a file compression program as described in the last section.

CAUTION

Not Under OSR 2 Windows 95 OSR 2 uses the FAT32 file system for the boot disk (drive C:). As of this writing, you can't use DriveSpace to compress or add a compressed drive to a FAT32 hard disk under Windows 95. To verify whether or not a hard drive uses the FAT32 file system, right-click the drive icon in the Windows Explorer or a My Computer Window, then click **Properties**. If the Type: listed on the General tab is Local Disk (FAT 32), you cannot compress the disk with DriveSpace.

Follow these steps to compress a floppy or removable disk:

1. Click the **Start** button, point to **Programs**, and point to **Accessories**. Point to **System Tools**, and then click **DriveSpace**.

2. The DriveSpace dialog box appears, showing you a list of the drives you can compress. Click the letter of the drive that holds the floppy or removable disk to compress.

3. Open the **Drive** menu and select **Compress**.

4. Drive Space displays graphs showing you how much free space the drive currently has and how much space it will have after compression (see Figure 5.5). If you are compressing a large hard disk, the graphs are confusing. From the graphs, you'd think you're going to lose disk space; however, if you look in the lower-right corner of the dialog box, you'll see that after compression you will gain a new uncompressed drive that more than makes up for the free space you're about to lose.

5. Click the **Start** button. A dialog box appears, cautioning you to back up your files, if any, before compressing them. Assuming you already did this (or you're feeling very lucky), move on to step 6.

6. Click the **Compress Now** button, and wait until the compression is complete. Depending on the size of the compressed drive and the amount of data to be compressed, this can take from several minutes to several hours.

7. When the compression operation finishes, the Compress a Drive dialog box displays results, as shown in Figure 5.6. Click **Close**.

8. To make sure your system will automatically mount (let you open) compressed floppy or removable drives, open the **Advanced** menu, and click **Settings**.

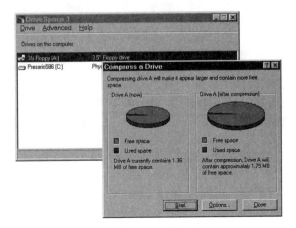

Figure 5.5 Compressing a floppy disk.

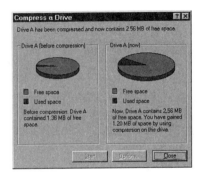

Figure 5.6 The results of compressing a floppy.

9. Make sure the **Automatically Mount New Compressed** Devices box is checked. Click **OK**, and then quit DriveSpace. DriveSpace will now automatically mount compressed disks that you insert in a drive if you double-click the drive letter in Explorer or My Computer.

Adding a Compressed Drive to a Hard Disk Under the Original Windows 95 Release

You can compress all or most of your C: hard disk if you want to if you're using the original Windows 95 release (and therefore not the FAT 32 file system). But I believe a better approach is just to create a new, compressed drive with some of the free space left on your hard disk. So, for example, if you have 100M of free space left, you can compress 50M of that space to form a new drive as drive H: (or another drive letter). Here are the advantages to only compressing part of your hard disk:

- You leave your system files alone, so there's no danger of corrupting them.
- You leave your system and program files uncompressed, meaning your programs will continue to run well. Compressing program files can slow down a program's performance.

CAUTION

Safety Back Up   Before you add a compressed drive to a hard disk or perform any big disk operation, it's still a good idea to back up the data on your disk. See Lesson 14 in this task to learn how to create and use backups.

To add a compressed drive with some of the free space on an existing drive, start DriveSpace. Click the drive whose free space you want to convert to a new compressed drive. Open the **Advanced** menu, then choose **Create Empty**. Change any settings you wish in the Create New Compressed Drive dialog box, such as changing how much space the compressed drive will use or what its drive letter will be, and then click **Start**. The time it takes to compress the file will depend on how much space you compress. When the compression finishes, if Windows prompts you to restart your computer, click **Yes**. The compressed drive will now appear as a new drive icon (H:, or the letter you specified) in Explorer and My Computer.

This lesson showed you how to find more disk space by clearing out old files, zipping files, and using compression. The next lesson explains how to find and repair errors on a damaged disk with ScanDisk.

Using ScanDisk on a Damaged Disk

This lesson shows you how to repair a disk that has errors using the ScanDisk utility.

Check a Disk for Errors with ScanDisk

With Windows 95 on your computer, you have a powerful ally available: the ScanDisk program. This handy little program checks the integrity of your hard disk drive (and floppy disks too, though that isn't done as often), as well as all the files on it. For example, if the computer is having trouble reading the contents of a file, sometimes ScanDisk can locate the problem and fix it.

In addition, ScanDisk can survey the entire surface of your computer's hard disk, looking for trouble spots. If there's a glitch on the surface of the hard disk —whether or not data is there—ScanDisk can spot it. The ScanDisk program can then "mark" the bad spot so that it will never be used to store data. And if the bad spot already contains data, ScanDisk can often recover it and move it to an undamaged area, preventing data loss.

 TIP **Scan Routine** You should use the ScanDisk program's Standard option at least once a week to check the integrity of your computer's hard disk drive. Perform ScanDisk's thorough scan once a month.

There are different ways to start ScanDisk, depending on your preferences and where you are when you need to use it. I cover all the options, next.

Running ScanDisk with the Start Menu

Like other system utilities, you can start ScanDisk from the Start menu, and run
a scan using these steps:

1. To fix a floppy disk, insert the disk into one of the floppy disk drives and
close the door (if necessary). To scan your hard disk, skip this step.

2. Click the **Start** button, point to **Programs**, point to **Accessories**, point to
System Tools, and then click **ScanDisk**.

3. The ScanDisk dialog box appears, asking you to pick a disk to check. Click
the letter of the drive you want to check, as in Figure 6.1.

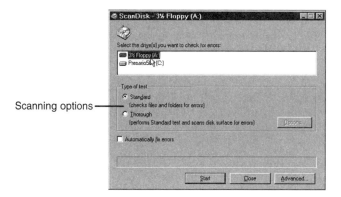

Figure 6.1 Select the drive to scan and scanning options.

4. To have ScanDisk check for and repair only file and folder problems, click
Standard. If you want ScanDisk to also check for bad places on the disk,
click **Thorough**.

5. To have ScanDisk repair errors without asking for confirmation, check the
Automatically Fix Errors check box. (If you leave this unchecked, ScanDisk
will let you choose how to repair the error. For example, if ScanDisk finds
a lost file cluster, it lets you decide whether to delete the cluster or save it.)
In most cases, you can select the **Automatically Fix Errors** option without
any problem.

6. Click the **Start** button, and ScanDisk starts checking the disk, informing
you of its progress, as in Figure 6.2. If ScanDisk finds a problem, it either
corrects the problem or displays a prompt asking you how you want to
correct the problem. Follow the on-screen instructions until the operation
is complete.

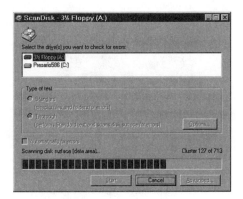

Figure 6.2   The progress bar at the bottom of the ScanDisk window keeps you apprised of the scan progress.

7. When ScanDisk is done, it displays a log of all the problems it found and corrections it made. Click the **Close** button, and then click **Close** again to quit.

Thorough and Long   For hard disks over 1 gigabyte, running a thorough scan will take an hour or even longer. Plan this type of scan only when you have a little down time on your hands.

CAUTION

Running ScanDisk from Explorer or My Computer

You can access ScanDisk directly from My Computer or Explorer. Insert a floppy to scan, if needed, then start Explorer or My Computer. Right-click the icon for the drive to scan. In the Properties dialog box, click the **Tools** tab to display its options (Figure 6.3). Click **Check Now** to open ScanDisk.

Running ScanDisk in DOS Mode

When you're troubleshooting a problem with your system, you may not always be able to boot to the Windows 95 desktop. You may have to boot to the command prompt (DOS) mode, or worse yet, use your startup disk to boot.

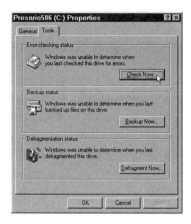

Figure 6.3 You can access ScanDisk via a disk's Properties dialog box by clicking the Check Now button on the Tools tab.

In these instances, you need to run the DOS-based version of ScanDisk, using one of these two methods:

- If you can log onto your C: drive, do so. Type **scandisk** and press **Enter** to scan the C: drive. (If scandisk doesn't run, change to the \Windows\ Command folder and try running it from there. Type **scandisk a:** and press **Enter** to scan a floppy.
- To run ScanDisk from the startup disk and scan drive C: from the A:\> prompt, make sure the startup disk is in drive A:. Type **scandisk c:** and press **Enter**.

When you use one of the two methods just mentioned to run ScanDisk, the ScanDisk screen that appears will look different than its Windows counterpart. Don't worry. It performs the same scanning and repairs under DOS that it did under Windows. Also note that under Windows 95 OSR 2, the DOS-based ScanDisk will start automatically in most cases when you perform a cold boot, or if your system didn't shut down properly. You'll need to press a key to initiate the scan, and when the scan concludes, Windows will start as usual.

This lesson showed you how to use ScanDisk to find and repair errors on a disk. The next lesson explains how to troubleshoot other disk and file issues.

Fixing Other Disk and File Problems

This lesson shows you how to resolve other disk and file problems that can slow down your work.

Dealing with a Jammed Floppy Disk

A disk is jammed when you can't get it out of the disk drive, and it does happen to the best of us. The most common reason for a jammed disk is that the disk was inserted incorrectly. This is especially true of 3.5-inch disks, which contain a metal slide that can get jammed inside the works of the drive. Another common reason for jammed disks, especially the 3.5-inch variety, is a disk label that's come off. The label catches on the inside of the drive, and prevents you from pulling the disk out.

If you are the victim of a stuck disk, use the techniques listed next to try to extract it from your computer disk drive. Warning: Even if you are very careful, there is the possible risk of damaging the disk.

Don't Be Brutal   For a *really* stuck disk, you may need to take your computer into the repair shop. If you tug and press too vigorously, you could break the drive.

CAUTION

- If the drive is the 5.25-inch variety, open the latch and try to wiggle the disk free. Sometimes, you can help extricate the disk by repeatedly opening and closing the latch.

- If the drive is the 3.5-inch variety, push the release button all the way in and try to grab the disk with your fingers. If the disk doesn't come out far enough, try gently grasping it with a small pair of pliers. Don't pull so hard that you damage the drive or disk.

- If the disk still won't budge, you may need to remove the computer's lid in order to reach the disk drives inside. Once the computer is apart, you may be able to manually free the obstruction that's keeping the disk from coming out.

- On 3.5-inch disks: If the metal slide was caught in the drive, more than likely it is now bent or damaged. Once you remove the disk do *not* reinsert this disk into the drive, or it will get stuck again. The disk is not totally ruined, however. Carefully pry the metal slide from the disk. It is only there to protect the disk and is not absolutely required. Be careful not to touch the exposed disk or you may lose your data. Once the slide is off the disk, insert the disk and copy its contents to a new undamaged disk. Verify that the copy is good, and then throw away the damaged disk.

Handling Disk Error Messages

When you're trying to copy files to a disk or read from a disk, errors may occur, particularly when you're using a floppy disk. Though floppy disks do have a protective covering—especially the hard plastic covering on 3.5-inch disks—they can become damaged or fill up will files. Follow the guidance in this section to learn how to deal with particular problems you see.

The Computer Says a Disk Is Write-Protected

You *write-protect* a disk to protect against making unwanted changes to it, such as deleting or overwriting valuable files on the disk. Most disks are write-protected for a good reason. For example, most application disks come write-protected so that you can't hurt the disk when installing the application. In addition, sometimes you might write-protect a disk that contains important files, such as a disk with backup copies of your files. If you try to copy or save a file to or delete a file from a disk that's write-protected, Windows will stop the operation and inform you of the write-protection, as shown in Figure 7.1.

Figure 7.1 This error message informs you that Windows can't write to the floppy disk. Other Windows 95 error message boxes look like this one.

TIP   **Error Boxes**   When a message box informs you of an error, click **OK** to close it and take the steps you need to deal with the error.

So, before you remove write-protection from a disk, double-check the disk's current contents to make sure you'd be comfortable with losing them. When you're sure you want to write to this disk, go ahead and remove the write-protection. For 3.5-inch disks, slide the write-protect tab so you can no longer see through the hole in the disk. For 5.25-inch disks, remove the sticker that covers the notch on the side of the disk. Then retry the copy or save operation.

TIP   **Permanent Protection?**   Some older 3.5" disks that were used as program disks have the sliding tab removed, so that you can't unprotect them. If you're ready to recycle such a disk, though, you can cover the hole with a piece of opaque tape. Just be sure to fasten the tape securely so it doesn't stick in the drive.

"Error writing to or reading from disk in drive."

This error message usually appears after you hear your floppy disk drive grinding unnaturally. The drive is trying its best to use the floppy disk, but it's not having any luck. The disk is probably bad, and you'll have to throw it away. Before you fling the disk in the nearest trash can, try to recover any files it may have:

- Try copying and files that you can read from the damaged floppy disk to your hard disk or to another floppy disk. (If you can't copy successfully in Windows Explorer or My Computer, try opening a DOS window,

changing to the folder where you'd like to copy the files, and using the
copy a:*.* command to copy the files.) Any time the system has trouble
reading or copying a particular file (at the DOS prompt, you'll usually get
an error message prompting you to choose how to proceed—press **I** for
Ignore), make a note of it. Even though you might successfully copy the
file at some point, that file may be damaged; on the other hand, you'll have
a clear picture of which files are damaged and which are probably safe.

- If you have Windows 95, click the **Start** button; point to **Programs**, **Accessories**, and **System Tools**; and then click **ScanDisk**. Scan the floppy disk
for errors.

In Windows 95, you will get an error like this if you try to format a disk and you
have a My Computer or Explorer window open that's displaying the disk's
contents. Simply close the window and continue with the formatting process.

Drive Not Ready or General Failure Errors

If you see a **Drive not ready error**, it's usually because you tried accessing drive
A before inserting a disk (or, if the drive has a door, you forgot to close the
door). Insert a disk, close the door if there is one, and press **R** or click **Retry**. If
that doesn't work, try another disk that you know for sure is formatted (such as
a disk with data already on it). If the problem persists, turn your computer off
and check under the hood (inside the system unit) for a disconnected or damaged floppy drive cable. If the cable's disconnected, consult your documentation
to verify its proper connection (it usually plugs into an adapter card for the
floppy disk), and plug it back in. If it's damaged, get help from a qualified
service technician.

If you get a **General failure reading drive A** message, you inserted a disk but
the disk was not formatted (or it has a flaw). Windows 95 will prompt you to
format the disk. Do so, unless the floppy disk has data on it. If the disk already
has data on it, *don't* format it. Instead, use ScanDisk to check the floppy for
problems, as described in the last lesson. Lesson 14 in Part II gives more coverage about formatting.

No Hard Disk Formatting   When you're working in Explorer or My Computer, you can't format your hard disk; you'll see an error message telling you
Windows cannot format the drive because it contains Windows files that are in

CAUTION

use. However, if you issue the format command at the DOS prompt and then accidentally press **Y** when you're warned that formatting will remove everything on your hard disk, your disk will reformat an you'll lose everything on the disk.

Can't Find the Tape or Removable Drive

Windows 95 or a program like a backup program might flash an error message telling you that it can't find your tape backup drive or a removable drive. Many such drives—especially those that connect via a parallel port—require that you have a tape or disk cartridge in the drive when you turn on the drive and your system. So, try turning off the drive (and your system if needed), inserting a tape, and turning everything back on. The system or application should then be able to find the drive.

Dealing with a Disk that's Full

If you try to save or copy a file to a floppy and get a message that the disk is full, use a different disk, or delete files from the disk before you try to save additional files. On a hard disk, it is good practice to use no more than 90 percent of the total space. Your computer needs some space for temporary files, and if you don't provide this space, you might encounter serious problems.

If you use Windows 95, your hard disk may not be full; it could be that the Recycle Bin is filled with deleted files. If so, Windows will usually prompt you to empty it to free up more room on the hard disk.

If you get a disk full message while trying to save a file to your hard disk (and your Recycle Bin is already empty), you might have to save the file to a formatted floppy disk for the time being. Then move some data files (files you create) off the hard disk to floppy disks to free up some space. Also check the steps listed for freeing up disk space given in Lesson 5 of this part.

For a more permanent solution to an overcrowded hard drive, consider installing a newer, bigger hard drive. (See Lesson 10 in Part V, which explains how to add an additional drive to your system.) Most applications nowadays gobble up hard drive space; there never seems to be enough. Or you might add a Zip drive, as described in Lesson 9 of Part V.

"Sector not found"

The magnetic material on a disk is organized into tracks and sectors to help your computer organize and track the pieces of a file. A bad sector error means the

521

disk has a bad spot on it. The bad sector isn't a big problem unless there's some data saved to that sector, in which case you might lose the data. You may be able to recover the data using ScanDisk, as described in the last lesson.

If the error occurred on a floppy disk, try to recover any data from the disk (using ScanDisk), and then throw the disk away. On floppy disks, if one sector goes bad, it's likely that additional neighboring sectors will follow suit sometime soon. Rather than risk losing data, discard the disk.

Hard disks are too expensive to throw away (and bad sectors usually are not a sign of the demise of neighboring sectors), so the best thing to do is use ScanDisk to scan the hard disk. It locks out any bad sectors so your computer won't try to use them again.

A Disk Seems Slow and Really Thrashes a Lot

Run a defragmentation program. Windows 95 has a utility called Disk Defragmenter that will solve your problem. After using your computer for a while, space on the hard disk becomes fragmented, meaning that files have been broken up and placed in pieces at various points on the hard disk. When parts of a file are scattered all over your hard disk, it's more difficult (and time-consuming) for your computer to retrieve the file when needed. Over time, fragmentation gets worse—until you finally notice a real difference in speed.

Thrash When you can hear a disk (especially a hard disk) searching and searching to read parts of files or write parts of files, the disk is said to be thrashing.

A defragmenter such as Disk Defragmenter pulls all the pieces of each file together, placing them on neighboring areas of the disk. This makes it easier (and faster) for your computer to read the files. Consult the next lesson to learn how to work with Disk Defragmenter.

Tackling Tricky File Problems

Human errors can occur when you're working with files, especially if you've had a long or hectic day. Look in this section for fixes to frequent faux pas.

You Accidentally Deleted a File

Windows 95 moves deleted files to the Recycle Bin, from which you can restore the deleted file (provided you haven't emptied the Bin already). See Lesson 11 in Part II to learn how to use the Recycle Bin. The only exception is for files deleted from a floppy disk. The Recycle Bin does not keep track of those. To recover a disk you deleted from a floppy, you need to run a utility program for recovering deleted files. The Norton Utilities includes such an undelete tool. Just make sure you use the utility to undelete the file before you copy any more files to the disk.

You Accidentally Dropped the File into the Wrong Folder, but You're Not Sure Which One

If you misplace a file in Windows 95, follow these steps to locate it. First, click the **Start** button, point to **Find**, and click **Files or Folders**. A dialog box appears, asking you to type the name of the lost file or folder. Type a name in the **Named** text box, pick the disk you want to search from the **Look In** drop-down list, and then click the **Find Now** button. Windows searches the selected drive for the specified file or folder and displays a list of items that match your search instructions.

If you're looking for a document file in Windows 95, you can find recently opened documents on the Documents menu. Click the **Start** button and point to **Documents**. Windows shows a list of files you've recently worked on. Click the file to run the program used to edit the file, and then open the file in that program.

If the file you're looking for has no extension (or you can't remember it), insert an asterisk at the end of the search file name. For example, type **myfile.*** to search for all files that start with MYFILE and end in any extension. You can also use the question mark (**?**) wild-card character to search for files. For example, **M????.*** finds all files whose name starts with M, has five or fewer characters, and ends in any extension.

One trick I often use to find misplaced files is to run the application I used when I created or saved the file. Then I open the **File** menu. Sometimes, the file is listed at the bottom of the menu. If I don't see it, I select **Save**. The application usually displays a dialog box showing the name of the directory where the application saves its files. Nine times out of ten, my lost file is in that directory.

My File Disappeared from the Screen

Often people "lose" files by closing (or minimizing) the window that the file is in or by opening another window on top of it. If the program you're working in has a Window menu, open it; chances are the file's name will appear at the bottom of the menu. You can display the file by clicking its name.

If you turned off your computer without exiting the program first—or if your computer crashed or suffered a power outage—the file probably *is* gone. You may be able to salvage the file (or parts of it) by running SCANDISK (or, if you use only DOS, **CHKDSK /F**) and telling the program to save the parts of the files it finds. You can then open those files in a text editor (such as Windows Notepad) to see what they contain. Look for these files in the root directory of the drive you checked. Recovered files are named *FILEnnnn*.CHK (where *nnnn* is a number from 0001 to 9999).

Some applications back up your documents automatically as you work. When you run the application after a system crash, the application gives you the option of recovering your lost file. But even if your application doesn't offer this valuable feature, most applications create backup files for each file you save. You may be able to recover your work by opening the backup file. (Backup files commonly have the same name as the original file, but they use the .bak extension.)

To avoid losing files, always exit a program before shutting down your computer. Most programs have a safety feature that asks if you want to save your work before exiting. If you shut down your computer when your program is running, you bypass this important safety net. Also, get into the habit of saving your files periodically as you work (that is, if your program doesn't automatically do that for you).

This lesson reviewed particular file and disk error messages and gave you steps for solving the problems. The next lesson covers how to use Disk Defragmenter to reorganize data on a disk and make it more efficient.

Making a Disk More Efficient with Defrag

Use the steps in this lesson to run Windows 95 Disk Defragmenter, which will optimize your hard disk for better performance.

Reviewing How a Disk Stores Files

Your programs and files are recorded in concentric circles of magnetic material on the surface of the hard drive. When you copy or save files, it is the disk operating system (DOS) portion of Windows 95 that works with the File Allocation Table (FAT) that determines where on your PC's hard disk to place them. Basically, DOS looks at the first empty space on the hard drive and tries to place the file there; the FAT tracks where the file is placed. (For more on disks, files, and the FAT, see Lesson 3 in Part 1 and Lessons 8 through 11 in Part 2.)

Now suppose you delete files from the computer's hard disk drive. This process leaves "holes" (empty clusters where parts of files used to be). When you save a new file to the disk drive, your computer tries to use up these empty clusters. To make the situation even more complicated, suppose there's no empty group of clusters large enough to hold a particular file. Then the file has to be split up and stored on non-adjacent clusters (clusters that aren't *contiguous* or next to each other). When this happens, the file is said to be *fragmented*. In fact, this is the most typical situation, especially on hard disks.

As you save and delete files on the disk, clusters break up into smaller and smaller groups. When a file is fragmented, the FAT becomes even more important. The FAT is basically a table that tracks each file's pieces. For example, here are the steps your computer has to take to open a file:

1. Suppose you're working with a program and you use its File, Open command to open a file. The program starts by talking with the Disk Operating System (DOS) under Windows 95, telling DOS to get the file.

2. DOS looks at the FAT file and finds out the location for each of the clusters that makes up the file.

3. The program starts to read the file: A signal tells the read/write head of the drive where to find the first cluster, and the drive reads the cluster's contents into RAM. A signal then directs the head to the next cluster, and so on, until the entire file is in RAM.

You can imagine what can happen to the clusters on your computer's hard disk drive after a while. As you save and delete files and the groups of available clusters become smaller or are further away from each other on the disk, large files can be strewn in wildly-separated clusters on the surface of the disk. To read such files, the FAT has to tell your computer to jump all over the hard disk drive to assemble all of its pieces.

One or two fragmented files are usually no problem. But a lot of fragmented files can seriously degrade the performance of your computer. Each time the file is chopped apart, the computer must work that much harder to read the file from the hard drive. In many cases, all this jumping around slows down the computer and decreases performance.

Optimize a Disk with Defrag

Windows 95 offers a handy utility program called Disk Defragmenter. (Windows 3.1 does not come with such a program; if you use Windows 3.1, you will have to exit to a DOS prompt and use the Defrag command—if you have DOS 6.0 or later). The Disk Defragmenter nickname *Defrag* comes from the job it does: The utility *defragments* fragmented files. In other words, it reassembles your files and places them in adjacent sections on the hard, floppy, or removable disk. Despite its complex-sounding names, this utility is actually easy to use. It guides you through the entire defragmenting process (which is often called "optimization") step-by-step. It will even suggest the level of optimization your disk needs in order to be more efficient. You can even defragment a floppy or removable disk if your system seems slow in accessing its files.

 TIP **Time, Time, Time** Defragging your hard disk can take an hour or more. Although you can run other programs while Defrag runs, your system might work very slowly. My advice is to plan your defrag for the evening or other period when you don't need your computer.

You should start running Disk Defragmenter regularly as soon as you fill about a third of the space on your hard disk. Follow these steps to use Disk Defragmenter to defrag a hard disk under Windows 95:

1. Click the **Start** button, point to **Programs,** and point to **Accessories.** Select **System Tools,** and then click **Disk Defragmenter.**

2. A dialog box appears, asking which disk drive you want to defragment. Open the **Which Drive Do You Want to Defragment?** drop-down list and click the desired drive, as shown in Figure 8.1. You can defragment all your hard disk drives by clicking **All Hard Drives.**

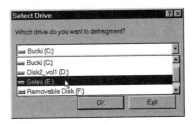

Figure 8.1   Select a disk to defragment.

3. Click **OK.** Another Disk Defragmenter dialog box appears, indicating the percentage of file fragmentation on the disk and telling you whether or not you need to defragment the disk now.

4. (Optional) Click the Advanced button to Display the Advanced Options dialog box (see Figure 8.2). To make the defrag operation proceed a bit more quickly, you can click either **Defragment File Only** or **Consolidate Free Space Only,** or turn off the **Check Drive for Errors** check box. Click **OK** to finish your options changes.

Figure 8.2   These options affect how fast and thorough the defrag operation is.

5. Click the **Start** button.

6. Defragmenter first checks your drive for errors. If it finds any, it will prompt you to run ScanDisk. Follow the prompts to do so, then repeat steps 1-5 to restart Disk Defragmenter.

7. Defragmenter starts to defragment the files on the disk. You can continue to use your programs, but they will run more slowly. If you need to temporarily stop Defragmenter (in order to run a program at full speed), you can by clicking **Pause**. When you're done, click **Resume** to start Defragmenter again.

8. (Optional) If you want to see a graphical representation of Disk Defragmenter's progress, click the **Show Details** button. You can then click the **Legend** button to see what each of the colored boxes on-screen represents, as shown in Figure 8.3. You can click **Hide Details** if you no longer want to view the Defrag operation.

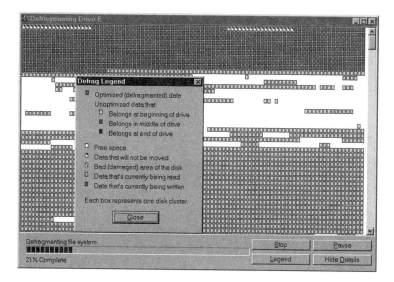

Figure 8.3 Get a graphical view of the defrag operation.

9. When you get the message saying that defragmentation is complete, click **Yes** to quit Disk Defragmenter.

 TIP **Another Start** You also can start Disk Defragmenter from Windows Explorer or My Computer. Right-click the drive you want to defrag, then click **Properties**. In the Properties dialog box, click the **Tools** tab, then click **Defragment Now**.

TIP   **FAT32**   The FAT32 file system used under Windows 95 OSR 2 is more efficient than the older FAT16 file system used under the original Windows 95 release and older Windows versions. Basically, the FAT32 file system is better designed to handle hard disks over 512M or so. FAT32 can use smaller clusters for those larger disks, so the FAT can manage the disk space more effectively. So, you may find that need to defrag your hard disk much less frequently under OSR 2.

Defragmenting a Compressed Drive

If you compressed a floppy disk or your hard disk or added a compressed drive to the disk (see Lesson 5 in this part) under the original release of Windows 95, you can still defragment it. (You can't compress a FAT32 hard disk under Windows 95 OSR 2, but you can compress floppies and removable disks.) In fact, you should defragment a compressed drive about as often as you might a noncompressed drive—if not *more often*. Because your compressed drive is really just one big file, defragging it will allow the computer to access the information in this large file more efficiently. You should also defrag the uncompressed portion of your hard disk), in order not to compound the problem.

This lesson explained how to improve a disk's operating efficiency by using Disk Defragmenter to reorganize the files and free space on a disk. The next lesson provides help for solving keyboard problems.

Handling Keyboard Problems

This lesson provides suggestions you can try if your keyboard stops working or gives you other problems.

Jump-Starting a Keyboard that Won't Work

If you've connected your keyboard properly and have installed the right driver for it (see Lesson 2 in Part 5), it should work without any incident. However, if the keyboard doesn't start working immediately when you install it or it stops working later, try the fixes here to revive it.

Turn your computer off and make sure your keyboard is plugged securely into the keyboard port (usually at the back of the system unit). Also make sure the cord is connected securely to the keyboard; you might have to flip the keyboard over to do this. Then turn on your computer. (Never connect or disconnect a keyboard or any other device when the computer is on.)

If the keyboard still doesn't work, check the following:

- Is the computer locked? Many computers come with a lock and key most people never use. If you keep the keys in the lock, however, someone might have turned the key for fun. After unlocking the computer, you usually have to press a special key to proceed with the boot operation.
- Turn off your computer, unplug the keyboard from the computer, and check to see whether any pins in the keyboard plug are bent or pushed in.

(If you had to force the plug at all when you plugged the keyboard in, you may have inadvertently bent some pins on the connector.) You can usually repair the plug with a pair of long-nose pliers and a gentle touch. Be careful when plugging the keyboard back in.

- If the keyboard doesn't work in Windows 95, double-click the **Keyboard** icon in the Control Panel (you can display the Control Panel by double-clicking **My Computer** and then **Control Panel,** or choosing **Start**, **Settings**, **Control Panel**). Click the **General** tab to see which keyboard Windows is set up to use. Click the **Change** button to change the keyboard type (you may need the setup disk that came with the keyboard to install the driver).

- If you can't bring your keyboard back to life, maybe it's fried (or maybe the keyboard cord is damaged). If you have access to another keyboard, plug it into your computer and see if it works. If the other keyboard works, your keyboard is dead. You can take the keyboard to a repair shop to try to get it fixed, but it's probably cheaper to just buy a new one and install it yourself, as described in Lesson 2 of Part 5.

Correcting a "Keyboard Not Found" Message

If you see a *Keyboard not found* message as your computer boots, either your keyboard plug popped out of its socket, or your computer is locked. Check the lock first. If that doesn't solve your problem, turn off your computer and make sure the keyboard is plugged in. Some keyboards have a connector on the keyboard, too (the connector looks like a phone connector); check this connection while you're at it.

Correcting Unexpected Behavior When You Type

If your keyboard is up and running, there are only a limited number of problems that can effect how it works. Check this section to find solutions to life's little keyboard annoyances.

Everything in UPPERCASE

If everything you typed appears in uppercase letters, you pressed the Caps Lock key by mistake. The Caps Lock indicator for your keyboard will be lit (see Figure 9.1). Press **Caps Lock** again to return your keyboard to normal.

CAUTION

Use Lowercase Online By the way, if you're "talking" to someone on an online service (conversing by typing), it's considered bad manners to type in all uppercase letters—it's the equivalent of shouting. If you want to emphasize a word online, enclose it between *asterisks*.

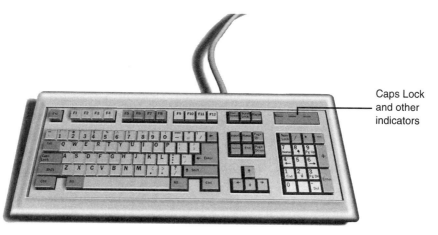

Caps Lock and other indicators

Figure 9.1 Check to see if Caps Lock is lit. If so, press Caps Lock again to turn it off.

Typing Replaces Existing Text

If characters you type are typing over existing text, you've changed from Insert mode to Overtype mode. In Insert mode, all text is inserted at the insertion point position, and surrounding text is adjusted to make room for the new text. In Overtype mode, everything you type replaces existing text. Many applications have an indicator in the status bar that lets you know when Overtype mode is on, as shown in the example from Word 97 in Figure 9.2. In most applications, you can switch back to Insert mode by pressing the **Ins** key. If that doesn't work, check the documentation or the application's Help system to determine how to change modes.

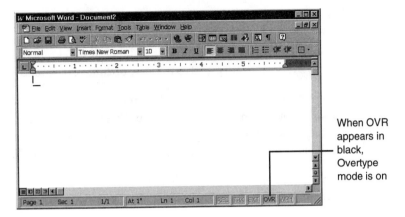

When OVR appears in black, Overtype mode is on

Figure 9.2 Some applications tell you if you've turned on Overtype mode.

A Key I Press Behaves Unexpectedly

Some keyboards have a Remap feature that allows you to make one key act like another. Advanced users like to remap keys to customize the keyboard and make it a real time-saver. The rest of us dream about replacing our keyboard with one that has no Remap key.

If you happen to remap a few keys, you can bring them back to normal. Press the **Remap** key, and then press the key you remapped twice. This essentially maps the key to itself. On a Gateway AnyKey keyboard, you can return the entire keyboard to normal by pressing **Ctrl+Alt+Suspnd Macro**.

TIP   **Sticky Keys**   If a key gets sticky, it can remain slightly "pressed" after you use it. For example, if your Ctrl key sticks and then you press another key, your computer might act like you pressed a keyboard shortcut (such as Ctrl+A). If you're seeing these types of symptoms, try the steps for cleaning the keyboard, both in Lesson 13 of Part 1 and in Lesson 16 of this part.

It's Beeping, not Typing

If your keyboard works but makes the computer beep at you when you type, it could be that the *keyboard buffer* is full (the buffer holds approximately 15–20 keystrokes). Maybe the computer is busy performing some other task and can't give the keyboard its full attention yet. Wait until the computer is finished with whatever task it's performing, and then try typing again.

If you wait a sufficient amount of time and you're still getting beeps, maybe you're pressing the wrong keys. Some applications beep if you click an option or press a key that's not currently available. If you know you're pressing the right keys, save your work and exit the application, and reboot your computer.

If the problem persists, turn off your computer and check your keyboard connections. If the keyboard is securely connected, maybe the wiring inside the cable is damaged, or maybe your keyboard is on the blink, in which case you can install a new keyboard, as explained in Lesson 2 of Part 5.

This lesson explained how to diagnose and fix problems with your keyboard. The next lesson helps you do the same for the mouse.

Tackling Mouse Problems

This lesson reviews common mouse problems and provides potential solutions.

Fixing a Mouse that Doesn't Work at All

If you don't even get a mouse pointer, first shut down the system and make sure your mouse is plugged securely into the correct port. Unplug it and plug it back in, if needed, to make sure the connection is firm. You should never unplug and plug in the mouse while the system is on, especially if your system uses a PS/2 mouse and mouse ports, as some desktops and notebooks do. It isn't safe for you or your system, and you'd need to reboot after doing so, anyway.

If the connection is fine, check the following:

- Is the mouse pointer just off the screen? It's possible to move the mouse pointer beyond the corners or edges of your screen, so that you simply can't see it. Roll the mouse on your desktop to see if you can bring the pointer into view.

- On your notebook, is the pointing device fastened securely? When the mouse/pointing device attaches to the side of the laptop system, it's easy to knock it loose. Even if it appears to be securely connected, you may need to restart Windows or even reboot to get Windows to find the mouse again.

- When you connected the mouse, did you install a mouse driver? Connecting a mouse to your computer is not enough. You must install a mouse driver that tells the computer how to use the mouse. Lesson 2 in Part V explains how to install and set up a mouse.

- Have you recently installed a graphical game? Some game and entertainment programs, especially those written for Windows 3.1, install their own screen drivers, causing problems within Windows, including a disappearing mouse. So check your display driver setup (right-click the desktop, click **Properties**, and use the options on the **Settings** tab) and verify that you have the correct driver installed for your monitor.

- Do you have the mouse problem in Windows 95? To change a mouse setting, press **Alt+F4** to close any windows that are in your way. Then press **Tab** until **My Computer** is highlighted and press **Enter**. Use the arrow keys to highlight the **Mouse** icon, and then press **Enter**. If you can't even get the mouse pointer to appear, press **Ctrl+PgDn** to select the **General** tab, and then press **Alt+C** to select the **Change** button. Use the down arrow key to select the mouse manufacturer. Press **Tab** and use the down arrow key to select the mouse model you have. Press **Enter** to save your change. (The last section in this Lesson provides more help about mouse pointer problems under Windows 95.)

- When you installed the mouse driver, did you specify a COM port? When you install a mouse driver, you might need to specify which port the mouse is plugged into: COM1, COM2, COM3, or a special mouse port. If you pick the wrong port, your computer won't be able to find your mouse. Run the installation or setup program again and select a different COM port. You must reboot your computer after selecting a new COM port.

- Make sure the mouse driver is loading. Reboot your computer, wait until you see the message **Starting Windows** and then press and release the **F8** key. Choose the **Step-by-Step confirmation** option to step through the startup commands. You should see a message like **Mouse Driver Loaded**. If you see something like **Mouse Not Found**, you probably have the mouse connected to the wrong port (or the driver is set up to use the wrong mouse port under Windows 95; most newer systems don't load a DOS-level driver at all).

- Look for a Readme file in the Mouse folder. Some mice have strange quirks that are documented in a README.TXT file. Look for such a file in your Mouse folder, open it, and read it. In Windows, use Notepad to read the file. Then go to the DOS prompt, type **CD \MOUSEDIR** to change to the mouse directory (substitute the real name of the directory for *mousedir*), and type the command **type Readme.txt I more**. The **I more** switch tells DOS to display one screen at a time.

Fixing a Jumpy Mouse Pointer

If a mouse pointer doesn't flow smoothly from point-to-point on-screen or it is very difficult to control, there are a few different techniques you can try to resolve the situation.

First, turn off your computer and clean your mouse. This process was covered in Lesson 13 of Part I. In fact, dirt within the mouse is the most likely culprit of mouse performance problems. If you have pets or eat a lot around your computer (although as a practice, you should avoid eating and drinking around your system), you should clean the mouse frequently to remove hair and crumbs.

 TIP   **Mousepad Alert**   Also inspect your mousepad for oily or dirty areas. Dirt and oil slicks on a mouse pad can cause the mouse roller to travel at inconsistent speeds or skip. Wash the mouse pad with warm soapy water and let it dry thoroughly before using it again.

If you clean the mouse and you're still having trouble, open your Config.sys and Autoexec.bat files; make sure you have only one mouse driver loading. If you find a mouse command line in both files, add **REM** plus a space before *one* of the commands. For details on how to edit Config.sys and Autoexec.bat, see Lesson 3 in Part V. If you have an older system that loads a DOS-level driver and you're having trouble with Mouse.exe and you have a Mouse.exe (or Mouse.com) file, remove the Mouse.sys command from Config.sys, add the Mouse.exe (or Mouse.com) command to Autoexec.bat, and then reboot your computer.

If that doesn't work, contact the mouse manufacturer and make sure you have the latest mouse driver (the program that tells your computer how to use the mouse). Microsoft, Logitech, and other mouse manufacturers constantly improve their mouse drivers to correct for bugs that crop up in the latest programs.

In other cases, you may find that the mouse pointer is simply difficult to see, making it difficult to control. In Windows 95, you can turn on pointer trails to make it easier to see the mouse pointer. Double-click the **Mouse** icon in the Control Panel. Click the **Motion** tab and click the **Show Pointer Trails** option, as shown in Figure 10.1. On some systems, you also can increase the size of the pointer by clicking the **Pointers** tab and selecting **Windows Standard (Extra Large)** from the **Scheme** list box. Click **OK** when you're done selecting options.

Pointer Trails Pointer trails are little copies of the mouse pointer image that trail behind the pointer to give a greater sense of where the pointer is and where it's headed.

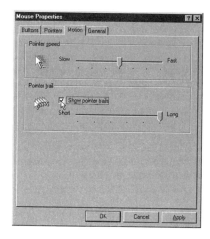

Figure 10.1 Turn on pointer trails to make the mouse pointer easier to follow.

Slowing Down or Speeding Up the Pointer

Mouse speed pointer speed is a matter of preference in most cases, but the quirks of your system or the type of software you're using can lead you to want to make a change. For example, when some mouse pointers are set to full speed, a small mouse motion can send the pointer zooming off the edge of the screen. If you're just typing a lot of text, you might not need fine mouse control, but if you're formatting and editing and need to position the mouse carefully, you might want better mouse pointer control.

To adjust the speed of your mouse pointer, double-click the **Mouse** icon in the Control Panel (**Start**, **Settings**, **Control Panel**). Click the **Motion** tab and adjust the **Pointer Speed** setting (see Figure 10.2) by dragging the pointer left or right. Click **OK** to finish your changes.

TIP **Quicker Double-Clicker** If your mouse doesn't seem to be working when you double-click, try adjusting the double-click speed. Double-click the **Mouse** icon in Control Panel, click the **Buttons** tab, then drag the slider for the Double-click speed. You can test the speed in the test area, then click **OK** to accept your changes.

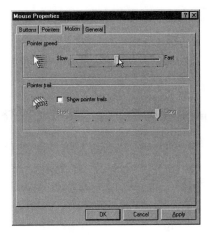

Figure 10.2 Adjust the pointer speed to fine-tune mouse control.

Making a Mouse Work Under Windows If It Stops

Mouse problems under Windows 95 can be frustrating, because a mouse is an essential tool for working with the Windows 95 interface. So, if you do encounter problems, look in this section to get your mouse back to work.

Windows 95 Keyboard Survival Shortcuts

If you can't use your mouse, you can't click, which is a problem when accessing commands at the Windows 95 desktop. So, here are some keyboard shortcuts that can help:

- To close open program windows, press **Alt+F4**.
- To open the Start menu, press **Ctrl+Esc**.
- To select an icon on the desktop, press **Ctrl+Esc**, then **Esc**. Use **Tab** or the arrow keys to highlight the icon you want, then press **Enter**.
- To open Control Panel, press **Ctrl+Esc**, use the **Up Arrow** key to highlight the **Settings** choice, press **Right Arrow**, then press **Enter**.
- To select an icon in Control Panel, use **Tab** or the arrow keys to highlight the icon you want, then press **Enter**.

539

- To select dialog box controls, press Alt+ the underlined selection letter in the control name. Then, you may need to press the Spacebar to toggle a choice on or off, use the arrow keys to make a choice, or type a selection.
- To move between tabs in a dialog box, press **Ctrl+PgDn** or **Ctrl+PgUp**.

Getting the Mouse to Work with Windows 95 Applications

First, make sure the mouse is set up on a COM port (or a PS/2 port if your system uses a PS/2 mouse and port). Then, make sure you have the correct mouse driver loaded.

In Windows 95, you can change your driver by using the **Mouse** icon in the Control Panel. With your keyboard, press **Ctrl+Esc** to open the Start menu, then select **Settings**, **Control Panel**. Use the arrow keys to highlight the **Mouse** icon, and then press **Enter**.

Press **Ctrl+PgDn** to select the **General** tab, and then press **Alt+C** to select the **Change** button. Press **Alt+A** to display all available drivers. Use the down-arrow key to select the mouse manufacturer. Then press **Tab** and use the down-arrow key to select the mouse model you have (as shown in Figure 10.3). Press **Enter** to save your changes. (You may need the setup disk that came with the mouse to install the driver.)

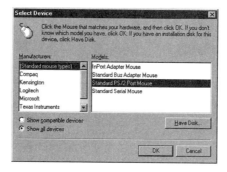

Figure 10.3 Check your mouse driver, and select a new one if needed.

 TIP **No Conflicts** You also can check for conflicts between the mouse and another device under Windows 95, then adjust the settings for one of the devices to remove the conflict. See Lesson 3 in Part V to learn how to check for device conflicts.

Fixing the Mouse After You Install a New Modem

Mice and modems both use COM ports. Normally the mouse uses COM1 and the modem uses COM2. If your mouse and modem don't seem to get along, they're probably set to use the same COM port. Leave the mouse port setting as is, and try changing the setting for the modem. Here's what you do:

1. If you have an internal modem, look at the back of it for a set of tiny switches. These switches let you change the COM port setting for the card itself.

2. If you find the switches, write down their original positions, and then flip the switches to select a different COM port (try **COM2** or **COM4**). (If you don't see switches, you might have to go inside your computer to change jumpers on the modem card; consult the documentation.)

3. Once you've changed the COM port on the hardware, you must change it in the telecommunications program you're using. This can be a fax program, online service, Internet program, HyperTerminal, or whatever program you use with your modem. In America Online, for example, you click the **Setup** button, select **Setup Modem**, and then click the COM port setting.

   In Windows 95, you can change the modem's COM port setting by selecting the **Modems** icon in the Control Panel and selecting the **Diagnostics** tab (you can change tabs by pressing **Ctrl+PgDn**). Press **Alt+H** or click the **Help** button to run the Modem Troubleshooter. The Troubleshooter will ask you a series of questions to help you identify the problem and fix it.

Helping the Mouse Work with DOS Applications from Windows

If your mouse works fine in Windows applications, but freaks out when you try to run a DOS application from Windows, try the following fixes:

- If the DOS application is in a window, press **Alt+Enter** to run it in full-screen mode. If you can use the mouse in full-screen mode, set up the application so it will always run in full-screen mode. In Windows 95, you can make a DOS application run in full-screen mode by exiting the program, then right-clicking the program's startup command in Windows Explorer or My Computer. Select **Properties**. Click the **Screen** tab and click **Full-screen**. Click **OK** to save your change.

- Make sure the correct mouse driver is selected in Windows. Exit the DOS application, double-click **My Computer**, double-click **Control Panel**, and then double-click the **Mouse** icon. Click the **General** tab. If the correct mouse driver is not displayed, click the **Change** button, and then select the correct manufacturer and model. (You'll need the setup disk that came with the mouse to install the driver.)

- In Windows 95, you may have trouble using your mouse in a DOS application if you have QuickEdit mode turned on. To turn it off within a particular DOS program, exit the program. Right-click the program's startup command in either Windows Explorer or My Computer and select **Properties**. Click the **Misc** tab. Click the **QuickEdit** option to turn it off, and then click **OK**.

- If your problem is selecting text while running a DOS application in Windows 95, make sure that the program is running in a *window*. If it's running full screen, press **Alt+Enter** to put it in a window. Then open the **Control** menu, select **Edit**, and select **Mark**. Drag over the text you want to select and press **Enter** to copy it to the Clipboard. To paste the copied text, use the **Edit**, **Paste** command.

- Make sure only one mouse driver is running. If both Autoexec.bat and Config.sys contain a mouse command, use the **REM** command to disable the **DEVICE=MOUSE.SYS** command in Config.sys. Usually, Mouse.com (or Mouse.exe) works better.

- Use the latest version of the mouse driver. If you have an old mouse driver (say it's a couple of years old or so), contact the mouse manufacturer and ask for an updated driver, or visit the manufacturer's Web site (if there is one), to see if there's a recently released driver available for download). To find the version of the mouse driver file installed on your system, choose **Start**, **Settings**, **Control Panel**. Double-click the **System** icon, then click the **Device Manager** tab. Click the plus sign beside the Mouse icon, then double-click the name of the mouse model that appears. Click the **Driver** tab, then click the name of the driver file (if there's more than one) in the Drivers list. Then, look beside File version: at the bottom of the dialog box to see the version number for the driver file.

- Use the Plain VGA driver that came with Windows. You can change video drivers in Windows 95 by right-clicking a blank area of the Windows desktop and selecting **Properties**. Click the **Settings** tab, and then click **Change Display Type** to view the current video driver and change it, if desired.

This lesson helped you troubleshoot problems with your mouse. If you're having monitor problems, check the next lesson.

Addressing Monitor Problems

Read this lesson to see what you can do about common monitor problems.

Reviving a Dead Monitor

If you turn on your system and see nothing but the dreaded black screen, there are some basic steps you can try to address the situation. First, check the obvious:

- Are you running a screen saver or does your system go into "sleep" mode? Some screen saver programs blank the screen instead of displaying pretty pictures. Usually, the press of a key or a mouse move will end the screen saver and snap your screen back to life. And, a sleep mode, in essence, turns off the monitor. Usually, the monitor or system unit will have a special power or Power Saving light that lights up when the system enters sleep mode. Depending the type of system you have, you'll need to move the mouse, press a key, or press a special button on the system to exit sleep mode and resume working.

Asleep, Not Dead I've had experiences where sleep mode does actually cause the system to freeze up. If the same happens to your system, reboot, and it should work fine.

CAUTION

- Is the monitor plugged in and turned on? Your monitor should have a power indicator that lights when the power is on. Could the outlet be bad? If so, test the monitor in an outlet that you know is good.

- Crank up the brightness control. The brightness control is usually on the front or side of the monitor, making it easy to turn it way down by mistake.

- Maybe it's the connection between the monitor and the system unit. Turn everything off and check the connection between the monitor and the system unit (sometimes it wiggles free).

- Is the video card loose? Turn off the computer, open the case, and make sure the video card is seated firmly in its slot. If the card is loose, gently rock it back into place.

If the above fixes for a black screen don't work or you get a message about a video problem during startup, boot in Safe Mode to see if your display returns. Turn off your computer, wait a minute, and then turn it back on. When you see the message **Starting Windows 95**, press the **F8** key. A menu appears, showing a list of startup options. Select the **Safe Mode** option by pressing the number next to it and pressing **Enter**. In safe mode, Windows uses a basic video driver. If your display returns in safe mode, follow the instructions for choosing a new display type under "Clearing Up the Picture," later in this task.

If nothing seems to work, maybe your monitor is dead. If you have a friend or colleague who has a similar computer system, try connecting his or her monitor to your computer. If your friend's monitor works on your computer, you know that the monitor is the problem. Call the manufacturer (or a computer technician). If your monitor is working but is going pale around the edges, or shows a split screen for a while as the system boots up, the monitor is likely dying. If you notice these systems, and subsequently get the dreaded black screen, you can be fairly certain the monitor is dead.

Dealing with a High-Pitched Whine

If you just installed a new video card (Lesson 12 in Part V explains how), and your monitor starts to cry out in an unusually high-pitched and loud whine, turn everything off *immediately*. The card may be set to a higher resolution than the monitor can handle. Check the manual that came with the video card and the one that came with your monitor. Make sure the card is set to display at the same resolution as the monitor. If you can't stop the whining, turn the computer off and call a qualified computer technician.

If the monitor has always whined, maybe you just purchased a whiny monitor. Earplugs may be the only solution.

Clearing Up the Picture

If the monitor's picture isn't as clear as you'd like, either you have a low-resolution monitor, or your monitor is using a low-resolution video driver. If you have your VGA monitor set to 640×480 dpi and 16 colors, you can expect any graphics or movie clips to look pretty fuzzy and perhaps have grayed or blotchy coloring. If you have an SVGA monitor capable of displaying at least 256 colors, pictures and text should look more clear, even at the lower resolution (640×480 dpi). However, some newer monitors begin to look quite fuzzy if set at anything below 800×600 dpi and High Color (also called 16-bit color).

Windows 95 makes it easy to change resolutions and color settings, which you learned more about in Lesson 15 of Part II. Simply right-click a blank area of the Windows desktop, click **Properties**, and click the **Settings** tab. Drag the **Desktop Area** slider to increase or decrease your resolution. You may want to change the **Font Size** and the **Color Palette** settings as well. Settings of 256 colors and 640×480 are usually the minimum for displaying images clearly. Click **OK**, and restart Windows when prompted.

 TIP **Tiny Icons** When you increase screen resolution, the icons, graphic images, video clips, and other on-screen pictures actually look much smaller. (Think about it—you're cramming more visual area into the same space.) If the picture is way too small, you might try changing to a *lower* resolution display setting. For example, if you selected 1024×768, try changing to 800×600, 256 colors. Although your pictures won't look as sharp, you will be able to see them full-size.

If changing the resolution doesn't fix the fuzziness or if you're seeing weird patterns on the screen, you may have selected the wrong display adapter driver or monitor type. Right-click a blank area of the Windows desktop, click **Properties**, and click the **Settings** tab. Click **Advanced Properties**, and then check the Adapter and Monitor listed at the top of the Adapter and Monitor tabs (Figure 11.1 shows the Adapter tab). If one of the tabs displays the wrong device, click **Change**. Click the **Show All Devices** option and select the display adapter or monitor type you need. If yours is not listed, click **Have Disk** and insert the disk that came with your new monitor. Click **OK** and then **Close**. Click **OK** again, and restart Windows when you're prompted to do so.

Figure 11.1 Use the Change button on the Adapter or Monitor tab to choose a new driver for either the display adapter (video card) or monitor.

TIP **I Can't Get the Video to Work Right** If the techniques described in this Lesson don't help you clear up your display problem, check the Device Manager tab in the System Properties dialog box (double-click System in Control Panel) to see if the right video driver is installed or to see if there's a device conflict with the system video. (See Lesson 3 in Part V to learn how). If the driver is missing in the Device Manager, reinstall it. If there's conflict with it or a problem, try removing and reinstalling it.

If you restart Windows and it won't start or you get an error message about a display conflict, you picked the wrong Windows display driver for your display adapter. Trouble is, you can't see anything in order to fix the problem. You'll have to boot in safe mode to choose another display type.

In Windows 95, turn off your computer, wait a minute, and then turn it back on. When you see the message **Starting Windows 95**, press the **F8** key. A menu appears, showing a list of startup options. Select the **Safe Mode** option by typing the number next to it and pressing **Enter**. In safe mode, Windows uses a basic video driver. You can repeat the process described earlier in this section to pick a different display type (video driver) or continue working with the basic driver.

Banishing Screen Flicker

If your screen has a lot of flicker or "jumps" occasionally, either the cord that connects your monitor to the system unit is loose, your monitor is too close to a source of electrical interference, or you have an old interlaced monitor. To check the connection, turn off the system unit and the monitor. Then make sure the monitor cord is securely plugged into the back of the system unit; tighten the screws (if the cord has them); then restart the system.

If you still see a flicker, try moving the monitor a couple feet away from the wall or from another device that may be causing interference—a TV set, for example. Sometimes another electrical energy source can make the screen flicker. Fluorescent lights are another culprit. These lights have a flicker themselves, which can flicker at a different frequency than the monitor, intensifying the flicker effect. Or, the flicker might be coming from the lights rather than the monitor. Try turning off the fluorescent lighting, and using regular incandescent lighting.

If the screen still flickers, you probably have an old *interlaced* monitor. These monitors have an almost imperceptible flicker (like that of fluorescent lights). As the monitor ages, the flicker may become more noticeable. Sometimes you can solve the problem by selecting a lower resolution setting, but then your graphics will look lousy. Your best bet is a new monitor and a graphics adapter card.

Clearing Up Headaches from Your Monitor

Work is work, no matter how apparently physical it is. It can be just as tough on the body to spend long hours in one position (parked in front of a computer) as it can be to do physical labor—because your body has to strain to hold your head still as you look at the screen, while you're moving your hands and arms to type and mouse.

If you find yourself experiencing headaches every time you use the computer, here are some fixes to try:

- Try tilting the monitor to a different position or elevating it a little more, so that you're looking up at a slight angle.
- Make sure you blink normally as you work. Believe it or not, you can forget to blink while concentrating on your work at the monitor.

- Take breaks and do neck rolls every 15 to 20 minutes. Or, instead of neck rolls, blink, squeeze and open your eyes a few times, and focus for a few moments on points across the room to give your eyes a break from close-up viewing.

- Adjust the lighting, not the monitor. Sometimes headaches result from working in an area with poor lighting or that's lighted with fluorescent lights. In addition, some light sources (a lamp or window) can bounce light off your monitor, creating screen glare. Try positioning the monitor at a 90-degree angle relative to the angle of the light from any light source.

- If you have an old, interlaced monitor (they're rare these days), it might have an imperceptible flicker that may be causing the problem. Go out and buy a noninterlaced monitor; the additional expense will pay off in health benefits.

This lesson covered steps you can take if your monitor doesn't display or if it has display problems. If you have trouble printing, look at the next lesson.

Fixing Printer Problems

When you have printer woes, check for a solution here.

Troubleshooting When the Printer Won't Print at All

Usually, Windows 95 will flash an error message to you if the printer won't print. Make sure the printer is plugged in and turned on, and that the On Line light is lit (not blinking). Check that the printer has paper as well.

If everything checks out and the printer still won't print, look for the following:

- If you're printing to a laser printer from the DOS prompt or some older applications that don't offer good printer control, it typically won't eject the page until there's a full page of information to print. Press the **Online** button to take the printer offline (if needed to eject a page from your printer), then press the **Load/Eject/Form Feed** button to eject the page.
- If you have a tractor-feed mechanism on the printer, make sure the sheet feeder switch is in the proper position (for single-sheets or continuous forms).
- Check to make sure you've installed the printer under Windows 95. Click **Start**, point to **Settings**, and click **Printers**. An icon for the printer should appear in the Printers window. To ensure that a printer is set to print to the right port, right-click the printer icon, select **Properties**, and click the **Details** tab to check the printer port (see Figure 12.1). If needed, change the **Print to the following port** choice, then click **OK**. To ensure a printer is set as the default, right-click the printer icon, then click **Set as Default**. See Lesson 1 in Part 5 for steps on adding and setting up a printer.

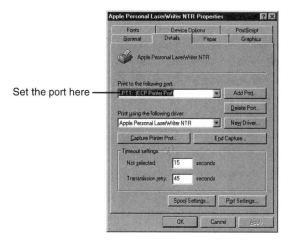

Set the port here

Figure 12.1   Make sure a printer is printing to the correct port.

- Check your printer choice in the application you're printing from to make sure it's sending the data to the right printer. Usually, the Print dialog box will display the selected printer near the top; you can choose another printer simply by opening that drop-down list. (Otherwise, there will probably be a printer button you can click to choose another printer.)

- Is the paper tray inserted correctly? If the paper tray isn't inserted all the way, the paper out light will flash. In this instance, pull out the paper tray, then push it back in until it locks into place (see Figure 12.2). In addition, the paper may not be in the right position to feed. If needed, adjust the paper in its paper tray or feeder until the paper out light stops flashing.

- Most laser printers have a long power-up sequence. While the printer is powering up, it can't receive any data. If you try to print during the power-up sequence, Windows will flash a printer error. Click **Cancel** in the printer error message box to cancel the print job. Turn the printer off, then turn it back on. After it powers up completely and its Online indicator comes on, try printing again.

- Is it a printer problem? To determine whether the printer has a problem, type **dir > lpt1** at the DOS prompt and press **Enter**. This prints the current directory list (you may have to press the **Load/Eject/Form** feed button to spit out the page from a laser printer). If it prints okay, the problem is in the Windows printer setup—or the application's setup. If the directory does not print (or prints incorrectly), the problem is probably with the printer. Most printers have a self-test; check the documentation to figure out how to run the test for your printer.

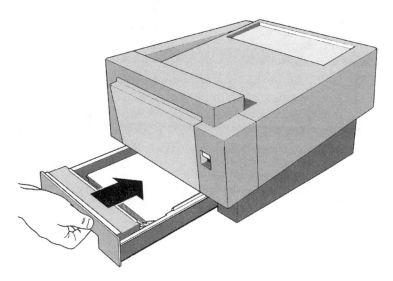

Figure 12.2 Double-check the paper tray by pulling it out and reinserting it.

If you've tried everything and the printer still isn't responding, your printed documents might be "stuck in traffic" in the print queue, described a little later in this lesson.

Eliminating Error Messages When the Printer Is Working

Some of the problems listed above cause Windows 95 to display an error message on-screen like the one shown in Figure 12.3. In other cases, the printer may print, but you may see the error message anyway. This usually means that your printer is a tad slower than Windows 95 is in sending the information to print. If you simply wait five seconds (as the message box itself states), the message will simply go away and more data will be sent to the printer. However, if you're printing large or graphics-intensive files, the repeated error messages might get in your way as you try to work with other files; you have to repeatedly click **Retry** to continue working.

Figure 12.3 Sometimes you'll see an error message box, even when you're having no trouble printing.

You can change a printer setting or two under Windows 95 to try to eliminate these error messages. Click **Start**, point to **Settings**, and click **Printers**. An icon for the printer should appear in the Printers window. Right-click the printer icon, select **Properties**, and click the **Details** tab (refer to Figure 12.1). Under **Timeout Settings**, increase the **Transmission Retry** entry. Click **OK**. If changing the Transmission Retry setting doesn't remedy the problem, redisplay the Details tab for your printer and click the **Spool Settings** button. Consult the documentation for your printer to see what changes may help here.

Documents Go To the Printer, but Don't Print

Your printed documents are sent to the *print queue*—a waiting line. Applications commonly send printed documents to a temporary waiting area and then feed them from there to the printer. If something goes wrong, the document has to stand in line until the printer is ready. If you keep entering the print command over and over, you end up with a long line of documents.

In Windows 95, you can quickly view the print queue by double-clicking the printer icon on the right end of the taskbar. The window for your printer appears, listing the print jobs it currently holds. (Consult Lesson 12 in Part 3 to learn more about working with print jobs.)

You may have inadvertently paused the printer somehow. Rather than trying to print multiple times and therefore only succeeding in filling up the print queue, click to open the **Printer** menu in the printer window, then click **Pause Printing** to remove the check mark beside that command. (If the print job itself is paused, which would be indicated in its listing in the window, you can click the print job. Then click **Document**, **Pause Printing** to resume the print job.) If you've printed to a printer connected to the network, the print queue might simply be extremely full. In this case, it might seem as if the printer is stalled, but it may simply be printing other users' print jobs. If the printer doesn't print your job after an extended period of time, check with the system administrator. The printer may be offline, or you may need an updated printer driver for your system.

You don't typically have to do anything to get Windows 95 to retry printing a document on which it might have paused; it'll do that on its own after a few seconds. To change the print order of the waiting documents (so one prints before some other one), just drag one up to the top of the list.

To remove a document from the queue, click it (or press Ctrl and then click to select multiple documents) and press **Delete**. (Doing that may cause the printer to stop if part of a printed page gets stuck in it. If that happens, press the printer's **Online** button, then the **Load/Eject/Form Feed** button to eject the page; or, turn off the printer, remove the page, and turn it back on.)

Straightening Out Garbled Printouts

If you get a bunch of foreign-looking symbols, you selected the wrong printer driver for your printer. In Windows 95, you can view the installed printer drivers by clicking **Start**, **Settings**, **Printers** to open the Printers window. Right-click the printer driver you want to use as the default and click **Set As Default**. If the correct printer driver is not displayed, double-click the **Add Printer** icon and follow the on-screen instructions. (See Lesson 1 in Part 5 to learn more about installing printer drivers.)

CAUTION

Switch It   At the end of Lesson 1 in Part 5, I explained how to add two printers to your system via an inexpensive switch box. To print to the printer of your choice in such a setup, you have to both select the correct printer from the application you're printing from and have the switch in the correct position. If these choices aren't in synch, you'll get a garbage printout. Make sure the application is printing to the right printer and that the switch is turned to the right printer, too.

If you have an off-brand printer, you can probably set it up to *emulate* (act like) a brand-name printer; that means you have installed the printer driver for the brand-name printer. In most cases, to set up the emulation on the printer itself, you have to pry open a panel on the printer and flip some DIP switches to turn on the emulation. The printer documentation tells you how to get to the switches, which ones you need to flip, and what position each one has to be in. You then select the printer driver for the brand-name printer.

If by "garbled" you mean that the print is too light or streaky, you may have to change the print cartridge or ribbon (or clean it). Before cleaning an inkjet cartridge, read the instructions. I once destroyed a $20 cartridge by swabbing the wrong area with alcohol. For a laser printer, make sure you rock a new toner cartridge gently as described in the instructions that come with the cartridge to distribute the toner before installing the cartridge. (In fact, you can remove it and rock it a few more times if the printouts are streaky for a fairly new cartridge, and then put it back into the printer.) Never store a new toner cartridge standing on end, which could greatly impact the distribution of the toner within it. And, don't touch the shiny roller that's inside the part of the cartridge that opens; doing so could damage the roller's ability to transfer the toner to the paper.

Correcting Grainy or Partial Printouts

Laser printers (and some inkjets) print an entire page at one time, storing the entire page in memory. If the page has a big, complex graphic image (or lots of fonts), the printer may be able to store only a portion of the page. The best fix is to get more memory for your printer, if possible. (This will also help your printer print more quickly.) Check your printer documentation to learn more about this possibility.

The quickest fix is to use fewer fonts on the page and try using a less complex graphic image. You can also try resizing a graphic so that it's smaller.

You might also try printing the document at a lower resolution. In most applications (and in Windows), you can choose a lower resolution through the printer setup. For example, in Windows 95, click **Start**, select **Settings**, and then select **Printers**. Right-click the printer icon and select **Properties**. Then click the **Graphics** tab and select the **Resolution** you want (see Figure 12.4). Click **OK** when you're through.

Figure 12.4 Adjust Graphics settings to help graphics print faster or better.

Printouts Don't Match the Screen

Fonts typically come in pairs—one font for the printer and one for the screen. If the *printer font* has no matching *screen font*, the application takes liberties and selects a screen font it thinks looks like the printer font.

To correct this problem, make sure you install both the screen and printer font for every font you use. Keep in mind that TrueType fonts (displayed with a **TT** on most Windows menus and in font formatting dialog boxes) consist of one font that controls both the screen and the printer. By using TrueType fonts only, you're sure to get in print what you see on the screen.

Removing and Preventing Paper Jams

When a paper jam happens, shut down the printer and remove the paper tray, if necessary to open the printer. Press the release button (Figure 12.5) if needed to open the printer, or lift the top of a dot-matrix or inkjet printer. Gently pull out the pieces of paper. If multiple sheets are jammed or the paper is really mutilated, remove a piece at a time. If you hear any internal parts straining or grinding as you pull, stop and consult a repair shop. If you see any remaining stuck bits of paper, fish them out with tweezers. Be extremely careful around the thin wires within a laser printer, though; they are brittle and can be damaged easily, resulting in the need for a costly repair. Put the printer back together and turn it back on. Once the printer's ready, Windows 95 will immediately resume printing to it, and should pick up where it left off. At worst, you may have to reprint a page or two of the print job.

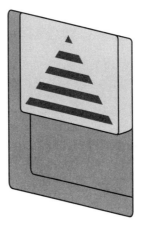

Figure 12.5   Press the release button to open your printer and clear a paper jam.

You can prevent most paper jams by loading the paper properly into the printer. With laser and inkjet printers, be sure not to fill the paper trays too full. Also, use the recommended weight and type of paper suitable for your kind of printer.

CAUTION

Paper Is Not Paper   With today's rising paper prices, inexpensive papers made for photocopiers might be a tempting bargain. However, low-quality papers can curl under a laser printer's heat or leave loads of paper dust in a printer. If you're having numerous paper jams and are using cheap photocopier paper, ante up for the good stuff to prolong your printer's life.

This lesson covered printer troubleshooting, giving numerous techniques for fixing printer problems, although those problems are less common than ever under Windows 95. The next lesson covers one last troubleshooting area—modems.

Making Your Modem Work

When there's a failure to communicate, consult this lesson for useful advice.

Waking up a Dead Modem

Today's modem technology is better than ever, and Windows 95 has more built-in communications features that facilitate proper modem operation. However, you still can experience difficulties from time to time.

If you try to dial another computer with your modem and nothing happens or if your communications program displays a distress signal saying that it cannot find the modem, try the following to determine the cause:

- In Windows 95, you can use the Modem Troubleshooter to fix any modem problems. First, display the Control Panel (click **Start**, point to **Settings**, and click **Control Panel**). Double-click the **Modems** icon, and then click the **Diagnostics** tab. Click the **Help** button. The Modem Troubleshooter screen appears, as shown in Figure 13.1. Answer the questions to determine the cause of the problem and to fix it.

- If you have an external modem, make sure the power is turned on and the modem is plugged into the serial (COM) port on your computer. Most internal modems have tiny switches on the back that you can flip to give the modem a different COM port setting. After setting the COM port, make sure the correct COM port is selected in Windows.

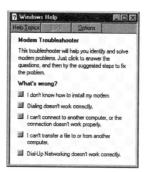

Figure 13.1 The Modem Troubleshooter is the best place to start to fix a modem problem.

- In most cases, your mouse is set up to use COM1, and your modem is on COM2. If your modem is set up to use COM3, the mouse on COM1 might conflict with it. (See Lesson 5 in Part 5 for a brief discussion of choosing COM ports.) Try changing the modem to **COM2** or **COM4,** if you can do so for your system. First, display the Control Panel (click **Start**, point to **Settings,** and click **Control Panel**). Double-click the **Modems** icon. Click the modem in the listing in the General tab, then click **Properties**. In the Properties window, open the **Port** drop-down list and click the new port. Click **OK** twice.

- If you can't change the port selection for the modem, try removing and reinstalling the modem driver. Lesson 2 in Part 5 explains how to remove drivers, and Lesson 5 in Part 5 explains how to set up the modem driver.

- To test your modem, run **HyperTerminal** (located in the **Accessories** group). In the window that appears, type **AT** and press **Enter**. If you get an **OK** message, your modem and COM port settings are okay. As a further test, type **ATDT** followed by your phone number and press **Enter**. The modem should dial, and you should get a message that says **Busy**. This tells you that your modem is capable of dialing out, and that the problem is probably with the modem setup in the application you're using. Check the settings in the communications program you're using to determine whether they're correct for your modem.

- To test the phone line, plug a regular phone into the phone jack and make sure you get a dial tone. Also, check the phone plug connection on the modem and phone jack. (I once encountered a brand-new modem that was missing one of the copper contacts inside the modem jack.) Make sure all the contacts are there, and that the cable you're using is in good shape. If those items are in order, dial 1 (as if you were starting a long-distance call), and listen for loud noise and hissing on the line. Line noise can keep the modem from connecting, and if you suspect this is the case, contact your local phone company to find out whether the lines can be repaired and the noise eliminated.

TIP **No Conflicts** If you try the above steps and the modem still won't work, you also can check for conflicts between the modem and another device under Windows 95, then adjust the settings for one of the devices to remove the conflict. See Lesson 3 in Part 5 to learn how to check for device conflicts.

Getting the Modem to Connect

In some cases, your modem may dial the specified number but never connect with the computer on the other end. You may have a problem with the number you're dialing or with the phone line. Check the following:

- Is the Line jack connected to the phone jack on the wall? Most modems have two jacks: one marked Phone and one marked Line. Make sure you connect the Line jack to the wall jack. (The Phone jack is often connected to your telephone, in cases where the modem and the phone are sharing the same telephone line.)
- Did you set up your application correctly for *pulse* or *tone dialing*? Pick up your phone and dial a couple of numbers. If you hear tones of various pitches, you have tone service. If you hear clicks, you have rotary (or pulse) service. Change the correct type of dialing for your modem's dialing properties.

TIP **Modem Setup** For more on setting a modem's properties and dialing properties in Windows 95, see Lesson 5 in Part 5.

- Do you need to dial a special number to get an outside line? If you work in an office, you may have to dial a 9 or some other number to get an outside line. Add this number, followed by a comma, before the phone number you want to dial, or set up the appropriate number in your modem's dialing properties.

559

- Is your communications program set up with the same settings as the modem to which you're trying to connect? Every communication session has three settings: data, parity, and stop bits. Typically, you'll use 8-none-1, but if you encounter problems connecting to a particular service, call them to check on their settings. You may also want to reduce the speed (bps rate) used in your communications program (or in your Windows 95 modem properties) and see if that helps.

- Disable call waiting if your phone line has that feature. In Windows 95, double-click the **Modems** icon in the **Control Panel**. Click your modem if needed in the **General** tab and then click **Dialing Properties**. Select the **This Location Has Call Waiting** check box and type the sequence needed to disable call waiting (such as *70,) or select the right sequence from the drop-down list. Click **OK.** If you don't know the right sequence to disable call waiting, check with your local phone company.

- If you have voice mail from your local phone company, the stutter that precedes the dial tone when you have a message prevents your modem from recognizing the dial tone. To overcome this problem, double-click the **Modems** icon in the **Control Panel**. Click your modem if needed in the **General** tab and then click **Properties**. Click the **Connection** tab, then click the **Advanced** button. Enter **S6=5** in the Extra Settings text box. Click **OK** twice, then click **Close** to close the open dialog boxes and accept the new settings.

 TIP **Busy Voices** If your modem dials and gets a busy signal, you'll have to try the call again later (your Internet connection will usually hang up and try again for you automatically). If the modem connects and you hear voices, it's dialed the wrong number. Verify the number, and check the phone number entry in your communications software. Some communications software, like the Dial-Up Networking connection created with the Internet Connection Wizard (see Lesson 2 in Part 4) enables you to set the modem to automatically redial when it encounters a busy signal. For example, double-click the **My Computer** icon on the desktop, then double-click the **Dial-Up Networking** icon. Choose **Connections, Settings**. Click to enable the **Redial** check box, then change the number of **Times** to redial and the **Mins.** (minutes) and **Secs.** (seconds) between redialing, if needed. Click **OK** to finish your changes.

Making a Modem Connection More Reliable

If your modem can successfully dial another computer and connect, you're getting closer. However, if the modem disconnects unexpectedly and repeatedly, garbage characters appear in your communications software, or you get error messages from the software, you might need to do some fine-tuning.

You probably have a problem with your telecommunications settings or with your login entries, so try these fixes:

- If you're trying to call a bulletin board or online service that requires you to enter a name and password, maybe your name and password entries are wrong (or you didn't pay your bills).

- Make sure you have the correct modem selected. In most applications, you can select the type of modem from a list. If your modem isn't listed, check the documentation to find out its *modem initialization string*, and then enter it manually. (The modem initialization string sets preferences for how the modem operates. For example, **ATM0** mutes the modem so that it makes no sound as it dials.)

- Try setting the bps rate (the speed at which modems transfer data) to a slower speed. Maybe the service or BBS you're calling can handle only 9600bps. (Most newer modems have an *automatic fallback* feature that enables the modem to drop to a slower bps rate automatically if necessary.) Your Internet Service Provider (ISP) can tell you the preferred speed setting for your Internet connection.

- Check the *terminal emulation*. The terminal emulation setting tells your computer how to act when connecting to another computer. This is usually DEC VT-100, but if that doesn't work, try a different emulation.

- Check the following communications settings in the Connection tab of your modem Properties window: data bits, parity, and stop bits. Most computers are set up to use 8 data bits, No parity, and 1 stop bit. Try to reconnect using these standard settings.

- Adjust the buffers (called FIFO buffers) that hold information as it comes to or goes from the modem. Double-click the **Modems** icon in the **Control Panel**. Click your modem if needed in the **General** tab and then click **Properties**. Click the **Connection** tab, then click the **Port Settings** button. Drag the sliders to the left (as explained in the dialog box) for a slower, more reliable connection. Or, if you suspect these settings have been changed from their defaults, click the **Defaults** button. Click **OK** twice, then **Close**, to close the open dialog boxes and accept the new settings.

- If the problems continue despite your best efforts to fix them, you may need to call tech support. Before you do so, you should try to log the modem's problems. To create a log file, double-click the **Modems** icon in the **Control Panel**. Click your modem if needed in the **General** tab and then click **Properties**. Click the **Connection** tab, then click the **Advanced** button. Click to check the **Record a Log File** check box, then click **OK** twice and **Close** once to accept your changes. When you use the modem, steps it performs and errors it encounters are tracked and saved in the file \Windows\ModemLog.txt. You can open this file in Notepad while you talk with tech support to discuss any error messages in the log.

CAUTION

Modem Bummer Some modems from lesser-known manufacturers simply don't work reliably. If you can't get a modem to stay connected or stop displaying garbage no matter what you try, you may be better off upgrading to a better brand.

This lesson provided help you can use to get your modem to work, connect, and stay connected. The next lesson offers guidance for backing up files on your computer with Microsoft Backup.

Creating and Using a Backup

In this lesson, you learn to back up files as a safeguard against loss or damage, and how to restore the files from your backup.

Backing Up Files with Microsoft Backup

As I've emphasized in several places in this book, the magnetic material on disks provides *semipermanent* storage. The very qualities that enable you to remove files from a hard or floppy disk when you want to also makes those files vulnerable to damage and errors. Because you use your computer to keep track of important information, you want to be able to trust that the data you feed into your computer will be there when you need it.

Unfortunately, there are no guarantees in life. Murphy is alive and well and living inside your computer, and he has a whole set of laws just for PCs. One goes something like this: "The odds of losing a file are directly proportional to the importance of the data it contains." It always seems that the more you need some scrap of data stored on your computer, the more likely it is that the computer gremlins just had that scrap for lunch.

To ward off such a catastrophe, you should make regular *backups* of the data stored on your computer's hard disk drive. You can back up your program files as well, but because you have copies of them already (on the program's original installation disks), you don't have to back them up.

 Backup A backup is not a copy of a file. Rather, numerous files are stored in a large backup file (with a special file format) called a backup set, archive, or backup volume. In some cases, the backup process compresses files

continues

continued

somewhat as it adds them to the backup set, but you can't count on the backup program to dramatically compress the storage required for the backup. Also note that a backup file is different from an archive, or compressed file (these are discussed in Lesson 5 of this Part). Archive files contain greatly compressed copies of files, to facilitate file transfer and storage rather than safeguard data.

TIP **Back Up the Back Up?** In addition to regularly backing up important files, you should also make copies of important data files you work with—and you should never store an important file on a floppy disk only. Zip drives and other removable drives make it easy to keep copies of files for safety's sake, and easy to move files to another system that has a Zip or other removable drive that's compatible with the one you use.

If anything happens to the data files you back up, you can repair the damage using the backup you made. Of course, you only use the backup if something awful happens to an original file; if nothing ever happens to the original, the backup is never used. It's just there for your peace of mind.

Windows 95 comes with a program called Microsoft Backup that you can use to back up the files on your system. (Or, you could buy another backup program if you prefer. Several are on the market for $50 or so.)

You don't have to back up all the files on your entire hard drive every time you want to create a backup. You have these backup options to choose from:

Full backs up all the files you select, even if they haven't been altered since the last backup.

Incremental backs up only those selected files that have been altered since the last backup.

Where to Store Backups

If your computer has a *tape backup* drive that is compatible with Windows 95, you can use it to make regular backups of your PC's hard disk. If you have a Zip or a Jaz drive or other removable drive, that will work just as well as a tape backup drive; but the removable drives and media are a bit more costly than a tape backup system. However, if your computer does not have a tape backup, a Zip, or a Jaz drive, you will need to use the floppy disk drives to create your backup files. Backing up on floppy disks is harder and more time-consuming, but such is the cost of doing business with a cold-blooded and finicky computer. Also, note that the more data on your computer's hard disk drive, the more floppy disks it takes to back it up. It is not uncommon to need 30 or 40 disks to store the complete contents of a 250 megabyte hard drive. For today's 1 gigabyte drive, expect to use four times as many disks or more. Because so many floppy disks are needed for a full backup of the entire hard drive, you might want to back up only certain files (such as data files) or folders. If something happens to your applications, you can always just reinstall them.

TIP **Backup Bonus** Tape backup drives and other types of removable drives often come with backup programs.

Running the Backup

Follow these steps to use Microsoft Backup to backup the files you select under Windows 95:

1. Click the **Start** button, select **Programs**, select **Accessories**, select **System Tools**, and then click **Backup**. Or, you can right-click the icon for the drive to backup in Explorer or My Computer, and click **Properties**. Click the **Tools** tab, and click **Backup Now**.

2. The first time you run Backup, a dialog box appears, providing an overview of the process. Read the information, and then click the **Don't Show This Again** check box (so it won't come up next time). Click **OK**.

3. Another dialog box appears, indicating that Backup created a file set (sort of a blueprint) for backing up all your system files. Read the message, click the **Don't Show This Again** check box, and click **OK**.

CAUTION

Tape It? You also might see a message box telling you that Backup looked for a tape drive and didn't find one. If you don't have a tape drive on your system, click OK to skip this message. If you do have a tape drive, it probably means you forgot to insert a tape before starting the backup process. Many tape drives must have a tape inserted to be recognized. Insert the tape, and restart the drive (or your system if needed). If you only restarted the drive without shutting down backup, use **Tools, Redetect Tape Drive** in Backup to have Backup recognize it.

4. The Backup screen appears, allowing you to start backing up files. To back up all the files on a drive, click the check box next to the drive letter, and then skip to step 8. To back up only selected files and folders, proceed with step 5.

5. Click the plus sign (+) next to the icon for the drive that contains the folders and files you want to back up. The tree expands to show the first layer of folders on the selected drive, as in Figure 14.1.

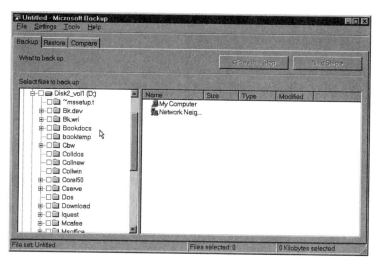

Figure 14.1   To backup selected files on a disk, expand its folder tree in the left pane of the Backup window.

6. To back up an entire folder, click the check box next to its icon. If you click the check box next to a folder that has subfolders, all its subfolders and files are selected.

7. To back up only some files in a folder, click the folder's icon in the folder tree on the left. Then click the check box next to each file and subfolder you want to back up in the file list on the right, as shown in Figure 14.2.

8. Click the **Next Step** button.

9. Backup asks which drive you want to use to store the backup files. Click the icon for the drive you want to use to store the backup files, as in Figure 14.3. This can be a floppy disk drive, a tape backup drive, a Zip or Jaz drive, a network drive, or another hard disk drive, but shouldn't be the same drive as the drive you're backing up.

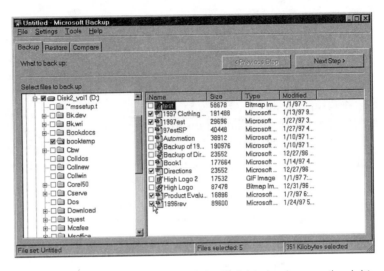

Figure 14.2 Select a folder on the left and the file(s) to back up on the right.

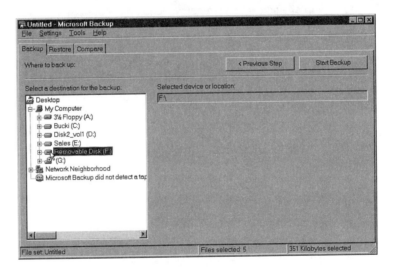

Figure 14.3 Tell backup where to place the backup file.

10. If you're backing up to a floppy disk drive, a Zip or Jaz drive, or other removable drive, make sure you have a disk in the drive. Then click the **Start Backup** button.

11. The Backup Set Label dialog box appears, prompting you to type a name for the backup set. Type a name for the backup set, and then click **OK**.

567

12. Backup starts the backup operation and displays on-screen instructions to help you complete the process. For full backups or backups where you've selected a substantial number of files, you may need to swap tapes or disks. When prompted by a message box asking for the next tape or disk, take out the old tape or disk, insert the new one, then click **OK**. Make sure your number the backup tapes or disks as the backup progresses, too, because you will need insert the tapes or disks in order if you need to later restore the backed up files.

13. When you see a message telling when the backup is done, click **OK**. You are then returned to the Backup dialog box.

14. Click **OK** to return to the main Backup window. Then open the **File** menu and select **Exit** to close the Backup program.

Slow Work Zone You can continue to work as Windows 95 performs its backup; however, your programs may work a bit more slowly. I prefer to back up at a time when I'm not working on my system.

CAUTION

Backing Up All Your System Files

Step 3 above noted that backup creates a file set for backing up your system (meaning both your data files and all Windows 95 and system startup files). To back up your entire system, you must use this file set during the backup. Just backing up your boot disk (drive C:) doesn't back up registry files and other system files.

Follow this procedure to use the backup set created by Microsoft Backup to backup your system files:

1. Start Microsoft Backup.

2. Click the **Backup tab** to select it, if needed.

3. Open the **File** menu, then click **Open File Set**.

4. In the Open dialog box, click the **Full System Backup** file in the file list, and then click **Open**.

5. Click **Next Step**, select the drive where you want to store the backup, and then click **Start Backup**.

6. Type a name for the backup set. Click **OK**, then follow the on-screen prompts to finish the backup process.

There's also an even quicker way to launch the system backup, but only if you have a tape backup drive attached to your system (because this method by default assumes that you're backing up to a tape drive, and you can't change that option):

1. Double-click **My Computer** on the desktop, then double-click the icon for drive C:.

2. Double-click the **Program Files** folder, then double-click the **Accessories** folder.

3. In the Accessories window, drag the **Full System Backup** icon over the **Backup** icon, and drop it to start the backup.

Figure 14.4   Drag the icon for the backup set onto the startup icon for backup.

4. At the message box asking you to verify the backup, click **Yes**.

5. Follow on-screen prompts as they appear to finish the backup. (Backup may minimize to an icon on the taskbar. Simply click it to restore the Backup window if you need to see what's happening.)

Restoring Files from a Backup

When you find that some of your files have been lost or damaged, you *restore* them from the backup set to your system. Microsoft Backup and other backup programs like it enable you to open your backup sets and select files to restore.

The restoration process is a bit simpler than the backup process, and it usually doesn't take as long. Normally you'll want to restore only one or two files that were erased (or otherwise met an untimely end).

569

Do note that the success of restoring a file to your computer's hard disk drive depends entirely on how "fresh" the file is. If you've deleted a file that you alter from time to time—the text of the book you're writing, for example—you will only be able to restore the file to the way it was the last time you backed it up. If you haven't backed up the file in two months, the restored copy will be two months old—and you might have lost two months' work. This is why making regular backups is so important.

CAUTION

Disk on Hand   Before you start to restore a file, make sure you have all your backup floppy disks handy (if that's the backup medium you use). During the restoration process, you will be prompted to insert specific numbered disks into the computer.

Follow these steps to restore files from a backup set:

1. If needed, make sure your backup tape is in the tape backup drive to ensure Microsoft Backup will recognize the drive.
2. With Windows 95 running, click the **Start** button, select **Programs**, select **Accessories**, select **System Tools**, and then click **Backup**.
3. Microsoft Backup starts, and you see the main window. Click the **Restore** tab.
4. A list of the drives attached to your system appears in the left pane. Insert your backup tape (if you haven't done so earlier out of necessity to enable Windows to recognize the drive), removable disk, or the last disk or tape of the backup set into the drive. In the **Restore From** list, click the drive that contains the backup disk or tape.
5. If there is more than one backup set name in the Backup Set list in the right pane, click the name of the backup set you want to restore, as in Figure 14.5. (Use the backup set name you entered when you performed the backup.)
6. Click the **Next Step** button.
7. The list on the left changes to show all the folders and files that are on the backup tape or disks. Under **Select Files from the Backup Set**, click the plus sign (+) to display the files in a particular folder.
8. To restore the contents of an entire folder, click the folder's check box in the **Select Files from the Backup Set** list. To restore only selected files in a folder, click the folder icon in the **Select Files from the Backup Set** list, and then click the check box next to each file you want to restore in the **Contents Of** list (in the right pane), as in Figure 14.6.

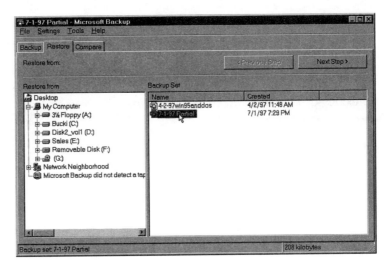

Figure 14.5   Click to select the backup set if you have more than one on a disk.

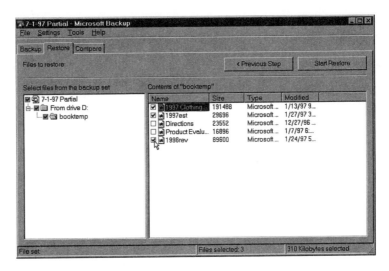

Figure 14.6   Click with the mouse to select the file(s) to restore.

9. Click the **Start Restore** button.

10. Select the drive or folder to which you want to restore your files, and then click **OK**.

11. If you are restoring from floppy disks, a dialog box appears, telling you which disk to insert. Follow the on-screen instructions until the restoration is complete. When you see a message telling you the restoration is finished, click **OK**. You're returned to the Restore dialog box.

571

12. Click **OK,** and you're returned to the main Restore window. Open the **File** menu and select **Exit** to exit the program.

This lesson demonstrated how easy it is to create safety backups of your vital files with Microsoft Backup, and how to restore files later when needed. The next lesson explains how to look for viruses on your system.

Handling Viruses

Review this lesson to learn how to protect your system against viruses and deal with them when you encounter them.

Handling Viruses

With computers, a *virus* is not a living microbe, but a program specifically designed by some bored programmer to cause damage to the data in your computer. No one really knows why people make the effort to create a computer virus (few ever admit doing so), but we computer users have to live with the fact that there are now several hundred known computer viruses out there—and any one of them could cause trouble for you.

Viruses can invade a personal computer in a number of ways. The most common happens when you use an "infected" program or file. You might obtain this program or file from a friend, or you might download it from an online service like CompuServe or from the Internet. It can even come from a commercial program you bought and installed on your computer, although that's unlikely.

Realistically (and fortunately), commercial software is seldom infected by a computer virus, and the same is true of programs available through online services like CompuServe, America Online, and Prodigy (but not the Internet!). Programs that might affect the reputation of a service or a company are checked before they are made available to the public. It is far more likely your computer will become infected by a program you get from a friend or associate.

Windows 95 does not provide its own antivirus program, but there are many such programs (also called virus checkers or virus scanners) available commercially and on the Internet. For example, Norton AntiVirus 2.0 for Windows 95—

sold in many catalogs and computer stores—has long been a leader in the field and retails for about $50. Another widely used (about 25 million users) and effective program is McAfee VirusScan, which you can buy from a store or catalog for about $45 or download from America Online, CompuServe, and the Internet (**http://mcafee.com**). In fact, the example screens shown in this lesson are from McAfee VirusScan. Another, newer virus checker that's on the market is called ThunderByte Antivirus.

TIP **Application Macro Viruses** It used to be that you could only catch a virus from programs. However, several "viruses" have been floating around that affect Microsoft Word files and now Microsoft Excel files. These viruses are transported in macros housed in seemingly harmless document files. One such virus, the Word "Concept" virus, converts an infected file to a template—so you can't resave the file as a document. Word 97 and Excel 97 now offer a feature that warns you if you're about to open a file that contains macros—decide whether to do so based on the source of the file. To turn on this protection in either application, choose **Tools, Options.** Click the **General** tab, check **Macro virus protection,** and click **OK**. This could be a trend. Keep your eye peeled for stories online and in other computer media about macro viruses and protections offered by software publishers.

Checking for Viruses with a Virus Checker

You should get into the habit of running your antivirus program at least once a month—more often if you regularly install new software on your computer or share disks with others. Here are the general steps for scanning your system for viruses with a virus scanning program (I'm keeping it general, because the commands will vary a lot depending on what virus scanning program you use):

1. Start the antivirus program in Windows 95.
2. Select the drive or drives to check. As shown in Figure 15.1, most programs let you scan multiple drives, including floppies and removable drives. In McAfee, you click a **Select** button, select a drive from the **Drives** list, then click the **Add Drive** button to add the drive to the list of Selections to scan. You can even use similar techniques in McAfee's Select Items to Scan dialog box (see Figure 15.1) to select individual folders or files for scanning. Click OK or the appropriate command in your program to finish the scan selections.

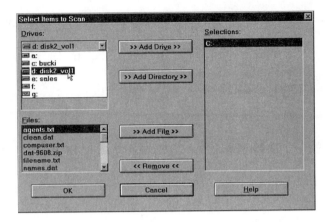

Figure 15.1 Select the drives to scan.

3. Start the scan. In McAfee, you click the **Scan** button or choose **Scan, Start Scan**.

4. After scanning your computer's disk drive(s), the program displays a Statistics report, which indicates the number and type of files it checked and whether any files were infected (see Figure 15.2). Review the report. (You may need to click **OK** to close the report in some programs.)

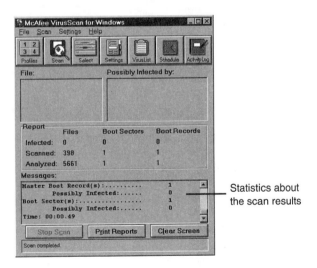

Statistics about the scan results

Figure 15.2 The scanner reports whether it found any infected files.

5. If the scanner did find viruses during the scan, print the report about the scan results. You may need this information if the virus scanner can't clean the virus and you need to contact the virus scanner publisher's tech support department.

6. Exit the virus scanner program.

Automating the Scan Process

Some antivirus programs can be set up to run in the background while you work on other programs, thereby providing you with 24-hour protection. Still others can be set up to run automatically whenever you insert a floppy disk. Consult your program's online help or documentation to learn how to schedule a scan. For example, in McAfee, choose **Scan**, **Schedule Scan**. Choose the appropriate settings in the When to Scan area (see Figure 15.3), then click the **Add** button in the Active Schedules area. Select the new schedule, choose your What to Scan Settings, and click **OK**.

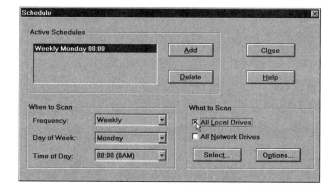

Figure 15.3   You can schedule regular scans in most virus scanners.

CAUTION

Can't Scan   Your computer must be running for the scheduled scan to take place. If your computer is shut down during the scheduled scan time, you'll need to run the scan manually after you boot. The latest version of McAfee now offers a ScreenScan feature; if you turn this feature on, it will automatically scan your system whenever your system goes idle and your screensaver appears.

Removing a Virus

If your system becomes infected with a virus, you may find it acting quite strange. It may not even start!

TIP **No Boot after Virus** If your system can't boot due to a virus, you'll need to boot your system with your startup disk, which you learned to create in the first lesson of this part. (Be sure to write protect the startup disk using its write protect tab—slide it so the hole on the 3.5-inch floppy closes; otherwise, the virus will likely infect the startup disk, too.) Once you can start up your system, contact the virus software publisher for advice about how to proceed. The company may be able to provide a DOS-based version of its software that you can run to fix the problem. Otherwise, you may need to do something more drastic like reinstall Windows and all your applications (or worse—reformat your hard disk and lose all your data) to recover.

Most virus programs not only scan for viruses, but also will clean them from your system, as follows:

1. Start the antivirus program in Windows 95.

2. Select the drive or drives to clean viruses from.

3. Select the cleaning options. For example, in McAfee, click the **Settings** button to display the Wscan Notebook of settings, and specify settings on the various tab. For example, the Action tab (see Figure 15.4) enables you to turn on cleaning and specify how to deal with infected files. Close the dialog box for setting options.

4. Start the scan. In McAfee, you click the **Scan** button or choose **Scan, Start Scan**.

5. After scanning and repairing, the scanner will report results. (You may need to click **OK** to close the report in some programs.)

6. Close the virus scanner.

TIP **Scan and Clean** Most virus checkers, including McAfee, will let you scan for viruses and remove them from your system simultaneously. Consult your program's documentation or instructions.

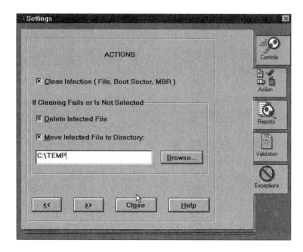

Figure 15.4 Turn on cleaning, and tell the virus scanner how to deal with infected files.

Keeping Your Virus Checker Up-To-Date

There are literally thousands of viruses. The current version of McAfee scans for more than 8500. New viruses creep into the computing world daily. To be able to scan for and eliminate all viruses, virus scanning programs need information about new viruses and how to identify and remove them. As such, most virus program publishers regularly provide updated virus lists to use with virus checker programs. You can usually download these lists from an online source, and quickly install them for use with the virus checker. See your program's online help to learn how to get and install such updates.

This lesson gave an overview of how to use virus checker software to find and remove viruses from your files and disks. The next and final lesson in this book explains how to recover from spills on a keyboard or mouse.

Appendixes

A Brief Buyer's Guide

This appendix offers contact information to help you better shop for a new system, upgrade components, or accessories for your system. The most contact information is provided, including Web sites, fax numbers, and tech support phone numbers, where available.

System Manufacturers

The following list provides contact information for several of the leading manufacturers of personal computers using the Windows 95 operating system. Several of these manufacturers also offer upgrade components such as CD-ROM drives and monitors.

Compaq Computer Corp.
http://www.compaq.com
800-345-1518; 713-514-0484
Sales: 800-888-5925
Fax: 713-514-4583
Tech support: 800-OKCOMPA

Dell Computer Corp.
http://www.dell.com
800-289-3355; 512-338-4400
Sales: 800-289-1180
Fax: 512-728-3653
Tech support: 800-624-9896

Gateway 2000, Inc.
http://www.gw2k.com
800-846-2000; 605-232-2000
Fax: 605-232-2023
Tech support: 800-846-2301

Hewlett-Packard Co.
http://www.hp.com
970-669-8000
Fax: 970-667-0997
Tech support: 970-635-1500

IBM (International Business Machines)
http://www.ibm.com
800-426-3333; 914-765-1900
Sales: 800-426-7255
Tech support: 800-237-5511

Micron Electronics, Inc.
http://www.mei.micron.com
800-347-3490; 208-893-3434
Sales: 800-388-6334
Fax: 208-893-3424
Tech support: 800-347=3490

Packard Bell NEC, Inc. (CA)
http://www.packardbell.com
800-733-5858; 818-865-1555
Tech support: 800-7333-4411

Sony Electronics, Inc.
http://www.sony.com
800-352-7669; 408-432-1600
Fax: 408-943-0740
Tech support: 800-326-9551

Toshiba America Information Systems, Inc.
http://www.toshiba.com
800-334-3445; 714-583-3000
Sales: 800-959-4100
Fax: 715-583-3645
Tech support: 800-999-4273

Internal Component Manufacturers

The manufacturers listed in this section sell components that are generally installed inside the system unit: floppy drives, hard drives, I/O (input/output) interface cards, sound cards, and video cards. Some manufactures sell upgrade components only, some provide components to full system manufacturers like those listed in the preceding section, and some do both. In addition to contact information, each listing indicates which of the upgrade components discussed in Part 5 of this book the manufacturer distributes. (Some manufacturers also distribute additional components like CPUs and motherboards.)

 TIP **No Number** If a particular kind of phone number (such as a sales or tech support number) isn't listed for a particular manufacturer, use the main number.

Adaptec, Inc.
I/O Cards, Sound Cards
http://www.adaptec.com
800-934-2766; 408-945-8600
Sales: 800-442-SCSI
Fax: 408-262-2533
Tech support: 800-959-SCSI

Aztech Labs, Inc.
CD-ROM Drives
http://www.aztechca.com
800-886-8859; 510-623-8988
Fax: 510-623-8989
Tech support: 510-623-9037

Boca Research, Inc.
I/O Cards, Video Cards
http://www.bocaresearch.com
407-997-6227
Fax: 407-997-0918
Tech support: 407-241-8088

BusLogic, Inc.
I/O Cards
http://www.buslogic.com
800-707-7274; 408-492-9090
Fax: 408-492-1542
Tech support: 408-654-0760

Chinon-America, Inc.
CD-ROM Drives, Floppy Drives
http://www.chinon.com
800-441-0222; 310-533-0274
Fax: 310-533-1727

CMS Enhancements
CD-ROM Drives
http://www.cmsenh.com
800-327-5773; 714-517-0915
Fax: 714-956-8156
Tech support: 800-555-1671

Creative Labs, Inc.
CD-ROM Drives, Sound Cards, Video Cards, Modems
http://www.creaf.com
800-998-1000; 408-428-6600
Sales: 800-998-5227
Fax: 408-428-2394
Tech support: 405-742-6622

Diamond Multimedia Systems, Inc.
Video Cards
http://www.diamondmm.com
800-4-MULTIMEDIA, 408-325-7000
Fax: 408-325-7070
Tech support: 408-325-7100

DSP Solutions, Inc.
Sound Cards
http://www.dsps.com
800-560-1817; 415-919-4000
Fax: 415-919-4100
Tech support: 415-919-4100

DTC
I/O Cards
http://www.datatechnology.com
408-942-4000
Fax: 408-942-4027

ENSONIQ Corp.
Sound Cards
http://www.ensoniq.com
800-942-0096; 610-647-3930
Fax: 610-647-8908

Fujitsu Computer Products of America, Inc.
Hard Disk Drives
http://www.fcpa.com
800-626-4686; 408-432-6333
Fax: 408-894-1716

Genoa Systems Corp.
Video Cards
http://www.genoayss.com
408-362-2900
Fax: 408-362-2998
Tech support: 408-362-2990

Hercules Computer Technology, Inc.
Video Cards
http://www.hercules.com
800-532-0600; 510-623-6030
Fax: 510-623-1112
Tech support: 800-323-0601

Hitachi America, Ltd.
Hard Disk Drives
http://www.hitachi.com
800-227-1930; 800-982-5815 (CA)
Fax: 408-727-8036
Tech support: 619-537-3000

Kingston Technology Corp.
Memory (RAM)
http://www.kingston.com
800-345-2620; 714-435-2600
Sales: 800-337-8410
Fax: 714-435-2699
Tech support: 800-435-0640

Matrox Graphics, Inc.
Video Cards
http://www.matrox.com/mga
800-361-1408; 514-685-0270
Sales: 514-969-6320
Fax: 514-969-6363

Maxtor, Corp.
Hard Disk Drives
http://www.maxtor.com
800-2-MAXTOR; 408-432-1700
Fax: 408-432-4510

Micropolis Pte, Ltd.
Hard Disk Drives
http://www.microp.com
800-395-3748; 818-709-3300
Fax: 818-718-5312
Tech support: 818-709-3325

MicroSolutions, Inc.
CD-ROM Drives
http://www.micro-solutions.com
800-890-7227; 814-756-3411
Sales: 800-890-7227, ext. 200
Fax: 815-756-2928
Tech support: 815-754-4500

Mitsumi Electronics Corp., Inc.
CD-ROM Drives, Floppy Drives
http://www.mitsumi.com
800-MITSUMI; 214-550-7300
Fax: 214-550-7424
Tech support: 415-691-4465

Nakamichi America Corp
CD-ROM Drives
http://www.nakamichi-corp.com
800-421-2313; 310-538-8150
Fax: 310-324-7614

NEC Technologies, Inc.
CD-ROM Drives
http://www.nec.com
800-NEC-INFO; 630-775-7900
Sales:P 800-284-4484
Fax: 508-635-4666
Tech support: 800-632-4662

Orchid Technology, Inc.
Sound Cards, Video Cards
http://www.orchic.com
800-767-2443; 510-683-0300
Fax: 510-490-9312
Tech support: 510-683-0323

Panasonic Communications & Systems Co.
CD-ROM Drives
http://www.panasonic.com
800-742-8086; 201-348-7000
Fax: 201-392-4441
Tech support: 800-222-0584

Philips Electronics, Inc.
CD-ROM Drives
http://www.pps.philips.com
800-235-7373; 408-453-5129
Fax: 408-453-0680
Tech support: 408-467-3628

Pinnacle Micro, Inc.
CD-ROM Drives
http://www.pinnaclemicro.com
800-553-7070; 714-789-3000
Fax:714-789-3150

Pioneer New Media Technologies, Inc.
CD-ROM Drives
http://www.pioneerusa.com
800-444-6784; 310-952-2111
Fax: 310-952-2100
Tech support: 408-496-9140

Plextor
CD-ROM Drives
http://www.plextor.com
800-886-3935; 408-980-1838
Fax: 409-986-1010

PNY Electronics, Inc.
Memory (RAM)
http://www.pny.com
201-438-6300
Fax: 201-438-9097
Tech support: 800-234-4597

Procom Technology, Inc.
CD-ROM Drives
http://www.procom.com
800-800-8600; 714-852-1000
Fax: 714-852-1221

Promise Technology, Inc.
I/O Cards
http://www.promise.com
800-888-0245; 408-452-0948
Fax: 408-452-1543
Tech support: 408-452-1180

QLogic Corp.
I/O Cards
http://www.qlc.com
800-662-4471; 714-438-2200
Sales: 800-867-7274
Fax: 714-668-5008
Tech support: 714-668-5037

Quantum Corp.
Hard Disk Drives
http://www.quantum.com
800-624-5545; 408-804-4000
Fax: 408-894-3218
Tech support: 800-826-8022

Reveal Computer Products, Inc.
Sound Cards, Video Cards
http://www.refeal.com
800-326-2222; 818-704-6300
Sales: 800-REVEAL-1
Fax: 818-340-9957

Samsung Electronics America, Inc.
Hard Disk Drives
http://www.samsung.com
800-726-7864; 201-229-4000
Sales: 800-656-2785
Fax: 201-229-4110

Seagate Technology, Inc.
Hard Disk Drives
http://www.seagate.com
800-SEAGATE; 408-438-6550
Sales: 408-438-8111
Fax: 408-438-7852
Tech support: 408-438-8222

SIIG, Inc.
I/O Cards, Sound Cards, Video Cards
http://www.siig.com
510-657-8688
Fax: 510-657-5962

TEAC America, Inc.
CD-ROM Drives, Floppy Drives
http://www.teac.com
800-888-4XCD; 213-726-0303
Fax: 213-727-7652

Truevision, Inc.
Video Cards
http://www.truevision.com
800-522-TRUE; 408-562-4200
Fax: 408-562-4066

Turtle Beach Systems
CD-ROM Drives, Sound Cards
http://www.tbeach.com
800-884-0190; 510-624-6200
Fax: 510-624-6291
Tech support: 510-624-6265

UMAX Technologies, Inc.
CD-ROM Drives, Video Cards
http://www.umax.com
800-468-8629; 510-651-8834
Tech support: 510-651-4000

Wearnes Peripherals Corp.
CD-ROM Drives
408-432-1888
Fax: 408-432-1884

Western Digital Corp.
Hard Disk Drives, I/O Cards
http://www.wdc.com
800-275-4932; 714-932-5000
Fax: 714-932-6498
Tech support: 714-932-4900

External Components Manufacturers

The manufactueres listed here sell components that can be external or optional: modems, monitors, scanners, removable drives, tape drives.

Boca Research, Inc.
Modems
http://www.bocaresearch.com
407-997-6227
Fax: 407-997-0918
Tech support: 407-241-1601

Caera Corp.
Scanners
http://www.caere.com
800-535-SCAN; 408-395-7000
Fax: 408-354-2743
Tech support: 800-462-2373

Canon Computer Systems, Inc.
Printers
http://222.ccsi.canon.com
800-848-4123; 714-438-3000
Fax: 714-438-3099
Tech support: 800-423-2366

Cardinal Technologies, Inc.
Modems
http://www.cardtech.com
Sales: 717-293-3049
Fax: 717-293-3055
Tech support: 717-293-3055

Citizen America Corp.
Printers
http://www.citizen-america.com
800-477-4683; 310-453-0614
Fax: 310-453-2814
Tech support: 310-453-0614 ext. 266

CMS Enhancments
Tape Drives
http://www.cmsenh.com
800-327-57773; 714-517-0915
Fax: 714-956-8156
Tech support: 800-555-1671

Datasonix Corp.
Tape Drives
http://www.datasonix.com/datasonix
800-328-2779; 303-545-9500
Fax: 303-545-9249

Diamond Multimedia Systems, Inc.
Modems
http://www.diamondmm.com
800-4-MULTIMEDIA; 408-325-7000
Fax: 408-325-7070
Tech support: 408-325-7100

Epson America, Inc.
Printers, Removable Drives
http://www.epson.com
800-289-3776; 310-782-0770
Fax: 310-782-5220
Tech support: 800-922-8911

Fujitsu Computer Products of America
Scanners
http://www.fcpa.com
800-626-4648; 408-432-6333
Fax: 408-894-1716

Hayes Microcomputer Products, Inc.
Modems
http://www.hayes.com
770-840-9200
Fax: 770-441-1617
Tech support: 770-441-1617

Hitachi Data Systems Corp.
Tape Drives
http:/www.hdshq.com
800-227-1930; 408-970-1900
Fax: 415-244-7647

Hyundai Electronics America
Monitors
http://www.hea.com
800-568-0060; 408-232-8000
Sales: 408-232-8000
Fax: 408-232-8146

Iomega Corp.
Removable Drives, Tape Drives
http://www.iomega.com
800-697-8833; 801-778-1000
Fax: 801-778-2743
Tech support: 801-629-7629

Lexmark International, Inc.
Printers
http://www.lexmark.com
800-358-5835; 606-232-2000
Sales: 800-438-2468
Fax: 606-232-2403
Tech support: 606-232-3000

Logitech, Inc.
Scanners
http://www.logitech.com
800-231-7717; 510-795-8500
Fax: 510-792-8901
Tech support: 510-795-8100

MAG Innovision Co, Inc.
Monitors
http://www.maginnovision.com
800-827-3998; 714-751-2008
Fax: 714-751-5522

MaxTech Corp.
Monitors
http://www.www.maxcorp.com
800-936-7629; 310-921-1698
Sale: 800-829-9605
Fax: 310-802-9605

Microsolutions, Inc.
Tape Drives
http://www.micro-solutions.com
800-890-7227; 815-756-3411
Sales: 800-890-7227 ext. 200
Fax: 815-756-2928
Tech support: 815-754-4500

Microtek Lab, Inc.
Scanners
http://www.mteklab.com
310-297-5000
Sales: 800-654-4160
Fax: 310-297-5050
Tech support: 310-297-5100

Motorola
Modems
http://www.mot.com/MIMS/ISG/
800-365-6394; 205-430-8000
Sales: 205-430-8296
Fax: 205-430-8296
Tech support: 205-430-8047

NEC Technologies, Inc.
Monitors, Printers
http://www.nec.com
800-NEC-INFO; 630-775-7900
Sales: 800-284-4484
Fax: 508-635-4666
Tech support: 800-632-4662

Nokia Display Products, Inc.
Monitors
http://www.intltech.com/nokia
800-BY-NOKIA; 415-331-0322
Fax: 415-331-6211

Okidata Corp.
Printers
http://www.okidata.com
800-OKI-TEAM; 609-235-2600
Fax: 609-778-4184
Tech support: 609-273-0300

Panasonic Communications & Systems Co.
Monitors, Printers
http://www.panasonic.com
800-742-8086; 201-348-7000
Fax: 201-392-4441
Tech support: 800-222-0584

Practical Peripherals
Modems
http://www.pracinet.com
770-840-9966
Fax: 770-734-4601

QMS, Inc.
Printers
http://www.qms.com
800-622-5546; 334-633-4300
Sales: 800-523-2696
Fax: 334-633-0013
Tech support: 334-633-4500

Reveal Computer Products, Inc.
Tape Drives
http://www.reveal.com
800-326-2222; 818-704-6300
Sales: 800-REVEAL-1
Fax: 818-340-9957

Samsung Electronics America, Inc.
Monitors
http://www.samsung.com
800-726-7864; 201-229-4000
Sales: 800-656-2785
Fax: 201-229-4110

Seagate Technology, Inc.
Tape Drives
http://www.seagate.com
800-SEAGATE; 408-438-6550
Sales: 408-438-8111
Fax: 408-438-7852
Tech support: 408-438-8222

SONY Electronics, Inc.
Monitors, Tape Drives
http://www.sony.com
800-352-7669; 408-432-1600
Fax: 408-943-0740
Tech support: 800-326-9551

Star Micronics America, Inc.
Printers
http://www.starmicronics.com
800-506-7827; 908-572-9512
Sales: 800-782-7636
Fax: 908-572-5095
Tech support: 908-572-3300

SyQuest Technology, Inc.
Removable Drives
http://www.syquest.com
800-245-CART; 510-226-4000
Sales: 510-226-4150
Fax: 510-226-4100
Tech support: 800-249-2440

TEAC America, Inc.
Tape Drives
http://www.teac.com
800-888-4XCD; 213-726-0303
Fax: 213-727-7625

Tektronix, Inc.
Printers
http://www.tek.com
800-835-6100; 503-682-7370
Fax: 503-682-2980

UMAX Technologies, Inc.
Scanners
http://www.umax.com
800-468-8629; 510-651-8834
Tech support: 510-651-4000

U.S. Robotics
Modems
http://www.usr.com
800-DIAL-USR; 847-982-5010
Sales: 847-982-5001
Fax: 847-933-5800
Tech support: 847-982-5151

ViewSonic Corp.
Monitors
http://www.viewsonic.com
800-888-8583; 909-444-8800
Sales: 909-869-7976
Fax: 909-468-3756
Tech support: 800-888-8383

Xircom, Inc.
Modems
http://www.xircom.com
800-438-4526; 805-376-9300
Sales: 800-376-9311
Fax: 805-376-9311
Tech support: 805-376-9020

Zoom Telephonics, Inc.
Modems
http://www.zoomtel.com
800-631-3116; 617-423-1072
Sales: 800-666-6191
Fax: 617-423-3923
Tech support: 617-423-1076

Catalogs and Other Resources

Here are a few companies that sell computer hardware, sofware, and supplies
by catalog. Simply call a company to ask for its catalog:

Global
http://www.globalcomputer.com
800-8-GLOBAL; 770-339-9999
Fax: 770-339-0033

MEI/Micro Center
http://www.mei-microcenter.com
800-634-3478
Fax: 614-486-6417

PC Connection
http://www.pcconnection.com
800-800-5555
Fax: 603-446-7791
Customer service: 800-800-0011

Power Up (TigerDirect)
http://www.tigerdirect.com
800-335-4055
Fax: 305-228-3400

Tiger Software (TigerDirect)
http://www.tigerdirect.com
800-888-4437
Fax: 800-782-1435

In addition, if you search the Web for computer sellers, you'll find hundreds of retailers that sell online or via fax or catalog—including reputable national chains like ElekTek and CompUSA.

Other Online Resources

The Web is becoming a very popular place, and with millions of Web sites, it can be pretty overwhelming. This short list of sites will get you started exploring the World Wide Web.

Site Name	Site Address	Offers...
Windows95.com	**http://windows95.com**	Tips, driver updates, free software and more for the Windows 95 operating system.
Shareware.com	**http://www.shareware.com**	Links to thousands of shareware programs.
ZD Net	**http://www.zdnet.com**	Includes links (Ziff-Davis) to popular Web site online computer magazines.
CNet	**http://www.cnet.com**	Excellent source of computer information; contains a wealth of product reviews.

Site Name	Site Address	Offers...
Sandy Bay Software's PC Webopaedia	http://sandybay.com/pc-web/index.html	Definitions of obscure computer terms.
Stroud's CWS Apps List	www.stroud.com	Stroud's Consummate Winsock Apps List contains up-to-date information on the hottest utilities and Internet tools.

Where and How to Get Help

Every computer setup is unique, with various components from various manufacturers and numerous types of software. So, this appendix is not designed to list every potential resource. Instead, it's intended to give you some direction in seeking help if you encounter a problem.

TIP **See Part VI** Of course, if you're having a hardware problem, you should consult Part VI of this book and try the remedies there.

If you're in a position where you find you need help from another source, follow the general steps detailed next.

1. If you encounter catastrophic problems with a new system or software, take or send it back to the company that sold it to you.

A brand-new system should boot and run smoothly, and new software should install and start up without big problems. Most reputable dealers will take a system or software back—no questions asked—within 30 days of the purchase. Check the policy of the vendor you're dealing with before buying.

My sister recently bought a laptop with a memory upgrade. When she installed the RAM, the system at first displayed fatal error messages, then stopped booting. She took the system back to the store, and learned that there was a problem with the RAM upgrade, and that other users had returned systems with the same problem. (Oddly, the computer store was prohibited from recalling the RAM, because the RAM manufacturer was denying that its product was flawed.) My sister got a new system, and was even given $300 back, because the system model went on sale between the time she purchased and returned the first machine.

Similarly, if you get a fatal error while installing a new program or it simply won't boot after you install it, it may not be your fault. Check first to ensure you have the right version of the program. If you buy the upgrade version of a program (rather than the full version) and don't have a program installed on your machine that qualifies you for an upgrade, the program will not install completely—and it won't tell you that the problem is that you can't use the upgrade version. In addition, although CD-ROM disks are more stable than floppies, you can on occasion get a bad or scratched CD.

 TIP   **Stop Payment**   Buying your system with a credit card can help you if you encounter a lemon system. If you dispute the charges with your credit card company backing you up, the vendor you're dealing with may become a bit more cooperative.

2. Register your product immediately.

You should complete and return the manufacturer's or software publisher's registration card (or online registration) immediately to ensure you'll be qualified for online support.

3. Thoroughly search the documentation and online help.

This step isn't intended to insult your intelligence. Rather, it's intended to point out that documentation and online help isn't perfect. Information might not be indexed under the topic name you expect, for example. For hard copy documentation, check the index and table of contents, and also flip through sections that cover a topic that may be related to the problem you're having—a tip box might shed some light on the issue for you. To duly search online help, make sure you use the Index and Find features (if available) as described in Lesson 6 of Part II. Also search for more than one term. For example, if you're having file saving problems, search for "file," "disk," and "saving." If you're getting a particular error message or number, search for that message or number specifically.

In addition, many documentation booklets and online help systems now offer a troubleshooting section with specifics about the product you have. You should always review and try the advice in a troubleshooting section before you call tech support.

 TIP **Read Me** The most up-to-date troubleshooting help often appears in a file named Readme.txt (or other names like Read.me, Readme.doc, and so on) on the setup or install disk for a program or hardware component. Check for a file like this in addition to checking online help and the documentation.

4. If you don't need an immediate answer, search online.

Chances are that someone, somewhere has had the problem you're having. There are various resources online. Some are sponsored and monitored by software publishers and hardware manufacturers. Others represent the efforts of a service or group of users trying to provide helpful information.

There are a few different types of troubleshooting help you may find online:

- **File fixes.** Smart companies try to fix program bugs, and often release "patch" or "bug fix" files. Simply download the patch and install it as directed on your system.

- **Tech support libraries.** Companies track problems reported by users in tech support calls, as well as the solution. You can search an online library for the problem you're having and an appropriate fix.

- **Places to post questions.** You can post a question about your problem in a message area, or even e-mail directly to a tech support representative or system administrator. Note that you may get no response to a general posting, and an e-mail response may take a few days. Plus, you'll have to check repeatedly for responses to your issue.

There are several different kinds of online resources to check for the information I just described:

- **BBSs.** Many software and hardware manufacturers run a technical support BBS (Bulletin Board System) that you can dial into with your modem (using Windows 95 HyperTerminal). Check the documentation for a BBS number, or look in online help.

- **Web sites.** Many company Web sites offer a technical support area, which is where you can access tech support libraries. For example, Appendix A lists the Web sites for numerous hardware manufacturers.

- **Newsgroups.** Again, larger companies administer Internet newsgroups about their products. Search for a newsgroup whose name includes the company name or product name. You also can find user-administered newsgroups about general topics like computing.

- **Other online services.** Both CompuServe and America Online offer general sections with computing help. In addition, each offers forums (discussion areas) and libraries of help about specific products, usually administered by the manufacturer. Search your online service for the name of a particular manufacturer, software publisher, or product to find help.

5. For help now, call technical support.

If you've tried checking out resources on your own, have quizzed your geek friends without result, or need an immediate solution (because a product won't work at all, for example), it's time to call tech support.

Before you do, you need to understand how tech support often works in this day and age, particularly for major software publishers. Free tech support is often only provided for 30 to 60 days, starting from the first "incident," or tech support call you make. This is why it pays to use the preceding steps to resolve a problem on your own before placing a tech support call and starting the countdown on your free support. After your free support has expired, you usually have two support options: paying "by incident," where a flat fee of $25 or more is charged to your credit card; or under a prepaid support plan, where a fee of $75 or more is charged to your card for a year or so of unlimited calls. (You may also find 900-number services, where you're charged by the minute.)

 Incident   In the world of tech support, an incident is a problem you call into tech support. Even if it takes several calls between you and tech support to resolve the problem, the exchange is considered a single incident. The tech support person will usually give you an "incident number," which you'll need to provide in all correspondence and repeat calls about the problem.

Check the documentation or online help for your product to find the tech support number for the type of tech support you want (free, by incident, or pre-pay plan). Then, before you call the tech support number, take the time to gather or jot down the following information, which the tech support representative will ask for when you call:

- **Product serial number.** You need this to verify you're qualified for tech support, if free.
- **Personal information.** You'll need to provide, at a minimum, your name, phone number, and e-mail address.
- **Incident number.** If your problem can't be resolved in a single call, during subsequent calls, make sure you also have the incident number provided by tech support during your initial call.
- **Credit card.** If you're paying by credit card, have it handy.
- **Specific notes about your problem.** Write down details about the circumstances under which the problem occurs (what you're trying to do with the system), the exact wording and number of any error message you see, and what steps you've already tried to fix the problem on your own.

TIP　**Long Distance**　Remember, free support isn't free if the tech support number is a long distance call. That's why it pays to gather the information noted above before you make your call.

To get the most out of tech support, follow directions exactly, even if it means packing up a new system and sending it back to the manufacturer. Tech support can't be helpful unless you cooperate.

6. Buy a book.

Tech support can get expensive. If you're having repeated problems getting steps to work, it may be more cost-effective for you to simply buy a better resource. Que's *Special Edition Using* line of books contain the best in-depth resources on the market.

7. If all else fails, find a repair shop (if the company that sold you the system or software doesn't have one).

Tech support help is good, but it can't solve every problem, such as retrieving data from a hard disk that's kaput, or fixing a printer that's shredding paper. To find professional help, look under "Computers" in the phone book. Call for an estimate before you take your system or component in, and consider making an appointment with the service person so that you can describe your problem completely when you drop off the component. If that isn't possible, type up or write out detailed notes about the problem, add your name and phone number, and tape the information to the component.

Before you drop off the component, also make sure you understand the repair shop's warranty (on both parts and labor) and payment policies.

Index

621

"Keyboard Not Found" error
message, 531
Keyboard Properties dialog
box, 409, 411
Keyboard Properties tab, 410
keyboards, 32-34
adding, 407-411
beeping, 533-534
choosing commands with,
125-126
cleaning, 96-97
commands
copying files with, 179
moving files with, 180
moving folders with,
180
moving information
with, 265-267
comparing, 33
computers, attaching, 408
connecting, 89
ergonomic, 407
insert mode, 532-533
installing, 408-409
keys, 32-33
alphanumeric, 32
Alt (Alternate), 33
arrow, 32
Ctrl (Control), 33
Esc (Escape), 33
F (Function), 33
numeric, 33
languages, selecting, 411
laptops, attaching, 408
overtype mode, 532-533
Plug and Play, 408
plugs, checking, 407
remapping, 533
Repeat Delay slider, 410
Repeat Rate slider, 410
resizing windows with,
120
selecting folders with, 155
settings, 410-411
shortcuts, 258-259, 539-540
for field-based
programs, 256

for grid-based pro-
grams, 256
for text-based pro-
grams, 255-256
troubleshooting, 530-534
keys, 32-33
alphanumeric, 32
Alt (Alternate), 33
arrow, 32
Ctrl (Control), 33
Delete, 170
editing text boxes, 133-134
Esc (Escape), 33
F (Function), 33
F1 (fast help), 140
Insert, 259
Num Lock, 255
numeric, 33
Remap, 533
repeating speed, 410
shortcuts, 128
sticky, 533
kilobytes, 23
Kingston Technology Corp.
Web site, 586

L

labels, 191
Language tab, 411
languages, keyboards, 411
laptop computer, *see*
notebook computer
laptops
keyboards, 408
mouse, 408
Large Icons command (View
menu), 157
Large Icons toolbar button
(Windows Explorer), 159
laser printers, 43, 401
launching
Internet Explorer, 334-336
Internet News, 387
leasing computers, 78
left pane window (Windows
Explorer), 154

left-clicking mouses, 113
Lexmark International, Inc.
Web site, 593
libraries (technical support),
602
licensing fees, 358
Line up Icons command
(View menu), 163
links, 340-342, 355
address preview, 341
Download Now, 355
exploring, 341-342
files, downloading,
354-356
troubleshooting, 342
list boxes, 132, 134-135
selecting items from,
134-135
List command (View menu),
157
List toolbar button
(Windows Explorer), 159
lists
bulleted
creating, 285-286
customizing, 286
removing, 286
contact, 305-306
Look In, 137
newsgroups, updating,
390-391
numbered
creating, 285-286
customizing, 286
removing, 286
word
building, 142-143
rebuilding, 143
Lithium Ion batteries, 68
Load/Eject/Form Feed
button, 549, 553
loading
e-mail programs, 369-370
Internet Explorer, 334-336
Internet Mail, 370
Internet News, 387

Check out Que® Books on the World Wide Web
http://www.quecorp.com

As the biggest software release in computer history, Windows 95 continues to redefine the computer industry. Click here for the latest info on our Windows 95 books

Make computing quick and easy with these products designed exclusively for new and casual users

Examine the latest releases in word processing, spreadsheets, operating systems, and suites

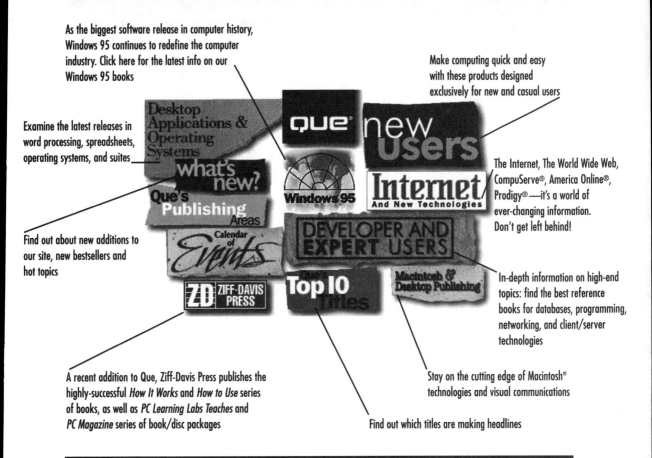

The Internet, The World Wide Web, CompuServe®, America Online®, Prodigy® —it's a world of ever-changing information. Don't get left behind!

Find out about new additions to our site, new bestsellers and hot topics

In-depth information on high-end topics: find the best reference books for databases, programming, networking, and client/server technologies

A recent addition to Que, Ziff-Davis Press publishes the highly-successful *How It Works* and *How to Use* series of books, as well as *PC Learning Labs Teaches* and *PC Magazine* series of book/disc packages

Stay on the cutting edge of Macintosh® technologies and visual communications

Find out which titles are making headlines

With 6 separate publishing groups, Que develops products for many specific market segments and areas of computer technology. Explore our Web Site and you'll find information on best-selling titles, newly published titles, upcoming products, authors, and much more.

- Stay informed on the latest industry trends and products available
- Visit our online bookstore for the latest information and editions
- Download software from Que's library of the best shareware and freeware

Complete and Return this Card
for a *FREE* Computer Book Catalog

Thank you for purchasing this book! You have purchased a superior computer book written expressly for your needs. To continue to provide the kind of up-to-date, pertinent coverage you've come to expect from us, we need to hear from you. Please take a minute to complete and return this self-addressed, postage-paid form. In return, we'll send you a free catalog of all our computer books on topics ranging from word processing to programming and the internet.

Mr. ☐   Mrs. ☐   Ms. ☐   Dr. ☐

Name (first) [   ] (M.I.) [ ]   (last) [   ]

Address [   ]
[   ]

City [   ] State [ ] Zip [   ] [   ]

Phone [ ] [   ] [   ]   Fax [   ] [   ] [   ]

Company Name [   ]

E-mail address [   ]

Please check at least (3) influencing factors for purchasing this book.

Front or back cover information on book .... ☐
Special approach to the content .... ☐
Completeness of content .... ☐
Author's reputation .... ☐
Publisher's reputation .... ☐
Book cover design or layout .... ☐
Index or table of contents of book .... ☐
Price of book .... ☐
Special effects, graphics, illustrations .... ☐
Other (Please specify): _____ ☐

2. How did you first learn about this book?

Saw in Macmillan Computer Publishing catalog .... ☐
Recommended by store personnel .... ☐
Saw the book on bookshelf at store .... ☐
Recommended by a friend .... ☐
Received advertisement in the mail .... ☐
Saw an advertisement in: _____ ☐
Read book review in: _____ ☐
Other (Please specify): _____ ☐

3. How many computer books have you purchased in the last six months?

This book only .... ☐   3 to 5 books .... ☐
2 books .... ☐   More than 5 .... ☐

4. Where did you purchase this book?

Bookstore .... ☐
Computer Store .... ☐
Consumer Electronics Store .... ☐
Department Store .... ☐
Office Club .... ☐
Warehouse Club .... ☐
Mail Order .... ☐
Direct from Publisher .... ☐
Internet site .... ☐
Other (Please specify): _____ ☐

5. How long have you been using a computer?

☐ Less than 6 months   ☐ 6 months to a year
☐ 1 to 3 years   ☐ More than 3 years

6. What is your level of experience with personal computers and with the subject of this book?

	With PCs	With subject of book
New	☐	☐
Casual	☐	☐
Accomplished	☐	☐
Expert	☐	☐

Source Code ISBN: 0-7897-1423-x

Which of the following best describes your job title?

Administrative Assistant .... ☐
Coordinator .... ☐
Manager/Supervisor .... ☐
Director .... ☐
Vice President .... ☐
President/CEO/COO .... ☐
Lawyer/Doctor/Medical Professional .... ☐
Teacher/Educator/Trainer .... ☐
Engineer/Technician .... ☐
Consultant .... ☐
Not employed/Student/Retired .... ☐
Other (Please specify): _____ ☐

8. Which of the following best describes the area of the company your job title falls under?

Accounting .... ☐
Engineering .... ☐
Manufacturing .... ☐
Operations .... ☐
Marketing .... ☐
Sales .... ☐
Other (Please specify): _____ ☐

9. What is your age?

Under 20 .... ☐
21-29 .... ☐
30-39 .... ☐
40-49 .... ☐
50-59 .... ☐
60-over .... ☐

10. Are you:

Male .... ☐
Female .... ☐

11. Which computer publications do you read regularly? (Please list)

_____
_____
_____
_____
_____
_____

Comments: _____

Fold here and scotch-tape to mai

MACMILLAN COMPUTER PUBLISHING USA
A VIACOM COMPANY

Technical ----: Support:

If you need assistance with the information in this book or with a CD/Disk
accompanying the book, please access the Knowledge Base on our Web
site at **http://www.superlibrary.com/general/support**. Our most
Frequently Asked Questions are answered there. If you do not find the
answer to your questions on our Web site, you may contact Macmillan
Technical Support **(317) 581-3833** or e-mail us at **support@mcp.com**.